As a frequent writer for Ain't It Cool News, VERN has gained notoriety for his unorthodox reviewing style and his expertise in "the films of Badass Cinema." As detailed in this book, his review of the slasher movie *Chaos* earned him a wrestling challenge from its director; his explosive essay on the PG-13 rating of the fourth *Die Hard* movie prompted Bruce Willis himself to walk barefoot across the broken glass of movie nerd message boards to respond. His previous book, *Seagalogy: A Study of the Ass-Kicking Films of Steven Seagal*, did indeed shake the very foundations of film criticism, garnering rave reviews and featuring in TIME magazine. Guillermo Del Toro, the director of *Pan's Labyrinth*, called Vern "a National Treasure". He lives in Seattle.

'YIPPEE KI-YAY MOVIEGOER!"

WRITINGS ON
BRUCE WILLIS
BADASS CINEMA
AND OTHER
IMPORTANT
TOPICS

VERN

"YIPPEE KI-YAY MOVIEGOER"
WRITINGS ON BRUCE WILLIS, BADASS CINEMA AND OTHER IMPORTANT TOPICS

ISBN 9781848563711

Published by
Titan Books
A division of
Titan Publishing Group Ltd
144 Southwark St
London
SE1 0UP

First edition March 2010
10 9 8 7 6 5 4 3 2 1

Designed by Martin Stiff.

Visit our websites:
www.titanbooks.com
outlawvern.com

Publisher's Note:
This publication has not been prepared, approved, licensed or endorsed by Bruce Willis, or any entity that created or produced any of the films or programs discussed in this book.

Did you enjoy this book? We love to hear from our readers. Please e-mail us at: **readerfeedback@titanemail.com** or write to Reader Feedback at the above address.

To receive advance information, news, competitions, and exclusive Titan offers online, please register as a member by clicking the "sign up" button on our website: www.titanbooks.com

A CIP catalogue record for this title is available from the British Library.

Printed in the United States of America.

'YIPPEE KI-YAY MOVIEGOER!"

WRITINGS ON
BRUCE WILLIS
BADASS CINEMA
AND OTHER
IMPORTANT
TOPICS

VERN

TITAN BOOKS

CONTENTS

5: TANGENTS

6: IT'S NOT SUPPOSED TO BE HAMLET

7: THE ISSUES

8: THE ARTS

9: MISCELLANEOUS

10: FILTH AND SLEAZE

11: TALES FROM VERN'S BLOODY CRYPT OF PHANTASMOGORIFYING HORRORS

12: THE MANY FACETS OF BADASS CINEMA

Aug 31 1999, 12:00 am
Newsgroups: rec.arts.movies.current-films
From: outlaw_69@my-deja.com
Date: 1999/08/31
Subject: WHO'S SEEN DIE HARD?

anybody? —vern

INTRODUCTION
by Vern

If you're reading this you might've heard of me from my book *Seagalogy*, or my contributions to the Ain't It Cool News web site. More likely you never heard of me at all and are just now realizing that whichever book by an author beginning with 'V' you meant to pick up, you got the one next to it. But please hear me out pal. Whatever nonsense you were looking for, this nonsense is way better. It is a collection of movie reviews that will make all other collections of movie reviews suffer from jealousy and low self-esteem. And I don't feel good about that because all of the books should get along and not go around backstabbing each other, but life's a bitch, you know?

I am not a professional movie critic, I'm just some asshole. Until publishing a book I never got paid a dime for any of these reviews. But for the last ten years, for some reason, I've dedicated my life to writing about movies. I started with moronic scribblings on newsgroups (see above), expanded into a crude free website on Geocities.com, then became a regular on the aforementioned The Ain't It Cool News and wrote the also aforementioned acclaimed book about the films of Steven Seagal.

This book is not Willisology. *Yippee Ki-Yay Moviegoer* is about the love of all types of movies, and I couldn't think of a better symbol for that than my man Bruce. When I first saw *Die Hard* I couldn't believe that comedian from *Moonlighting* had just starred in the greatest American action movie I'd ever seen. (I still consider it #1). But by the time he was getting acclaim for his quiet performance in *The Sixth Sense* he was so associated with action movies that he surprised people again. The lesson is to be good at what you do, but do more than one thing. Bruce has been many things to many people: an iconic screen wiseass, a badass action star, an underrated dramatic actor, an inspiration to victims of male pattern baldness, a tireless advocate of Seagram's Golden Wine Cooler. I would like to be the Bruce Willis of film criticism. I don't play harmonica though just to be up front here.

You probably have some ideas about what a film critic is, either good or bad. I don't really see myself fitting in with most of those guys. I'm not into the consumer reports type reviewing you see in newspapers and some commercial web sites. You know, the short little formulaic reviews where they give you a plot summary and tell you if it's recommended or not. I'm more in line with the long-winded *New Yorker* types and academicians who want to explore a movie in context with film history and American culture, who want to explore what makes movies work or not and examine the themes of genres and subgenres. But I'm still kind of a weirdo in those circles because although I do like documentaries and that "new wave" they had in France that one time, I am more likely to fixate on, say, slasher sequels of the '80s or action movies starring former professional athletes.

I'm not fuckin around here, I believe a well-rounded film lover oughta have something to say about Jean-Luc Godard *and* Jean-Claude Van Damme. And okay, so maybe I have more expertise in the latter, but that's an area that has not been studied as much. In this book I will discuss the works of Brian Bosworth and Alejandro Jodorowsky and everything in between, and I will hopefully treat them with the same level of sincere respect. If you read my Seagal book you know what I'm about — hopefully these reviews will make you laugh, but not at the expense of legitimate insights into the films, and definitely not in some smarmy sarcastic kind of way. I might be writing about a type of movie that you think is ridiculous but please realize that I genuinely love these types of movies.

I don't see many critics out there standing up for the genres and issues I care about, or even treating film criticism as the artform that I think it should be. So in my mind I'm John McClane and the world of film criticism is Nakatomi Plaza. I'm an off-duty individual who happened to be in a certain place at a certain time — I won't pass judgment on whether it was "right" or "wrong" — and I knew nobody else was gonna fuckin do it. So even though I'm unarmed and I have no shoes on I walk over the glass and take care of business using my unorthodox methods and sardonic quips. And I guess Al Powell would be all the nice people who email me all the time, helping me out from the outside, believing in me when no one else does. I'm not sure who Argyle is. I'll have to think about this metaphor a little more.

Anyway, thanks for hearing me out. I hope you will purchase this book and subsequently enjoy it. If you flip through you'll see it covers a pretty weird list of movies and filmmakers. Who the hell does a book that discusses both Julie Taymor and *The Gingerdead Man*? Only me, I guess. But don't worry. These aren't necessarily supposed to be the most important movies there are, but they're some of the best reviews I've done over the years and they hopefully bring up larger points about movies (and even society) as a whole. In short, all smart people buy this book, and no dumb people. Sorry dumb people, maybe next time. If you are a professor please assign this book to your class. Also buy it for everybody for birthdays and holidays. Help me out here buddy I think you know it's the right thing to do.

CHAPTER ONE
WARRIORS

You and I are thinkers. We are book readers and writers. We like to analyze and mull over shit. Some of us may be fighters also, but we remain thoughtful. We are not barbarians. This chapter is not about us.

This chapter is about men forged in the heat of battle and what not. I'm talking about individuals who excel in the use of the swords, the throwing stars, the chains, the two-by-fours with a nail in it. Their stories are presented here in chronological order.

These men are experts in murder and mayhem, geniuses of assassination and stealth. They know how to punch, to kick, to stab, to phalanx, to use a pommel horse. Some of them are loners, some travel in packs. They are Spartans, Warriors, Baseball Furies, ninjas, Olympic gymnasts. They are physical beings, creatures of destruction. If they are ever creative, it is only in the innovative ways that they are destructive. The only time they are inside their head is when some other savage fucker shot an arrow or threw a knife at them and they have to pull it out of their skull.

Some of them don't fight beneath a flag or even behind a code, they just exist to defeat their opponents. Their shields, their denim vests or ninja masks are everything they believe in. Those are the men we are here to discuss. Today we speak of the warriors.

Actually come to think of it these are some stupid motherfuckers, but they seem pretty cool in movies.

Make no mistake about it, it's hard out here for a Spartan. A lot of these bastards, they're "baptized in the fire of combat." They grow up having to fight their dad all day, and I mean really fight him. You thought your dad pushed you too hard at hoops, well at least he didn't beat on you until you fucked up. These guys, the beating is the actual practice. It's their culture.

In some of the other neighborhoods, like Arcadia for example, you can grow up to be a potter, a sculptor or a blacksmith. In Sparta, you're a soldier. But you don't even get to talk about it, like "What do you do for a living?" "Oh, I'm a soldier. I'm baptized in the fire of combat." In Sparta, they ask you what your trade is you gotta yell out "WHOO WHOO!" or something. You are highly trained in combat and in grunting.

Basically, you're trained your whole life to fight, and you learn that the best thing in the world is to die "a beautiful death" in battle. If it's not that great of a battle then forget it, it has to be a really good battle, and then if you die, that's awesome. No mention of 72 virgins, or the afterlife at all, unless "Tonight we dine in Hell!" is meant literally, which is debatable.

But then after all that training they might not even let you fight. First of all, you have to have a son. Not just a bun in the oven either, it has to be a born son to carry on your name. Bloodlines are a big deal to these people. And then there are body image issues to deal with. There are some serious pecs and six packs on these Spartans. I don't know if shirts were invented yet or not, but they don't wear shirts. You can imagine that if you didn't have pecs like that you would feel pretty fuckin worthless. You'd look like a freak.

Even worse, what if you literally *are* a freak? Like this one guy, I forget what they call him, but he is Walt Disney's Hunchy, from the movie *Walt Disney's The Hunchback of Notre Dame*. The guy looks like the Toxic Avenger after he broke his spine in a car accident, and he's trying to fit in with all these fuckin Adonises. He's a Spartan, so obviously he's trained his whole life and he can fight like nobody's business, but because of his birth defects he can't raise his shield to the proper phalanx height, so they won't let him help. It's like those guys that wanted to help out in WWII but they got rejected because of their eyesight or something. Except this guy can't get laid either. And because of their whole macho culture he thinks he has to redeem his father by killing. Everything in Sparta is about killing. He can't open up a hospital and name it after his father, that wouldn't do it.

I really wondered during the movie what exactly these Spartans do when they're not fighting. If it's not a war, it's training the kids for war. Okay, so there's some sex, but it's "I'm about to leave for war" sex. They definitely got some great warriors in this joint but I bet there's not shit to do during peace time. You can't even climb a tree because there's dead bodies nailed to it.

For women, I don't know, it might not be as bad. They have to stay at home and they have to worry about their husbands and sons dying, but they are given more human rights than in some of the other cultures. A Persian messenger is offended when the Queen speaks to him. More importantly, King Leonidas looks at the Queen and waits for an approving nod before he sets off a war by killing the sexist bastard. There is still room for advancement but at least there's a little bit of power there, like Hillary Clinton when she tried to get us health care.

One thing that definitely sucks about being a woman in Sparta: it's too god damn cold. You can tell because their nipples are always rock hard.

And the worst thing for both sexes: having to hear about Sparta and Spartans all the fucking time. *We are Sparta! Spartans, prepare to fight! In Sparta we do this, in Sparta we don't do that. Spartans are like this, white people are like that. Sparta Sparta Sparta Sparta.* They NEVER fucking shut up. Half these guys, it's like they don't even have names, the King calls them "Spartan." Not even an occasional "buddy" or "pal" or "chief," everybody is a nationality. "Hey Arcadian," or "Hey Persian." I mean, I have a name, dude. I guess it's good that Sparta means so much to the King, but jesus. ANYTHING you talk about that much, you're gonna get on somebody's nerves. Get a hobby, dude.

I also get a sense there's some bigotry going on here. I mean obviously King Xerxes and the Persians really are planning to enslave Sparta, so the Spartans have every right to fight back. But why does the first guy they kill, and the most joyfully evil guy they encounter, gotta be the only two

African-Persians they ever run into? This one dark skinned guy cackles satanically and then his whole face digitally turns ink black except for his eyes. And I'm sure it's an homage to the drawings in the comic strip this is based on, but jesus.

I bet they're pretty progressive about gays, though. True, some nationality or other gets called a bunch of "boy lovers," and I'm sure it bugs some of these guys that Xerxes has fruity looking painted on eyebrows. But I think most would agree that this movie would make a good double feature with *Dreamigirls*.

It also reminded me a little bit of *Apocalypto*. It has less pretense of being actual history (even though it's based on an actual battle) because it's more stylized and has a couple monsters in it. But it's another macho, balls-to-the-wall action movie. And just like in *Apocalypto*, the invading army are a bunch of assholes sporting more bling than Bishop Don Magic Juan. How do they go to the bathroom with all that shit on?[1]

From the looks of it everything is better in Persia. They got more numbers, they got fancy boats, they can cover their chests, they get to ride pimped out elephants and rhinos instead of shitty old horses. They have crazy orgies and even hunchbacks are invited. The King is such an asshole he rides around in a parade float carried on people's backs. And he uses them as stairs when he wants to get off. Rich bastards flaunting their Liberace lifestyle. Spartas don't like it. They grew up rough, they're straight outta Sparta.

Another one this reminded me of was the first *Conan* movie. Because it's macho as hell, it's a good simple story about brawn and not so much brain, and it takes place somewhere between the real world and fantasyland. The people who look like monsters are supposed to be inbreds, and there's no dragons or talking birds or nothing. Only seagulls that snack on dead bodies.

Walking out of the movie I heard some guys saying there was no story, it was just fighting. I don't think they meant this as a bad thing. But they're wrong. This is actually a very old and very good story, the story of the 300 Spartans and 6,700 of their close friends who thought it was

---

1 This reference might be older than a lot of my audience. Let's put it this way: it's a quote from a Keenan Ivory Wayans movie.

a good idea to fight hundreds of thousands of invading Persians. It's a story, but it's a story freebased to its purest elements. These guys are fighters, they fight. They got a good strategy. They got a simple philosophy. And they kill some motherfuckers, actually a lot of them. Some of the battle sequences are pretty impressive, there are some long, elaborate slow motion shots where Leonidas runs through a crowd chopping up who knows how many Persian motherfucks in a row.

According to my sources, *300* is based on a comic strip by Frank Miller, same guy who did *Sin City*. The comic strip is inspired by the movie *300 Spartans* which is based on the actual historical events of the battle of whatsisdick in 480 BC. I don't know much about any of these things so I consulted my Nerd Issues Correspondent. He hasn't read the comic strip (he doesn't like stories where capes are worn in a legitimate historical context) but he says this is a landmark comic book movie because it's the first one to credit a colorist (Lynn Varley) for creating the source material. Man, that's progress. I wish Dr. King was here.

Anyway, my guy hasn't read it but he heard the movie exactly captured the artwork from the strip, like *Sin City*. If so I think they did a better job of making it seem like a real movie than *Sin City*. This whole movie is stylized, right down to the blood sprays that are animated to look like ink splattered on a page. But it has more depth to it, it looks more like a real world that these people actually live in. Even if it's really a blue screen. They got some more *Dick Tracy* makeup in this one but it's not the main characters, the main characters are real people.

And I have to give credit to this Gerard Butler, who plays Leonidas. He's not like a Daniel Craig or somebody who's gonna conquer the world with his charisma. But he's convincing as the baddest motherfucker of the 400 BCs, the guy you'd follow on a suicide mission. And with that pointy beard he sure looks a lot like crazy fuckin Mel Gibson. (Prediction: Gerard Butler in *Mad Max 4*.)

I liked this movie. I'm not gonna say I loved it, but it was very enjoyable. These days you don't see this tone too often — it's an action movie that's dead serious, not a bunch of wisecracking, but it's not at all pretentious. It's not trying to trick you into thinking it's more than just a bunch of patriotic musclemen throwing spears and trying not to get hit by arrows. There are numerous great badass moments, including when the Spartans build a wall out of dead people, and when they bury some suckers under the wall of dead people. There's some good tough talking too, and at least some of it is taken from the accepted historical accounts of the event. When the Persians tell the Spartans to hand over their weapons and Leonidas says to "Come and get 'em," it's not an action movie cliché, that's supposedly what he said.

To me it's kind of like *Gladiator* except nicer to look at, with battles where you can follow what's going on, and it's shorter and less pretentious so I had more fun and didn't feel insulted by it.

The director is Zack Snyder, his second movie after the surprisingly good *Dawn of the Dead* remake. So we know now that wasn't a fluke, this is a guy who can make a fun and cool looking movie with some good violence for the whole family. ("ARE YOU ENTERTAINED?") The question now is if he has a brain in his head, or if he's just working on some really good filmatic reflexes. First he took probably the most thoughtful of all the modern horror classics and remade it as a movie about nothing. Now he makes a movie that non-judgmentally tells about a society of nationalistic killing machines. I'd say he's definitely a good director but can we call him an interesting director before we know if the guy ever, like, *thought* about stuff before? I'm not sure, but if the next one is empty too I'm gonna have some suspicions. You can't eat cotton candy for every meal of the day. But for breakfast and lunch, I guess that'll be okay.

THE WARRIORS

I gotta be honest. As good as *The Warriors* is it's not quite the amazing masterpiece I like to remember it as. What makes it good is mostly on the surface: the different gangs and their gimmicks, the bleak rawness of everything from the cinematography to the John Carpenter-ish analog keyboard music, and the dead seriousness of all the characters in the face of this exaggerated world where thugs patrol the streets in baseball uniforms and gangs seem to outnumber law abiding citizens by a thousand to one.

This is all more than enough to make it some kind of minor classic, but my memory was being pretty charitable to the storytelling. I always loved the mythological simplicity of it: Cyrus calls a meeting to try to unite all the gangs, some prick assassinates Cyrus and blames The Warriors, now these nine guys have to cross New York on foot to get back home before the other gangs kill them. It's a good old fashioned odyssey or a gauntlet or whatever.

But watching it this time I don't think Walter Hill keeps the momentum of that journey from point A to point B. Or the simplicity. He splits up the group. They don't even realize at first that everyone's after them. And half of them keep getting distracted by the eternal search for pussy. This is pretty funny when they try to hook up with the girl gang called the Lizzies and they don't seem to notice the obvious fact that the Lizzies are not, you know, into guys. If only that homophobic prick Ajax was there, he calls everybody "faggot" all the time so maybe he would've picked up on it. Anyway, there's some meandering, it doesn't really build like it could, when they get to the beach on Coney Island to face off with their enemies maybe you should feel more like they've been through Hell and back.

But I'm kind of nitpicking. I like the whole tone of this movie. Everybody looks so serious all the time. Warriors rarely smile. They're macho like Spartans, they have a code they stick to stubbornly. Like the scene where they have to go through Orphan turf but there's a whole political negotiation first. And it's decided that all they have to do is take off their vests, they can't go through in uniform. But they refuse. They'd rather fight and maybe die than take off their colors. It's not clear if they'd be allowed to just turn them inside out like they made kids do with their Spuds Mackenzie shirts in the '80s. And if it had been the Baseball Furies or the mime gang would they have had to clean off their face paint?

One of my favorite touches is the DJ played by Lynn Thigpen, only seen as a pair of lips talking into a microphone. She's in cahoots with the Riffs so she dedicates records as coded messages to the gangs about the mission to kill The Warriors. For example she plays 'Nowhere to Run, Nowhere to Hide' at the beginning. She plays a lot of white rock music, I guess in deference to the multi-culti makeup of the gang. Unfortunately there was no song called 'Sorry We Fucked Up and Had Everybody Trying To Kill You (Tonight)' so she had to play something a little less direct at the end, I'm not sure what it's called.

That's probably why the government is always worried about terrorist suspects sending coded messages through the media — they've seen *The Warriors*.

The Warriors are anti-heroes. They're not good people and they're not any more heroic than most of the other gangs. But you can side with them because of the odds against them. You can tell it's hard out there for a Warrior. Watching the movie again I realized my life these days is really nothing like the Warriors, for example I generally wear a shirt. But I think all of us can find some part of our life to relate to their predicament.

Let me tell you a story. This has very little to do with *The Warriors* but it will be cathartic to write it, so bear with me. Right after I watched the movie I went across the street because I had to mail a bill I'm late on. I live in an apartment building but I have to move out pretty soon because it got bought out by some asshole company that's "renovating" the apartments and jacking up the rent, pricing us all out. So there are always these young rich couples moving in. As I was coming back in the building I saw this couple having trouble carrying a dresser up the stairs. For some reason the man was at the top and the woman was on the bottom and I felt like I would be an asshole just to walk past them. So I asked if they needed help.

"Would you really do that?" the woman asked gratefully. So I helped her lift her end, which was empty and not as heavy as I thought it was gonna be. But suddenly there was a loud metal clang as a bunjie corded hand truck fell from beneath the dresser, the tape they had across the drawers gave, some of the drawers fell open and my fingers got crushed between I don't know what.

My first thought was to apologize, but I didn't because my second thought was why the fuck are these people carrying a dresser with the drawers still in and facing down and then being surprised when they fall open? I thought they were just carrying a dresser up the stairs like a normal person would do, it didn't occur to me they would be trying some weird scheme where you roll a dollie up some stairs so you don't have to take the drawers out. So maybe I should've been looking closer, but I feel that those sorts of carts are durable enough to take a fall and nobody should be crying about it.

I dislodged my fingers, we pushed the drawers in, turned the chest sideways and the woman angrily thanked God that nothing was damaged. The guy said, "You can set it down." I was ready to go but I thought maybe he needed to rest.

I stood to the side for an excruciating half minute or so as they stared me down and I realized that they were blaming me for this incident. I was ready to carry the damn thing to wherever they needed it, it would only take a couple minutes, I could probably do it by myself if they're gonna just stand there. But "It's okay, you don't have to help," he said impatiently. "We'll figure something out."

"I can help, it's not a problem, but—" I trailed off as I realized what he meant was they were waiting for me to leave.

I ducked into my apartment in disbelief and undeserved shame. What the fuck? They didn't even get it into the building, they weren't allowing me to help. A total stranger trying to help some yuppies move into the same building he has to move out of because he doesn't make as much money as they do. And I really like this place too, I wish I could stay. Even if it had been my fault — and even if harm of some kind had been done — sure, it would be awkward, you don't have to say "thank you," but show some fuckin manners. Don't put it on the good Samaritan. At worst I am a well-intentioned Samaritan. But at least in Samaria we take the damn drawers out before hauling the shit up the stairs.

Man, that bummed me out, put a wicked hex on my whole night, even though I had just watched *The Warriors*! Thanks a lot. Welcome, neighbor. I hope you enjoy paying $500 more than I did. Just so you know — they got rid of the on-site manager when they bought the building. Last month some drunk puked right there where you won't let me move your dresser from. Nobody cleaned it up, we just waited for it to rain. True story.

At first I thought damn, that was a Larry David moment right there. But then I realized no, that was like *The Warriors*. Blamed for a crime I didn't commit. And blamed by the people who actually did it. We've all been in that position of having the hammer come down on us and we didn't even do anything. That's why I am a Warrior. And you too are a Warrior. We all are Warriors. Except personally I am against "runnin a train" on some lady, I don't know about you guys but that seems pretty wrong to me. Otherwise I am a Warrior. The Baseball Furies are also pretty good although it would be a pain in the ass putting on all that face paint. So I am a Warrior. And I *will* come out and play.

NOTE: This review is based on the original DVD release of The Warriors. *I made a point not to watch the director's cut special edition, where Walter Hill went back and added cheesy comic book frames as transitions.*

ENTER THE NINJA

This week I followed an anonymous tip to take a look at an individual named Sho Kosugi. This guy starred in a series of ninja movies and was said to be a missing link in my badass studies to date. I looked him up and found that *Enter the Ninja* is also known as *Ninja 1* because it begins a series, so I started with that.

The movie opens promisingly with the badass in question, Mr. Sho Kosugi, in full ninja uniform, standing in front of a black void, demonstrating every weapon he knows. Nunchakas, throwing stars, arrows, daggers, grappling hook, blow gun. You name it, he spins it around or shoots it. The guy is obviously good and it's kind of cool how he is basically doing show and tell for you throughout the opening credits. It might as well be some Ninja How-To video. But then all the sudden a ninja in all white flies onto the screen and "kicks" him in the head (although it doesn't look like he makes contact at all).

Then we go into the opening scene, where this White Ninja fights Sho Kosugi. I call him White Ninja because not only is he wearing all white, but you can tell by his eyes that he's a white man. White Ninja faces Sho Kosugi and his men (red ninjas), who chase him through the woods, over a waterfall, into a temple where he bows to an old man and then chops off his head.

Up to this point there is no dialogue, no explanation. But I think it's pretty clear what's going on here. White Ninja is mad because everybody makes fun of him for being White Ninja. Nothing against us white men, but we are not the best ninjas, in my opinion. It's just not one of the things we're good at. So to shame him for his whiteness the other ninjas call him White Ninja and force him to wear an all white ninja outfit. This is clearly a mocking gesture because why the hell would you wear a white ninja outfit unless you were going to assassinate somebody in the snow, or in DMX's all-white apartment from *Belly*? Otherwise you stick out like a sore thumb, as demonstrated when he runs through the trees. There's a reason why polar bears live in the snow and brown bears live in the woods, but ninja logic doesn't follow nature, I guess. It is anti-nature. My guess is they tricked him and told him that wearing all white means you're the most powerful ninja. And he fell for it.

To be fair, an argument could be made for an all white ninja outfit being a "Just Don't Give a Fuck" type of boastful ninja maneuver. As if to say *I will wear an all white outfit and* still *disappear into the shadows.* Maybe the rank of White Ninja is the second highest ninja honor behind Reflective Fluorescent Orange Ninja. Well, if so this White Ninja clearly didn't earn that honor. He's good for a white man, but as far as we can see he couldn't even do 1/8 the shit Sho Kosugi did in his show and tell. This guy is a punk. Then he chops off an old man's head.

Well don't worry, turns out it's all fake, it's a trial for Ninja School. A final exam to prove that he's a master of ninjitsu. Sho Kosugi's character Hasegawa (namesake of former Seattle Mariner Shigatosi Hasegawa) however doesn't agree that the white man should get this honor and he's real pissed. And it's no wonder, when White Ninja takes his mask off he turns out to be the Italian actor Franco Nero. Despite his '70s white-karate style mustache, Franco Nero is not a martial artist or a master of ninjitsu, no matter what he may tell you. He knows less martial arts than Dolemite or Billy Jack in the first two *Billy Jack* movies (including *Born Losers*).

Now unmasked and openly mustached, White Civilian Ninja leaves Japan and goes to Manila. An old war buddy named Frank sent for help because some assholes are trying to squeeze him out of his property. So most of the movie is about Nero without his ninja outfit acting as a one-man army warding off the various thugs that come after his buddy.

You can't really take the movie very seriously because the casting is so phony. Why do so many movies take that route of wanting to show some culture, but only by having a white guy infiltrate that culture? Some day there will be *American Sumo* starring James Gandolfini and *The Last Geisha* starring Sandra Bullock. Anyway, at the end Nero has to face Sho Kosugi in a ninja duel and it's just ridiculous. It's like if Ben Affleck had to play a muay thai boxer who competes with Tony Jaa. And then not only would the plot call for Ben Affleck to win the duel, but Tony Jaa would announce that Affleck had beat him with honor and would ask him to cut off his head. I don't buy that from Ben Affleck and I don't buy it from Franco Nero. (Although Franco could take Ben, even now.)

That casting guarantees that the movie is mostly good for laughs, but director Menahem Golan (of the infamous Cannon Group, also directed *Delta Force*) delivers all kinds of fun badass moments. There's a good scene where Frank goes to talk with one of the guys who's after his property. While he's coming into the mansion White Ninja sneaks around (still not in ninja outfit) killing or knocking out all the security guys. Later, the bad guy signals for his security. Only six guys come out, he gets embarrassed and has to figure out what happened to the other fourteen. Then White Ninja and Frank only have to take on the remaining six.

After the big fight they go to the bar, where Frank reveals that lately he can't get it up for his wife Mary Ann (Susan George). It's kind of weird because okay, some guys are trying to steal your property, in that case you can call on the skills of a ninja. But now you're telling him you can't get it up? I don't see how he can hel— oh. Wait a minute.

Indeed, Mary Ann uses her own amateur ninja skills to sneak into White Ninja's bed. So you see, this really is a guy who travels around the world helping people.

Eventually the bad guys stop fucking around, they find out that White Ninja is a ninja so they hire their own, Hasegawa. Hasegawa kills Frank and kidnaps Mary Ann. White Ninja paces around the ranch yelling "Mary Ann! Mary Ann!" and then suddenly it cuts to him with the full ninja outfit armed with every sword, bow, blow gun, ninja star and smoke bomb he can carry. This is a hilarious cut because he hasn't had the ninja outfit since the first scene in the movie. That's the kind of badass momentum I like. Golan knows there is no need for the dramatic suiting up scene. You kidnap a woman, you gotta deal with a fuckin NINJA. In costume. That's just what happens.

Now, on this particular mission of revenge, it turns out that the White Ninja costume really is useful. He sneaks into the villain's building, which is lightly colored and lit naturally by sunlight. The white costume is more camouflaged than traditional black would've been. Plus, all the bad guys wear white suits, so if you saw White Ninja out of the corner of your eye you might think he works there. White Ninja needs that extra advantage because he is Nero, not a stunt double, and he's not very graceful.

The bad guy isn't there, but his right hand man tells White Ninja "Mr. Venarius has been expecting you." They get in the car and drive to the cockfighting pit where, for some reason, Mr. Venarius is waiting. Even though everybody knows White Ninja's name and what he looks like, he rides in the car wearing the full ninja costume and mask, which is awesome. Right hand man gets out of the car to tell Venarius they've arrived, and when he goes back to the car White Ninja is gone and all the security guys are piled up dead everywhere. Nero is not very convincing doing ninja moves on screen, but off screen — perfect. Good job, White Ninja.

It may be disrespectful for me to call this guy White Ninja (his name is actually Cole.) But Venarius knows his name too, and he just calls him "Ninja." At least I specify which ninja I'm talking about. Later there are smoke bombs, the Right Hand Man gets an arrow through his right hand, and then White Ninja fights Hasegawa and wins way too easy.

The last scene is pretty funny. Nero (back in his civilian persona) is talking to somebody about what he'll do next, and he implies that he might be doing some more ninja murders. Then he looks at the camera and actually winks, and it freezes. You always gotta appreciate a Wink and Freeze Ending, but this one's especially funny since there is a whole series of NINJA movies, but Nero isn't in the other ones. Sho Kosugi is.

Enter the Ninja is no *Enter the Dragon*, and not a very good showcase for Sho Kosugi. He seems good but they don't show enough to make a proper judgment of his level of badassness. Still, it's a good time, I recommend it.

BY POPULAR DEMAND!
VERN REVIEWS THE GYMKATA DVD!!²

I believe Donald Drunko was the name of the wiseguy talkback newsie who kept bugging Harry and Moriarty to review the *Gymkata* DVD, and then roped me into it. If so this is for you, Drunko. Don't get me wrong, I was happy to perform this important service. Number one, I am a positive individual so I try to give back to the community. Number two, I always meant to see this horse shit anyway.

Gymkata is the 1985 picture by Mr. Robert Clouse, director of *Enter the Dragon, Black Belt Jones, China O'Brien* and various other American martial arts pictures. Unfortunately he must've hit upon some hard times during the Reagan years because here he is rehashing *Enter the Dragon* but instead of finding a cool new martial artist to star in it, he got a gymnast. Kurt Thomas was a world champion and was expected to win a gold medal in the 1980 Olympics, but the US team boycotted over the Russian invasion of Afghanistan. If he had gone maybe he would've won, but maybe he wouldn't have and people woulda been disappointed, the shine woulda been gone on him and nobody would've wanted to make *Gymkata*. What I'm saying is this movie and Osama bin Laden are both unintended consequences of the same conflict. And I can say objectively that the better of the two is *Gymkata*. *Gymkata* is better than Osama bin Laden.

Now, a lot of you may not know this about me but I have a little inside knowledge of this material because I was involved in competitive men's gymnastics, qualifying for three regional competitions and placing in two between 1977-1982. Because of this background, my experience viewing *Gymkata* may be a little different from— nah, just fucking with you, actually I forgot there even was such a sport as men's gymnastics so bear with me if I make any incorrect statements.

Based on the novel "The Terrible Game"³ by Dan Tyler Moore, *Gymkata* is the timeless tale of, well, *Enter the Dragon* but with all the good elements replaced by bullshit. It starts out intercutting the dude

---

2 I don't know why but whenever I send a headline to The Ain't It Cool News it goes online with 300% more exclamation points.

3 I'm no fan of that sport either, but calling it "the terrible game" seems needlessly harsh.

spinning on bars with some guys riding horses (what is this, an Ed Wood movie?) but then becomes *Enter the Dragon*, with some prissy government bureaucrat guy recruiting Kurt to go to some backwards fictional country in Eastern Europe called Parmistan and compete in a deadly tournament. But instead of Bruce Lee you get fucking Kurt Thomas. Instead of the most iconic martial arts scenes ever put on film, you get some asshole spinning around on a bar pretending to kick a dude. Instead of a martial arts tournament you get an obstacle course race (in the movie they call it "The Game," but in modern society we call it "*Real World/Road Rules Challenge*.") Instead of a great villain like the metal-clawed Han, you get the Clouse regular Richard Norton, who just looks like any other bearded white karate dude from the '80s except he has a little braid on the back. And a dangly earring. Instead of cool henchmen like Bolo Yeung and Sammo Hung, you just get some dipshits in executioner masks that are supposed to be ninjas because they shoot arrows every once in a while.

A lot of people forget this, but *Enter the Dragon* has a good supporting cast too. Bruce is obviously the main show, but Jim Kelly is in there and he gets some good lines. And you even got John Saxon. This one has a bunch of nobodies that get one line before they get impaled, fall off a cliff or are found dead without you even getting to see it. So there's nobody to carry the gymnast. He's gotta stand on his own two feet and that's something the guy just can't do. Maybe the most telling moment is when the race begins and he is immediately in last place and running like a girl. After about twenty feet he falls down for no reason, and a big dude named Thorg (Bob Schott, another Clouse regular) notices so he turns around and kicks him in the face.

Let me repeat that. The so called martial arts hero of this movie is such a fucking sissy that he can't run twenty feet without collapsing to the ground and getting kicked in the face. And this isn't at the beginning before he toughens up, this is the start of the climactic race. Maybe they shoulda got Mary Lou Retton to star in this thing. This is what we get in a permissive society that allows *The Karate Kid* to become a major cultural milestone. That's why even though *Enter the Dragon*, *Black Belt Jones* and *The Big Brawl* all had funky as hell theme songs, this one doesn't. The score is fine (especially considering the era we're dealing with) but it has no funk. Because it stars Kurt Thomas. It doesn't deserve funk.

See, gymnastics are obviously a good skill, all the great martial artists do flips and shit. But the thing is this guy can only do the flips. The kicks and the punches are not so convincing. Worse, he just looks like a complete dipshit. There is nothing tough about this guy at all. And that's why America loves it.

Okay, I had to criticize this movie for being such a low point for Robert Clouse, but I can completely understand why some of you people love this movie. I'm not sure it's up there with *Roadhouse* or *On Deadly Ground* in laughs or admirable sincerity, but this is definitely a funny straight-faced action movie. I mean, at one point Kurt Thomas gets chased down an alley and finds a bar perfect to jump up on and spin around. At another point he is surrounded by a crowd of criminally insane cannibals, but happens to be sitting on a stone something or other with handles just like a pommel horse, so he starts gymnasticking everybody in the face. This is good shit.

There's also some good lines. Like the guy who says, "Well, there's just a little anti-American sentiment running around. But I think—AARGH!" as he is suddenly hit with an arrow. Or Kurt's secret agent dad, who turns out to actually be alive, hugs him and says, "It's great to see you! You'll never know how—AAH! AHH!" as he too is suddenly hit with an arrow.

Also, I counted at least five parts where somebody is thrown off something tall and does a funny dubbed scream.

Most of the non-gymnastics action scenes aren't as funny. But there's a pretty entertaining section where the race goes through "the village of the crazies," where Parmistan sends their criminally insane. These guys just stand around laughing and making bird sounds and they attempt to mutilate any outsiders. I'm not clear whether this is what they do 24-7 all year round or if they just pull out all the stops once a year when The Game comes to town. But this is crazy town so some crazy shit goes down here. A guy in a monk's robe gestures to come through a door, and Kurt (who, by the way, is a complete idiot) is about to follow. Then the guy turns to open the door and we see that the back of the robe is cut open to reveal his bare ass. Which means he's crazy.

These crazies have some good ideas though. They send vicious dogs after Kurt, which would make the Olympics more entertaining, but they don't listen to the crazies, they're stuck in their boring old ways. Kurt also gets chased through a pig pen and has to climb over pigs, but as far as I can tell they are just regular pigs and not crazy pigs that have been cast out. As Kurt climbs out a window he looks down and sees the crazies about to stab Thorg with pitchforks. Kurt has this look on his face like he knows he has to intervene, this guy tried to kill him but it is only right to save his life, and then maybe all will be forgiven and they'll work together to survive this deadly challenge. But that's not what he does, he just watches as they kill Thorg. Remember, this is Kurt Thomas we're dealing with, he's not gonna be able to save somebody unless doing a flip or spinning on a pole is what can save them. Even then, he might boycott.

The part I really don't get is the weird guy with the blank expression standing up against the wall. After a while he turns around and you realize the weird face you've been staring at is made out of rubber and attached to the back of this guy's head. But I don't think it's supposed to be a mask, I think he has two faces, like Barbra Streisand's mirror. So they send people with birth defects to the village of the crazies too? This is very strange for this type of movie, I gotta commend it. However, having just watched *El Topo* again recently I'm thinking they could've gone even further. Maybe a dude covered in bees jerking off or something, I don't know.

In the end of course Kurt wins The Game, and some text on the screen tells us that the government got their way and was able to use Parmistan to launch a "Star Wars" defense satellite. In *Enter the Dragon* they're actually accomplishing something, stopping Han from murdering women. In *Gymkata* they just want to send up an SDI satellite. Of course, now it's twenty-two years and billions of dollars later and we know that "Star Wars" is a scam — it still can't tell the difference between a missile and a balloon that got away from a birthday party, even on a clear day, and how's it gonna shoot down a boxcutter or a suitcase bomb? So in retrospect we can see the cruel irony of The Game. All those lives, all those arrows, for what? To pad some pockets and send up a useless satellite. Unless maybe they use that satellite for cable TV now. Who knows. Maybe they died so we could watch *Crank Yankers* and shit.

Gymkata was released on DVD as the result of an annual Warner Brothers promotion where amazon.com allows people to vote for the release of movies from a group of WB catalog titles. I know there were multiple online *Gymkata* get out the vote campaigns, but don't get too excited. It was one of twelve movies they chose, it didn't exactly win the gold medal. It did beat out a pretty good movie called *Carny*, starring Robbie Robertson from The Band.

Knowing the fan response, WB pulled out all the stops for this DVD, including interactive menus, scene selections, the whole works. On the chapter index your selection is signified by a little ninja star, which is nice since there are no ninja stars in the movie but there obviously should've been. Other extras include an FBI warning, the original trailer, which has some really funny narration, and a trailer for *Dukes of Hazzard: The Beginning*, with a new Daisy Duke that looks more like Catherine Bach. ("The Duke boys are back — for their first adventure." Whuh?)

One thing they definitely did right, they used goofy vintage artwork from the original release instead of doing some new photo collage that would hide what the movie actually was. I don't know why they don't do that more often — it's easier for them to do, it looks way better, and it's more honest. I also appreciate that they included an English subtitle track. Some of the Seagal movies lately they haven't bothered, and I can't always tell what everybody is mumbling about.

The original 1.85:1 aspect ratio is sumptuously transferred, looking better than *Gymkata* has ever looked (probably, I don't know) and also better than *No Retreat, No Surrender* has ever looked.

Anyway, thanks Drunko or whoever it was.

CHAPTER TWO
THOU SHALT NOT LIE WITH CARTOONS AS WITH LIVE ACTION

In 2006, China's State Administration of Radio, Film and Television shocked the world by issuing a ban on programming featuring live action actors beside animated characters. At first glance it seems like a bizarre new form of prudishness in a country already doing a good job of confusing the rest of the world (for example they reportedly banned the movie Babe for featuring talking animals).[4] But what if they have a point? What if the continued blurring of the line between live action and animation goes against God and nature? I don't think they address that in the Bible, but it's in the movie Cool World for what that's worth.

Look man, I'm very liberal, especially in social matters. But I gotta admit I'm pretty closed-minded towards this cartoon-loving. In Japan they got a whole industry of pornographic cartoons, and I'm not sure I understand how live action dudes get off on that, but I guess they must. Maybe I'm just old fashioned but I think a live action person should fall in love with another live action person. None of this frame-by-frame stuff. Gives me the heebie jeebies.

---

4 On second glance, or reading the whole article, you realize it's just a roundabout way of protecting the traditional 2-D animation studios in China, which are threatened by these techniques done better in other countries. But it's more fun to pretend they're offended by the friendship between Michael Jordan and Bugs Bunny.

Walt made Mickey Mouse and Minnie Mouse, not Mickey Mouse and Minnie Driver.

But I don't know, maybe I'm mellowing out in my old age. I recently saw a Muppets special where Miss Piggy was treating Kermit like shit, as usual. No surprise. But then Uma Thurman, playing an airline employee, was openly flirting with Kermie. And he either didn't pick up the signals or just ignored them, because he's loyal to Piggy. But he's out there trying to help some poor kids while Piggy is in town clothes shopping for herself, occasionally taking breaks to nag him on the phone. Kermit clearly needs to leave that bitch, she's no good and she doesn't deserve him one bit. I was so disappointed in him for not saying "fuck it" and leaving with Uma. I know that's puppets and not cartoons but I think it's similar. Maybe this old dog can learn some new tricks of acceptance.

I never really realized this was an issue for me until I was going through my old reviews and noticed that this theme just kept popping up. In this chapter you'll see me struggling with the topic from many angles including the morality of live action/animated couples, the unnatural biology of a society of animated cars, and the hideous abominations that come about when computers try to create real people or give a cartoon cat real fur. But then to show that I'm not a complete zealot I'll end with two reviews where it's pretty obvious I'm sweet on some ladies who clearly have some cartoon ancestry in there somewhere.

ENCHANTED

I like to think I'm a pretty tough individual, even on a cellular level. So I don't usually watch movies like this and I don't usually get sick. A year or two ago I got some crud that really knocked me out, so while I was laying there a useless husk of my regular self I decided that God had opened a window — a window of opportunity for me to watch *Kill Bill Volume 1* and *Volume 2* in a row. The movie seemed even better in one sitting and I was healed the next day. Thanks God. You got good taste in movies.

So the next year when I got real sick I did the same thing, with the same success. Only trouble is when I got sick again this month and it was the worst I had in years. My *Kill Bill* treatment had been too recent, I didn't know if it would work and I didn't want to overdo it and create a *Kill Bill*-resistant supervirus. So I watched a bunch of other DVDs I had laying around.

But nothing worked. The shit was stuck in me. I watched a lot of movies but they were hard to enjoy, they somehow left a bad taste in my mouth and brain. On about day three, laying there in my feverish state, I became some kind of naturopathic theorist. My ideas were so revolutionary I could've been one of those doctors interviewed on *The Secret*. I decided that *Kill Bill's* power was a two-tiered regimen: its classic fight scenes and high quality filmatism got my adrenaline level up, but it was the sweet ending, with the lioness crying in happiness that her cub has been returned to her, that really did the trick. The pure joy raised my metabolism or my anti-bodies or my something-something... you know the thing. The thing that makes you healthy, in my opinion. That meant what I needed was not the usual mayhem I watch but some kind of fluffy sweetness.

So I crawled to the video store and when I came back it turned out I had rented Walt Disney's *Enchanted*.

You and your whole family will be enchanted by *Enchanted*. You'll have a magical time. If you and your family ever dreamed of fucking a magic cartoon princess whose best friend is a squirrel then *Enchanted* is a dream come true. Is what Gene Shalit might've said. But personally I did not like *Enchanted*, I was disenchanted with it. (Take that Shalit you fuck.)

What this is is a high concept romantic comedy by way of a tribute to the old Disney animated movies from before they got all concerned about the environment and told everybody to draw on computers instead of paper. Its heart is in the right place I guess but they don't have the skills to pull off what is really only a halfway there idea: an animated princess from a non-existent Disney fairy tale movie (depicted through actual hand drawn Disney animation) is sent through a magical portal and appears in live action (depicted by Academy Award nominee Amy Adams) in the "real" New York. There is no way to predict whether her naive ways will make it impossible for her to survive on the mean streets and it will turn into a *Death Wish* movie real fast or if she'll bump into dreamy Patrick Dempsey just before his wedding and teach him to slow down and learn the lessons of a magical cartoon from another dimension so that he can stop working too hard and be happier and ditch his woman for a better looking lady who barely has a brain and literally doesn't belong on this plain of existence but talks to animals and turns every day life into musical numbers. It could go either way, take your pick.

Dempsey of course is a divorce lawyer (how will he ever learn about love?) and a single father to a young girl (oh, what a sweet guy) and when his daughter spots live action Princess Giselle and her giant ball gown stuck on a billboard that she thinks is her castle he rightfully assumes she is a lunatic or perhaps a very, very well dressed and made-up crack ho. He tries to help her (like Eddie Murphy would do) and brings her to his apartment but then his fiancée thinks he's fucking her (*Three's Company*) and also Giselle ruins his drapes by making them into a dress, then humiliates him by singing as they walk through the park together. Of course, all the everyday New Yorkers they run into love her and instinctively take part in her musical numbers. It's only the cold, shriveled heart of the leading man that can't see that the magical toys of Mr. Magorium's Magical, Magical, Magical Emporium are full of imagination, wonder and dazzle. Or that might've been a shitty trailer I saw, but anyway this guy at first doesn't understand the lessons of cartoon fairyland until something happens that makes him believe, and I will not give away what it is that happens. Because whatever it was I fell asleep during it. But when I woke up he presumably had learned that she is actually a cartoon and because she's so nice and caring and knows how to enjoy life he starts to fall in love with her anyway.

Now I don't want to seem like a backwards guy or some kind of anti-cartoon bigot like Bob Hoskins in *Roger Rabbit* but I have to say that I am against this live action guy marrying this cartoon. There are a lot of issues here, for example we learned in the movie *Cool World* that if a live action guy fucks a cartoon girl it will destroy the very fabric of cartoon/live action reality. So guys, keep your dick in your pants. Or if you are a cartoon like Donald Duck then put some pants on. I know many live action youths had a thing for a cartoon lady such as a Betty Rubble or a Penelope Pitstop but that doesn't mean those cartoon gals should come into the world of live action and that you should marry them. First of all Betty is already happily married to a nice hard working guy and has a kid, so that's fucked up. Second of all, if you married Penelope Pitstop can you imagine, you couldn't even drive to the store without some asshole grabbing your wife and tying her to some railroad tracks. What a pain in the ass. I know that opposites attract and everything but you gotta take into account if your lifestyles are compatible or not. A regular guy marrying a cartoon princess is like a spider marrying a fish. It's just not gonna work.

In fact "opposites attract" is an important phrase to bring up because I think today's acceptance of live action/cartoon love goes back twenty years to Paula Abdul's famous video 'Opposites Attract.' If you're too young to remember I will just say that Paula Abdul, the judge from *Star Search* or whatever it's called now, was once a famous R&B pop singer and this was a video where she danced around and sang a duet with an animated rapping cat sporting a high top fade and a wifebeater. He's also a very talented dancer who tap dances, moonwalks and, ironically, does the Roger Rabbit. In the video they sing about how different they are — one only watches movies, the other only watches TV (?), one has a more serious demeanor than the other, one goes to bed early while the other one stays up all night freebasing cocaine and having huge orgies on the roof of the house ("I party all night" the lyric says), only one of them smokes, one of them steals the covers while the other is very courteous about the covers, etc.

So they list a lot of different things but they leave out the most important ones. For example, I don't want to assume too much but I have a hunch that Paula Abdul uses a toilet while MC Skat Kat shits in a box. If I'm right about that then you gotta admit that is a pretty fuckin big lifestyle difference in my opinion, they shoulda mentioned that in the song. To be fair, if they were out on a farm somewhere and MC Skat Kat had to shit he would probably dig a little hole and shit in it and then he would bury it. It would be way worse if she was dating Goofy. But you can see in the video that he lives in some sort of urban environment where it would be difficult to find a place to dig a hole for shitting in. In the concrete jungle he is equal to Goofy.

Anyway the important thing is I looked up Paul Abdul's bio. Her mom was a concert pianist, she wasn't raised on a farm. Paula studied broadcasting, left to become a Laker Girl, then she left that to become the choreographer for Janet Jackson's videos and for movies (she worked on *The Running Man, Action Jackson* and even did Tom Hanks's giant keyboard dance in *Big* — no shit), and she already had three other huge smash singles by the time she made the catfucking video. So she was most likely used to some high livin. What I'm getting at is that in the circles she ran in those days I'm pretty god damn sure she wasn't accustomed to dating people who shit in a hole in the backyard or in a box in the laundry room. Maybe that was part of the attraction, the whole bad boy/forbidden fruit thing, but I don't know man. That oughta be a dealbreaker, in my opinion.

Now, I've seen the stand up comedy. I know that men are from one planet while women are from a different planet from the one the men are from, that women go to the bathroom in groups, men are always scratching their balls while they watch football to ease the pain of the women using their credit cards to go shopping (by the way that last one happens in *Enchanted* — his daughter has his credit card "for emergencies" like going dress shopping with a magical cartoon princess). But even though your lady or fella is gonna have different interests and tastes from you I'm telling you, there should be some overlap there. If not you're gonna be miserable. This I fear is the case for Patrick Dempsey. I feel sorry for MC Skat Kat being a one-hit wonder, but he should thank the Egyptian cat gods that Paula ditched him for Emilio Estevez. That relationship would've driven him over the edge, next thing we'd hear he was stuck up a tree or ODd on catnip somewhere. Opposites may attract but that doesn't mean they should stick.

Yes, Princess Giselle becomes a live action woman when she comes to New York. So that probably solves the *Cool World* dilemma. And makes this whole enterprise more biologically feasible. And yes, she could probably be trained to use a toilet, although they most likely did not have that technology in her castle. It is also true that Amy Adams is gorgeous and adorable. So I can't really blame Dempsey for falling for this one. They don't make 'em like Amy Adams in live action world.

But still, I mean jesus. This is not a human being. This is a one-dimensional, one joke cartoon character. Dempsey is supposed to be an adult human being with responsibilities such as a job and a human daughter he is expected to raise. He is in a long term relationship with another adult human being. And he makes the decision to instead spend his life with a lady who doesn't understand anything at all about the world around her or even what time period she's in, but she does love fancy dresses and can dance around with animals and sing songs about kissing. That is not rational on this dude's part. What are they gonna talk about once he's tired of talking about true love? And is he gonna let all her animal friends come over for dinner or is it gonna eventually be too much for him? Sure it's cute at first, and she's less annoying than Snow White, but still, she'd get on anybody's nerves after a while. You can't have Christmas all year.

And you know what, even if you were gonna be a jackass and marry a Disney character you might be able to do better than this. Because if *Princess Giselle* was a real Disney movie it would be one of the worst ones. It's not even a real fairy tale, it's just a cheap rip-off of *Sleeping Beauty*. It's the old movie-within-a-movie problem — if you had a good idea for a movie you would make a real movie out of it, so the fake movie is always gonna suck. And they didn't want to waste an actual fairy tale on these bookend cartoon scenes. So instead they just have a lady and some animals and a doofus prince that rescues her from a troll (thankfully without a Scottish accent or farting) and an evil queen. They did get a couple things right to make it seem like a real Disney movie — the villain is a celebrity voice (Susan Sarandon) and plummets to her death (spoiler). But still. Who wants to see a non-specific fairy tale movie?

And by the way, if you're feeling bad for Dempsey's human fiancée, don't worry about it. She gets dumped but then she falls in love with the cartoon prince and goes to live in the cartoon world. Guess she hated her job, family, friends, home, reality, even her skin which she is willing to replace with drawings.

I know how to suspend the disbelief but for me this concept was too much, I can't accept that not one but two sane individuals would marry cartoon characters from another dimension. I don't buy it.

But a lot of people did, and the movie was very well reviewed for such a sitcom concept. There's exactly one reason why it was considered passable at all, and her name is Amy Adams. I honestly don't think there's another actor in the world who could've played this role without looking like an idiot. Everything about Amy Adams from her perky nose to her perfect doll hair really does make her look like a VIP member of the Disney Princess Club. She doesn't even look like a Disney princess come to life, she's not one of those gals in the Disneyland parades. She looks like the actual living being who the character was based on. And she talks and sings like it too. And she's great at playing these innocent, uncynical characters. If I were her I'd worry about getting typecast, but since this kind of seems like the role she was born to play I guess she might as well run with it.

I don't keep track of the ratings but Amy Adams is so lovable I think she may be America's Top Sweetheart, and if so I'd just like to point out that I predicted this years ago. Most people never caught on to her until her Oscar-nominated performance in *Junebug* in 2005. But guess what, early in 2001 I was onto her lead role in the straight to video *Cruel Intentions 2*, of which I wrote:

"The rest of the casting isn't too bad. The Catherine is no Sarah Gellar but you could get used to her, I guess."

You see that? "You could get used to her, I guess." And years later the whole world would get used to her. By the way when I said she's "no Sarah Gellar" I think I just meant she would not be in *Southland Tales*. So I'm way ahead of the curve on these things. I was practically psychic on that one.

In conclusion, don't fuck cartoons.

THE POLAR EXPRESS 3-D IMAX SPOOKARAMA

A few years back I wrote a piece called *Final Fantasy: The Spirits Within (Working title: Boring: The Movie)*. In the piece I talked about the wrongness of computer animators trying to create photorealistic human characters. I argued that no matter how real they looked they would never look completely real, because they wouldn't be able to walk quite right, or have a human soul, etc. I guess I didn't mention it in that piece, but there was a scene in the movie where two realistic human characters kissed, and it was like watching mannequins go at it.

(For your information, there's a porno called *Real Doll: The Movie* where pornographic professionals like Ron Jeremy stick their penises inside ten thousand dollar silicone sex dummies. That movie is disturbing in a different way from *Final Fantasy* because the dolls are not moving and their faces don't look alive. So it looks like these guys are having their way with dead bodies. But picture two of the dolls going at it with no animate objects involved. Then picture a rated PG version of that. That's the scene in *Final Fantasy*, I guess. It's not natural.)

Well nobody seemed to care back then but now many of the ideas I presented in that piece have worked their way into the mainstream, as reviewers of the new computerfied Robert Zemeckis Christmas fantasy *The Polar Express* have criticized the creepy, dead-eyed look of its overly realistic computerized cartoon characters. Japanese roboticists have even expanded on my theories, calling it "the uncanny valley" where your ability to relate to a robot or cartoon character suddenly plunges as it gets closer to humanity. So Mickey Mouse is our buddy but final fantasies give us the willies.

The Polar Express is a big pile of technological show offery which uses many methods no ordinary human being could defend. Why exactly would anybody make a movie starring actors, with computer animated characters made to look as much as possible like the actors? Couldn't we just eliminate the middle man and have actors? The movie was made I guess by having Tom Hanks and the other guy from *Bosom Buddies* wear magic space suits that control computer characters within the world of the computer (or "matrix," or "tron.") So it's not really animation as much as it is a high tech puppet show. You got the *Star Trek* prequels then *Sky Captain* and then this is the next step, but it's still not quite a cartoon.

The one and only way to see this movie is in Imax 3-D where available. This gimmick amplifies the creepiness of the movie but also makes it into a long theme park ride, a series of artfully designed dioramas, rollercoasters and waterslides. The people don't look entirely real, but neither do the fuckin pirates or haunted mansions, do they? It's amazing how far a big set of battery-powered goggles will go to make ol' Vern forgive and forget the valley of the uncanny dolls. I mean for the most part this is a well-told kiddy fantasy story with great atmosphere, so I didn't mind zooming around peering through windows and cracking through ice and watching the pretty 3-D snowflakes fall. I'm as surprised as you are that I am here to tell you that when it's in 3-D, it's really not that bad.

But I guess I can take partial credit for this one. I know in my heart, and I think you know this also, that Robert Zemeckis read my *Final Fantasy* piece. He still went the wrong way (just make cartoon characters look like cartoon characters, asshole! It's not hard to figure out) but at least he learned from my other final fantasy criticisms.

1. The walk. You'll remember my main complaint was that they would never duplicate the human walk. The crafty bastard did just that by capturing the actual human walk into the brain of a computer. They still have problems with characters looking weightless standing on top of a high speed train but at least their legs move at the right speed.

2. The voices. One of the most ridiculous aspects of *Final Fantasy* was hearing recognizable celebrity voices coming out of realistic human faces that do not match the celebrity. So Steve Buscemi's voice comes out of a boyish Jason Priestley type. Having read my piece, Zemeckis made all of the characters voiced by Tom Hanks actually look like Tom Hanks, so it wouldn't be too distracting. It's more like he's pulling a Peter Sellers. Glad I could help bud.

This is a children's fantasy story about a kid with no name who is starting to not believe in Santa Claus. He wants to believe but does not, so I guess he's agnostic. It's Christmas Eve, he's laying in bed and the magic of Imax 3-D makes you feel like you're hovering four inches away from his rubbery-skinned, milky-eyed face. Made me kind of uncomfortable. But to be fair, the animation on the kid is not that bad. His voice is the kid from *Spy Kids*, who is a good kid actor but is he a two-time Academy Award winner? Fuck no. So they got Tom Hanks to do the movements. The kid from SPY KIDS does not have the kind of acting experience required to move like a real kid. Tom Hanks does. Sorry kid from *Spy Kids*, maybe come back when you're older. You're a voice actor, leave the motion performance to the grown ups.

Anyway, a huge train shows up right next to his house, and a Tom Hanks Engineer sort of hassles the Tom Hanks kid into getting on. There are other kids there and the thing is headed for the North Pole for reasons nobody has explained. The Tom Hanks engineer is concerned that they might be late, which would somehow ruin Christmas. And the kid keeps fucking things up, pulling the emergency brake or losing a girl's ticket out the window or risking a horrible death by climbing around on top of the fast moving train. The engineer is no Willy Wonka but it's the same kind of magical/threatening children's story. At one point they even think he's gonna toss a little girl off the back of the train because the kid lost her ticket.

Along the way of course, a bunch of magical shit happens. The kid (Tom Hanks) meets a hobo (Tom Hanks) who has a campfire on top of the train and gives him a drink of disgusting dirty coffee. It later turns out the hobo is a ghost, which of course means the kid drank ghost coffee. That definitely raises a lot of questions about the digestion of ghost coffee but unfortunately we will never really learn the deal with that unless maybe there's a part 2.

I would also like to mention that the computerists have not yet found a way to duplicate the human mustache.

For the most part, the characters did not look as creepy as I was expecting. At least the main kid wasn't. But then he gets on the train and this little girl is smiling at him. And I don't know what they did but I swear to christ this little girl character looks like she has two glass eyes. Other than that, she looks great. But the two glass eyes kind of freaks you out. Maybe this was intentional, and there is some implied backstory of dual eye injury that ties in to the magic of jingle bells or whatever, I don't know. I have read a lot of the bible but not all of it.

Anyway I was going right along with it, but as soon as I got to the girl with the glass eyes I started to lose my connection to the computer world. I started to go offline. And suddenly I realized that these were not actual kids. They moved exactly like actual kids but they didn't look right. And I realized what they were was kids dipped in molten rubber, then airbrushed and wigged and given glass eyes. So there are actual little kids in there controlling the rubber outer layers from within. What a weird fucking thing to do, Zemeckis.

Somebody in Hollywood has to figure out that they gotta take advantage of this. These filmatists are trying to make realistic humans and accidentally made them creepy. So why not use this technology for a character who is actually *supposed* to be creepy? I think Stanley Kubrick actually wanted to do that in *A.I.* but since *Final Fantasy* did not exist yet I'm not sure if he really understood what a great idea he had. (And why the fuck do these mad computer scientists think that a horrible computer/cartoon abomination like Garfield or Shrek is CUTE? I know you guys stare at numbers all day but jesus, you must be fucked in the head trying to pull that shit.)

Anyway, after a brief rubber kid-induced panic attack I got used to the computer people again and from then on it was okay. They do the best job on the two train workers who keep trying to fix the lights or the brakes as the train and its occupants hurtle towards magical yuletide doom. They are a little more cartoony than the kids are (one of them hangs from the other guy's long beard) and they really seemed to me like Pirates of the Caribbean — 3-D and rubber but created by artists, not scanned into computers.

But there are a couple other problems with the movie. There are a couple of musical numbers, which fits in this kind of story, but most of the songs are awful. The only part I liked in the sappy kid duet on the back of the train was when the retarded guy sitting in front of me started to unexpectedly sing along. The actual score, by Alan Silvestri, is easier to take. I don't know about you but I think the score for *Edward Scissorhands* is a good wintery piece of music, so it was a good idea for Silvestri to blatantly rip off that score for this movie.

And by the end it is easy to overload on talk about The True Meaning of Christmas and Believing In Santa Claus and the Magical Magic of Christmas Magic and Crap. Even though they are more restrained about that shit than you expect them to be.

I gotta mention also, there is something a little weird about a movie where Tom Hanks is hiding behind every wall. In this movie, you are Tom Hanks, your dad is Tom Hanks, you get a ride from Tom Hanks, then you meet the ghost of Tom Hanks, you find out Santa Claus is Tom Hanks, and you even grow up to have the voice of Tom Hanks. One of the very few people who is NOT Tom Hanks is Steven Tyler, who has a cameo as a singing elf. So it is easy to wish that it was a complete Hanksworld. Other than that cameo the filmatists carefully created an old fashioned world with Roy Rogers slippers, classic space pajamas and vintage

Christmas carols playing on vinyl and piped into every corner by, well, pipes. But I guess they figured Steven Tyler is hundreds of years old and could really be from almost any time period.

There is also something a little off about Santa when you see him at the end. His face is a thin and pale Tom Hanks and he has a holy glow that makes him look part Santa, part Jesus. He seems like a nice guy though. He gives kids presents and all that. I should probably leave him alone.

This time of year everybody wants a piece of that Christmas magic. At the Seattle Center where I went to watch this movie there was a sign for the Washington Mutual Holiday Ice Rink. What better way to celebrate the birth of Jesus and/or Santa Claus than to ice skate indoors in honor of a particular bank. Also Camel cigarettes has just introduced delightful new limited edition warm toffee and mochamint flavors that create the type of yuletide cancer the Lord probably would've wanted to die from if he hadn't gotten nailed to that cross for our sins. (Mel Gibson's dad, if you're reading this, notice that I did NOT say nailed to the cross by the Jews. You need help dude.)

I kind of expected *Polar Express 3-D* to be the same kind of Christmas magic, the kind that comes with tie-ins and coupons and is made by computers for $150 million and is uncomfortable and weird to look at. But I think the baby Jesus will be happy to hear that it's not all that bad. It really isn't a shitstain on His holiday. I'm not saying Jesus would like it necessarily, but obviously he would forgive it. Me too, Jesus. Me too.

THE BEOWULF 3-D IMAX EXPERIENCE

Beowulf is the new "motion capture" weirdly computerized sword and sandal 3-D movie from Robert Zemeckis. He's using the same technology and directational style as *Polar Express* but it will go over better because that one was for kids, this one has a bunch of stabbings and monsters and a part where Virtual Angelina Jolie gives a handjob to a sword, so that means it's more sophisticated and adult.

Ray iWinstone voices the blond he-man of the title. Anthony Hopkins 2.0 plays the old king, Robin Wright Penn's likeness plays the princess from the fuckin *Shrek* movies, and John Pac-Mankovich does his usual distractingly weird performance as some asshole who is pissed off about something or other. Also you got Crispin Glover inhabiting the monster Grendel and a very good computerized duplicate of Angelina Jolie's head as Grendel's hot mom.

I guess they ran out of comic books and '70s horror movies to remake, so this one is based on an epic poem from 700 AD. All I knew was a dude named Beowulf fights a monster named Grendel, so it was a fresh new story for me. But some 1300 year olds might say it's raping their childhood, because apparently co-screenwriters British-guy and *Pulp-Fiction*-guy-besides-Tarantino throw in a pretty big reinterpretation. In this one the king fucked Grendel's mom (take that Grendel!) and in fact is Grendel's dad. And Beowulf fucked Grendel's mom too (ooh, snap!) and the dragon he fights at the end is his son. *Ha ha, your son is a dragon!*

The weird thing is that this modernization of the ancient poem actually makes it more politically incorrect. I mean, that shit is fucked up. The whole story is about some dudes going to a cave and fucking a demon and then lying about it and killing their own poor bastard sons. On the surface they seem like fairly noble kings, but their way of absolving themselves of their past sins is to murder their own children. King Anthony Hopkins could've solved this whole problem if he would've bought Grendel some ear muffs and let him hang out at the castle. I know he's a fucked up Elephant Man looking giant with no genitals who likes to bite people's heads off and hates merrymaking, but I'm sure if you get to know him he's pretty cool.

The main villain is Angelina Jolie Robot as Grendel's Mom (or "Beowulf's Baby Mama" I believe they call her in the credits) and her brand of evil is to look real sexy and lure people in to fuck her. I'm not sure how it works because you can see that she has no vagina, but I guess they figured something out. Admittedly she does fly down to the hall and kill a bunch of dudes *Predator* style, but that's only after they murdered her retarded son. She's like Pamela Voorhees without the sweater. Anyway, the emphasis is definitely on "oh jeez, she's so hot, how can I not fuck her?" The ol' male fear of female sexuality. And the fear of the consequences of sex, and the responsibility of fatherhood. They cannot turn down the magical golden cave pussy, but then they're ashamed of the sons it creates. I guess politicians have always been the same.

You know, now that I think about it the main villain is not the king's baby mama, it's the king's johnson. In fact, that would be a good title for the movie, *The Kings Johnson*. No apostrophe because there are two kings, it's a double meaning. They would have to rename him Beowulf Johnson though for it to really work.

Actually I read on Wikipedia that the manuscript of the original poem is not titled, it just has become known as *Beowulf*. So in my opinion it was always meant to be called *The Kings Johnson*.

The Kings Johnson only think with their johnsons. The Queen (Robin Wright Penn OSX) seems like she's supposed to be really nice and loving, but she gets passed on to Beowulf like property, and then he sleeps with some younger girl anyway. I mean he used to go around on adventures fucking mermaids and shit, so that's the lifestyle he knows. If this whole thing was gonna turn out less tragic, one of these King Johnsons needed to man up and have a more mature relationship with his woman. The Anthony Hopkins King Johnson should've done the right thing and married Grendel's Mom and helped her raise Grendel into a more respectful young man with more self-esteem. I'm sure Grendel's Mom would've settled down a little if she got married. She's a smart lady and ahead of her time, she invented stiletto heels you know. I don't think she could've breast fed Grendel though, unfortunately. That might be part of the problem with that boy.

Before I go on, I gotta say, you should go see this movie in 3-D right now. I can't vouch for the digitally projected 3-D they are using in some theaters, but the Imax version is great. It's a fun movie but the 3-D and the Imax sound is half of the experience. On video the stupid idea of using computerized dummies instead of human beings will be much more distracting.

See, here's how the movie is made. It would be nearly impossible to film Anthony Hopkins making a speech in live action, so instead they have him make the speech while wearing specially designed scuba gear and with hundreds of little dots glued on to his face, and then they spend two or three years having a team of computer scientists create a multi-million dollar computerized simulation of him standing there making a speech. Through this miracle of technology he looks like rubber but he's wearing a robe and not scuba gear! There is no trace of the scuba gear at all! Amazing! I don't know how people even made movies before this was invented, must've been a huge pain in the ass.

So now the movie has some of the subtlety of an Anthony Hopkins acting performance, but with the not-being-real of animation. So it's part of the best of one out of two of both worlds. This technology was also a good way to get Angelina Jolie to appear completely nude, although the technology is apparently not good enough yet to give her nipples or a vagina.

Like with *Polar Express*, I sort of got a kick out of the creepy stiltedness of this completely misguided approach to animation. It's a good novelty, like those *Thunderbirds* puppets they used to have. But I know that's not what they're going for, so I don't know what the fuck they're thinking making a movie this way. I love what Zemeckis does with the camera, constantly flying up to a God's eye view, pulling back from the hall into the rafters, into the sky, into the clouds, and into Grendel's cave for a closeup of the back of his fucked up head, all in one shot. Or the way in *Polar Express* he followed a girl's ticket as it flew out of the window of the train, got captured by a bird, trampled by wolves and fell off a cliff back into the train.

But is that camerawork really a good trade off for having characters that are an abomination against God? Yes, they've improved it since *Polar Express* but it's still distracting as hell. John Malkovich still looks like he's either blind or not looking in the right place. Most of the characters have realistic heads and weirdly stubby, blobby bodies. Even the horses look kind of like dwarves. (Guess they couldn't get a horse into scuba gear.) There's a crowd scene that really creeped me out, because it's so obvious that nobody in the crowd is really standing in the same place or looking at the same thing and nobody knows how to create a realistic standing-watching-a-guy posture. And things are always dropping or being carried or flying through the air with no sense of weight at all. How hard is it to just flip an actual gold coin? I guess it's some of the same problems you have with live action movies these days, since so much is done with green screens. But what about the hair? When the characters are talking to each other should I really be ignoring what they're saying and thinking they must have a hell of a conditioner in 700 AD to give their warriors such perfect, doll-like hair?

But I don't know, maybe that was how they described it in the poem.

Also, I'm not entirely convinced that you can't do shots like that in a live action movie with effects. Yes, it would be hard and require a lot of computers, but I think you could do it, and probably for cheaper. I mean, Peter Jackson did shots like that in *Lord of the Rings*, following the moth around. The only differences are 1. Peter Jackson had to plan it before shooting it, instead of letting the effects people figure it out later and 2. it's not as distracting and creepy.

So *Beowulf* is a crazy and misguided movie, but it's also a fun time. I enjoyed it. There's a lot of good spectacle here. Beowulf tells a story where he fights a bunch of sea monsters and it's pretty crazy, he's stabbing their giant eyes with his sword. The most hilarious shot in the movie is him tearing out from inside a giant monster eyeball, then puffing out his chest and yelling "I. AM. BEOWULF!!!" Top that, *300*. It's gotta be one of the most violent PG-13 movies ever made, but they shoulda gone for rated-R just for the sake of nudity. Not just because of Angelinabot's Barbie anatomy, but because Beowulf fights Grendel butt naked, and there's no way to take it totally seriously when they keep using conveniently placed objects to cover him up. Obviously Zemeckis didn't see *Eastern Promises*. That's how it's done, fella.

The best part of the movie is Grendel. I expected a big mean monster, but you immediately feel sorry for this guy. He's giant but he's pathetic, he's a fucked up Elephant Man looking motherfucker with parts of his insides exposed, weird bumps and slime and scales all over him. He has super-sensitive hearing so the loud noises make him flip out, and he's screaming and crying the whole time he's attacking. The design of him is blobbier and cartoonier than he oughta be but it's still a great monster because you get the tragedy just looking at him. Poor guy, it looks like it hurts just to be alive. Plus he still lives with his mom. And she's always bringing new boyfriends to the cave. Not fun.

And I think Zemeckis, despite all the shit I'm giving him about this stupid process, is doing a lot of cool stuff with it. I like his storytelling. I love the scene where Grendel comes back up to the cave and his mother is talking to him, and the whole scene is from the point of view of the mom, coming up out of the lake, one of those killer's-eye-view shots like in horror movies. But then at one point a 3-D tentacle comes out from behind the camera and caresses Grendel's deformed face. Pamela Voorhees never did that.

In fact, I think this movie is gonna give more kids nightmares than any other in recent years. Poor fucked up fifteen foot deformed naked man kicking the door down, running around screaming like he's on a speed binge, tearing people in half, biting people's heads off, impaling them on chandeliers, carrying their limp dead bodies up to a cave so his mom can fuck em. Grendel will be the *Wizard of Oz* flying monkeys of 2007.

So maybe it's not a great movie, but it's a good theme park ride. I think I might go on it again.

UPDATE: I did go on it again, and I can now vouch for the Real-D digital 3-D version. Looks like the digital projecting technology is finally catching up with the hype. It looks real nice, quite possibly a little clearer than the Imax version and for me it had less ghosting. I still prefer the giant screen and the sound system of the Imax though. But either way if you can see it in 3-D it's gonna look good. Also I thought of another alternate title for it: *Caves With Benefits*.

GARFIELD
the asshole cat

Man, what a fuckin week. On Tuesday Bush got either "re"-elected or re- "elected," and I've been stumbling around muttering to myself ever since. Stabbing at my porridge with my spoon, staring blankly out the window, mouthing the word "why" to myself over and over again. One thing I know, there are some things in this world that just cannot be explained. Sometimes bad things happen to good people. Sometimes people vote for a president that couldn't be trusted to put on his own pants. And sometimes a guy gets the blue state blues, walks around town in a daze, suddenly finds himself at home having rented the movie *Garfield* not really knowing how or why. I know for a fact this happens because you're lookin at the guy who it happened to. Me. It was weird.

What this is is a movie based on the popular comic strip from the 1980s called *Garfield*. Like all comic strips it is not funny and about a talking animal. This is a cat called Garfield who is orange. The thing about Garfield, he is real fucking fat, he eats lasagna. That's funny because real cats eat cat food, but this one also eats lasagna. Also he says "I hate Mondays" at the beginning although this does not turn out to be important. But it is that sort of detailed characterization that makes him, you know, Garfield. I guess.

I mean, think about it. Why the fuck is a cat gonna hate Mondays? Especially this particular cat, this Garfield. What he does, he sleeps, he eats, etc. For a cat, even a talking, dancing asshole cat like this, he is not gonna give a fuck if it's Tuesday, Thursday, the 12th of February, anything. It doesn't matter. He doesn't have to work. He doesn't have to get out of bed. Every day of the year is the weekend to him. There is no beginning of the week for a cat with that particular lazy asshole cat type of lifestyle. Even when he is expected to eat a mouse, he just fakes it. There is no fuckin reason this cat even knows what Monday is, let alone hates it. And yet he says it explicitly that he hates Mondays. You see. That is why it is funny. Because why would he hate Mondays. Oh, that Garfield the asshole cat. He hates Mondays.

The weirdest thing about Garfield, he looks like some kind of fucked up Nazi medical experiment or something. Like they took an ordinary cat but painted him bright orange, surgically removed his skeleton, injected him with fifteen pounds of human assfat and then gave him a new plastic skeleton with a skull designed to contain a pair of huge, wet, human eyes the size of baseballs. I don't think that's really how they did it for the movie, but that's what it looks like. They might've used a real cat wearing a padded suit or something but I think it was probably computers. But I think this is a poor and unethical use of computers. You gotta make up your mind if it's real or cartoon, you can't do both. It is real unnatural to see a wacky cartoon cat wearing real fur.

Anyway, Garfield is a cat who lives with his owner John. This is a guy who has no job or activities. His only interests are his pets and the hot veterinarian he's had a crush on since high school. In the opening shot we see a collection of photos of John, and in every single one he is holding Garfield. Now it would be weird enough for a guy to be that obsessed with his cat, but especially this particular cat. Because this cat is a total asshole. He steals John's food, flushes the toilet when he's in the shower, destroys all of the furniture, constantly pushes the puppy off the chair, scratches him, or beats him with a pillow, even bullies the other cats in the neighborhood. He just watches TV all day and never leaves the house. He eats too much, he burps too much, he sleeps too much and insists on having his own bed and even a god damn teddy bear.

And he fucking whines. He is constantly complaining from the first minute of the movie to the last. Nothing is good enough for Garfield. He hates everyone and everything. Except himself. John pampers him so much he even makes home made lasagna for him, and lasagna is a pretty time intensive pasta in my opinion. But even *that's* not good enough for fucking Garfield. And he makes bad puns too. He makes Elvis jokes and *Jerry Maguire* references. He says lines like "I think I'm going to blow cat chow chunks" and "maybe I'll get a CAT scan."

When Garfield disappears for a while, you'd think John would breathe a sigh of relief. But he's like one of those common law wives you see on *Cops* all the time, he thinks he loves his abusive cat because he says, "I can't live without Garfield."

Another thing that is weird, Garfield never shuts up (he has the voice of Academy Award nominee Bill Murray) but John has no idea that he talks. Only animals can hear animals talk, not humans. But paradoxically, animals *can* hear humans talk. Whooooah. It's not explained if the humans can see that Garfield's mouth is moving or that he is always gesturing and dancing around and crap.

At first I couldn't tell if John could hear Garfield or not, so when I realized he couldn't, I started thinking maybe there was some twist where John is actually a ghost, or Garfield is actually a ghost. I'm not sure which way it would work.

Anyway, since this is a movie about pet animals, that means a bad guy is gonna steal a dog. It happened in *Air Bud* and it happens here. And it's Garfield's fault, so the one positive thing he does in the movie is go clean up his own mess. For the first forty-five minutes nothing really happens, he just sits around the house, sort of a slice of life kind of deal.

I almost thought it was supposed to be like *Friday* but with a freaky looking obese asshole talking cat. Then the puppy gets stolen, and this Garfield finally gets up off his fat cat ass and makes the courageous move of leaving the god damn house. Then he goes on an epic adventure that involves going to a building where the dog is, etc.

A lot of the comedy in this movie is Garfield runs around, he falls, there is screaming. At one point he runs up a lady's dress. And then he'll say something about an HMO or a primary care provider or something like that. Because what would a cat know about health care? That's why it's funny. Ha ha, the cat said HMO. It's like in those cartoons where they put in jokes that the adults will understand and the kids won't. But here it's not jokes, it's just words.

In a way this is the perfect movie for the 2004 election. Garfield is a horrible, useless asshole bully. But the music tells us he's some kind of charmer and I guess the movie made a bunch of money. So apparently everybody loves this asshole. There is nobody on Earth that could explain why Garfield is supposed to be a lovable character, but there he is. Just like Bush with his 51% mandate. Hooray. God bless America. I think that's what it's supposed to be about, isn't it?

No, probably not. But the key to the meaning of *Garfield* may lie in presidential history. President James A. Garfield was only president for 200 days before he died. He was shot by a lawyer who thought God told him to do it. The bullet itself didn't do much damage, but the doctors couldn't find it in there. They had Alexander Graham Bell make them a metal detector to find it, but he mistakenly detected the springs in the mattress beneath the president. The doctors dug around so much they created a huge infected wound which caused the heart attack that killed Garfield. Which, hmmm, I'm not sure if that has any parallels to the story in this movie.

Man, I gotta be honest, I don't think I really *get* this movie *Garfield*. I'm not sure what the deal is. I listened to some of the director and producer commentary track but they never really get into explaining what the deal is. I mean, I guess they sort of do. In one part the producer says, "Now, this is a really fun sequence in the picture, because Garfield is about to destroy the lasagna." That pretty much explains this movie, I guess.

CARS

As you know I'm not one for the cartoons but somehow I ended up seeing this new one called *Cars*. What *Cars* is about is cars. However they are not any ordinary type of car like you've ever seen before, they are living cars. And when I say that I am not even talking about a *Knight Rider* or *Herbie the Love Bug* type of scenario here, I am talking about an entire society devoid of human life, but dominated by living, feeling cars with weird eyeballs on their windshields. They can make gestures and they can use their tires sort of like hands, and they have jobs, etc. Even the insects of this world are cars, but there are regular non-car plants.

These cars have not only created a civilization, but their civilization has been around long enough that the good old days are gone. The story is about Lightning McQueen, who is apparently not named after Steve McQueen despite his brave service to the cause of cars in *Le Mans* and *Bullitt*. Thanks a lot, assholes. Lightning is a hotshot race car, basically a NASCAR star without a driver. Because he's a stubborn egotistical asswipe of a car he fucks up and blows his huge lead making the big race a three-way tie. One of the other racers is played by Michael Keaton but he looks like the Burt Reynolds of cars. Anyway Lightning has to go to California for another race and because he's a celebrity he doesn't even bother to drive there himself, he goes inside his friend, a Mack truck played by Cliff from *Cheers*. Basically, he is inside his friend's ass, but you can't completely blame him because the inside of his friend's ass looks like some kind of luxury apartment.

But then Lightning gets lost and ends up stranded in a small town along Route 66 where he learns valuable car lessons and helps revive a dying way of car life, etc.

This movie maybe isn't quite as effective as the other movies by these *Toy Story* people, but it does work. And part of the appeal is the incredible attention to detail, even in the filmatism. For the parts about car races they take on the frenetic tics of sports broadcasting, with flashy camera moves and onscreen graphics and with car commentators and corporate sponsors. There is an entire audience of thousands of cars. Then when it gets out on the road it slows down and there is actual atmosphere. Somehow they really capture the feel of driving out on the highway at night. And when they get to the town, I think it's called Radiator Springs, there are these quiet establishing shots with a yellow traffic light slightly buzzing as it blinks on and off. Even the sound effects are perfect. They had to figure out the sound of tires rolling around as cars "walk" along having a conversation.

And the computery animation is far beyond what we've seen before — the different kinds of lighting, the reflective (or rusty) surfaces of the cars. And the world around them looks like reality. I mean, there were previews for four or five other computer-animated movies before the movie, all of them about talking animals, but not cars. Animation-wise, *Cars* looks like it's about ten years ahead of those other ones.

So I think whether or not you should see this movie all depends on whether the premise freaks you out in a good way or a bad way. It's cuter than *Polar Express* but in some ways weirder. I mean, a world of cars? It's kind of a freaky premise and it brings up questions here and there, questions that are not answered in the movie. I mean the main thing I wondered was how do cars reproduce? Do they mate, or do they just build other cars? They gotta reproduce somehow because the founder of the town is an antique Henry Ford type deal (you see him in statue form) so there are definitely generations of cars. And thank God, because we want car society to go on bravely into the future.

If cars have parents, do they look like their parents? Or is it just kind of random? Could a bus screw an ice cream truck and pop out a Lightning McQueen? If Lightning and his Porsche girlfriend have a baby what will it look like, half race car and half Porsche? Do they start out small, and if so, why didn't we see any baby cars like that in the movie?

And if you think about it, it gets deeper than that because you have to wonder, is a race car born a race car or does he make a lifestyle choice and then grow into a race car? I guess he's probably born that way but what if he doesn't like to race? Doesn't being born a certain type of car seem like sort of a curse? Isn't there something inherently depressing about a world where your entire way of life is predetermined upon birth? What if Mater (played by unfunny fake redneck "Larry the Cable Guy") didn't WANT to fucking tow cars? What if he wanted to be a fire truck? Too bad, he's a tow truck, he's fucked.

Unless maybe he could get customized, but I don't know what car society's view is of that sort of thing. If a ride gets pimped, is that the same as plastic surgery, or is it a natural process? Does it mean you're a sellout, or an individualist?

I know your job isn't your whole life, a tow truck can have hobbies outside of towing. But work definitely seems important to these cars. Most of them seem to own their own businesses. They definitely have a whole car economy going, I'm just not sure how it works exactly. We know they sell tires and gas to each other, and money is mentioned. But we never see any money. If they really have money, where do they keep it, in their glove compartments? Does the money have a picture of a car on it? How do they hold it with those big round tires? Obviously they don't have debit cards, 'cause how the fuck are they gonna type in their PIN numbers?

You know what would really suck? Being a train. There's a living train in this movie. I hope that guy can get off the tracks, otherwise he's got the rawest deal of anybody. Being a train must be like knowing for sure you're gonna work for KFC for the rest of your life.

You have to wonder how exactly this civilization is gonna progress. They don't like to drive everywhere themselves, but other than that one truck's ass they don't seem to have any other form of transportation. Maybe the train's ass, but I'm not sure if he's hollow. In the future will cars begin to build other cars to drive in? They already built a road-fixing machine, so clearly it's not out of the question for cars to build and operate machines. Would living cars driving inanimate cars cause an ethics debate? Or would it just be creepy?

Where does their gas come from? Does it come from dinosaur fossils like ours did? What type of cars were the dinosaurs of car world? What does a car fossil look like? Are their chassis on display in museums?

Have cars gone to space yet? I guess there must be living space shuttles. Will they ever discover life on other planets, and if so will the life be cars? Maybe just microscopic spore cars on Mars?

Because the founder of the town is no longer there, we know that cars can die. But do they die of old age or do they only die in wrecks? Do they feel pain? How far can a mechanic ethically go in saving an ailing car? How many parts can be replaced before a car is no longer himself? In other words, what part holds a car's soul?

And hell, as long as we're talking about the car soul we might as well hit on religion. Is there such a thing in car world? An all-powerful being who built the cars? Is there a car Jesus? Maybe the Tucker Torpedo? Are there different religions and hell, do they have wars? I guess there must be tanks off somewhere fighting wars. So it's kind of like our army, there's a whole class doomed to military service and all the Suburbans and Volvos and everybody get to stay home and not worry about it.

I'm assuming there's war in car world because I'm assuming there's religion and if there's car religion there's car war. But when will it end? How can you have peace when you have members of your society born as tanks and bomber jets and shit? Isn't it kind of a self-fulfilling prophecy? And if you stop war, isn't it unfair to these individuals, to erase their whole purpose in life? They were born that way. Who are we to judge what they do?

Other than those few questions everything is pretty much answered, not a bad talking car movie at all, I would recommend it.

MARY POPPINS

You know how politicians are always saying lately that we don't need to just worry about helping the people on Wall Street, we need to help the people on Main Street? Well one time I was at Disneyland, walking down Main Street when suddenly Mary Poppins rushed by with an entourage of kids trying to get her autograph. Not the real Mary Poppins, (because she is a fictional character in my opinion) and not Julie Andrews, but the Disneyland Mary Poppins. And I was surprised to find myself thinking *you know what, Mary Poppins is kind of hot*. Nobody wants to get to an age where you start to think a nanny from an old Disney movie is kind of hot, but it happens to the best of us.

And it was kind of like a door opened up there full of new possibilities, because then I realized actually back then Julie Andrews was kind of hot too, not just modern day Disneyland Mary Poppins. And she had those little hats and a talking umbrella and shit. I know a lot of men are intimidated by women who are more capable than them, but I would not be against dating somebody who can fly and sit on a cloud. I don't know what her capacity is for carrying other people and putting them on clouds and all that, I guess that would have to be addressed. But it's pretty cool that she can do that. I would call that a point in her favor.

Well I apologize if this information shatters any illusions about what a hardcase I am, but recently I watched the movie *Walt Disney's Mary Poppins* showing at a local theater. Long story. But that was kind of a revelation too because I never really gave it much thought before, but I realized this is a pretty fuckin good movie as far as that type of thing goes.

If you haven't seen it before or don't remember it too well, Andrews plays Mary Poppins, magical nanny riding carousel horses etc.

There's a famous scene where Mary interacts with animated penguins and what not, but even apart from that this is the Disney live action movie that's most integrated with their world of animation. Everything in the movie from Mary's costumes to the house with sails and a cannon on top to the stylized London cityscape looks like it was designed and manufactured by Disney artists. No half-assing it. And then it's got those catchy songs, and they go off into magical worlds inside a chalk painting, they do a dance number on the roof, they get covered in ash but not in a *War of the Worlds* type of way. So it's easy to see why everybody is charmed by this movie.

But what I noticed this time is there's more going on than that. Even taking out the fantasy elements, the whole idea of this movie is alien to me. I don't know about you, but I never knew anybody that had a nanny. I don't live in a place where people hire other people to raise their kids for them. The parents in this movie are sympathetic, but they're stupid. The dad, obviously, is too obsessed with his job at the bank, he is not good to his family and has to learn his lesson.

(See, you thought that first sentence where I mentioned Main Street/Wall Street made no sense, but now you go back and it turns out I was making this Disneyland reference but then also I was laying the groundwork to start talking about the themes of the movie and see we got this banker, that's where the Wall Street comes in, and there's this whole thing going on with the gap between the classes... go ahead and take a minute for it to sink in there, I don't want anybody's minds to explode from how deep it is. So ease into it please.)

The mom is cool because she's really into the women's suffrage movement, she comes home and sings a song to her maids to get them riled up about women's rights and how they must fight to create a better world for their daughters. But then as soon as she hears her husband she puts all the paraphernalia away and warns everybody to shut up. "You know how Mr. Banks feels about the movement." She reminds me of people today who are really excited about the environment or stopping the war or something and their hearts are in the right place but it's really more of a hobby and a series of bumperstickers than something they're going to put themselves on the line for.

We never hear Mary comment on the women's suffrage movement, and it's almost like she doesn't need it because she's such a strong and self-assured woman, she clearly does what she wants and takes absolutely no shit from anybody, knowing exactly how to manipulate her boss to get what she wants with minimal confrontation. On the other hand she can't vote, so she should probably use her magic powers to improve Mrs. Banks's rallies or something.

But the movie is more about class than about gender. Little Jane and Michael are these rich kids but they hate being nannied, they like to run off late at night, it's how they cry out for attention. And the interesting thing is that all their friends are the servants and the working class — the maids, the chimney sweeps, the street performer, the beat cop. Bert changes jobs every day which makes him adventurous but also suggests things aren't as easy for some people as they are for the Banks family. He's always hustling for a buck and making the world happier, like with his sidewalk drawings, but he's never gonna own a house and a nanny and an army of maids. When he does his one-man-band gig in the park the rich people stand around, delighted, and then when he holds out his hat they won't make eye contact and they suddenly have to go polish their money or something.

But the lives of the working class are like a thrilling adventure to the children. While the bankers sit in their heavily staffed homes worrying about work, the chimney sweeps are having a huge dance party on their roofs, enjoying an incredible view of London that the bosses will never get to see. Maybe there's a sense of tourism there, these kids hang out with the workers but go home to a comfy bed. But the chimney sweeps also get

Mary's endorsement. She's of the servant class like they are but she literally lives on a cloud and seems to control her own destiny (and has some pretty nice dresses) so she could probably be out on the town with some handsome rich fuck if she wanted. Instead she's on the roof with them or in the park with Bert.

The other thing going on is there's this whole sad undercurrent to the movie. As much as it's about fun and songs and better parenting and what not, there's also an element or two of tragedy and unrequited love and shit. Because first of all, Bert is clearly infatuated with Mary Poppins. We got no idea where he knows her from or how long it's been since he's seen her, because she lives the lifestyle of a nomad, a drifter or a cloudsitter. But when she shows up he's so fuckin happy, and he sings this song 'Jolly Holiday' about how much he likes being with her. You don't sing about holding somebody's hand and how your heart starts beatin' like a big brass band if you're not enamored of the lady. And in case you don't get the picture he starts listing off all the other gals he's been with and how they're not as good as Mary — I count twenty names.

And why not? Mary is a fun lady. You're telling me you wouldn't want to hang around with her? This is not an *Enchanted* situation where she talks to birds and doesn't know better. Mary Poppins can talk to birds AND fit into modern society. She can make a carousel horse go rogue, she can make a plume of chimney smoke into stairs. That's what she does when she's on the job, taking care of kids. But she also enjoys rum. Who knows what she does in a twenty-one and over type situation. So of course Bert wants to have as many jolly holidays with her as he can get.

But Mary tries to play it like she thinks they're just friends, she praises Bert for not wanting to "press his advantage." And she's not blind, she fuckin knows the poor guy is crazy for her. But she doesn't tell him "I don't like you that way," she just kind of feigns ignorance.

I'm not trying to accuse Mary Poppins of being a tease. For a minute I did think this was pretty cold for her to string him along like they're on this date when clearly he has strong feelings and she pretends not to notice. But maybe there's a good reason for this when you consider the other tragic part of the movie. For some reason Mary has resigned herself to this life of traveling around helping families. She becomes closer to these kids than they are to their own parents, then as soon as there's an improvement she leaves. And she acts like she doesn't care but there's one shot where she's looking out the window as the dad is finally shaping up with the kids and she looks like she's holding back tears. But not "that'll do pig" type happy emotional tears. She loves these kids and wants to stay but her own happiness is not the priority for her. She sacrifices herself to go around helping these rich people.

Who knows how long she's been flying around doing this, making a difference, and probably breaking the hearts of Berts all around the world. I'm sure she could list off twenty dudes too. But since she knows she has to leave maybe it's for the best. Maybe she even loves Bert back, but she can't tell him that and then fly away. She doesn't want to be a deadbeat.

I wonder what made Mary Poppins this way? Did she have shitty parents who didn't pay attention to her in a cloud mansion somewhere? So she's like Batman, she has to dedicate her life to a mad crusade to prevent this from happening to other kids? I don't know. But she feels strongly about it. No wonder when the day is gray and ordinary Mary makes the sun shine bright. I mean I don't know what value there is in this but I saw the movie and it hit me pretty hard, I was thinking about it so I thought I would mention these things.

Nah, I don't really like it though, that was all a big joke. Right guys? Who likes that kind of crap anyway. Not us right guys?

X-2: X-MEN UNITED

Dear Mystique,

Hey sugar it's me Vern. Remember me, I reviewed your first movie "the x-men" and even though I don't read that comic strip shit, I enjoyed the picture. Well I gotta say although the title "x part 2 x-men united" is pretty terrible I also enjoyed your part 2. It doesn't have the same "I can't believe this isn't total shit" surprise factor but instead it has these characters that I enjoyed in the first picture and it tries to add more depth and drama and convolutedness to their adventures and what not. like a comic strip book.

But the reason I'm Writing to you mystique is because you are my favorite mutant now. Don't get me wrong, I still think Young Clint Eastwood is great as Professor Logan Wolverine, the art teacher at X-Men Community College. There is another X-Man called Rogue but she's not really a Rogue, she always sits at the same table as Iceman and Fireman. Professor Wolverine is the real rogue, he wanders around in the snow by himself uncovering his past and going on adventures and shit. Who knows what happened between part 1 and part 2, he could've saved an injured baby polar bear, or he could've gotten in a fight with a yeti, or got buried under an avalanche and had to melt his way out by banging his metal Freddy Krueger claws against each other to create heat. I mean anything could've happened, as long as it is snow related. Anyway he's the real rogue, so when he goes to the X-Man school to try to find beer, all the kids follow him around because he's cool. I liked when he said "You picked the wrong house, bub." That was pretty tough.

Most improved X-Man goes to Storm, played by Halle Berry. Her wig looks a lot better and I guess the oscar made her try harder. She's actually kind of scary this time when she gets the weather control going.

Also that new German guy Kurt is pretty cool. I mean I'm cool with mutants, I totally don't even care that the guy has that tail and everything. I mean I would totally hang out with blue skinned people to be frankly honest. I probably, you know I'm not a mutant but I'd probably be one of those guys that hangs out with mutants and it's like, when I'm around them I don't even remember who is a mutant and who is not a mutant. I'd be like...

Hey, you know that guy Kurt? Kurt Vagner? You know, the German guy?
Kurt? German guy Kurt. I don't know, what does he look like?
I don't know how to describe him, I mean, he's kind of short I think, about this tall. Medium length hair. You know, not long at all, but it's not like a crew cut or anything. He's got a lot of tattoos, he wears like a leather jacket and striped pants.
Hm, I don't know, are you sure I know this guy?
Yeah, Kurt. You know. With the accent. And he's real religious, always saying prayers.
I don't know.

He has a rosary, I think he was raised by gypsies though. He said he used to be in the circus. You know he's, he's the guy that teleports all the time, and leaves this cloud of inky blue smoke.

Oh, you mean the blue guy with the devil tail. Nightcrawler.

Oh yeah, he is blue, isn't he? Yeah, that's Kurt. Kurt Vagner. He's a cool guy.

The one disappointing thing about Kurt, that opening scene where he attacked the president. When he didn't kill him and just left a "mutant freedom now" ribbon I thought he was my fuckin hero. I thought he was some revolutionary like John Brown. But then it turns out he's just being mind controlled by Stryker.

Now that Stryker guy, that guy's a real asshole but I coulda warned you, Mystique, because that's Brian Cox. He's always playing assholes now, or pedophiles at least. I don't fuckin trust that guy. I coulda told you that guy's a bad guy and he has some magic formula to control the mutants and his son was a mutant who he tried to "cure" (can you believe that shit?) and now he has a vendetta so he is building his own "cerebro" machine and kidnapping Dr. X-Man to use him to concentrate on all of the mutants in the world at once so that he can commit telepathic genocide.

Now let me tell you why I liked this movie: this is a movie for our times. I mean I can relate to the idea of a militarist maniac manipulating the government for his own hateful, extremist agenda. I like how the X-Men are a badass underground civil rights group who try to use non-violence when necessary. I'm into that. But I mean you guys are cool too, nothing against you guys. I have to admit it was you guys who stopped the passage of the Mutant Registration Act. The X-Men saved the humans from Magneto but you and Magneto saved the mutants from the humans. I was curious though, as long as I have you here, what's the deal with you impersonating that senator? How did you convince his family that he's still alive? Do you like show up at the house and then you're like, "Oh shit, I forgot my good tie at the White House, I'll be back in a couple of weeks." I don't know, whatever you did you fuckin pulled that one off. Kudos.

By the way, I know you're mostly interested in the mutant issues but I was wondering maybe if you get a chance, you and Magneto could look into this USA PATRIOT act that we have and the part 2 that they're working on. The "patriot" act is our own Mutant Registration Act, but it encompasses a lot more. They use it to justify roundups of immigrants, and then they lock them up for months or years without charges or lawyers and eventually deport them (*de*port, not teleport). They also do this trick where non-citizens from the middle east have to come register. If they don't register, they can get arrested or deported. If they do register, they'll get locked up without charges or deported. It's fucked up man. This is also the act that gave Stryker the right to raid that X-Men school, and to lock those little mutant kids up in a pit. They're doing the same thing in Camp X-Ray Guantanamo Bay. But instead of "little kids" they call them "juvenile enemy combatants." If he wanted to, Stryker could've searched the school without a warrant and without telling anybody. He also could've checked all the X-Men's library records and if the librarian tried to tell anybody that he did it, he or she woulda been arrested. That's the Patriot act for you.

I don't know what you could do now, because if you morphed into Bush or Ashcroft or any of those guys, and then you actually did something good, people would be pretty suspicious. I don't know, I know this thing already passed but, you know, whatever you can do.

Anyway, that's why you guys are cooler than other comic strip characters, you fight against the system. You fight cops and soldiers and you fuck with politicians and you get shit done. You don't waste your time flyin around in some fuckin cape tryin to stop muggers. Shit especially you, you let it all hang out, you just walk around naked, do flips, slither around on the ground and all that crap. I love that crap. And that was pretty cool when you turned into Rebecca Romijn-Stamos. She was great in *Femme Fatale*. Isn't she married to some goofball from *America's Funniest Home Videos*? Anyway you X-Men and Magneto-ites, you have strong opinions and some of you are more radical than others (right on sister). I mean I know I'm a human but like I said in my first review I think you guys got a good point about the fuckin humans. I don't agree with everything Magneto does but he seems like a cool guy and it's cool how he always has this blue naked chick (you) standing behind him.

You guys really have the same goal as the X's, you just have a different opinion about how to get there. And I think the X's understand that, that's why Dr. X-Man visits Magneto in prison, and did you notice that when you busted him out and met them at that campfire they didn't waste time trying to find out if they trusted you, they just went into action. That was cool.

I mean it's a good movie. It gets kind of convoluted at the end because it's so complicated and you start to wonder about all these powers, like what is the deal with Dr. X-Men being able to freeze the whole world like in *the Matrix*? I don't get it. Also it would've been a better cliffhanger if after their little talk, the president went ahead and read the speech anyway, declaring war on the mutants. Not that I want a war on you guys but that would make a more exciting part 3 wouldn't it? Oh well, I liked in the first one how they left Wolverine's past unresolved, and they did the same thing here with Jean Grey's growing magic super powers. I'm not stupid man, I know she's not dead and since I heard all the nerds whispering something about "Phoenix" I guess that's where she's gonna turn up, Arizona.

But enough about Jean Grey, I mean she's a looker for sure but she's always whining about her headaches and stuff, plus between her husband and Professor Wolverine she has more than enough man. No Mystique, I am more interested in you and let me tell you why. It's not because of your looks although I like your pretty glowing yellow reptilian eyes, your bright orange slimy hair and your gorgeous blue scaled naked skin. No, it's like that Fox show with the masks, I like you for your personality.[5] You've got a mischievous sense of humor girl I like that. Like when you were seducing Wolverine, I know it was in a closeup and hard to tell but didn't you turn into Rogue for a second to tease him about his uncomfortable relationship with teens? That was good stuff, you know he's into barely legal. Also how you freaked out that janitor by walking past him looking like him.[6]

I know you don't have a lot of respect for men, you might be hard to always get along with but I don't know man I feel like maybe I could change you, settle you down a little but you'd still be a strong woman and

---

5 This was a reference to some Fox reality show involving masks or something. It has been forgotten forever and replaced with other shows of equal or greater stupidity.

6 I guess I'm not the only one who still likes *Darkman*.

you could still kick my ass. I mean I don't think I'll ever need you to bust me out of prison but you gotta appreciate a woman who COULD do that if she needed to. That was a nice thing to do Mystique.

The part that impressed me the most was when you were talking to Kurt by the campfire. And by the way I could tell this impressed Kurt too, but some nerd told me you're his mom, is that true? Anyway Kurt asked why you don't just look normal all the time since you can, and you said, "We shouldn't have to." Right on girl. I like you just the way you are. Just don't shoot me up with metal so Magneto can tear it out of me.

Think about it Mystique. We could be magic together if you were real. Either way, I can't wait to see you in part 3.

Love always,

Vern

CHAPTER THREE
BLOW THINGS UP REAL GOOD

The artistry of action cinema doesn't get enough credit. Even fans of the genre tend to downplay the skills and talents of the people who made their favorite movies, saying that they only want to see car chases and explosions and don't care about anything else. But the truth is that violence alone does not make an entertaining movie, otherwise everybody would equally love Bruce Willis in Die Hard *and Anna Nicole Smith in* Skyscraper. *Even a lowbrow, formulaic action movie requires a certain touch to work well with audiences. It needs the right tone, the right rhythm, the right characters, and yes, sometimes a really good explosion will help. But not always.*

In this chapter we'll look at a variety of action movie types and acknowledge the talents that go into them. This will include a few respectable studio movies, and a whole bunch of lowbrow ones most people would never give the time of day. (They don't need the time anyway, they are responsible enough to wear a watch.) The selections here also pay tribute to the inclusiveness of action movies, where many of the greats did not follow the traditional path of an actor or filmmaker, but were originally known for something entirely different. For example we have action stars who started out as football players, bodybuilders, or stuntmen. We also have a stuntman turned master director of action and an action movie legend turned producer and director of crazy movies.

Of course, there is no better way to start out a chapter on action movies than with a particularly good one that uses the cheap stunt of including the word "action" in the title.

ACTION JACKSON

Every once in a while I'll get in a gentlemanly argument with a motherfucker about whether Michael Bay single-handedly ruined the future of action cinema forever, or whether he's just an asshole. And invariably a Bay-defender will claim that although his movies are not fun to watch and you don't know what's going on while you watch them, Michael Bay "blows things up real good." I think the idea is supposed to be that Regular Folk like to watch a big fiery explosion with no brains involved and if you got a problem with that you must be some kind of snob.

Well I am not a snob and I think you guys know that. The problem is that in my opinion he *does not* blow things up good. He blows things up and then by the camera placement and quick cuts forces us to wonder whether we are in fact watching an explosion or a closeup of Billy Bob Thornton's shoe or perhaps the reflection off a bead of sweat dripping down Josh Hartnett's Adam's apple.

So let me tell you who blows things up good: Craig R. Baxley. He's a stunt co-ordinator (he did *The Warriors*) turned director. He first directed on *The Dukes of Hazzard* but *Action Jackson* is his first theatrical work.

Carl Weathers plays Jericho "Action" Jackson,[7] a Detroit police sergeant recently demoted from Lieutenant. Why was he demoted? BECAUSE HE RIPPED A GUY'S ARM OFF. That is how you know this is gonna be at least an okay movie. Even better, he defends his action by saying, "He had a spare." The bad guy is the one-armed man's dad, Craig T. Nelson from *Coach*, and you know he's a bad guy because he's got Al

---

[7] I should mention, a lot of people have trouble with this title because of the way it almost rhymes. It doesn't rhyme but it comes so close that you gotta assume they *thought* it rhymed. A lot of my buddies won't even watch it unless it gets re-released as *Action Jaction*. But if you pay attention there's one character who seems bothered by this too and seems more comfortable with "Axin' Jackson."

Leong (*Die Hard*) as his limo driver. Just like you know Action is a cop because he has Bill Duke as his boss.

The story is generic '80s cop movie shit: Action thinks that the rich auto manufacturer father of the sex maniac whose arm he ripped off is assassinating union bosses, so he teams up with the guy's wife (Sharon Stone, *Above the Law*) and his junkie mistress (Vanity) to investigate. Then he gets framed for murder, etc. etc.

All that's kind of boring, and it's a little disappointing that we never get to see him face down the one-armed sex maniac. (Maybe they were saving that for part 2.) But the movie is completely worthwhile for its peppering of pure Baxleyism.

My first exposure to Baxley as a director was *Stone Cold* starring Brian Bosworth. I remember a part in there where a motorcycle flies out a window. A lot of directors would've stopped right there. But he has the motorcycle collide with a helicopter. That's awesome, you can't get any better than that, can you? Well, yes, because then the helicopter crashes and lands on a car, and the car blows up. That's Baxley for you, he's a second unit director turned first unit. So he's always looking for ways to juice up the action. In the opening scene of *Action Jackson* some thugs come to murder a union boss. In this scene alone there is more glass broken than in any Seagal movie save for *The Glimmer Man*. And at the end of the scene they shoot the guy with some kind of explosive shell, and he catches on fire. And then he falls out the window. And he plummets from a skyscraper, on fire, and lands on a table where some people are having dinner below. (Somebody could've said, "Be careful, the plate is hot.")

Those type of touches aren't non-stop, unfortunately. Action has to do some investigating and what not. In fact, there was a point almost halfway through the movie where I started thinking I don't know, for a guy called Action Jackson he sure doesn't see a lot of action. As soon as I thought it, Vanity asked him, "Hey, why do they call you—" and just then a guy tries to run over Action in a taxi cab.

This leads to what I believe is the first ever high-speed car chase where the guy chasing forgot to bring a car. Action Jackson runs after the guy and manages to keep up for several blocks. Then he climbs onto a parked car and does a spectacular flying leap onto the taxi, leading to the standard *T.J. Hooker* "holding onto the top of the bad guy car" routine. (Unlike T.J. Hooker, Action Jackson states out loud that it was probably a bad idea.) When the car finally stops he shames the driver into trying to run him over instead of just shooting him. That's a brilliant stroke because what he does is run up the front of the car and do a flip off of the car. The driver takes his eye off the road to figure out what the hell just happened and when he turns back he's about to crash into a parked car. And like many movies of this type, instead of trying to steer away or hit the brakes, he just holds his hands up to cover his face. A total quitter. Anyway, his car launches into the air, spins, crashes into the side of a garage, tears through the wall, and crushes a couple of cars inside the garage. (Sadly, it does not explode. But I guarantee you Baxley tried. There must've been a safety issue or something.)

The climax of the movie takes place at a big party held at the bad guy's mansion. There is a guy swinging on a string of Christmas lights. There is a guy impaled. There are some knifings. Action finds out that Craig T. Nelson has Vanity at gunpoint in his bedroom, so he has to act fast. Instead of wasting time by running up the stairs, Action steals the Ferrari-like car that this guy manufactures, and rams it into the house. Then he drives the car up the stairs and into the guy's bedroom. This is the closest we will ever see to a movie where a sitcom star is run over in his own bedroom. But Action gets out and fights Craig T. hand-to-hand. It's okay, because the car is still there the whole time. It's still weird to have a fight in a bedroom if there's a car parked there.

Craig T. Nelson makes a pretty good bad guy. He's mostly the rich asshole type but in order to have a fight scene at the end there is one scene earlier to establish that he knows how to fight. He's at home sparring with a young, muscular Asian guy, so you figure he is having his martial arts lesson. But you figure wrong. After he defeats the guy he says "Lesson's over" and walks away. I guess you could argue that he is better than his teacher but I assume this is supposed to mean that he actually is a martial arts teacher in his spare time. I guess either way is pretty cool.

Sharon Stone is okay, she gets more to do than in *Above the Law* where she just whines and cries. Contrary to what some dude said on IMDb, she does not get naked in this one. Vanity does get naked and shoot up, if you're into that. She is more the female lead in this one. She also performs a couple songs but one thing I have noticed, she was not as good without Prince. I don't want to be controversial but in my opinion Prince was the real talent behind that whole deal.

A lot of people enjoy bad puns and one-liners in their '80s action movies and if that's what you're into, there is plenty to offer here. And I mean I'm talking terrible one-liners. The worst is probably when Vanity's huge bodyguard appears out of nowhere to rescue Action Jackson. He jumps down from a catwalk and says, "Hello, I'm Mr. Ed!"

What the hell does that mean? It doesn't make any sense as a pun, as a literal statement, even as a reference. What does a big bodyguard dude have to do with a talking horse?[8] A total non-sequitur.

Another one I don't get, in the same scene Action Jackson says, "Chill out," and then blowtorches a guy. How does that work? You can't say the opposite of what you're doing, that doesn't count as a pun. Later he does a better job when he says, "Barbecue, huh? How do you like your ribs?"

(A lot of people catch on fire in this movie, by the way. It's the kind of thing where if you bump into some electrical equipment you will immediately burst into flames.)

Baxley was even better by the time of *Stone Cold* (his third movie) but I liked this one too.

STONE COLD

As you know I have a professional interest in the old B-action pictures. I like your Seagals, your Swayzes, and your etceteras. That's why somebody asked me Vern, do you know about this guy Brian Bosworth though. I said are you kidding me? Let me answer your question with a question. Did I live in Seattle in the year 1987? Of course I know who the damn Boz is. He was on the Seahawks and the local media acted like he was Jesus Christ Hisself, coming down from Heaven with a sacramental football and a new haircut. The haircut of course was a bleach blond mullet with

---

8 On subsequent viewings I've learned that the character's name is Ed, but turning that into a Mr. Ed reference is the kind of lame joke you expect out of somebody's elderly uncle, not a guy in an action movie.

designs shaved on the side, sometimes a full color Seahawks logo. It was called the Boz cut. I guess you could say he was the Dennis Rodman of his time. Known for his calculated outrageous fashion and In Your Face Attitude, he was a phenomenon with the kids. The white Mr. T. People copied the haircut, they had pro and anti Boz t-shirts, they even had this poster that said "Land of Boz" and showed him going down the yellow brick road with a bunch of kids dressed as him (Bozkins, probably). He was a real big fuckin deal for all us retards[9] here in Seattle.

Only one problem was, he never played that good. He kept getting injured and retired after three seasons. But his career was insured so he got rich off it all. After that score he figured, what the hell, maybe you can pull this same shit off in movies. Moved to L.A. and made *Stone Cold*. And it should've been obvious just from that background that this was gonna be a real good bad action movie.

The movie opens in a grocery store where a group of Troma-style insane biker criminals are robbing the joint and terrorizing the shoppers with machine guns. But they start to panic when they realize some dude (Brian Bosworth) is just ignoring them and continuing his shopping. Remember after 9-11, everybody was all scared and they told us the one way we were gonna show these terrorists what fucking time it was, was we were gonna go back out there and shop, buy products, etc. This is the same exact thing, the fuckers just freak out. They send guys after him but he uses canned food to foil them. He acts real cocky and he's wearing a leather trenchcoat with big shoulder flaps like a samurai or an evil space villain would wear. I mean, Seagal must've been so jealous when he saw this coat. When the cops show up they're sayin shit like, "Oh Jesus, what did you do this time Joe, you're still on suspension!" So you know he's a Cop Who Plays By His Own Rules. In these type of movies it is heroic to be a self-absorbed asshole who everybody at the workplace hates.

So far so good, but it's during the credits that we realize this is something special, a bad action movie with a little more crazy energy than expected. I mean there's a pretty good part where a judge gets blown up

---

9 I try not to use that word anymore, because it's not fair to kids who actually have to deal with that disability. I could just rewrite it, but I don't want to be Steven Spielberg taking the guns out of *E.T.* So I'm leaving it in, but my sincerest apologies to the mentally disabled for lumping them in with me and other Brian Bosworth fans.

while he's fishing. But the topper is before that, a little scene, maybe about four or five seconds long, consisting of only three shots. First you got a smiling minister baptizing a baby. Next shot, you got a big bald dude firing a shotgun at the priest. Then finally you got the minister flying through the air and crashing through a stained glass window. I didn't notice until the second time I rewound it that when the glass shatters you can barely make out the rest of the biker gang sitting outside like they're watching a play.

I mean they just hit you with that scene out of the blue and then move on like it's nothing. It's important to the plot, because the baldy gets forty-five years in prison, and a showboating D.A. is trying to get it changed to a death sentence, and that's what the gang is angry about throughout the movie. They act like he's a political prisoner or something. I mean, all he did was shotgun a Baptist minister in front of a baby. Is that a crime? They never explain why the fuck this guy wanted to blow away a minister in the middle of a baptism. I mean there must've been some reason I bet.

Anyway, the Boz is a typical Alabama cop, except that he has a Boz cut and lives with a giant lizard, and probably lives in L.A. The FBI somehow holds the singlehandedly-stopping-a-grocery-store-robbery/takeover incident over his head to force him into an undercover job, using his expertise in biker gangs. He has to infiltrate The Brotherhood, which I don't know if it's the same gang as robbed the grocery store, but these guys are killing religious leaders and selling drugs and hooking up with the mafia and who knows, probably smuggling human organs. All kinds of bad shit. So you see it is a heavily researched and highly realistic examination of modern day bike gangs.

The Boz renames himself "JOHN STONE" and teams up with an uptight and obsessive-compulsive square cop (Sam McMurray), then goes to a bar and picks a fight with a guy named Ice who's a big shot in the Brotherhood. It's kind of like throwing rocks at girls on the playground though because they invite him to the rally and he becomes some kind of junior probationary member. Anyway Ice is William Forsythe, playing another great lunatic like he did the same year in *Out For Justice* (arguably Seagal's best picture). This guy is such a fucking weasel. I love him. His overacting goes so far over the top that it loops back around under the bottom and then flips back to over the top again, like a little kid getting pushed way too hard on a swing set. This time he's a greasy, bearded longhair so his mad eye gleam makes him look like Manson (in *Out For Justice* he's an insane mafia wannabe on a suicidal killing spree/crack binge).

So William Forsythe becomes Stone's rival in the gang, but we need an even better villain for the leader so, obviously, it's Lance Henriksen as Chains. (There are also other gang members with such one-word names as Gut, AWOL, Tool, Trouble and Mudfish.) It's great to see Lance Henriksen with long hair and a goatee, walking around with a sleeveless vest and no shirt. He plays a lot of damn villains and a lot of them are pretty much the same character, but this time he's lower class and he gets to have a different look.

If you ever get chained up, what you do, you pick up a stone and start pounding on the chain until it breaks. Stone and Chains are born enemies, two bones chipped off the same skeleton and cast into the sea in opposite directions, fated to one day drift together and collide again. Chains is Lance Henriksen, so he's a lanky freak with deep, cold eyes, his face covered in more lines than a map. Stone is Brian Bosworth, so he's a smooth, shiny, golden haired meatball. One look at these guys standing next to each other and you can understand why Chains would hate that smarmy muscleman bitch.

I mean think about how perfect it is. Here's Lance Henriksen, such a talented character actor with such an interesting face and strong presence. Working his ass off for decades, never getting cut a fuckin break. *Dog Day Afternoon* looked like it was gonna be the big one, but it never made him a household name or gave him the kind of clout he needed to be able to pick and choose his roles. Shit, even after *Aliens*, he doesn't seem to be able to turn anything down. Including everything from *Wes Craven's Mindripper* to *Alien vs. Predator* to *Stone Cold*. He later got that TV show *Millennium* for a while, but at this time the best he could hope for was action movie villain roles like this one and *Hard Target*.

So that's Lance Henriksen in one corner. And then in the other corner you got this bland jock who has to wear a silly coat and paint the side of his head to seem interesting. They made a huge deal out of him, paid him piles of dough, and he didn't deliver at all. Got rich off of hype and good agents, not off of talent. So he blew it at football, has no experience in acting... what the hell, let's give him the starring role in a movie! The first Brian Bosworth vehicle.

I don't blame you Lance Henriksen. Kill that fucker.[10]

I got some beef with some of these villains though man, the way they run their operations is so incompetent. I mean what the hell kind of robbery was that in the opening anyway? You got a big team, you're risking murder one and wasting a bunch of machine gun bullets on a measly grocery store job? I mean there's probably pretty good cash in those tills for a one or two man job, but not with this kind of split. Especially in this day and age when most people are gonna be paying with credit. Only people that use cash are just buying a Pepsi or a Snickers or something. So either they didn't put too much thought into the economics of this job or, more ominously, they just don't give a fuck. They do this shit as a leisure activity.

The mafia is pretty inefficient here too, they attack one of the biker gang's runners and steal the bag of money from a shakedown they did. And it's only four hundred! (Musta been all in nickels judging from the size of the bag.) The damage Stone does to their car before they get away is gonna cost more than $400. That's just not a good crime there, guys.

But that's either here or there, or whatever the saying is, that they say. Anyway the director is Craig Baxley of the Baxley stunt family. He started out as a stuntman and stunt coordinator/second unit director. Started out directing on *The A-Team*, then started doing movies like *Action Jackson*[11] and *I Come in Peace*.[12] I guess it must be his background in stunts that gives this one that extra spark. I mean I've seen so many generic takes on this exact type of material but this one is more memorable. There are lots of little touches that take it further than you expect. A guy gets hit in the face, he's gonna flip all the way over. A guy gets shot, he's gonna go flying ten feet through the air, maybe fall out a window and crush the top of a car. A vehicle moves, it's gonna explode.

---

10 Let me be clear, I really don't want Lance Henriksen to kill Brian Bosworth. I would consider myself a Brian Bosworth fan. I just really got into the mentality of the character while writing this one. I take this shit seriously.

11 Yeah, yeah, I know, we've been over this information before.

12 But what about this, huh? Didn't mention that title before. This is new information. Get off my back, pal.

This is a movie with the big action finale inside the Mississippi Supreme Court, during a trial. There are motorcycles driving around the halls, burning rubber on marble floors. When Stone pulls a matador maneuver on one motorcycle it crashes out a window, collides with a helicopter and explodes, causing the copter to fall down onto a car, which explodes also and scorches some other cars (too bad it didn't make those explode too).[13]

In the middle of all this you got Lance Henriksen gleefully machine gunning everybody in the court room, dressed in a priest outfit.

When Stone's uptight partner is forced to kill Chains, Stone just gives him a smile like, "I'm beginning to like you, man." Don't be a pussy Sam McMurray, having to kill a guy in a priest outfit in the middle of the supreme court building couldn't be that traumatic. I don't know, maybe Stone regrets treating the whole thing so lightly. That's one of many possibilities of what he might be thinking about during the awesome end credits where he struts out of the courthouse, blood dripping down his face, staring off thoughtfully in the distance as everybody else scrambles to make sense of the mayhem.

In my opinion, *Stone Cold* is in the upper tier of this type of movie, the ones you want to watch over again and share with your friends and what not. Brian Bosworth wasn't a keeper, but this movie was. And now the Boz cut will live on forever. If they ever put this out on DVD.[14]

COMMANDO

Commando is a rare commodity — a Schwarzenegger picture on a low enough budget to feel like the early Seagal and Van Damme pictures. The good ones, though. Schwarzenegger plays John Matrix, the perfect name for an ex-special forces muscleman who lives in a cabin out in the woods with his daughter Alyssa Milano. (Who is the boss, anyway?

---

13 This is worth mentioning twice per book in my opinion.

14 In June of 2007, *Stone Cold* finally became available on DVD in the United States, paving the way for the election of the country's first black president.

I never did figure that out.) She doesn't want him going on dangerous missions anymore so he stays home and spends his days chopping wood and feeding deer with her. Luckily, before he gets too bored with this Snow White lifestyle some other soldiers he used to be knee dip in the shit with kidnap his daughter as a way to force him to assassinate some South American leader or other. So he gets to go to war. And to be honest he looks more comfortable running around with camouflage paint on than he does feeding a deer. We all have our little things we're good at, you know

If the deer-feeding scene or Joel Silver's name on the credits didn't tip you off that this is gonna be a good one then the plane scene will. Matrix and one of the bad guys get on a commercial flight headed for the assassination. John Matrix — pretending to be way more high-maintenance than you would expect from a guy named John Matrix — asks a flight attendant for a pillow and blanket (no sleep mask though) and inquires how long the flight will be (about eleven hours). When no one is looking he snaps his captor's neck, poses him with the pillow and blanket like he's asleep, sneaks into the cargo hold and climbs out onto the landing gear just as the jet is taking flight. He jumps off as soon as he's over swampland, lands safely and sets the timer on his watch for eleven hours. Ladies and gentlemen, *Commando*.

So of course Matrix has to kill a bunch of guys to get to his daughter — the sweet simplicity of classical action movie structure. Nobody ever mentions Matrix's giant muscles, which as usual he must've been born with since we never see him pumping iron. But because of his He-Man build he does a lot of things a normal sized commando couldn't do believably such as tear a seat out of a car, carry a huge log on his shoulder supported by one hand, carry a guy around by his ankle, pick up a phone booth with a guy in it and throw it, and push over a car that's on its side. (Well, I guess that last one anybody could do, but they would be scared to do it.) Also he swings on some kind of streamer and jumps on top of an elevator. And later when he gets arrested Rae Dawn Chong rescues him by firing a rocket at the truck he's in, so it blows up and he doesn't. Because he's John Matrix.

There are several notable bad guys here. There's Dan Hedaya with a bad South American accent. There's Bill Duke, always menacing even when he's a good guy. Here he's trying to kill Matrix (later they'll be teammates in *Predator*). But the main guy is Vernon Wells, best known as Wez from *Road Warrior/Mad Max 2*. He's kind of a mid-level villain, but he does wear a chain mail vest, which you don't see every day. And he has the line, "John, I'm not going to shoot you between the eyes. I'm going to shoot you between the balls."

The fights are real good super powered type fights where they punch each other through the air and throw each other through walls. There is one of those traditional smash-through-hotel-wall-and-scare-people-having-sex type fights. At the end Matrix impales Vernon Wells with a big pipe and somehow steam comes out of the pipe so he says (SPOILER) "Let off some steam." The very next shot is little Alyssa Milano smiling as if she enjoyed it. At first I thought this was just bad editing, but then I remembered that despite her not wanting her dad to go on missions she did tell a bad guy that being returned to her father would be "not as nice as watching him smash your face in." So she is kind of a messed up little girl — she's worried about her dad being put in danger but she loves to watch him horribly mutilate people, it is one of her primary interests along with deer-feeding.

I don't remember if I saw this one in the '80s or not, but now I understand why it's one of the more famous Schwarzenegger pictures. The director is just some dude who did *Class of 1984* and *Firestarter*, so it's no great directorial work like *Predator* or something. But it doesn't fuck around. The kidnapping happens early on, then he immediately pulls that great plane escape and there is never too long in between those types of crazy action sequences. There's also a lot of funny dialogue both of the clever and the corny varieties. I'm gonna have to give some credit to screenwriter Steven de Souza and producer Joel Silver, since they also did *Die Hard*. Back then those guys knew how to make an entertaining action picture.

By the way, my friend Mr. Armageddon tells me that the fictional South American country Val Verde is also where the dictator is from in *Die Hard 2*. IMDb trivia says it's also mentioned in *Predator*. And that John Matrix kills eighty-one people in the movie. Jeez, I must've missed some of those, I better watch this again.

PREDATOR

Predator starts out with a shot of an alien spacecraft jettisoning a shuttle towards Earth. We just see it from the distance, there's not a lot of detail visible, but we don't live under a rock, so we know what's going on here. The extra-terrestrial hunting enthusiast known only as "Predator" is arriving on Earth. The human characters in the movie get all the screen time, but Predator gets the first shot, so we know this is really his story.

Like *E.T. the Extra-Terrestrial*, *Predator* doesn't give us any backstory on the alien star. All we know is the guy is no botanist. Maybe an exotic meat salesman. It almost seems like an alien remake of *First Blood* because you got this one crazy alien maniac out in the jungle by himself, taking on a couple platoons' worth of elite soldiers and doing a pretty good job of it. John Rambo did some sick shit but he didn't skin a bunch of guys and hang them upside down from the trees. He didn't pull out people's spines. So Predator's got one on John. You even get the scene where Predator, like John, is wounded and has to do some makeshift surgery on himself. The only difference is he uses advanced alien technology to heal himself instead of just crudely sewing himself up.

And that's actually our key to understanding what this Predator dude is all about. If this guy was REALLY the great hunter he obviously thinks he is, he wouldn't be fucking CHEATING by using advanced alien technology. The guy is making himself invisible, using laser cannons, all this shit. This seems more like Dick Cheney style bird torture than actual legitimate hunting. It's not until the very end that Predator takes off his helmet and weapons and takes on Schwarzenegger man-to-man. But he probably wasn't planning that from the beginning, he probably either got the idea from Billy when he threw down his gun, took off his shirt and cut his face, or from Dutch when he did the same kind of thing. That macro take-off-your-shirt-and-throw-down-your-weapons shit is contagious when you're out there in the jungle away from civilization. But make no mistake about it, this Predator asshole is just some rich spacetourist coming here for some thrills. You don't fly all the way to Earth for hunting unless you got some serious money in your account. That opening shot of the shuttle firing off of the mothership and heading for Earth? That's the Predator Luxury Vacation Cruiser bringing Predator to Earth for the Deluxe Big Game Hunting Package. I mean come on. Let's not glamorize this guy.

On the other hand, I gotta be fair. We don't speak predator and we don't know what happened on that ship before he blasted off. Maybe they got in a big argument and he said *fuck this*, got in an escape pod and shot off to Earth with both middle fingers blazing. Then he landed in the jungle and the soldiers there pissed him off, one thing led to another and the next thing you know there's some skinned earthlings hanging from the trees. I mean I'm still leaning toward the rich tourist theory, but in the interest of fairness I gotta acknowledge "disgruntled Predator on a rampage" as a possibility.

Predator made the 2006 revised Badass 100 list, which is why I decided to re-watch it for the first time since the 1980s. I guess I owe some of you boys an apology because I've talked some shit about *Predator* now and then, and it turns out you were right, this is a pretty good movie. I liked it at the time but I figured that was just the '80s talking. And it's true, this is clearly an '80s movie. You got Arnold Schwarzenegger (R-CA) with his thick accent, somehow getting away with playing "Dutch," the leader of a platoon of elite American soldiers. We had our own special brand of excess back then so a soldier couldn't just be tough, he had to be fuckin Mr. Universe, apparently spending all his time working out instead of going on missions. And we were fascinated with firepower back then so the best character in the movie, Blaine, played by Jesse "The Body" Ventura (I-MN), had to carry around a giant gatling gun he apparently pulled off of a helicopter (I'm not sure if it's bigger than the purposely ridiculous "Big Fucking Gun" from the movie *Doom*, but it's comparable). There's one laughable scene where everybody just stands around firing machine guns and shit into the woods, firing a *Hard Boiled* amount of bullets for a couple minutes at some innocent trees. Because back then we loved machine guns and we wanted to see as many bullets fired as possible, no precision required. Also, you got some terrible one-liners ("Stick around") and reliance on the heat vision and camouflage effects that aren't really as cool now as they seemed at the time. And I gotta be honest, I never knew the Predator was seven feet tall until I watched the behind the scenes documentary. Maybe they shouldn't have given him that giant helmet. So I'm against the helmet.

But that was the kind of stuff I was remembering when I wrote the movie off. All the good stuff I forgot is what made the World Badass Committee rate the movie so high this time around, and they were probably right. The number one reason is that it's very well directed by John McDIEHARDTiernan. With somebody else it could've easily been a cheesy monster movie with guns, but McTiernan knows what to do. The production values are great. It's shot more like a serious war film than a horror movie. Instead of some cheeseball keyboard score or noodly guitars like you get in a lot of movies from the era, you got a menacing score by Alan Silvestri, that BOMP-BOMP... BOMP-BOMP... type of score like *The Terminator* or Basil Poledouris. It sounds like a mix between a theme song and the footsteps of a giant coming toward you.

And then the other thing is, you have a great ensemble of badasses here, and you know it as soon as the helicopter shows up with the team of special ops guys. First you got Jesse the Body, who spits out a big mouthful of tobacco and says some macho bullshit, but you don't really care how dumb the line is because Jesse the Body has such a cool voice. (Unfortunately his dialogue in the movie is pretty minimal.) Then you have Bill Duke, who I guess is supposed to be Jesse's best friend, although I didn't know that until he was all broken up over Jesse's laser-death. And you got Carl "Action Jackson" Weathers in the #2 badass slot, the CIA guy that recruits them all for this mission. The new discovery for me was Sonny Landham (R-KY), who I don't remember from all the other movies he's in, but he has a deep voice like Jesse and adds a tough guy edge to the mystical Native American warrior stereotype. (The making of documentary claims that the insurance company forced them to have a 7 foot bodyguard on set at all times to protect everyone from Sonny, but I can't find any evidence of why this would be necessary.)

Also you got Shane Black (writer of *Lethal Weapon*) as the conspicuously less muscled guy on the team who tells jokes about large pussies, and one other guy.

And of course Arnold. I'm not against the guy as an actor, I really like *Total Recall* for example, and *Conan*. But I don't worship him like some people. You know what it probably is, it's like Mickey Mouse. The guy is such an icon, so synonymous with action movies, that after a while you've looked at him too many times and he's lost all meaning. But still, it must be acknowledged, he's cool in this movie. He smokes cigars a lot, which makes him a COMPLETELY DIFFERENT character than what Arnold would often play, in a movie without cigars. At the end, after the spacetourist has murdered all his friends, he goes primal. He builds a bunch of booby traps and tiger pits and shit, he covers himself in mud, he picks up two huge torches and screams into the jungle like some kind of fuckin mad sasquatch on the loose. With the subtitles on, it should say COME HERE YOU FUCKIN TOURIST I WILL PULL OUT THOSE SPACE-DREADLOCKS ONE BY ONE, FORCE YOU TO EAT THEM THEN WAIT FOR YOU TO SHIT THEM OUT AND THEN FORCE YOU TO EAT THEM AGAIN, AND THAT IS THE NICEST THING I WILL DO TO YOU YOU DIRTY SONOFASPACEWHORE.

It makes no sense that putting mud on his face would prevent him from being seen by heat vision. At the very least Predator is gonna see his eyes. Unless maybe he's wearing contacts and the heat vision is powerless over contacts, but I think they would've mentioned that if it was supposed to be the case. Oh well. The magic of cinema.

I like Arnold in the movie but Jesse the Body definitely steals the show while he's there. The guy is so macho and arrogant that he becomes charming. The line "I ain't got time to bleed" obviously comes to mind. And he has a cool hat. Honestly, a lot of people wouldn't be able to pull off that ridiculous gun, "Ol' Painless," but Jesse does it. They have on-set interviews with him on the DVD and he is so proud and braggadocios about the gun that it's clear he's the guy confident enough to pull it off.

Also, I read a little on Jesse's political career and it sounds like he definitely beat Schwarzenegger in the governing department. I don't agree with all of his views but he sure impresses me more than most politicians. Am I reading this wrong, or did he really give a tax refund and STILL get mass transit constructed? I wish he was mayor of Seattle. He also apparently supported gay rights, medical marijuana and third parties (obviously). At one point there was a bill to promote the Pledge of Allegiance in public schools. I'm sure every other governor in the country would've signed off on it and got a little extra shine on their American flag lapel pin. But Jesse vetoed it and said, "I believe patriotism comes from the heart. Patriotism is voluntary. It is a feeling of loyalty and allegiance that is the result of knowledge and belief. A patriot shows their patriotism through their actions, by their choice [such as voting, attending community meetings and speaking out when needed]. No law will make a citizen a patriot."

In *Predator* he chews tobacco and says, "Bunch of slack-jawed faggots around here. This stuff will make you a god damned sexual Tyrannosaurus, just like me." Same guy.

But even though Jesse is my favorite on the team, you gotta give the movie credit for how solid the whole team is. I mean, The Terminator, Apollo Creed, Jesse the Body, Bill Duke and this Sonny Landham guy all in one elite force? That's a hell of a lot closer to a real Dirty Dozen than you usually get in an action movie, especially in the '80s. And when the action goes down it's some good stuff, partly thanks to my man Craig R. Baxley. *Predator* is important because of its place in Baxley's career. It was the first time he got to be second unit director on a feature film. And I don't think it's a coincidence that it was also his last movie as a stunt coordinator. A year later, he and Carl Weathers went off to make *Action Jackson* together. And the rest is Baxlistory. Which is a real word, in my opinion. Look it up.

Anyway, what I'm saying is: welcome to the Badass 100, *Predator*. I didn't think I'd ever say this about a Schwarzenegger-fighting-an-alien movie, but I approve.

PREDATOR 2

After watching *Predator* for the first time since the '80s and realizing that it's actually a good movie, I decided to watch *Predator 2*. I never seen this one before and I knew the reputation wasn't too good. More ominous, instead of John McDIEHARDTiernan the director is Stephen *Lost In Space* Hopkins. Not lookin good.

But damn if the opening isn't a scorcher. It starts out with the familiar Predator POV heat vision in the jungle... but as it pans across you realize it's not the jungle — it's the outskirts of Los Angeles. THE URBAN JUNGLE! In the futuristic year of 1997. (Think about it: a Predator is loose in Los Angeles at the same time Snake Plissken is looking for the president in New York. Meanwhile, the Spice Girls are topping the charts and *Titanic* is breaking box office records.)

Anyway the scorchin part is when the Predatorcam flies across the city and finds some TFM (total fuckin mayhem) goin down on a city block. It's a shootout between cops and a gang of maniac Colombian drug dealers, but it's a bigger war zone than the one that Dutch and his special ops team went into early in *Predator*. You got flaming cop cars, wounded cops and motorcycles laying all over the street, cars blowin up and flippin through the air, machine guns firing every which way, cops running around with metal shields, and reporters (including Morton Downey Jr., remember him?) frantically trying to broadcast the play-by-play. When our hero Danny Glover shows up his colleagues tell him that they don't have all their guys there because some of them are in the other shootout going on somewhere else in town. This is not a great movie, but it's a truly great opening, picking you up by the hair and dropping you right into the thick of things.

So you quickly get the idea that maybe 1997 L.A. is not the best place to be a non-Predator. One might even consider it to be a total fuckin hellhole. And there's a lot of details to show that throughout the movie, like the way everybody always has sweat stains on their armpits and their chests. (I guess there's a heat wave, which fits with what was said in the first movie about Predator tourists choosing to vacation in hot places.)

The cops end up chasing the gang into a building, where by some kind of dumb fuckin luck a Predator decides to hop through a skylight and skin the motherfuckers. So the cops come in and can't figure out why there's about ten thousand bullet shells on the floor and a bunch of dead, skinned guys with no bullet holes. It's like one of those whodunit murder riddles except there's no puddle of water so you know they weren't killed with icicles. But before Danny and his team get much of a chance to figure things out the feds (led by Gary Busey, *Under Siege*) take over the investigation.

By the way this would be as good a time as any to mention that I have heard three separate reports of Gary Busey being spotted driving a red Cadillac convertible around Seattle. The sightings took place months apart, so he probably wasn't just in town shooting a movie here. I guess the common sense assumption would be that he either has a house here or has a relative or special friend that he visits here a lot. But my theory is that these sorts of sightings take place all over the country, because he just drives all over the country in his convertible between filming movies. And he loops back here now and again. Or it could even be some sort of mystical apparition that appears in times of great change or turmoil. The Gary Busey convertible vision is a portent of doom.[15]

And in the case of *Predator 2* the actual physical presence of Gary Busey is a portent of jurisdictional disputes. But of course Danny doesn't give up that easy, he keeps investigating with his team of Ruben Blades, Maria Conchita Alonso and the rookie, Bill Paxton. But when they go visit the Jamaican posse the same exact shit happens — the Predator skins em before the cops get there.

That's a real good cast there but I gotta be honest, they are not utilized as well as Jesse the Body, Bill Duke and Sonny Landham in part 1. Busey plays it surprisingly low key (he can't be too much of an asshole because his character was supposed to be Dutch before Schwarzenegger turned it down). Partly because the team is not as badass, partly because the direction is not as good, and partly because they're in a city instead of out in a jungle covered in mud, the story does not build as well as in the first one. Every once in a while you see a Predator on a fake looking set, like when he poses with a skull on top of a building and gets struck by lightning. He looks like he should be holding a flying-V guitar in that shot. And after that epic opening it seems a little wimpy to have one of the big action setpieces take place in a meatlocker. Also if the Predator can only see heat, how does he even know there's a side of beef hanging there (they say he snacks on beef from slaughterhouses)? And why does he still see in computervision after his mask comes off? And how did he know the "you're one ugly motherfucker" line from part 1? This isn't supposed to be the same Predator back from the dead, is it? Maybe he saw *Predator* on video.

In defense of this new Predator tourist, he does seem a little more honorable than his predecessor. Admittedly, he's still using advanced alien

---

15 Whether or not a Gary Busey sighting is a bad omen, a *Seattle Weekly* cover story later tipped me off that my friends had not seen the real Busey but in fact Jeff Swanson, a Seattle native whose weird resemblance to Busey seems to cause a commotion everywhere he goes.

technology against humans, which is still cheating. In fact, it seems like he's constantly showing off new weapons every time he kills somebody, like James Bond or Jason Voorhees. But he does have honor and we know this because he decides not to kill Maria after his x-ray vision tells him she's pregnant. Also, please note that he uses the x-ray to look at her innards, not her boobs. What I'm saying is this guy is a true gentleman.

At the end Danny finds the Predator ship, including the mantle where he keeps his trophy skulls. They got a t-rex on there and an Alien skull from the out-of-Predator's-league-you-would-think *Alien* series. And next to that is a human skull. And you have to wonder why they even bother. I know there's that cliché about man being the most dangerous game, but let's be honest. After hunting tyrannosauruses and alienses this guy is basically just squirrel hunting at this point. Or at best fishing.

But Danny is one hell of a fish or squirrel, so he ends up beating the Predator right there on his own ship. Suddenly ten Predators turn off their camouflage and appear around him, a real OH SHIT moment. Instead of making a wisecrack like, "Oh damn, is it really 9:30? I gotta get home and iron my work shirts," Danny utters the overly confident line, "All right, who's next?"

Lucky for him these Predators

a) follow a strict code of honor where they must respect him for defeating their bro in a fair fight
b) always thought that Predator he killed was kind of a dick anyway, or
c) didn't see what happened because they have that crappy heatvision

… so they just give him an antique musket from the 1700s as

a) a symbol of their respect for his warrior skills, or
b) a gag gift to confuse him. I mean seriously, a musket? What's that all about?

… so he just leaves. The end is cool too because he has to jump Dutch-style but instead of a self-destruct atom bomb he's escaping the flames from the space ship's space engines. Then he climbs out of the dirt and stumbles through L.A. looking like a zombie, carrying that antique musket given to him by aliens. He's probably not the first dude to ever wander around L.A. covered in dirt and carrying a musket that he believes was given to him by aliens, but he must be one of the first to be well-founded in that belief. He tells the feds not to worry, they'll get to see a Predator again some day. In those naive days there was no way to anticipate them seriously doing *Alien vs. Predator* so it probably seemed like a nice idea.

I actually kind of like this idea of Predators coming to Earth throughout time. Wouldn't a good part 3 be to have a young Predator fighting dinosaurs as a rite of passage? No dialogue (maybe subtitles), you side with the Predators, and it's all shot *Walking With Dinosaurs* documentary style. They could do something weird and unexpected like that that wouldn't make very much money, or they could make some moronic piece of worthless dog shit that taints the legacy of both this series and the *Alien* series, that makes the same small amount of money. It's hard to say which direction the geniuses of Hollywood will go, we'll just have to wait and see, could go either way.

Predator 2 is not nearly as good of a movie as *Robocop* but it has the same idea of exaggerating the madness of modern life to create the setting for the movie. The movie came out in 1990 which, as I explained in my review of *I Come In Peace*, is still the '80s as far as I'm concerned. So you got a lot of things that remind you of the '80s: the aggressive, exploitative reporters (which seem current today but were probably based on shows from the time like *A Current Affair* and shit), the *Marked For Death* style, voodoo lovin Jamaican drug gang (who are so superstitious they think the Predator is a ghost), and even a reference to Bernard Goetz (a Goetz-looking guy pulls a gun on subway muggers — then every other passenger also pulls out a gun). I don't think the movie is really a satire, and it might've been more effective if the plot did have some small thing to say about life in 1990, but I still think it makes for an interesting movie. I wish somebody would make a movie like that today. God knows there's a whole lot of shit to work with.

All that stuff dates the movie in kind of a good way, but there's also some shitty '80s style humor that probably should've been left behind in time. I mean do we really need a Predator that says "Shit happens" before he falls off a building? (.ON KCUF :rewsna [hold book up to mirror to see answer]) Also you get some of those dumb little moments like he almost kills a kid but the kid offers him candy, and a wacky old lady finds him in her bathroom, and that type of shit. Now, I like both of these movies but this is the perfect example of why this *Predator* series did not deserve to be held on the same pedestal as the *Alien* series. Sure, they made some mistakes in *Alien* parts 3 and 4, but even at that point they never had a wacky old lady character, much less one who finds an alien in her bathroom and tries to swat him with a broom.

Still, I'd say it's an underrated sequel. Nice to see them taking it in a different direction than the first one. The Predator's head is still too big though, I still can't tell he's so tall. Let's do better on the proportions next time, fellas.

THE PROTECTOR
REAL TITLE: TOM-YUM-GOONG
SHOULD BE THE TITLE: WHERE ARE MY ELEPHANTS?

Well, I can't say I didn't know what I was stepping into. The import DVD of the newest Tony Jaa movie (from the same director as *Ong-Bak*) has been circling around forever and a day now but I never got around to seeing it. Now the Weinsteins have unleashed their bastardized and cut-up version across the screens of America. I knew it was probably gonna be dubbed, I knew it was shortened (that's what the Weinsteins do: buy other people's movies, then cut parts out of them), and I knew it was re-scored.

And it was actually that last part that reeled me in like a suckerfish. Because in the newspaper ads it says in giant letters, almost as big as the title: "MUSIC BY RZA."

I knew it was wrong to take somebody's movie and re-score it just to sell tickets to marks like me, but still. Muay thai and RZA beats, right? Sounds like a good Friday afternoon at the Cinerama.

And okay, it was. The movie is definitely worth seeing if you're a fan of martial arts. It's very similar to *Ong-Bak*. Once again Tony Jaa is a naive, rural traditionalist. But instead of the head of a Buddha statue being stolen from his village, it's two elephants (one adult, one baby) that his family are sworn to protect. This isn't some gimmick like that movie with Bill Murray. Elephants are very important in Thai culture and history, Jaa comes from a long line of elephant trainers, and he actually owns two elephants in real life. One of his big breaks as a stuntman was as a double for Sammo Hung in a commercial where he had to roll off an elephant's tusks onto its back, and it's cool to see him do a few of those types of tricks here.

Language-wise it's a real mish-mash. A lot of it is in the original Thai, some of it was already in English (since it takes place largely in Sydney, the Vancouver of Asia), then for some reason some parts are dubbed into English. I'm not sure what the thinking is — there is more than enough subtitles to scare away the illiterate Neanderthals who they assume all Americans are, so what's the point of fucking up parts of the movie by dubbing it? Who are you trying to please there?

There was probably an explanation for how he goes from his father being killed and his elephants getting swiped to facing down the criminals responsible, but if so we're gonna have to go steal those scenes back from the Weinsteins. *Ong-Bak* had a generic but nicely executed story to string the fight scenes together, but this one (in its current form) has most of the string cut out so it gets confusing. People will say "Who cares, I just want to see the fights! FIGHT! And PUNCHING!" which is understandable. But the context for these scenes, I'm sure, was already there. It takes more work to cut them out than to not cut them out and now it makes it seem like Thais are a bunch of crazy retards[16] who make movies where suddenly for no reason the main character is in a flooded, burning temple fighting a capoera guy and a seven foot bald muscleman. And yes, this scene is awesome but am I crazy to ask for some basic explanation of how the fuck Tony got into this situation? It would be one thing if they made the movie like this in the first place, but to take somebody's pre-existing, internationally popular movie and turn it into nonsense is kind of cruel.

There aren't (at least in this version) as many great stunt-related scenes

---

16 Sorry again.

as *Ong-Bak*. There's a good high-speed boat chase. He runs up a fence or two. There's not anything comparable to what I thought was the best part of *Ong-Bak*, the chase through the market where he jumps over and through an series of pointy obstacles (knives, barb wire, etc.) But the fights this time are arguably even better. They don't seem quite as blunt and hard-hitting, but they're beautifully choreographed and thrilling. Jaa knows the power of posing — the forms his body goes into between the hits is almost more important than the hits themselves. (The same principle as funk music, where the emphasis is on the 1 note. Ask Bootsy about it.)

There are at least three classic fights. Two of them involve Nathan Jones, a scary bald muscleman just shy of seven feet tall, so he's more than a foot taller than Jaa. This guy just grabs Jaa by the head and throws him across the room, it's like some kind of super *X-Men* or *Blade* battle but you can tell these are both real guys. I guess I saw Nathan Jones in the Jackie Chan movie *First Strike*, but here he has a little more personality than your typical Jackie Chan villain, just because when Tony punches his head ridiculously hard Jones laughs and says "YEAH!" I'd love to see this guy in some more movies — luckily he's in an upcoming *Most Dangerous Game* rip-off from prestigious WWE Films.[17]

The most Jackie Chan-esque fight is the one where he fights a bunch of dudes on rollerblades and bikes, as well as a *Road Warrior* type on a four-wheeler. There's all kinds of leaping into vans and through windows and up walls and shit. And you know he's not using wires or stunt doubles, although I'm not sure it's all real. For example did he really run up that glass window that, in the same shot, the four-wheeler crashes through? I don't know, some of that stuff is probably fake. Not that I'm gonna whine about, just trying to be honest.

But the most impressive scene, and one that will definitely go down in history, is a continuous one-take Steadicam shot that goes on for more than four minutes as Tony Jaa fights his way up four stories to the guy he wants to face. As far as I could tell it was really done in one shot, although I've read there's a little digital enhancement as far as broken windows.

---

17 Unfortunately the movie (*The Condemned*) completely wasted Jones, barely using him and shooting him in such a way that you couldn't even tell how tall he was.

Still, he beats up a ridiculous amount of people, throwing them down stairs, over ledges, through windows and doors. Someone who has the DVD will have to go through and tally how many people and pieces of furniture are broken. But if you thought that scene in *Oldboy* was impressive, well, look out.

And all I could think is THANK GOD this guy was watching Bruce, Jackie and Jet while he was growing up and doing his thing. Jackie and Jet are getting old and compromised now. I think they still have some magic but it clearly can't last forever. So it's good to have a possible heir to the throne. Tony's persona is a little like Jackie's, because his voice and face are so boyish it's hard to imagine him playing something besides a naive, innocent hero. But like Jet he's more serious and he tries to work elements of his Buddhist beliefs into the storylines.

At least as *The Protector* there's not as much humor as in *Ong-Bak*, which is kind of a bummer. The guy who played Dirty Balls is back, this time playing an Australian cop who arrests Jaa and then ends up on his side. I hope he always co-stars with Jaa because they play off each other well, they're opposites. This guy is short and wide, doughy instead of chiseled, out of shape, and his eyes look tired. He doesn't really get to be funny in this one but he still has a funny air about him. Way to go, Dirty Balls.

I thought there was a Jackie Chan walk-on too, but then I read it was only a lookalike. Sure looked convincing to me. Also, this must not've been on purpose but I swear there's a Rosie O'Donnell celebrity lookalike who you see eating a scorpion with chopsticks.

The miniscule amount of story that is in here is pretty cool. I love that he's doing it all for the elephants and he has a stronger emotional reaction to the death of an elephant than even the death of his own father. He keeps asking (in Thai) "Where are my elephants?" which is why I think that should be the title. It's like *Not Without My Daughter* or *Get Away From My Sister*. There's a great moment where he bursts into a big business press conference, baby elephant at his side, and yells "You killed my father! And you stole my elephants!" You don't see that every day.

So I don't regret seeing the movie, and if amazing fight scenes is all you need, you shouldn't miss it. But I do feel bad about supporting these assholes butchering somebody else's movies this way. They left Disney and started their own company, it's the perfect opportunity to start over with a clean slate and leave behind the horrible Miramax history of buying foreign films, leaving them on the shelf for years, bullying anybody who tries to sell imports in the U.S., then if they ever release them half the time they cut out half an hour and sometimes they change the title and the music and dub it.

Oh yeah, and as for the music. I was almost willing to let them massacre this thing if it was gonna mean that next great RZA score I've been waiting for since *Ghost Dog*. But yet again, it's a god damn lie. I'm calling you out Demon Dave style, RZA. THIS IS MY REALITY, RZA. If RZA is gonna score a movie, MAKE SURE RZA FUCKING SCORES THE MOVIE. Let me give you some examples.

Ghost Dog is RZA scoring a movie. One of the best scores of all time.

Kill Bill is not RZA scoring a movie. It's RZA helping compile a real good soundtrack. Okay, I'll forgive you because it works great for the movie.

Blade Trinity is not RZA scoring a movie. It's some other dude with RZA adding a little techno.

Unleashed is not RZA scoring a movie. It's RZA producing two half-assed songs that appear on the credits.

So you'd think I would've given up on these claims one or two disappointments ago, but here I was again believing the "MUSIC BY RZA" advertisement. This time he might've really done the score (it's credited to him and another guy, not the original Thai composers, so I assume they collaborated). But it sounds EXACTLY like anybody else's score. Lots of keyboard violin sounds and *Mortal Kombat* percussion. Even some cheesy rock guitars here and there. There's nothing wrong with the score, it's fine, but nobody in the world would have listened to this and guessed it was by RZA. And when I say nobody in the world, I am including RZA. I am convinced that even he would've listened to it and when they told him he made it he'd say, "What? When did I make that? That doesn't sound like me."

Which would be fine if they hired him to score it in the first place and he wanted to waste his talents making a generic score and disappointing legions of fans and making babies cry and disgracing the legacies of Ol' Dirty Bastard and the late Ghost Dog. But there was already a score on this movie when they brought him in. WHY IN FUCK'S NAME are you gonna replace the old score with a RZA score UNLESS IT SOUNDS LIKE A GOD DAMN RZA SCORE? And then you advertise that RZA did the score as if some RZA fan is gonna go to hear this score and is gonna be happy with it. Are you DELIBERATELY trying to piss us off?

Here's what you do, RZA. Your pal Quentin Tarantino put his name on the movie just by adding a "QUENTIN TARANTINO PRESENTS" logo at the beginning. Otherwise, he didn't change the movie. That's all you gotta do, "QUENTIN TARANTINO PRESENTS..." and then "ALSO, RZA PRESENTS THIS AS WELL..." That's all you need, you don't have to waste your time replacing the score. Unless you're gonna give us some Wu-Tang.

I'm gonna pull out the big guns here to make my point. I'm gonna pull out *Die Hard*. Do you think *Die Hard* would be better if they "tightened" most of the story and just had the parts where he blows up the helicopter and the elevator shaft and hangs the guy on the chain? Would that faster pace give you a hard-on? How about if some of the dialogue was dubbed into, say, Japanese, the entire score was redone and some of the classical music was replaced by Asian pop songs? Would that be better, the same, or not as good? Do you think Japanese audiences would like it better that way? If so, would you think they were morons?

A real world example: *Shogun Assassin*. Okay, I can see how that's a fun movie if you didn't know where it came from. But they just edited together the violent parts from two separate *Lone Wolf and Cub* movies and dubbed that into English. The real movies are equally violent but also beautiful, mythic stories. The whole series made number 2 on our Badass 100 list, that's just behind the Man With No Name trilogy as the greatest badass cinema of all time. And yet to this day I meet people who won't watch the actual movies, they just know the version where they cut different swordfights together.

I believe that releasing a movie like this is an attack on multiple cultures. First of all, it's an attack on Americans because it's making the assumption that we are morons who are afraid of subtitles and have such short attention spans that we refuse to watch a storyline unfold in our action movies. When Miramax released Jackie Chan's underrated *Who Am I?* they not only cut out some of the storyline, they actually cut out some of the action scenes! What is this fuckin obsession with movies being short? If it's so important for you to only release short movies then why not only buy short movies? That way you are saving a lot of time, energy and resources, and you're also not being a big fuckin ignorant asshole. Everybody wins.

And then if you're not tired from mutilating somebody else's movie you will have more energy to come up with the new American title, and won't embarrass yourself with this *"The Protector"* bullshit. I mean, how braindead are you fuckin people, you got a movie about a guy protecting an elephant and you can't come up with a better title than that? A title that, by the way, was already used for a widely hated Jackie Chan American vehicle. But I don't think they're using it as an homage to that, I think it's an homage to the time they renamed Jet Li's *My Father Is a Hero* as *"The Enforcer."*

Which brings me to my next point. I think these releases are also kind of racist, or at least xenophobic, or at the very least disrespectful toward the artform of martial arts cinema. These guys don't give a shit about the characters and stories, they don't WANT there to be characters or stories. They just want to sell us an Asian minstrel show. They figure if these silly Asian guys can flip around and kick each other fast enough then American morons will eat the shit up. The more generic the better. If it happens to have a distinctive title and concept FOR GOD'S SAKE be sure to hide that in the marketing. *My Father Is a Hero* starred a little boy who is not shown or mentioned on the box for their version. *Tom-Yum-Goong* is about saving elephants and they don't even show that on the poster or the ads. God forbid somebody remembers which movie this is six months from now. *"The Protector*? Is that the one with Van Damme and Natasha Henstridge? Or the one with the wrestler saving his wife from Robert Patrick? Or is it a John Grisham?"

At the very end of the movie a narrator, who I assume is supposed to be Sgt. Dirty Balls, describes Jaa's character as an old fashioned guy who cares about tradition. He says that some people may make fun of Tony for that, but he is basically the greatest guy ever so fuck you (paraphrase). Ironically, the Weinsteins are dubbing that into the movie at the same time that they are cynically slicing pieces out of it to make it more modern and fast-paced and retarded.[18] Because nobody likes that old fashioned "let's explain what the fuck is supposed to be going on in this movie"

---

18 I'm still sorry.

bullshit. Oh well. I guess that's the post-post-ironic world we live in.

So see the movie, but if you have access to the real version (or if you're willing to wait to see if they consider it worthy of inclusion on the American DVD) I'm betting that's better. Both as a movie and for the soul of America.

P.S. The Brits apparently call it *Honour of the Dragon*, which is arguably even worse.

TO LIVE AND DIE IN L.A.

I always knew the title to this one, because of that song by Wang Chung. But I never knew what exactly it was about. Turns out it's loosely based on a novel by this guy Gerald Petievich. He was in the Secret Service, and the book was inspired by some of his experiences. So it's supposed to be about the weirdness of that job, where one day you're protecting the president of the United States and the next day you're working for the treasury department, so you're just chasing some dude with counterfeit twenties.

This movie has the thumbprints of great filmatism smeared all over it. It has the kind of opening I'm a sucker for, the kind that throws you in the middle of something, sets the tone, then goes into the opening credits. Like a preamble or an overture. The main character Richard Chance (William Petersen) is on security detail for a Reagan speech (you just hear Reagan's voice off screen, they don't have Martin Sheen or anybody playing him). The guys are just kind of killing time when he notices something odd that leads him to the roof, where he finds an Islamic suicide bomber. (Oh, shit.) He's not able to talk him down but his partner climbs up the side of the roof and yanks the guy by the leg so that he explodes in mid-air, like a big balloon full of blood and chunks of meat. Then the two sit on the edge of the building to think about what has just happened. Chance says, "Let's go get drunk and play cards" and it cuts into a stylish opening montage showing various images from the movie and that represent L.A.

One sign of greatness: the title is printed in a font so big the title has to be split up to fit on the screen. This generally means the movie is gonna be awesome. I'm sure some shitty movies have figured that out and use big fonts to fake everybody out but as a general rule title filling entire screen = good movie.

More reasons it's great: It has a compelling lead who you haven't seen in many movies. (I kept wondering why I haven't seen this guy in other stuff before I figured out he was the dude from *CSI*, only young and McConaughey-esque.) It has the confidence to abandon the plot to focus in on details, like the long montage illustrating step-by-step the process of counterfeiting bills. It has some knock-you-on-your-ass-and-then-help-you-half-way-up-but-then-say-'psyche'-and-drop-you-back-on-your-ass-and-then-a-car-drives-by-and-splashes-a-puddle-on-you action setpieces. I think maybe the big car chase even tops director William Friedkin's own *The French Connection* with its escalating mayhem, thrilling car POV shots and the way it's both an exciting action scene and a major turning point for the characters. I didn't know that the L.A. river basin was done before *T2*, or that wrong-way-on-the-freeway was done before *Ronin*.

And it's unpredictable. You don't necessarily know where it's gonna go. Things don't unfold exactly how they're supposed to. For example, Willem Dafoe is this scary villain, but every time he gives somebody a beatdown he almost gets the tables turned on him first. He's not untouchable. He gets his ass beat. The hero is vulnerable too, and flawed. But not a total fuckup. He's heroic enough that you think he's gonna learn a lesson and stop treating his girlfriend/informant so shitty. But let's just say he might not. He has a dark side.

All of the actors are really good in this movie, most of them early in their careers, too. John Turturro for example had only played a few small roles before he stole the show here as a guy they nab with counterfeit money, and might get taken out before he can snitch. There's also a good part for Steve James, the guy that played Michael Dudikoff's sidekick Curtis "Before 50 Cent" Jackson in the *American Ninja* movies.

On the DVD there's a deleted scene that Friedkin says he doesn't remember why he cut, and he wishes he could put it back in the movie but the only footage of it is a crappy video. The scene would've been near the end of the movie. Chance's partner Vukovich (John Pankow) is about to go to the big climactic showdown. But first he goes to some apartment building. You're not sure what he's doing. He knocks on a door and a woman we've never seen in the movie comes out. It becomes apparent from the conversation that this is his wife, but they're separated. And he tells her he wants to patch things up. But it's late at night, he seems crazy, he knows she doesn't want him there, so she tries to get him to leave, and they get into an argument.

It's a great scene and it's not in the movie, but it would've fit right in there. That's the kind of movie we're dealing with, a movie that does have an exciting, dangerous showdown, but first wants to take a little detour about a character's life. What's wrong with it, what he wants to fix about it. And at the same time it shows you just how scared he is because obviously he wouldn't be doing this if he wasn't thinking he could die.

Friedkin reminds me a lot of Michael Mann. Both of them are these macho guys directing macho guy movies, making buddies with cops and criminals who they use as technical advisers, bragging about their adventures on their commentary tracks. On *Thief* Michael Mann hired a real safecracker so he could show how a safe is really cracked, on this one Friedkin hired a real counterfeiter so he could show how money is really counterfeited. According to IMDb trivia, Mann even tried to sue Friedkin over this movie, claiming it was a ripoff of *Miami Vice*. (He lost, then he drank a mojito.)

But Friedkin is less pretentious and makes movies with a quicker pace. He's more interested and skilled at putting thrills in his movies. And he seems slightly less full of himself. Very slightly. *To Live and Die in L.A.* was not a big hit but seeing it now I think it was very influential. I'll be damned if little twentysomething Shane Black didn't have this movie on the brain when he wrote the first *Lethal Weapon*. It even has the partner about to retire who says "I'm too old for this shit." And it has a slick style that I think sort of mutated into the Tony Scott pre-midlife crisis style. Hell, maybe even the midlife crisis Tony Scott style, because every time they show a title on the screen it uses a different font. That's the 1985 version of flying subtitles and attack of the Avid farts. But it's kind of cool.

By the way, Friedkin found William Petersen in theater, but he had done one movie role before: he played a bartender in *Thief*.

You know, people have been recommending this one to me for years, and there was at least one close call before. I went to the video store with the intent of renting it. I had the box in my hand. I ran into a buddy who's into shit like this and I asked him, "You said this one was good right?" And of course he said it was, and while talking it up he mentioned that the soundtrack was by Wang Chung. I didn't know it was gonna be that kind of party, so I put it back.

But I'm here to tell you that even for those of us who don't necessarily wanna have fun tonight, and who most certainly do not want to Wang Chung tonight, this is a good picture. I don't generally like something to be dated to the '80s, and especially musically. But this one captures the era well, coming across more like a great period piece or time capsule than like something that's dated. And the soundtrack fits that real well. They only sing on the opening title track and the rest of it they just sit there and keyboard away and it works real good for the mood. And I don't think this could be intended but the associations I have with that kind of cheesy '80s white people keyboard music perfectly captures the heart and soul of the setting and the topic of counterfeiting. It's slick and electronic (fake), it's trying to be hip, it probably has a ponytail and sunglasses on.

Matter of fact, I can't really say this captures the essence of that side of L.A., because I've never lived there, but based on the times I've been there this really does a good job of capturing how it all looks to me. At any rate it's a very solid and original crime/action/police procedural type movie. Everybody have fun tonight.

MAD MAX BEYOND THUNDERDOME

Beoynd Thunderdome has always been the red-headed stepchild of the Mad Max series. Everybody loves *Road Warrior*, on account of it being one of the best movies everybody has ever seen. So if Miller just rehashed it but added a new Joe Pesci character or something then everybody probably woulda been happy. Instead he expanded on the universe, he took the story in another entirely new direction and a lot of people still aren't ready to follow.

I hadn't seen this movie in years and I actually remembered it being more different than it really is. In fact, I was thinking there weren't even cars in this one. I just remembered planes and pig shit and that song by Tina Turner. I thought it wasn't as good as the other two but that it got a bum rap. Seeing it again — well, okay, it's my third favorite, and there is a section in the middle that I had a problem with, but it needs to be said that this is a *great fucking movie.*

When you think of Mad Max you think of fast cars. Max lost his Interceptor in part 2 but you know he's gotta get himself a new ride, right? In the opening scene he is traveling through the desert but either his engine doesn't work or he's out of gas because his customized truck is being pulled by camels. Before we even know it's him though a pilot (Bruce Spence, not playing the gyro pilot from *Road Warrior* as far as I can tell, that's just what pilots always look like in the desert) flies down low, knocks him off the car, then jumps in and steals it from him. So we're just a couple shots into the new movie and Mad Max is a pedestrian. And he's gonna stay that way until the climax.

Also Max has a pet monkey. And long hair like Braveheart.

Max follows his vehicle and monkey into a gated post-apocalyptic community called Barter Town. This is like the city where Lord Humungus would go to bars if he was into that type of thing. It's an incredibly detailed society full of crazy individuals with mowhawks and feathered headdresses and armor made out of junk. This part sort of reminds me of *Star Wars* in the way it shows you this fully inhabited world. Tina Turner is the boss (actually, the "Auntie"), she lives in an elevated house, and the place is run on methane that comes from pig shit shoveled by slaves in a subterranean pig farm. (Not one of the better vocations, in my opinion.) They won't let Max in to get his car because he has nothing to barter, but then they find out he's a badass so Auntie hires him to off somebody. And he goes undercover as a pig shit shoveler to scope out the target, a retarded giant named Blaster who works in conjunction with a dwarf named Master who runs the pig shit factory and therefore thinks he's the cock of the walk.

This of course leads to the famous Thunderdome of the title. You know, it's like that one Tupac video. It's a cage where Max fights Blaster while suspended from ropes, they swing around and can grab different weapons from the dome. The only rule is "two men enter, one man leaves." There are crowds who chant this and lustily watch the violence, but it's not just gladiators to them, it's *The People's Court*. This is Auntie's system of law.

The way the crowd mindlessly chants the laws is pretty good satire. They keep chanting "two men enter, one man leaves!" until Auntie convinces them that Max can't leave because of another law, "bust a deal and face the wheel," so then they start chanting that. At that point Max has to spin a wheel of fortune which chooses his punishment as "gulag," so then they start chanting "Gulag! Gulag!" The whole thing reminded me of a stupid thing that came up recently where this nineteen-year-old girl was busted for recording twenty seconds of *Transformers* on her digital camera. A theater employee saw her doing it and told the manager, who instead of telling her to stop called the police, who instead of saying "fuck you, we have jobs to do" arrested the girl, and then Regal Cinemas instead of trying to do something positive for humanity such as finding a way to stop having so much god damn advertising at movies decided to press charges against the girl. And she said she was making a clip to show her little brother to get him excited to come see the horrible movie. (He'll have to get a ride from someone else; she's banned from the theater for life.)

When I read that story it made me mad to think some girl could face a $2,500 fine and a year in jail just because she did a dumb, harmless thing in front of some schmucks with no souls who work for a corporate monolith run by evil robots. But what made it worse was when for some reason I read themovieblog.com, where John Campea's story "Girl Could Go To Jail For Recording Transformers — Should She?" actually I swear to God begins with the sentence "This is a tough one."

NO IT'S NOT A FUCKING TOUGH ONE. Anybody with a human soul or an ounce of common sense does not have to struggle with whether or not a dumb nineteen-year-old girl should get jail time for a blurry twenty-second recording of a movie. (Even if it is one of the most evil movies ever made.) And then the worst part is that most of the people in the comments seemed to agree that she should at least get a hefty fine. Because "stealing is stealing" and "the law is the law."

"BUST A DEAL AND FACE THE WHEEL! BUST A DEAL AND FACE THE WHEEL!" The chanting at the Thunderdome is dead on. There are plenty of people in this pre-apocalyptic wasteland who do not use things like personal morals or ethics. They don't want to have to take time to think things through in a thoughtful manner. They want to have a simple, catchy phrase that turns all situations into easy black or white, yes or no type problems. And preferably something bad will happen to somebody at the end, such as a fine, jail time or GULAG! GULAG! GULAG!

I know I got way off topic here and this part will seem dated when people read this review down the line. But consider it the end credits song. The Tina Turner songs on the opening and closing credits were clearly made in the '80s, the rest of the movie is pretty timeless.

Anyway, Max gets the gulag, so they tie him up and send him out in the desert on a horse. And because it's *Mad Max* they put a big paper maché cartoon head on him. I think Rob Zombie is the only other director who would do a scene like that. But Miller was there first.

Post-Thunderdome is the part that turned a lot of people against the movie. Passed out in the middle of the wasteland Max is rescued by a tribe of children who believe he's their savior, "Captain Walker". I think these kids were refugees that the real Captain Walker was bringing somewhere on a jet, but it crashed. He must've been the only surviving adult, so he went to get help, but never came back. The kids have a good thing going at a hidden oasis and have survived by hunting for meat and furs. But they've built up this religious belief about Captain Walker and an oral storytelling tradition where they "tell the tell" every night so the history won't die.

The other two *Mad Max*es, especially part 2, were much more about showing than talking. This section of the movie though is all about words and telling stories. The kids have a fucked up language because they don't have grownups to correct their grammar. So they talk about "the pocksy clips" that turned the world into a wasteland. They're in awe of "the video" and "the sonic" (a record player) and one kid has an old talking Bugs Bunny doll that still works, which is kind of like having a super rare Ferrari or something.

But even this part is about visual storytelling. Notice that as the storyteller "tells the tell" she has a pole with a big rectangle, like a movie screen, that she uses to frame cave drawings and other things she wants the audience to look at. Then they make Max look into a Viewmaster.

My only problem with the movie is the section where Max takes the kids into the pig shit farm, and they swing around on ropes and fight some guys. Some of that stuff is cool but what really kills it is the music. The score is by a new guy, Maurice Jarre instead of Brian May.

By the way, I always thought the score for *Mad Max* was made by the dude from Queen until I looked it up just now and learned that it's a different Brian May. Just like there's that guy George S. Clinton that scored *Mortal Kombat*, he's not the same George Clinton. But at least he has the courtesy of a middle initial. The guy from Queen should have to use a middle initial. He's been coasting off *Mad Max* for decades now and he didn't even have anything to do with it. Asshole.

Anyway Maurice Jarre does fine for most of the movie, but he's a little more traditional than Australian film composer Brian May. And in this particular section of the movie he goes way overboard with trying to make the kids' activities seem triumphant and majestic and shit. If he would've just kept his pants on everything would be fine but with him trying to tell us how fun and adventurous it is for kids to fight slavedrivers in a pool of pigshit the whole thing just comes across too cheesy. I know some of you guys have that same problem with the Ewoks, but to me that's different. Because when Ewoks knock multi-million dollar government war machines over with rocks and logs it has a clear thematic purpose, it's kind of the whole point of the story. Ass-kicking lost boys does not have the same depth to it.

This by the way is an early case of PG-13 sequel to rated-R series, like *Robocop 3* and *Live Free Or Die Hard*. But it didn't even occur to me until I noticed the rating on IMDb. I guess it helps that you have the same director and you also have him intentionally not rehashing the type of story from the other ones. So it's not somebody watering down the old formula. It's a different thing entirely.

Anyway, the kids on ropes part of the movie is over fast and then we get on to the more *Road Warrior* part where Max and friends are on a jet-powered truck on train tracks being chased by Tina Turner and her posse in awesome souped-up dune buggies that show the advances in roll bar technology that have taken place in the years since part 2. Eventually they meet up with that pilot from the opening scene and Max says *"You!"*

And you think "A ha! So it *is* the gyro pilot! He recognizes him!"

and then "Wait, no, he just remembers it's the prick who stole his car!" and then finally

"Oh, I guess he just meant 'You there! I'm talking to you! The guy with the funny hat. Yeah, you.'"

This is part of the playfulness of the movie and what confused people who wanted something more normal. If you pay attention I'm pretty sure they never refer to Max as Max in this movie. Even when he is introduced in the Thunderdome they call him "The Man With No Name." So that's the one part where it is openly acknowledged that they are trying to go a little Leone with these movies. Bruce Spence is part of that Dollars Trilogy tradition, where Lee Van Cleef is in part 2 and 3 but as different characters. Although Bruce Spence is obviously more of an Eli Wallach. At the end of *Road Warrior* they tell you that the gyro pilot became the leader of the Northern Tribe and that they never saw Max again, so they couldn't really put that character in this movie. But I'm sure George Miller wanted to work with him again so what the hell, there's another pilot that looks like Bruce Spence. And then he plays with you by having Max almost seem to recognize him.

One thing that's weird, George Miller actually co-directed this one with some dude named George Ogilvie. Apparently he was a theater director who Miller had co-directed with on a mini-series and they liked it so much they decided to do it on this movie too. Supposedly Miller concentrated on the stunts and action while Ogilvie was in charge of the performances. Probably it was really a scam so Miller wouldn't have to deal with all these crowds of mud-covered kids and pigs. "Hey Ogilvie, shoot this part where the kids swing on ropes. I'll be in Thunderdome with the grown-ups."

The thing is, if you compare this to his other movies, even the pig and penguin movies, it's clear this is the work of the same mind. So it's not like he's letting Ogilvie take over. He's just freeing himself up to concentrate on the part where the car goes flying through the air and crashes through another car or whatever.

I'm praying they end up making that *Mad Max 4* that got cancelled because of the Iraq war (good one, Bush) but if not there's something nice about the way this wraps things up. In the first one there is still some society, but it's turning into the wild west, and Max loses his family and humanity. In the second one it's post-apocalypse, the whole world has gone to shit and he's this amoral wanderer, but he ultimately does something good to help some people. Now in this third one "civilization" is coming back but it's not exactly rebuilding, it's a new and even more corrupt alternate society. But he helps these children, because he believes the children are the future, teach them well and etc. etc.

It's kind of ironic and sad though because the kids actually start out in sort of a paradise, but because of their religious beliefs or folk tales or whatever you want to call Captain Walker, they end up moving into the bombed out ruins of Sydney! I'm sure it's kind of cool to explore but that's no place to live. Who knows what they're breathing in there. Not to mention the radioactivity. They had some natural beauty and they traded it for the rotting remains of the man-made world.

At the end Max is on his own again, perfectly open to having another adventure, perhaps called *Fury Road*. But despite the magic of parenting he's doing worse than he was at the beginning of the movie. Tina Turner has kind of a bonding moment with him, or at least a "what the hell, I'm not gonna kill you" moment. So we last see Max out in the desert, a legendary hero, a messiah, a survivor... a guy with no car.

MEL GIBSON'S APOCALYPTO

Apocalypto opens with a wild pig being chased through the jungle. Eventually the group of hunters on his ass lure him into a trap that impales him on a set of wooden spikes. Victorious, the hunters step through the leaves and reveal themselves to the camera. They're Mayan so they're half naked, covered in ritualistic scars and tattoos, piercings through their noses and chins. We've seen guys like this in movies before, they're called "savages." I just saw a more fantastical version in the *300* trailer before this movie. You see these type of guys, they might as well be bloodthirsty aliens, you just can't relate.

But then they drop down to the ground and start cutting up the meat, whoo-hooing and laughing. And you realize, these are just some dudes. They could almost be high-fiving each other. The hero Jaguar Paw (who looks like Jada Pinkett) cuts up the parts and distributes them, and he tricks his friend Blunted (not a pot joke) into eating the balls. (See, that's why I knew I could call the pig a he in the first paragraph.)

This is a brilliant opening, because Gibson sets up what appear to be authentic ancient Mayans, speaking their real language, but also portrays them as ordinary relatable people. I can't think of many movies with Mayans in them, but if I could I'm pretty sure you wouldn't see them joking and laughing too much. They'd be serious, either angry or noble, speaking in mystical broken English. Of course, Gibson ends up overdoing it a little. By the time you're fifteen or twenty minutes in and Blunted is screaming in pain, dunking his dick in a water trough because of an outrageous *Police Academy* style prank, you remember that this was made by a talented man most people agree has lost his mind, and you wonder if he's ever gonna get on with it. Luckily, the wacky hijinks pretty much disappear, except for one "oh Jesus, what were they thinking?" reference to *Midnight Cowboy*'s famous "I'm walkin here!" scene.

Eventually trouble comes to Apocalypsia when an army of warriors with torches show up and start killing and kidnapping. You can tell the bad guys from the good guys because they've got way more Mayan bling. More scars, more tattoos, fancier hair dos, a lot of them wearing jawbones and skulls on their shoulders or heads. It's kind of a class thing, these guys are hotshot materialists from the big city coming and tormenting the laid back forest people. They take the adults (including Jaguar Paw and Blunted) to use as slaves or human sacrifices. The good news: Jaguar Paw manages to hide his pregnant wife and his little son in a hole. The bad news: they'll be stuck there for the whole movie, like those two whiny hobbits that were stuck in the tree for the whole *Lord of the Rings Part 2*.

Eventually the captives get trotted to a big pyramid where a huge crowd watches the royalty cut out their hearts and bounce their severed heads down the side of the pyramid. There are dudes whose job it is to catch the heads in little nets, which is kind of unfair. What if somebody in the crowd wants it? I guess if they were unhappy with the beheading they would throw it back and that would cause problems, so they need the net guys.

This is an amazing scene. There's a giant crowd shot that looks very digital but when they're just showing the front it's an impressive real crowd, and there's so much detail in this pyramid and the jeweled faces of the royal family. They even got a fat little spoiled brat prince. That's kind of a trip man, think about a spoiled little bastard from a rich family, now imagine he gets his entertainment by watching his old man cut out hearts and bounce heads down the stairs. Think about the sense of entitlement this little porker is gonna have. Makes ya sick.

Now, I don't think it's too much of a spoiler to reveal that Jaguar Paw ends up not getting his head bounced, instead he escapes. And the second half of the movie is the great half of the movie. Because the rest of the movie is one long foot chase. A group of elitist rich boy warriors keeps on Jaguar Paw's ass just like he did on the pig whose balls he cut off. It becomes about more than just one escaped dude because a sick little girl has prophesized that the "man jaguar" will lead the warriors to their doom or some shit like that (one of the few superstitious parts in the movie). Since there is no media at this time, he does not become a folk hero with people all around the Yucatan peninsula showing their support. Instead he jumps down a waterfall, dodges arrows and spears, etc.

Because it's Mel Gibson, it's a pretty brutal movie. You got people getting impaled, a guy getting his head bit by a jaguar, a fuckin badass maneuver using some kind of hornets or wasps, and poor Jaguar Paw running over a pile of about a thousand rotting headless corpses. Not to mention the corresponding heads bouncing down the pyramid. All this is good clean American fun, but some of it is pretty emotional too. Like when all the adults are being led away in bondage and the crying children stay behind on their own. (You don't find out what happens to them, though. Maybe that's part 2.)

It seems to me like there's a growing backlash against minimalism and simplicity in entertainment. Everything has to be complicated and overproduced. Nothing can be left ambiguous or unexplained. Characters have to fuckin talk and talk and talk. Nobody wants to just see an expression on an actor's face that explains more than words, because we're a bunch of fuckin babies that need to be spoonfed baby food. At least that's what it seems like to me when I hear people complaining about *Miami Vice* being boring or *Mission: Impossible 3* cleverly obscuring what exactly the weapon is that everybody's fighting over or *Children of Men* not wasting everybody's time by gratuitously explaining exactly how and why its women can't have babies. I mean, I like all kinds of movies but I am especially a sucker for cinematics like this where there's not much talking and not much standing around. To me this is pure cinema. It's pictures and they're truly in motion. Think *Mad Max*. Except on foot. And with less clothes.

The movie goes light on dialogue, light on subplots, light on backstory. The point is for this guy to fuckin run and get his wife and kid out of a hole before they get murdered by assholes or bit by monkeys. Everything else is beside the point. I like it.

I should mention, by the way, that a lot of the portrayal of Mayans in the movie is apparently horse shit. You would think if somebody was gonna go through the trouble to make a movie in the dead language of the Mayans they would also try to make it really accurate, but apparently not. I'm sure Mel probably thinks the Jews sabotaged his consultants, but... nah, just kidding. That was a cheap shot. Let's set the anti-Semite thing aside. I admire Gibson for making a movie about such an out of left field topic, and make it in the Mayan language, and not really make it about the Mayan empire, exactly.

Most of us won't be bothered because most of us aren't scholars of Mayan history. But those who are point out that the movie is combining art and architecture from hundreds of years apart, giving the characters weapons that did not exist at that time, depicting mass killings that historians don't believe ever happened, showing them rounding up villagers for sacrifice when really they sacrificed members of the royal family. And they even have the Mayans being spooked by an eclipse, which if you think about it is pretty ridiculous. I mean, what's the most famous thing about the Mayans? Their astrological calendar. The Mayans knew their fuckin astro-shit. Now, if it was me — I could see me getting spooked by an eclipse if I hadn't had the TV or radio on in a while and didn't know it was coming. But the Mayans? No way. They calendared that shit. They woulda known exactly when it was gonna happen, they woulda been out there waiting for the eclipse with their little paper viewer things. So a lot of people knowledgeable about the Mayan culture have complained about that.

I would also like to add that *Midnight Cowboy* did not exist until the 1970s or so, the Mayans did not have access to it and even if they did there was no electricity. Also, the movie does not show that the Mayans maybe invented chocolate, which is a pretty huge oversight. I forget where I read it but somebody once pointed out that Robert Zemeckis has two movies where he has a white man inventing black music. In *Back to the Future* Michael J. whatsisdick teaches Chuck Berry everything he knows. In *Forrest Gump*, Tom Hanks teaches Elvis everything he knows, he doesn't actually learn it from black musicians. At least Mel doesn't have a white man inventing chocolate, but still. Give the Mayans credit. Chocolate is delicious. I know it, you know it, Mel Gibson knows it. Who are we trying to fool here, Mel?

Anyway, you gotta watch this as some fantasy adventure like *Conan the Barbarian* or something, not as actual history. But if you can do that you got a good one here.

CHAPTER FOUR
PHILOSOPHY

Maybe a little philosophy would be good for us. Movies aren't only about things blowing up, they're just mostly about things blowing up. But sometimes the filmic artists use their chosen medium of expression as a tool to explore the different ways of thought that are available and what not. For this chapter I have chosen a few movies that might not get the credit they deserve as philosophical movies, plus one that is explicitly about that shit but not necessarily in a good way in my opinion.

KNIGHTRIDERS

Folks, this week I'm gonna cut right to the chase. I have just seen a movie that is new to DVD that is VERY likely the BEST FUCKIN MOVIE EVER. This is a movie many of you have probably never seen and hell I never even HEARD of this piece until the other day however it is, for those of you just joining us, the BEST FUCKIN MOVIE EVER.

Now I have been tallying and calculating votes for the top 100 Badass Films of All Time and this picture has not received one vote. And I'm not complainin because this is not a Badass picture per se. It is more of a drama than an action film and is more about feeling and sentiment than about attitude and breaking a motherfucker's arms or whatever.

The name of the picture is *Knightriders*, a film directed by George A.

Romero in 1980. It was one of those movies that did very poorly at the box office and was never heard of again.... until it came to DVD and most people discovered that it was the BEST FUCKIN MOVIE EVER.

The picture opens with a whisp of mystical medieval flute and a black raven flying through a forest. A young Ed Harris and a pretty gal wake up naked in the woods. Ed bathes in the pond, meditates on his sword. He puts on his armor, the gal puts on her crown. She stands behind him and embraces him. The music grows triumphant as he pulls down his face shield and revs up his motorcycle.

Yes, this is a picture about knights who ride motorcycles. And that is only one of the reasons why it is the BEST etc. etc.

Ed is King Billy or Sir William, the leader of a troupe of individuals who travel around the country and hold renaissance fair type deals. This is where everybody dresses up like knights and monks and shit and pretend it's hundreds of years ago. They sell swords and maces and wine and all this type of garbage. It is basically the same as *Star Trek* conventions only without action figures or that fucking kid from *Trekkies* with the camper shaped like a spaceship.

The reason why this type of behavior is considered acceptable to ol' Vern is on account of the motorcycles. You see the main attraction is that they joust on motorcycles. There is a whole lot of motorcycle stunts in this movie — people crashing into cars, flying into lakes, going off of ramps. They even got a motorcycle that gets loose and smacks right into a gal in the audience. This is good stuff as far as knights on motorcycles type stunts go.

And yet, like I said, this is not an action picture. It is really a melodrama and a poem about living by your ideals. Most of these characters are just a bunch of real good friends, a bunch of hippies and bikers who like to dress up in armor and joust together. But the King takes it a little more to heart. He is an individual who really stands up for his beliefs. He refuses for example to pay off the cops who threaten to shut down the show if they don't pay. Instead he tells them to shove it up their ass. Then he willingly goes to jail until things are straightened out and makes a solemn vow to the cop that some day he will kick the shit out of him. And King Billy lives by his word.

The code of honor theme really starts rolling when a little kid shows the King a motorcycle magazine with pictures of the knight riders and asks for his autograph. Billy refuses to sign it and says that he is not about that.

Afterwards the Queen argues with the King. The troupe is running out of money. Embracing fame does not mean compromise. Why couldn't he be nice to that kid who idolizes him.

"That kid... that, that kid... thinks I'm Evel Knievel!"

"That kid thinks you're Billy Davis. Sir William the knight. You're his hero."

"I'm not trying to be a hero! I'M FIGHTING THE DRAGON!"

This is when you first realize that the King is a little bit, uh, fucked in the brains. He's one nut short of a sack. But maybe you have to be crazy in order to be a purist in this world, in order to really do what is right for your heart and what not.

The story is mainly about how a sleazy entertainment agent discovers the troupe and tries to turn them into a hot "act". A group of disillusioned knights led by Sir Morgan (Tom Savini, who was so great on the commentary track for *Maniac* as well as this one) takes up the offer and we see the clash between the ones who "get a spiritual fix" out of the knightrider lifestyle and the ones who are willing to give that up if it means glamour and money and floating around smoking pot in swimming pools with hot chicks (and one fat one).

But it's not what it sounds like. Hell I am a Writer but I don't know how to do justice to this one with the words. It's not an exploitation movie and its not really funny. It is 145 minutes long and it is sad and moving and reaffirms everything I believe in and reminds me to stand up for my ideals 24-7.

You know how all those dudes feel about *Braveheart*? You know who I'm talking about. Well that is how I feel about *Knightriders*. One reason why it is the best fuckin movie ever is because of its sincerity. It is sort of like how *Billy Jack* is an action movie with all those corny left wing ideals mixed in. Well this is the same kind of thing with better writing and acting and directing and especially singing, and not quite as corny. And with knights on motorcycles.

George A. Romero obviously made this film as a reflection of his life as an independent filmatist. The cast and crew were living this lifestyle and enjoying it. It becomes very personal and real and if you listen to the commentary track on the DVD you can tell that they really believed in this. And hell, they should.

Most people start out life with dreams of all the great things they want to do. They want to write movies or do ballet or be the first bank robber to be widely accepted by the mainstream or whatever. But then as they get older and they realize that they're not as talented as they always thought and things aren't as easy as they had hoped they give up and settle in to their 9-5 and forget about chasing dreams and even resent people who do. This movie is about doing the opposite.

The character Merlin is a doctor who quit medicine to become a mystical healer and storyteller for the knightriders. The backgrounds of the other characters is not revealed but I think King Billy may be a former pro motorcycle racer who quit the life to follow this dream. *Fight Club* says that we've been raised to believe we'll become rock stars and movie gods, but we won't. This movie says that we can, but FUCK THAT. Why would we want to? Instead we should carve out our own lifestyles. We should dedicate our lives to the things we like best, regardless of money. We should be knightriders. Outlaws.

The movie plunges us into this lifestyle and shows us why it's so good. These are people who like to joust and swashbuckle and build weapons and sit around the campfire singing 'Sygnifyin' Monkey'. They like to chase the bikers that steal their rubber axes and trick them into crashing their bikes. By the end you have so much invested in the lifestyle that anything that threatens to fuck with it upsets you. Sir William is a symbol for the true outlaw hero we should aspire to be, because he lives his entire life by his own code of honor. He refuses to buckle down to pig oppression, to sell out for money, to live any other way. He takes all of the substance of being a knight of Camelot and gets rid of all that sissy horse riding shit because he is so good at riding motorcycles instead. And unlike *Fight Club* or *The Beach* the Knightrider Club does not go sour, and will live on forever. God damn I love it.

This is a truly beautiful and poetic knights on motorcycles movie, one of the best you will ever see and god damn it if it didn't make ol' Vern cry. I love this fucking movie. I mean it, I love the shit out of this movie. It is the BEST FUCKIN MOVIE EVER. Take this movie, add in a couple of

Clint Eastwood and Steve McQueen's best, and you have everything I know and believe about what it means to be a man. Minus what I learned in the can.

I don't want to give away anything else but please, if you are in the mood to see a GREAT FUCKING MOVIE please rent this bitch and let me know what you think. Hell, I'm gonna put it all on the line — if you rent this movie, and you think it sucks, I give you my 100% guarantee that I will call you a retard.[19]

"I mean it's real hard to live for something that you believe in. People try it and then they get tired of it, like they get tired of their diets, their exercise or their marriage. Or their kids. Or their job. Or themselves. Or they get tired of their god. You can keep your money you make off this sick world, lawyer, I don't want any part of it."

Hell, the other knights have a point when they talk about ways to earn some money to help the group survive. I sure know how they feel. But I would like to live by Sir William's code. If you think I'm getting tired of it, or leaving my ideals behind, please let me know. Send me an e-mail or throw a brick through my window I don't give a fuck. I want to live by the outlaw code. I'M FIGHTING THE DRAGON.

Knightriders forever.

HOLY MOUNTAIN

Plot summary: When a dwarf with no hands or feet and some little kids try to stone a naked dude they found passed out, pissing himself with his face covered in flies, the naked dude and the little guy smoke a joint, hug and become fast friends. So they go into town, where tourists laugh and take pictures of the troops executing school children, and they watch the frogs and chameleons re-enact the conquest of Mexico in a model city. Also the naked dude looks like Jesus and these guys drug him and make a cast of him and he wakes up surrounded by hundreds of duplicates of

---

19 Offer no longer valid.

himself so he screams and smashes them but takes one and carries it around for a while and later he eats its face off and ties it to a bunch of helium balloons and sets it free. He hangs out with twelve hookers in matching see-through black outfits. One of them is an old lady, one is a little girl and they also have a chimpanzee. Some people might call it thirteen hookers I guess, but I'm old fashioned so I'm gonna assume the chimpanzee is just an associate and not a professional.

But when the Jesus guy puts a knife in his g-string and rides a hook up into a giant orange tower to try to assassinate the Alchemist (Alejandro Jodorowsky) it could change the course of his life forever. A deadly game of cat and mouse could happen maybe, or a suspenseful who knows what. Explosive revelations about the past could hold the key to the future. I don't know. You really can't turn *Holy Mountain* into a tagline but the point is, Jodorowsky asks the guy if he wants gold, he says yes, then he makes him shit in a bowl. Then he burns the shit and the guy sits in a big glass case and breathes in the fumes of the burning shit and his sweat drips into a tube and they pour it through some other tubes and eventually it crystallizes and then turns into gold. And Jodo hands him a chunk of gold that used to be his shit and you just know the guy is thinking *I shoulda had a bigger breakfast.*

But that's only the beginning. Believe it or not this movie actually has a clear plot and structure. It really is the craziest movie I've ever seen. This could be the Adult Pleasures movie you pay fifteen bucks for when you stay at the Interzone Best Western. But it's not just a bunch of random psychedelic bullshit. I'm not gonna lie and claim I can make heads or tails of, say, the part where an old dude has boobies and then they turn into tiger heads and spray milk all over a dude's face. (I think it has something to do with society. Or relationships, maybe.) But for the most part I think this movie is on my wavelength, I get what is going on here.

Once the naked Jesus dude (who unfortunately is called "The Thief" in the credits instead of "naked Jesus dude" — this may be the one concession Jodorowsky made to the mainstream) gets inside the Alchemist's orange tower (not a penis, by the way, just a tower) it turns into some kind of occult ritual with these beautiful stylized sets that are shot from a bird's-eye-view and rotate around. The place is pretty stripped down but I'd still say the Alchemist is living large since he has this beautiful naked tatooed black lady bodyguard working for him, and he has a throne made out of two stuffed mountain goats and a bathtub with a live baby hippo in it. I mean, this would be a fuckin spectacular episode of *Cribs*. Anyway he brings the thief onto a giant turntable that spins around and points at seven different life-sized naked wax sculptures of the other people who he's going to take on a journey to the Holy Mountain. But there's also a pelican walking around on the turntable. Okay so Ice-T has a shark tank, that might top the pelican, but not a lot of people have a pelican and a baby hippo. I think he might have a buzzard or something too. But it figures I guess — you turn enough shit into gold you're gonna buy some exotic animals. It can be a very profitable vocation, alchemy.

This is basically the second section of the movie, where each of the characters represented by the wax sculptures introduce themselves and their planet ("My name is Sel, my planet is Mars.") I've never been sure if they are literally supposed to be from that planet, or if it's some zodiac thing. The Alchemist says that they are "thieves, like you" but they don't turn out to be the kind of thieves that steal little pieces of gold. They are corporate thieves — a guy who makes beauty products (including artificial faces and asses) an arms dealer, an architect with a very unique approach to low income housing (coffins), a manufacturer of toy guns and GI Joes, a government financial adviser, etc.

Seeing this movie at the Grand Illusion theater here in Seattle, this was the part where the audience finally loosened up and realized it was okay to laugh. This is an extension of that town at the end of *El Topo*, where the rich old ladies had slaves and their husbands had whores shipped in in crates. I love this type of surrealist approach to satire — we see so much weak satire these days where it's too damn obvious (this guy represents Bush, this lady represents Ann Coulter) or it just isn't accurate. Jodorowsky's satire is outrageous, nightmarish broad strokes in a fantasy world that have a clear truth to them. So you nod your head at the arms maker creating psychedelic designs on guns to appeal to hippies or the toy lady training kids from birth to hate Peruvians in case there's a war against them in the future.

Once everybody's introduced themselves, the Alchemist leads them on a quest to climb the summit of the Holy Mountain to kill the nine Immortals and steal their secrets. Obviously, killing the nine Immortals is the kind of thing we can all relate to, we know exactly what this means. If not, just think of *City Slickers II: The Legend of Curly's Gold*. Those assholes go ride horses or whatever and it teaches them the value of, you know, to savor it or, you know, learning the wisdom and what not, etc. etc. Is it about actually finding the legend of Curly's gold? No, it's about looking for the gold. In the end, they throw the gold in the river and then self-immolate (just guessing, I haven't seen that movie). Anyway same exact thing here except instead of Curly's gold you have the nine Immortals, instead of Billy Crystal you have a dude with a mowhawk who cuts people's balls off with scissors and collects them in jars. And then instead of riding horses they hump a mountain. The details are different but the substance is the same. Every rock has a soul.

[TANGENT: This brings up something somebody asked me about, and it occurred to me too watching it this time. If you've seen it maybe you can give your opinion. The Chief of Police says that 999 officers have already had their balls cut off, but then he says it's a Sanctuary of 1,000 Testicles. But the question is, shouldn't it be 2,000 Testicles? Well, there are a lot of possibilities. Maybe for the first 500 ballsacs he didn't think to use formaldehyde so they went bad and he had to throw them out, but he still wanted to honor their sacrifices by mentioning their numbers. Or maybe he only cut off one ball, it's not really clear until we get a remastered DVD and can pause and zoom.[20] Also a possibility: all the officers have one ball, like Lance Armstrong. Or maybe it is a mistranslation or script error, but those seem far-fetched. Anyway, enough about ball counting.]

I think the Alchemist knows from the beginning that it's all about the journey, just the experience is gonna enlighten the hell out of these pricks just like Billy Crystal before them. Think about it. This is the Alchemist, this is the guy who turns shit into gold. And he's taking these corporate vampires and enlightening them. Same thing. Shit into gold.

Also one of the prostitutes (a really gorgeous one, not the old lady or the little girl) and the chimpanzee follow the thief because they love him. So any time it's getting too deep into alchemy and tarot symbols don't worry, there will be a funny shot of a monkey wearing clothes at some point.

---

20 There is now a remastered DVD but to be honest I have not yet paused to count the balls.

I love this movie. It's honestly one of my favorite movies. It's the *Die Hard* of surrealist alchemy comedies. This is the first time I've seen it projected on a screen. This print was still dubbed and did not appear miraculously alchemically remastered. It didn't have all the pubic hair blurred out like on the Japanese release though. But it was fucking great. I couldn't stop smiling while I was sitting there, wondering if these other people in the theater hated it. I heard one dude sighing impatiently several times, but maybe he just has a breathing problem.

My buddies Moriarty and Scott Swan wrote a *Masters of Horror* episode where everybody's trying to find a print of a movie that has only screened once and when it did it drove everybody crazy and they all killed each other or themselves or something. That was what I always figured a public screening of *Holy Mountain* would be like, but somehow this was a normal moviegoing experience. I would've liked if somebody had released ants or baboons in the theater, but no dice. Nobody even got up and left in frustration. I think people liked it.

As I was leaving the movie I heard some young people comparing the movie to Matthew Barney's, agreeing it was more fun to watch and had more of a story. It would've been funnier if they were crying and all they had to compare it to was *Little Miss Sunshine* or something, but still. It was nice to know that the kids dig Jodorowsky.

There is no other movie like *Holy Mountain* and there probably never will be. It is some crazy shit you can't believe is really on film, but at the same time it's watchable and enjoyable. Listen to the youth of America, they have spoken and they prefer Jodorowsky to Barney. If we could have one of those shows where kids pay money to text message a vote for a meaningless contest of some kind, the kids would totally vote for *Holy Mountain*. And all the profits would go to buying tiger heads to replace old men's boobs.

If you are a Sandra Bullock/Meryl Streep type of individual who sometimes doesn't like a movie because it's "too weird," this will probably cause your eyes to bleed and you will lose all feeling in your extremities and when they find you you'll be naked in a fountain downtown munching on fistfuls of caterpillars. Who knows where the fuck you got 'em, you were just in the mood for caterpillars. So check it out. It finally comes out on region 1 DVD May 1st, 2007. If you are rich I suggest you pre-order 100 copies and give them to all your relatives, your pastor, members of the city council, etc.

It's weird, this has always been an elusive, mysterious movie that most people never heard of and you have to go to an underground freemason lodge and use a password to rent it. But starting on May Day 2007 a new era is upon us. With the help of Anchor Bay, we might be seeing this shit in Wal-Mart, or at least Best Buy. This is a dream come true for me, I have always thought this whole fucking nightmare that is American pop culture 2007 might pop like a balloon if we could just print up a couple hundred thousand copies of *Holy Mountain* (Excrement Into Gold Edition) and start re-molding everybody's minds.

The secret will be out. It won't have that mystique anymore, but it'll be cool to finally share this with everybody. Before long *Holy Mountain* will be as mainstream as *Napoleon Dynamite*. Guaranteed to be in stock at Blockbuster Video, or you get a coupon for free jalapeno Twizzlers from Pizza Hut. There's gonna be *Holy Mountain* ringtones, *Holy Mountain* valentines card, *Holy Mountain* Home Alchemy Kits, *Holy Mountain* Slurpee with a hologram of the Jesus dude getting his ass washed, limited edition prop replica of the crucified flayed lamb, t-shirts and lunch boxes and talking key chains with all the quotable lines like "Your excrement... you can turn yourself into gold" and "Rub your clitoris against the mountain" and of course my favorite "Your sacrifice completes my Sanctuary of 1,000 Testicles." People are gonna be quoting this movie so much you'll get sick of it, like *Austin Powers*. Some of those pricks who do the *Scary Movie* type parody "movies" will get some has-been dressed up dorf style to play the limbless dwarf in the WWII helmet kicking the Jesus dummy in the alley, there is a lot of spoofability there. *Saturday Night Live* will get more traction though with their reoccurring "Alchemist" character. Dressed up in Jodorowsky's duds and with a Peter Lorre accent, he goes around asking people if they have any extra poo anywhere they can give him. I don't know man it's hard to explain, you just gotta see it to understand how hilarious it is, I'm sure it's on YouTube.

Ladies and gentleman, 2007 will be the year of *Holy Mountain* and Jodorowskymania. Mark my words. You heard it here first.[21]

---

21 Okay, admittedly some of those things haven't happened. Yet.

GROUNDHOG DAY

Last week I reviewed this movie *The Ice Harvest* which I thought was only okay. And I think I blamed director Harold Ramis, who I accused of mediocrity. Then the other day, through coincidence or karma or something, I ended up watching *Groundhog Day*, which is the Bill Murray movie Ramis directed back in 1993.

I'd seen this movie before but I actually forgot how good it was, so I gotta give Mr. Ramis credit. I give credit where credit is due, and credit is due right here. Harold, here is your credit. Take it.

I'm sure you've seen this one before but if not here's the deal. Bill Murray is a bitter, cynical weather man who has to go to Punxsutawney to cover the Groundhog Day ceremony where they pull the groundhog out of a tree stump and pretend to ask him if he saw his shadow or not. Bill clearly hates this shit so he gets it over with and tries to get the hell out, but a blizzard (which he had predicted would not happen) strands him at a bed and breakfast.

The next morning he wakes up at 6 am hearing the same broadcast he heard the morning before, and thinks the radio station fucked up and played the wrong tape. But he looks out the window and there's no snow, and people on the streets are headed for the Groundhog Day ceremony again. And he goes downstairs and starts to have the same encounters with various locals that he already had the day before.

And the rest of the movie is about the increasing frustration, mischief and eventual enlightenment caused by his having to live the same Punxsutawney Groundhog Day over and over again (we don't know how long it lasts but it's definitely a long time — according to the DVD extras the writer originally envisioned it as thousands of years).

When I saw this before I liked it because it's a good *Twilight Zone* type premise and it's funny to see the way Bill Murray takes advantage of the situation, using his knowledge of events to rob banks or manipulate people, or using the lack of consequences to create mischief. He can lead the police on a chase or punch an old high school acquaintance in the face because the next day it will be undone and nobody will remember. And he can use the endless time loop to learn to speak French or play piano.

But now that I see it again as a more thoughtful, positive individual and a more astute motherfucker in the area of filmatic theory and practice, the movie takes on a much deeper meaning. The reoccurring day is not just a cool gimmick, it's also a reflection of the way he feels about his life. He is tired of repeating variations on the same old weather shit, going to the same places, surrounding himself with the type of people he hates. So he ends up literally having to relive the same day every day, and cannot escape these small town people because of the blizzard that strands him there. And the one person he really likes, his new producer (played by Andie McDowell) he has a hard time connecting with, first because he approaches it on a superficial/manipulative level and then because he only has one day of genuine bonding before she forgets it all entirely and he has to start over from scratch.

But over time he starts to change his attitude toward life, even this horrible repeating life. It's not just that he picks up hobbies and interests, and starts making a more sincere effort to have a relationship with Andie McDowell. That's what I remembered from before, he learns to do things to genuinely make Andie McDowell happy instead of just things that trick her into thinking he's cool. That's a good moral but I think there's more philosophy in the movie than just that. He also starts trying to help people he doesn't even know. To me the most moving scene is when he decides to start feeding and hanging out with the old homeless guy he's been walking past every day. The guy gets sick and dies, and you see how much this upsets Bill Murray. He won't accept it. He tries to figure out what it is that kills the guy so he can stop it from happening the next time.

To me that's the deepest thing about the whole movie. He lives in a world where there are literally no consequences to anything. The old man dies every day, but he's back again the next day, so it really doesn't matter all that much. And yet, instead of choosing to not give a shit and to continue indulging himself, Bill Murray decides he wants to spend his time by trying to make this guy live. And by catching the kid who falls out of the tree everyday and changing a flat tire that some old ladies get every day. He has no reason to do these things except to make the world a little better, to make today a happier day, to be a nice guy. And he does it. That's Jesus right there, that's Buddha, that's Santa Claus and probably Superman and Ziggy. Arguably Popeye. Maybe Zorro, I don't know too much about Zorro. Anyway, it's deep.

So I will follow Bill Murray's lead. There's no reason to take back what I said about Harold Ramis, since he never heard it in the first place, but I take it back. This guy, at least in 1993, was striving for excellence. It's nice to see a mainstream studio comedy with such an unusual gimmick (before Charlie Kaufman), but especially with one that has deeper meaning than just a clever hook for a movie. And I also gotta credit Ramis and co-writer Danny Rubin for not ruining it by trying to explain what caused the loop (a curse? some radiation?) or specifically explaining exactly what causes it to end. If he was a mediocre director he probably woulda worried that the audience would be confused and come up with some phoney explanation.

By the way, did you know there's an Italian remake of *Groundhog Day* called *It's Already Yesterday* or *Stork Day*? I wonder if that's any good.

Anyway, good job boys, a couple more movies like this and you won't have to keep coasting on your records of public service as Ghostbusters.

WAKING LIFE

It took me a while to get to this one because 1) cartoons are only for children and 2) it wasn't nominated for the best animated feature Oscar so it must not have been any good. So I watched *Jimmy Neutron* instead.

Actually that is all bullshit. I know this movie was beloved by critics and people alike. I even talked to one dude who hates all Richard Linklater's other movies but liked this one. As you probably already know this is a movie that Linklater shot on digital video, then had computer animators paint over the video in their computer programs and turn it into surreal computer art type business. What the plot is about is this kid is dreaming, but he can't wake up, and everywhere he goes people talk to him about free will or lucid dreaming or show off that they have some wacky quirk like they pretend their car is a boat.

Now let me tell you something. This is a completely original idea for an animated feature and I respect that. The animation style itself is also original and sometimes even looks good. Because of the software tracing over handheld video camera footage the backgrounds end up bouncing around like the whole city is built on the surface of a giant water bed, and everywhere you walk the trees and the buildings and the signs wobble around. Some of these shots, especially walking around on city streets, look stunningly beautiful and are a good totally phony way of portraying a dream life. (I mean seriously, have you ever had a dream that was anything like this animation in any remote way? Of course not.)

There are also some interesting ideas to ponder in this movie. And some of the acting is good, like the one scene with Ethan Hawke and Julie Delpy. A few of these actors know how to deliver this dialogue and make it sound like they're actually talking and not just spewing memorized lines. Also some of the scenes obviously are real professors talking about the type of shit that they, unfortunately for us, like to talk about.

I had to get that out of the way because there are things that I can respect about this movie ON PAPER but that does not in any way mean that it wasn't one of the most insufferable pieces of garbage of the year. I would have to say that despite some good scenes in there, overall I hated this fuckin movie.

Look, maybe you guys went to college, maybe you want to be back there talking to the worst bags of hot air you've ever known and consider that a good way to spend ninety minutes of valuable life. But don't put the rest of us through that. I took a Wednesday night writing class at a sort of hippie college so I've witnessed these kind of fuckwads firsthand. And I think anyone who has met these people in person knows that they should not be glamorized in cartoons. At this school they have what is called seminar. Everybody in the class is supposed to read about a book, and then they come and discuss it. They talk a little about the book but mostly go off on tangents about subjective vs. objective reality, existentialism, and what happened that week on *The Simpsons*. Well this movie is like *Seminar: The Animated Movie.*

Okay let me give you a different example. I was on the bus and all the way from downtown to my house there was this yuppie talking loudly on his cell phone to a friend who had just gotten back from India. "So tell me all about it! Was it really Indian? I mean did they have Persian rugs everywhere? Tell me!" He went on and on about did you go out of Heathrow and etc. and tried to make it clear to everyone on the bus that he was intimately familiar with the airports and geography of Europe and was very worldly and etc., although at no point did he demonstrate knowledge that India and Pakistan were believed to be at the brink of nuclear war and that the day before the U.S. had urged all Americans to leave.

Then the other day I went to a party and got into a conversation about *The Outfit* and then everybody started talking about what Truffaut and Godard do. And the day after that I went to a barbecue and listened to some guys talk about which hotels they've stayed at in Vegas, which casinos they felt were used as locations in the movie *Swingers*, which magicians they wanted to see, why the logos for NBA teams symbolize the downward spiral of the sport and why the NFL is the only legitimate professional sports league.

If I had a video camera and taped all these fuckwads[22] talking and then turned it into a cartoon, that might be quite an accomplishment for myself but I would not be cruel enough to release it in theaters and on DVD and expect people to actually watch it. These are the types of conversations a man or woman spends his or her life trying to avoid, except when high. I don't know if I've ever seen a movie before where I felt like I needed to nod politely and try to think of an excuse to leave.

I mean look, if you haven't seen this movie yet and I'm not convincing you, I have no choice but to pull out the big guns. Here are some actual quotes from the movie:

"I'm beginning to think that it's something that I don't really have any precedent for, it's totally unique, the quality of the environment and the information that I'm receiving."

"When I say 'love', the sound comes out of my mouth, and it hits the person's ear, travels through this Byzantine conduit in their brain, you know through their memories of love, or lack of love, and they register what I'm saying and they say yes they understand but how do I know they understand because words are inert, they're just symbols. They're dead. Y'know?" (In the next 10-20 seconds she also manages to use the words

---

22 I apologize — I don't know why I called all these people fuckwads. Except for the cell phone guy on the bus, I'm gonna go ahead and categorize that one as a fuckwad. Otherwise, no judgment.

intangible, spiritual, communion, and transient.)

"We are all coauthors of this dancing exuberance where even our inabilities are having a roast. We are the authors of ourselves, coauthoring a giant Dostoevsky novel starring clowns."

That's not the only entry-level pretentious literary reference either. Throughout the movie, people will be talking and slide into "Kind of like, D.H. Lawrence had this idea of two people meeting on a road..." blah blah fuckin etc. Or Philip K. Dick or you name it. A gal gives her idea for an "interactive soap opera" which comments on "consumerism and art and commodity." Paradoxes, paradigms, self-awareness. And yes, a professor talks about existentialism, fer cryin out loud. If you want to get the part of college that cannot be applied usefully, save your money and just watch this movie.

I'm not trying to say that these ideas are all full of shit or that these people are dumb or that thinking about things in different ways is not ever useful. Although, in the case of some scenes, that would be the truth. I'm just saying, this is a movie that made me want to back away slowly, and not make eye contact. These people are just like the asshole on the cell phone or the dudes who think the NBA logos are too cartoony — they think what they are saying is a lot more insightful and impressive to the listener than it actually is. And no amount of fancy computer cartoons can disguise that fact.

My idea of hell would be if this movie could follow you around and keep talking to you.

CHAPTER FIVE
TANGENTS

Critics who write for newspapers or magazines usually have to fit their reviews in a couple of columns, so they gotta trim the fat. But some people like to eat the fat. I like to include in my reviews different things the movie makes me think about, so I got a habit of going into rants or flying off onto tangents. It's probably a bad habit, but sometimes I end up liking the tangents more than the reviews. In this chapter I present some of my favorite reviews where I use the movie as an excuse to rant about society and what not. In some cases I'm talking about the movie business or sort of what the movie's about and in some I'm really stretching it.

FRIDAY AFTER NEXT

I really don't have much to say about this movie, so instead I will rail against our modern consumerist society. Thanks for your understanding.

I really feel old when I show up to a movie ten or fifteen minutes early. Sure I like to think I'm young in the heart and all that shit, but I still remember when moviegoing was a pleasant experience. Sure I am thankful for the innovations of digital sound and automatic ticket machines. But it's time to dump the rest of the cineplex baggage. These chains are all going chapter eleven anyway, why not jettison the extra weight?

So I walk in there, the old man, and I let this CD pretending to be a radio station introduce me to the latest contemporary R&B products. I'm pretty sure they have a camp somewhere where they raise these kids to groom them into soul-less, personality-less test tube warblers with prefabricated sexuality. They keep them naked in cages until the cameras are ready, then they throw each of them a plastic bag containing 1 (one) wireless microphone headset (does not work), 1 (one) pair white leather pants (low riding), one (1) $200 boutique t-shirt (one sleeve only), and 1 (one) rhinestone cowboy hat.

Then they throw them in the studio with whichever mainstream hip hop producer has had the most #1 hits in this particular business quarter, spend two months of postproduction overdubbing and electronically altering their vocal tracks, and *voila!* Suddenly the little curly haired kid from In Sink has a song that exactly mimics Michael Jackson. As soon as advertising, promotions, assistant promotions, corporate advertising, press relations and the payola department go over it, the single is ready. Quick, get this to the Cinematron Radio Network Popcorn Jam! We want Vern to have to listen to this garbage while he waits to see *Friday After Next!*

Sitting waiting for a movie, there used to be some kind of atmosphere there. They would play classical music, if anything. I'm not a big classical music fan but it makes for good atmosphere, it makes you feel like you're in a semi-classy establishment, with some sense of culture or at least a desire to let you relax. Not anymore. Now you have to get banged on the head with the *Clockwork Orange* assault. Coca-Cola rapes you in the eyes with their trivia questions (impossible to be stumped by, just so nobody feels left out) while the R&B gets you in the ear. Available now at Sam Goody. It's not just that this music is absolutely horrible and that I don't want to have to stop watching movies in order to avoid listening to it. It's also that I have to sit there and think about American culture's position, hanging from a cliff with a hook in its ass, being stretched deeper and deeper into the abyss, forever.

I mean I'm sitting there thinking about little Michael Jackson when he was in the Jackson 5. So charismatic and talented, so they turned him into a waterskiing squirrel. Come see the waterskiing squirrel, the dancing monkey, the BMX bear. Hear him sing about relationships, even though he's nine. He got older and he became such a superstar and he was starting to seem pretty weird but man that motherfucker could dance and he was still doing good music even if it wasn't as good as 'Off the Wall' was. So he was treated like royalty and women thought he was a "fox" and wanted to have sex with him even though he looked increasingly feminine and was always riding on a giraffe or holding a monkey or some weird shit. But as his music started to slide out of the public consciousness, as his perfectionism and fear got him spending years and millions on one mediocre album, as he got increasingly weirder and more mysterious and sinister, the press and the people got crueler. And now he's walking around in a man-made albino alien face, watching us through Diana Ross's eyes, wearing a black velvet surgical mask that protects his delicate mouth and his tiny nose with its little piece of hip bone protruding through the tip. I never thought I'd see the headline "Pop star dangles baby from balcony."

I mean look, this guy is still incredibly talented, and he's one of the only entertainers out there with a straight face talking about healing the world. But in exchange the world has left him an insane, baby dangling, desiccated alien corpse, and replaced him with some average kid with a funny hat and a bunch of computers. And we still wonder why he tried to buy the Elephant Man's bones.

Well I was probably the only one in that theater worrying about Michael Jackson but I wasn't the only one sick of listening to this god damn music. Every time a new song started I heard my fellow old men beside and behind me let out loud, anguished sighs. And then the real advertising began.

There was the Coca-Cola "refreshing film." Then the cell phone company reminding you to be polite, but still be an asshole with a cell phone. (Sorry about the brain cancer.) Then there was the obnoxious website trying to convince you, through the medium of bad comedy, that it is actually really difficult to get a ticket to a movie unless you pay extra to buy it online. (How do they expect this ad to work when everyone in the theater, by definition, was able to get into the movie? Well, by showing it before every single movie you ever see for the rest of your life. Maybe eventually you'll give in and accept their logic.) Then those lovable characters from *Men In Black Part 2: MIB 2* come on to mention Sony, Loews, enjoythemovie.com, *Men In Black 2* on DVD, and to say, "Sit back, relax, and enjoy this exclusive *Men in Black 2* show!" Which turns out to mean about fifteen seconds of outtakes where they forget their line and then start laughing. And that was followed up by another ad, this one for Volvo, explaining that they finally gave in and made an SUV.

More ads, more anguished sighs.

Then a trailer for some cartoon starts up. Finally, a trailer. But halfway through the narrator lets you know that also you can get a special Sony-Loews Coca-Cola KFC Taco Bell Gift Meal Super Pack of popcorn, soft drink and Viacom Nickelodeon movie ticket, all you have to do is get a receipt and go onto this website, to play some fun exclusive trivia games or some shit... long story short, this is not a trailer, it is more of an ad, advertising all of the corporate tie-ins to the movie instead of the movie.

By now, we should be ready for the trailers proper, right? No, first we have Spider-Man selling an electric toothbrush (I am not shitting you) and James Bond selling an electric razor and computer animated dudes with swords selling a video game. And when, after being advertised to death for the half hour since I stepped into the theater, I finally get a real god damn movie trailer, it gets stuck halfway through and the film melts on screen.

Which is fine. Those are fancy machines, and shit happens. But for five minutes, we sat and watched the surviving edges of the film, bubbling and dripping, still projected on the screen. Because it took that long for the projectionist to get there. They're taking in Spider-Man electric toothbrush dollars but they can't afford to hire enough projectionists, or pay or train them well. They have to have one college kid running sixteen projectors, selling popcorn and doing his homework at the same time. If it takes them that long to get to the non-moving, melting to death movie, how long does it take them to get to the one that's out of focus?

The good old days, man. One or two movies in a theater, not necessarily a mainstream hit, one projectionist keeping an eye out, no more advertising than "Let's all go to the lobby." They even gave you a free cartoon! And people didn't talk too much during the movies. If they had had cell phones, they would've known not to use them in a fucking movie theater. But now that seems like a thousand years ago, on another planet. And they wonder why people want to stay home and watch movies on DVD.

That's probably what you should do with *Friday After Next*, if you're interested. The first *Friday* was fresh, it had breakout roles for the straight man Ice Cube and the hilarious Chris Tucker. It started its own genre of hood comedies, it had a real good soundtrack of funk and gangster rap, it had a good message and it seems funnier and better made each time you watch it. Well the sequels don't have Chris Tucker and they're increasingly formulaic and don't seem all that much better than the *Friday* imitators.

At first this one seems like it might be reaching for new territory a little, because of the great animated credits and Christmassy orchestra score. But it quickly settles into the *Friday* formula, with Craig and Day Day (Mike Epps, Craig's cousin, introduced as the Smokey-replacement in part 2) needing a certain amount of money, Craig scoping out a hot chick from afar, everybody saying "You got knocked the fuck out!" whenever possible, Craig's dad having to take a shit real bad, etc. This time around they get Craig's mom from part 1 back, and his Uncle and the record store owner Pinky from part 2 back. But they can't get Dibo back so they replace Tiny Lister with another huge, bald muscleman named Damon,[23] who just returned from prison and still wants to rape men. Fer cryin out loud. And even when they try things that are new for the series, sometimes it's bad like Mike Epps wearing old man makeup to play another character. You don't want to be the new Martin Lawrence, man! Just cool it.

I mean, I enjoyed parts. Mike Epps is probably funnier than in the last one. There are a lot of good chuckles. And it's always good to see a movie like this, about guys who can barely pay their rent, and have to work at a strip mall, and get no respect, instead of about all those rich fuckers you usually see in movies. But the series has stretched itself too thin. It's time to try something else, Ice Cube. We'll see how *Barbershop 2* works out, I guess.[24]

---

23 I didn't know who he was when I wrote this, but Damon was played by Terry Crews who went on to appear in *Idiocracy, Terminator Salvation* (briefly) and *The Expendables*.

24 Actually I never did see how it turned out, I never watched that one. Anybody know how it turned out?

CRANK

No, this is not the one where Adam Sandler has a magic remote control that he uses to conquer the world, that's *Click*. This is *Crank*, this is the one where Jason Statham (the Transporter himself) is a hitman who gets injected by high concept poison. It's gonna kill him, but he figures out that it won't finish until his adrenaline rate goes down. So he tries to run around, have sex, do coke and get in shootouts until he is able to get revenge on the poisoner. So it's *Speed* in a guy, with a side order of revenge.

An inventive thrill ride full of imagination and wit that keeps you constantly involved as it builds to an unbelievable climax... would be a good way to do this movie. Instead they went the *Domino* route of "if you throw every stupid show-offy technique you ever saw in a commercial at the screen, technically it counts as entertainment." I think I know what they were thinking: he has to keep his adrenaline up, so the movie has to keep its adrenaline up too. But it's flawed logic. *The Jerk* is about a moron, but the movie doesn't have to be moronic. I don't think *Speed* had cameras flying around constantly to convince you that it's about speed. If you show a guy in a hospital gown zooming around on a motorcycle pursued by police, that is by definition somewhat exciting. But when you throw in unnecessary zooms and split screen and do a jokey flashback on one side and then freeze on a guy's goofy expression and then switch it to black and white and then zoom into Statham's chest to show an x-ray of his heart beating (a nod to the Furious Movement) AND you gotta throw in "exciting" guitar music made by a guy who used to be in Tangerine Dream who is now trying to rock out, it seems like you're overcompensating. It isn't exciting anymore, it's just annoying. To me it's another movie that has no build or rhythm at all, just the same frantic shit for eighty-seven minutes straight.

The responsible parties are two rookie directors who are small time actors and did effects on *Biker Boyz*. My guess is that one directed the movie and then the other one directed it again and then they edited the two versions together using a coin toss or dice to figure out which shot to use where. It's not nearly as bad as *Domino*, that's one nice thing I can say. I guess the difference is that it has that cool premise and it sticks to it. It's a simple, fairly streamlined story. I guess I can see how somebody might be interested to see him get his revenge if they could watch the movie without their mind wandering off to somewhere more peaceful.

On the other hand, I think they do kind of fumble the whole adrenaline rush concept by making him so casual about everything. When he drives through the mall chased by cops in the beginning, he is talking on the phone and doesn't seem to be even paying attention to the high-speed car chase he's involved in. That might be a funny way to show that he's seen everything, but doesn't that sort of contradict the idea that he's doing all this to terrify himself into staying alive? He sure doesn't seem like he's got any adrenaline flowing. Which is it? Unphased tough guy or adrenaline rush? You can't choose both.

The only other positive thing I can say (this is for you, Thumper's mom) is that it occasionally has a funny gimmick or over-the-top idea. The opening scene seems promising as he wakes up disoriented, finds a DVD that says "FUCK YOU" on it in Sharpie, puts it in and watches his enemy inject his unconscious body with the poison. In the part where he drives through the mall (not as good as in *The Blues Brothers*, by the way) I like that he somehow manages to get his car sideways onto the escalator. But then he stands on top of it and jumps off at the top of the escalator, which is kind of disappointing. I'm pretty sure the Transporter would've been able to get the car off the escalator and continue. Oh well.

Remember how I pointed out that the Transporter seems to have some weird racial issues? Maybe it's Jason Statham himself because he does it again, in this one he announces that he's gonna "kick some black ass" in order to provoke a bunch of guys so he can keep his energy up. But he has bigger problems in the woman department. He has this nice girlfriend played by Amy Smart (the dangerous babe on *Smith* if you saw that show before it was cancelled[25]) who doesn't even know he's a hitman. Again, he needs to keep his adrenaline pumping so he decides he wants to have sex with her on a crowded block in Chinatown. I don't know, maybe she's shy, so she says no. So he rapes her. But the way they go from "our hero is raping his nice girlfriend in public" to "this is a fun time at the movies"

---

25 Yeah, real helpful to try to explain who she is by referencing a show that was cancelled after 3 episodes.

is they show that she starts enjoying it and getting into it. I thought that old saw died with the westerns but no, here it is again, a great fantasy for any of you sickos out there: if you rape her good enough you'll win her over. Wonderful. This scene is supposed to be the comic highlight — you can tell because they have all these shots of the crowd watching as he screws her doggystyle, and then a tour bus of school girls pulls up to enjoy the show. And in case you, like the character played by Amy Smart, have already forgiven him for raping her — he decides to push it further by pulling out his phone and making a call during the sex. Which is, in my opinion, rude.

That reminds me of something completely unrelated to *Crank* that I want to get off my chest. I've probably written about cell phone etiquette before. I'm kind of a caveman or a Luddovite or whatever on this issue. I personally am not a cell phone guy. Usually I figure if it is important enough to call somebody, it is important enough to either be indoors or find a damn payphone. And I don't like the idea of walking around anywhere in the world and if somebody calls you you gotta decide whether to answer it or not. That's what leaving the house is for. You don't have to worry about that shit until you get home. And you never have to worry about your fuckin "minutes." But I'm not blamin you people, I completely understand why you want your phones, it is very convenient. And I will understand even better some day if I fall through a sinkhole or get trapped under a collapsing viaduct. I will reach for my hip and think "Where the fuck is my cell phone side-holster?" before realizing "Oh, that's right, I have never owned a cell phone." And then I will sit there for however long it is that man can live without water, considering whether or not it was worth it.

So you guys are probably smart to carry those horrible things, in an emergency you can always call for help or download the latest jamz from the Black Eye Peas. But since you're the ones playing with them I believe the burden is on you to institute a worldwide acceptance of common sense cell phone etiquette rules. I mean for God's sake, it goes without saying that you shouldn't make a phone call while doggystyling Amy Smart in front of a crowded square and a bus full of tourists as Mr. Statham does in this picture. How is it gonna be special for Amy Smart, or for the tourists, if you don't even have your mind on it? Multi-tasking may be valued in your office (or in this case hitman) job but there are some situations where your focus should be on interacting with other human beings (in this case Amy Smart and a hundred or so others) and not on showing off how many "tasks" you can stack up at once.

True story: a few weeks ago I was walking down a sidewalk and had to go around a young hipster couple passionately making out in an intentionally obstructive fashion. I saw them from half a block away, but it was only as I maneuvered around them that I noticed the dude was listening to his voicemails while he kissed her. Of course, this is not as bad as making a phone call during public sex, but it shows that the attitude does exist, these assholes really are that far gone. I guarantee you this guy I saw has the willingness and the ability to execute that type of bullshit. The threat is imminent.

Of course, the more common problem is assholes going into a bank or a 7-11 or what have you and expecting the poor clerk to be able to make a transaction with them while they are talking to somebody else about fixing the heater in the pool or who's gonna pick up the wine to have for dinner. It used to be they just looked down on the workers serving them or treated them like shit, now they are trying to avoid even talking to them or acknowledging their existence on this plane. As far as this guy's concerned he just paid a magic cash register for his Slurpee. He didn't even see the guy he gave the money to.

And the problem is even worse now with this type of phone that's getting more and more popular, and this is the real reason I wanted to go off on this tangent. As Jerry Seinfeld would say, what the holy fuckballs is up with those phones that attach to your ear? I don't know what it's called but it's a little silver headset type phone that actually ATTACHES into your ear AND YOU ACTUALLY KEEP IT THERE ALL DAY. I'm sorry but I have to use capitals to convey how fuckin nuts this is, italics doesn't cut it. I call these "Lobot phones" because that's what a nerd told me is the name of the guy in *Star Wars* who works for Billy Dee Williams and he has a cyborg attachment thing around his head. Lobot is Billy Dee's manager or something and he thinks he's pretty fuckin cool walkin around doing whatever you do with that cyborg head thing all day, and this is the same way for you weirdos with your Lobot phones. It used to be if you had a pager you looked important, then if you had a phone, now that is commonplace so if you want to look important you gotta have a phone ATTACHED TO YOUR FUCKIN HEAD. I sincerely hope that the next step is to get them surgically implanted, because maybe when your hair products drip into it and you get infected you will learn your lesson.

I mean seriously, have you ever considered the logic behind the Lobot phone? By wearing a Lobot phone you are announcing to the world that you spend more of your time on the phone than off, so it's just more convenient to have it in your ear all day. Or that the discomfort and looking like a fuckin jackass factors are overcome by the huge convenience of not having to take the phone out of your pocket to answer it. With a regular phone you have to pull it out of your pocket, you have to put it back into your pocket when you're done. Way too much of a hassle. Better to have a phone in your ear all day.

I saw a guy at a concert wearing a Lobot phone. Really? You're expecting a call during the show? What? *I can't hear you. There's loud music. I'll have to call you back. Don't worry, I have a phone attached to my head, it will be easy.*

And when you walk around in public with these things, down the sidewalks we pay for with our taxes, into the businesses where we expect to not have to deal with cyborgs, it can cause problems. Of course there is the now-familiar problem of hearing someone talking and having to determine whether they are talking to you, talking to themselves, or making a phone call. These are pretty noticeable, they look fuckin ridiculous, so when you see them on somebody you might assume they are making a phone call even if they're not. They try to talk to you and you ignore them because you think they're talking to their friend on the phone, then when you realize they are talking to you you try to get them to repeat what they were saying but by that time they actually *are* making a phone call. And then you realize they were trying to warn you you are about to fall into a sinkhole but they are distracted by their phone call so they forget and leave you there to die in the sinkhole without a cell phone or even an iPod to jam out to some new tracks or files or whatever. And you can take pictures because you have a digital camera but you can't send the pictures to anybody because you would have to hook it up to a computer first and attach them to an email, but you can't hook it up to a computer because there is not a computer there, you are in a sinkhole.

And speaking of being left to die in a hole, I believe I was talking about the movie *Crank*. If he hadn't raped her maybe it would be funnier later when she gives him a blowjob while he's in a high speed car chase, busting off shots out the window. Beat that, Tommy Lee. I don't know, this type of scene would be very impressive in a genuine hardcore porno, but in this context it just seems kind of sleazy. Then she stops abruptly without, you know, finishing. Just so you know how hilarious this is they have the sound of a needle scraping off of a record. Kids today might not know what that sound is, but it's from an old technology called the comedy machine.

I appreciate some of the crazy fantasy ideas in the movie, but because they're trying so hard to be over-the-top they end up not making the minimum amount of sense that would make the ideas work. For example, in a climactic confrontation with his enemies Statham points a finger at them instead of a gun, and they laugh. But when he twitches his thumb and mouths 'bang' the guy he's pointing at gets a bullet in the head, and everybody freaks out. What is this, a magic finger gun? No, it turns out it was THE GANG OF TEN OR TWELVE TRIADS STANDING TWO FEET BEHIND HIM HOLDING REAL GUNS! If only they had seen ten or twelve guys standing behind him they wouldn't have let their guard down.

That didn't work, but I was somewhat won over by the even more ridiculous ending where he pulls his enemy off a helicopter. He's gonna die anyway so he doesn't mind falling. But to make it more personal, he doesn't let the guy just plummet to his death — he strangles him in mid-air! The effects during this part almost look like *H.R. Pufnstuf*. After the strangling he realizes he's got some time before he hits the ground so he takes out his cell phone (here is another reason why it would be good to have one) and leaves a loving answering machine message for Amy Smart. This makes no sense on any level except story and character, and that's why for once it works. I liked it. Then there's another little touch at the end I liked. Nothing great but I can't give it away in case you actually watch this movie. You gotta have some kind of cheese at the end of this maze.

FULL DISCLOSURE: I hope you don't think I'm making a habit of this, but in fairness I gotta admit I watched this late at night and I fell asleep a couple times. From discussing it with other people I now know that I missed one really offensive part (accusing an innocent Arab cabdriver of being al-Qaeda so that people will attack him) and one apparently cool part (something about him being able to see the subtitles on the screen).[26]

WALKING TALL (2004)

The first thing you see in this movie: "inspired by a true story." The last thing: "Dedicated to the memory of Sheriff Buford Pusser."

In between, you got nothing to do with Buford Pusser, except a sheriff with a stick. See, that's what happens when you raise an entire generation on nothing but *Diff'rent Strokes* and Duran Duran. They get confused. They grow up, they start running things, but they got heads made out of oatmeal. It's like letting a dog mow your lawn. If you train it right, it might be able to push the mower around, but it's gonna do a really bad job by human standards. These kids today, they don't understand reality. To them, "reality" means you have to eat bugs and stab your best friend in the back to win money. So let me explain it to you knuckleheads. MOVIES ARE NOT REALITY. Because a movie was made in the '70s does not mean that it actually happened. If you make a remake of *Saturday Night Fever* or *Star Wars*, you can't say "based on a true story." You have to say "based on a movie you already saw."

A modernized version of a hollywoodized version of a true story is no longer a true story. Just like a remake of a movie that is not a true story, is not a true story, despite the advertising for that thing they released a while back that they claimed was *the Texas Chainsaw Massacre*.

The movie *Garfield* is based on a comic strip. It is not based on a true story. The movie *Super Mario Brothers* is based on a video game. It is not based on a true story. The thing you see on a TV or in a comic book — that

---

26 I tried to give it another shot later on. I don't know man, I really want to like this movie, it has some funny ideas in it, but it just can't pull it off. You ever seen a little kid defiantly take a shit on the living room carpet? And you know how in the second or two before the parents realize what has happened and start yelling at him he has that proud look on his face? That's exactly the look on *Crank*'s face.

is imagination and fun. The thing you are in right now, at your house? That is reality. Look out the window now. Reality. Got it? There's a difference.

As soon as you take one step outside of the border of Hollywood proper, none of this needs explaining. But the reason why it bothers me is because I guarantee you, there is not a single human being on this planet, or any other planet, that was or ever will be tempted to see the *Walking Tall* remake because they believe that it is a true story. That is some obsolete advertising rule that probably wasn't even entirely accurate when it was made up fifty years ago. Because of these types of cases, modern humans do not consider the tagline "based on a true story" to be trustworthy. So all you're doing is make people snort when you claim that your garbagey remake is based on a true story. So just stop it, guys. Leave us alone.

Anyway, the movie. In this version instead of Joe Don Baker as Buford Pusser coming back to his hometown in Tennessee, becoming sheriff and cleaning up the moonshiners, we get The Rock as Chris Vaughn coming back to his hometown in Washington state and cleaning up the crystal meth. And to be frankly honest, that is not a bad thing. I loved The Rock in *The Rundown* and he's great in this one too. Huge and menacing but completely charming. He has an inherent Good Guy quality about him, especially when he comes back and lives with his well cast parents. I especially like his interaction with his quiet father who for reasons we never learn is appalled by guns and did not approve of his son joining the military.

This movie is kind of a throwback in its violent anger against the decline of our communities into drugs and thuggery. But it has a little bit of a modern Washingtonian twist. The problems in the town come from the closing of the lumber mill where Vaughn's dad used to work. Vaughn's old acquaintance Jay inherited the mill but immediately closed it down and opened a casino (pretending to be 1/16th Blackfoot Indian). So now the town's entire economy is based on the casino, and even Vaughn's sweet ex-sweetheart works there as a peepshow pole dancer. There is one little bit that shows this is a symptom of a larger problem, though, when Jay goes into town to buy lumber and sees that the store where he always bought it is closed down (with an adult video store moved in next door). "There's a Home Depot up the street," his dad explains, non-judgmentally.

Anyway, Jay lets Vaughn and his friends come into the VIP room at the casino, and Vaughn seems skeptical but accepting of his hometown's new decadence. Like in the original, he sees his friend getting cheated at a dice game, but it's kind of more exciting here because he makes a big scene proving to a crowd that the dice are loaded. This leads to violence and mayhem, with a few gratuitous karate type moves on the part of the casino security, but for the most part it's a good fight and Vaughn ends up with the same multiple stab wounds that Pusser got (but offscreen, since it's PG-13.)

After recuperating, he finds he can't press charges because the sleazy sheriff considers the casino a "no fly-zone" and the matter settled. Before Vaughn can figure out what to do about it, his streetwise nephew Petey almost dies of a crystal meth overdose, and the kids say they got the drugs from the security guys at the casino. So Vaughn grabs a shotgun and drives to the casino in a rage.

This is the best part of the movie. He cocks the shotgun, and people in front of the casino start screaming. Oh my god, he's a maniac. He thinks for a moment, then comes up with a better plan. Tosses the shotgun back in the truck and grabs a 2x4 out of the back. (See? True story.) Then he goes in and just starts smashing all the machines, and beating the piss out of the security guys who come after him. Finally he tosses the lumber through a two-way mirror in the ceiling to reveal Jay watching from upstairs. So of course Jay is the lead villain here. He's played by Neal McDonough, which is not a name I'd recognize, but I bet you'd recognize his face from *Minority Report* or *Ravenous* or something. He's a big blonde meatwad who looks like either Paul Walker's evil cousin or how Ian Ziering pictures himself in his fantasies.

So after facing him down, Vaughn takes off. There's a great little scene where he tries to drive away, adrenaline pumping, like he just robbed a bank, with no hope of escaping the police. Not a car chase, just a short, token attempt at leaving.

But this is where the plot really kicks in, and where the trouble starts. While on trial for his crime, Vaughn makes the big speech about cleaning up the town, tears open his shirt to show all his stab wounds and announces that if he's acquitted he will run for sheriff and make sure this never happens again. Unfortunately he also works in a cornball line about "in this town, people used to walk tall." Get it? WALK TALL. Because it's called *WALKING TALL*.

They skip over the election and Vaughn is already sheriff. He fires the entire police department but hires his ex-junkie friend Johnny Knoxville (I think I saw this guy electrify his balls in the movie *Jackass*) as a deputy. So for the rest of the movie, they are the entire police force. Vaughn stays at the sheriff's department by himself, which is helpful so that he can have sex with his ex-girlfriend when she comes over, because there's nobody else there so it's not rude.

Earlier in the movie, his older sister was a police officer, but this never comes up again. So I can only assume that he fired his sister too. That's kind of harsh.

The new two-man police force immediately falls into corruption. I know they are going against bad guys, but they still shouldn't pull people over for no reason, break people's headlights, plant drugs on people, destroy their trucks while "searching for drugs," etc. That's not cleaning up Kitsap County, Sheriff Vaughn. That's just stooping to their level. And besides, didn't you learn anything from O.J.? You don't try to frame a guilty man, it doesn't turn out good.

But the movie is over way too fast to contemplate these issues. He quickly finds out that the meth lab is in the old mill, so he goes there and finds that the big cheese Jay also apparently works alone, standing there by himself waiting for Vaughn to show up. And this is where the wood symbolism kicks in.

You see, earlier in the movie we learned that the original good-hearted sheriff from when Vaughn left town eight years ago was killed by falling asleep and crashing into a tree (shades of the real Buford Pusser, who crashed his Corvette into an embankment). Before the casino, the town's economy was based on the lumber mill, where Vaughn's dad worked. And it was the mill that brought Vaughn back into town, remembering the smell of fresh cedar when he went to visit his dad at work when he was a kid, and wanting to get a job there. Even as sheriff he carries a piece of cedar with him, using it as his weapon and trademark. And now here he is facing down the owner of the mill, who is using the mill to make crystal meth instead of wood. And the bastard drops Vaughn down a chute, like he himself was a tree.

They fight in the mill, but quickly find themselves outside in the woods, Jay wielding an axe and Vaughn wielding a stick. So there it is — the woodcutter against the wood. Jay uses his destructive, man-made tool and Vaughn uses a gift from mother Earth herself. There he is, The Rock. The Wood. Summoning the power of The Tree, reaching its roots deep into The Earth, where it pulls out the strength of the good sheriff who died at the hands of the Tree those five months ago.

Or maybe I'm reading too much into it, I don't know.

Anyway, now that we've taken down the drugs and danced with the wood sprites, it's time for the other foot to come down. In the original *Walking Tall*, and in real life, the seeming victory is capped by horrible tragedy. Pusser brings his wife along on a call, and some guys drive by, shoot her in the head, and shoot him in the face. In both reality and movie his wife died, and in the movie he came out of the hospital defiant, his whole face wrapped in plaster, crashed his car through the side of the tavern and watched as the citizens pulled out all the furniture and started a bonfire. So if you've seen that movie, now you're ready for the climax...

Too bad. No tragedy. Story's over. The casino is shut down and the mill opens again. This is probably okay if you've never seen the original, but if you have, it's kind of like that feeling where you step off of a curb and you think the ground is right there but you misjudged it, it's about six inches farther down, and you almost fall on your face. Or when you're reading a book, and you don't realize there's an excerpt from another book at the end. So you finish off a chapter and you turn the page, anxious to find out what happens next... but you realize the book is over now, you just read the last page. And you have to go back and re-read it to try to get comfortable with the idea that this is the end of the story.

I still think The Rock is great, and Johnny Knoxville is a less annoying sidekick than *The Rundown*'s Sean William Scott. But this movie should probably be better. It's a good dumb movie remade as an okay dumb movie. But based on a true story, I guess, in a way, if you're dumb.

p.s. I liked on the TV ads, they showed the Rock breaking the *Walking Tall* logo with his stick. That was cool. That's not in the movie though.

CHAPTER SIX
IT'S NOT SUPPOSED TO BE HAMLET

You've heard it a million times before: somebody criticizes some lowbrow or mainstream type of movie and their friend defends it by saying, "Well, it's not supposed to be Schindler's List," or "Hey, it's not trying to be Henry VIII" or "Well, it's not supposed to win any Oscars." The idea is you can't hold everything up to the highest possible standards. For example a favorite of mine like Stone Cold *must be expected to deliver fun action sequences, but not to have a wrenching emotional performance by Brian Bosworth.*

Fair enough. As one of the leading proponents of the Steven Seagal oeuvre obviously I understand the concepts of working within a genre and not holding movies to impossible standards. But more often than not I think those clichés are used to dismiss legitimate criticism and I think they actually do those types of movies a disservice by implying that they actually can't compete on a level playing field. You're really going to call me a snob? I love this type of movie. So I hold it to certain standards. If there's an action movie and I say I didn't like it that probably means it didn't fulfill what I want out of an action movie. It doesn't mean I was expecting an intimate portrait of family tragedy and grief along the lines of In the Bedroom.

My Ain't It Cool News *review of* Transformers *was one of the most widely read and controversial I've ever done. It's a long, crazed rant and came across needlessly harsh to some people. See, I was angry — not so much at the movie as at hearing the same claims over and over again in reviews and talkbacks that this is all a summer movie is supposed to be, that you can not expect quality, intelligence, taste or basic storytelling competence in a summer movie and that in fact you are a snob and/or homosexual epithet if you even hope for such a thing.*

I believe summer movies can be expected to be good, and I can back that up by pointing to numerous high-quality hit movies spread across the 30 odd summers since Jaws *came out. So in this chapter I will unleash my fury on* Transformers *and follow with explorations of a few of the great summer movies of the past. And one that's just pretty good.*

VERN VS. TRANSFORMERS – ONE SHALL STAND AND ONE SHALL FALL...

THREE words for you about *Transformers*: Ho. Lee. Shit. Not as in "Holy shit, I was blown away, it was a blast as well as AWESOME!" but as in "Holy shit, society really is on the brink of collapse."

Usually if a movie is already playing in theaters I don't send my review here, I just use it at my geocities.com/outlawvern sight, but jesus, SOMEBODY had to say *something*. I can't believe how many positive reviews I have read of this. I think Harry's was the only negative I saw, but he was polite about it. I read Moriarty's review before the screening and I thought *wow, what if I actually like this movie?* Like me, Moriarty hates Michael Bay's movies from head to toe, style and content, and me and him agree on all kinds of stuff. I don't remember too many cases where I thought he was being too easy on a movie, at least not a big one like this (only one that comes to mind is the much smaller *Daredevil*). I never thought I would like this movie until I read his review. He had me about 80% convinced that it would surprise me and win me over, like *Live Free Or Die Hard* did. And I might have to seek counseling after enjoying those two movies in a row, but that's life.[27]

---

27 I'm not sure what I meant by that, other than questioning that maybe the movies I like aren't actually good and I'm just losing my sanity. But if I had it to do over I wouldn't write that sentence (or a lot of the other ones — this sucker is *long*.)

I've mentioned a few times before that I have a buddy who loves Michael Bay. But before you rush to judgment, let me say that he's not some stereotype that just loves to see things explode and hear black guys joke about being "negroes" while a camera rotates around them. This is a smart guy with varied tastes. He gives me tips on older action movies I haven't seen, but his favorite movie so far this year is some documentary I never heard of. He watches more movies than I do, and is much more fickle than I am. I could not possibly list how many movies I thought were good, or at least okay, that he out and out despised. But still, somehow, he loves that fucking Michael Bay garbage, especially *Armageddon* and *Bad Boys 2*. He describes *Bad Boys 2* as "the most hateful movie ever made" and always mentions how Bay's directing credit is over a shot of a burning cross. So his enjoyment seems like kind of a rebellious *fuck you* to the world, like a kid listening to punk rock or stabbing his grandparents in their sleep. He's been excited about this movie all year, and I've been shaking my head and grumbling about it. I definitely wanted to see it out of morbid curiosity, but felt it would be morally wrong to pay for it. I paid to see *Ghost Rider* because I thought it would be funny, and I still feel guilty about it.

So when my buddy invited me to a free screening of *Transformers* I couldn't resist. He said we had to have the area's biggest pro and anti Michael Bay forces together at the same screening. Sounds like a fitting sequel to my peace initiative from last summer where I watched *Bad Boys 2* and *Transformers The Movie* to set a positive example for the Israelis and Palestinians.

So it's fitting that the movie begins in "QATAR — THE MIDDLE EAST." (Need to establish location and tell the audience you think they're idiots at the same time? Try subtitles!) An American army base is attacked by a big robot. These guys are apparently trained in a similar manner to the soldiers from *The Hills Have Eyes Remake 2*, because they all just run away and don't fight. When you see all the military hardware fetishistically on display it seems kind of weird, because the robot doesn't look like it has a chance. But then some tanks fly through the air and you find out later that all but the handful of main characters were killed and nobody knew it was a robot that did it.

At this point I was trying. I secured my brain safely in a locker at the

Greyhound station like you're supposed to and I attempted to lower my standards. I am a guy who enjoys Brian Bosworth movies so why not enjoy this shit? Plus, if I'm gonna watch a Michael Bay movie again it might as well be one about robots. They won't joke as much as Martin Lawrence and they'll either look cool or funny. At least the effects are in good hands. And ever since I heard Michael Bay was hired for this job I thought it was tailor made for him. The dude is obsessed with sports cars and looks like he has never felt a human emotion, so how could you do better than hiring him to make a huge expensive movie where the main characters are cars? It's like God made up The Transformers just to get some use out of Michael Bay.

But Michael Bay told God to fuck off, and he went and made a movie about people. After that opening attack you get literally an hour of kiddie movie horse shit about Shia LeBeouf being a nerd and trying to hit on the adult car mechanic Maxim cover girl with a troubled past from his high school. He buys an old yellow Camaro which turns out to actually be a robot from space in disguise. I don't know if I need to explain this to you guys, but Transformers are robots from space and you know those Cirque Du Soleil type weirdos in the car commercial who contort themselves into the shape of a car? It's like that, they crash land on Earth and are worried people will make fun of them so they pretend to be cars and planes and shit to fit in. Anyway, for the first hour of this movie his car is alive but mostly is not a robot, he just causes a ruckus by driving around doing donuts and playing funny songs on his radio.

I have learned while this movie was being made that many grown adults grew up on this toy cartoon and hold its characters and concepts deep in their hearts, and were concerned about their portrayal in the movie. And I myself revere the filmatic language, and was worried that I would get dizzy and confused by Michael Bay's double-flip-off approach to editing and camera movement. Well let me tell you, he probably blows it on both counts, but both are entirely irrelevant. By the time the movie gets to a second robot or action scene it's already way too late to turn things around. This painful first hour shows that the movie's main problem is the same one as *Bad Boys 2*: constant, embarrassingly unfunny jokes. Is it too difficult to take anything seriously anymore? Everything's gotta be wacky: Shia has a little dog with a cast and he feeds it painkillers.

He rides a pink girls' bike and crashes in front of the girl he likes. A robot pulls his pants down so he's in his boxers. Anthony Anderson eats a bunch of donuts. Bernie Mac's mom flips him the bird. A fat guy dances. When robots attack later, there are lots of half-assed "jokes" about little kids saying "cool!" or comparing it to *Armageddon* or thinking a robot is the tooth fairy. The "jokes" are more rapid-fire than a DTV Leslie Nielsen movie, and with an equal or lesser success rate. Even in that opening robot attack they don't have the discipline to take it seriously for sixty fuckin seconds, they have to have the guy from *Turistas* who looks like Johnny Knoxville on the phone arguing with a cartoonish Indian operator (ooh, topical) while Tyrese keeps yelling something about his left ass cheek. The music sounds like John Carpenter or *Terminator* but the composer seems to be the only one making any effort to create drama. Everybody else is assuming the effects people will put that in later.

For a movie produced by Spielberg it's surprisingly low on awe. People are supposed to be surprised to see robots, but they always turn it into jokes. There's not one second in the movie where you believe people are really reacting to seeing robots. In *Jurassic Park* or in *War of the Worlds* or many other Spielberg movies, you believed these people really were having their minds blown by what was standing right in front of them. In *Transformers* they say things like "It's a robot. You know, like a super advanced robot. It's probably Japanese," and you're supposed to laugh.

And half the time nobody even notices the robots. I should mention there is one other robot in this part of the movie, a little bad guy robot who makes wacky troll noises while hacking into the Pentagon computer. I think he's supposed to be the cute comic relief character, a bad idea since there is no drama or tension to relieve. He crawls around, over and through hundreds of humans waving his many limbs all over and making loud grunts and power tool noises without ever once being detected. Either these robots are invisible or the people in charge of our national security are even more incompetent than anyone ever imagined.

So you got this hour of waiting for it to get to the god damn robots, and then when it happens you realize you don't like them that much more than the people. Admittedly, they are the one thing that makes this more watchable than the other Michael Bay movies. From the ones I've seen I think this is his worst movie, but it's bad in a more fascinating way, like a

$200 million version of that TV show *Power Rangers*. After a good hour fifteen of failed jokes, the probably-meant-to-be-serious introduction of the good guy Transformers is finally laugh out loud hilarious. They just look so fucking silly posing and saying their names and they talk in voices just like the old cartoons, so it almost seems like one of those meta-ironical type movies like *Fat Albert* or *The Brady Bunch* where TV characters come to life in the "real" world to show how goofy they are. And this is one of the great "did I really just see that?" moments when one of the robots says something along the lines of "Yo yo yo wussssUUUUUPPPP Autobots REPRESENT![28]" and I don't think he was eating robotic chicken or watermelon but I swear to you on my mother's grave that he started breakdancing. And I'm sure black stereotype robot was in other parts of the movie but the next time I was sure it was the same character was at the end when Optimus Prime was casually holding his broken-in-half corpse like it was the pieces of a plate he dropped.

But before it gets to the fighting, buckle up for a whole lot more "comedy." There's a section, probably originally planned as a sitcom pilot but then used as part of the movie, where the robots hide in Shia's backyard. They break things and say "funny" lines and try not to be spotted when Shia's parents look out the window. This seems to support the "Transformers are invisible" theory because they're fucking fifty feet tall and shaking the earth with every step but nobody sees them. In fact, they might be like the Velveteen Rabbit or whatever the children's story is where only a kid can see them and adults can't because they don't have the magic of childlike innocence in their hearts or whatever. Anyway, Shia is able to get into his bedroom and his parents accuse him of jerkin off, and you can imagine all the "comedy" "gold" they are able to squeeze out by riffing on that one. I think it's supposed to be funny to see the serious Transformers characters involved in this sort of wackiness, but since they have not yet been portrayed in a serious light there is nothing to contrast it with.

At this point the movie is beyond feature length and then they introduce a new villain, John Turturro as a Men In Black type agent under

---

28 The actual line was "What's crackin' little bitches?"

the mistaken impression that he's being funny. His performance is over-the-top enough to fit in in a movie like *Space Jam* or *Rocky and Bullwinkle*, that is what they would like to do with his talents. And it keeps cutting away to a parallel storyline about a team of NSA analysts (all shaggy-haired twentysomething hipsters) and secretary of defense John Voight and Anthony Anderson playing Kevin Smith's character from *Live Free Or Die Hard* and a giant alien cube discovered in ice by Shia's great great grandfather. And all the robots are here on Earth to find a pair of glasses, which are in Shia's bedroom in a backpack, so it should probably have taken thirty seconds of screen time to get to them instead of ninety minutes. There is a part that I almost think I might've dreamed but I remember it so vividly, where there is a cartoon BOING! sound and then there's a long shot of one of the robots proudly pissing all over John Turturro. This guy has toiled away in independent film for decades, done so much great work and in order to get a pay check he has to get R. Kellyed by a fucking cartoon robot. I'm not sure if it's supposed to be funny or if it's supposed to be sexy but it failed on both counts. And then all of a sudden Shia's car/robot/pet gets shocked and dragged away on cables and the score turns into violins like it's *Schindler's List*. It is an understatement to say that this heartwrenching music is not earned. It's like if Jennifer Love Hewitt's character in *Garfield* found out she had cancer and we were expected to get choked up.

Towards the end the movie starts to be more about Transformers. But if any of the filmatists were interested in turning them into actual characters they must've been too busy running errands or something to add that into the movie. Optimus Prime is pretty funny because he speaks almost entirely in platitudes. My guess is they didn't have time to write or record dialogue for him so they just used a key chain where you push buttons and different Transformers soundbites come out. His voice is awesome, the only thing resembling gravitas in the movie. He is shamelessly corny and old fashioned, while every other element of the movie is trying to be irreverent and self-aware. So it's so out of place you gotta laugh any time he speaks.

I guess this is the part that people wanted, the BIG ACTION SEQUENCE where robots chase a boy carrying a cube over buildings. Some robots do flips and fight each other. The effects are obviously very expensive and somebody worked a long time on making them, so way to go, E for Effort. But I think the Lord would agree with me when I say Jesus Christ, if this is what you guys consider exciting action sequences I don't even know how to relate to you anymore.

Imagine you took apart a whole bunch of cars, mixed the parts up and welded them all together into a giant ball maybe fifteen or twenty feet in diameter, then rolled it down a hill. Shoot that in close-up and you got every fight scene in this movie. I'm sure the Michael Bay style is a huge contributing factor, but I'm pretty sure you could've shot these fights with a stationary camera like a boxing match and I still would have no clue what the fuck was going on. I am no expert on robotics but to my untrained eye, these robots look like shit. Their designs are so overly complicated you can't tell which part is which. One robot (I think a bad guy robot, but not sure) goes flipping through the air in slow motion and while staring at it I was not entirely sure which end was up. There are scenes that are close on Optimus's face while he's talking where I could not even make out a face. I never knew which robot was which or who was a good guy or bad guy or what vehicle was what robot. Luckily Optimus has a shiny blue part on him, occasionally I would see shiny blue and know that hey, that's Optimus! I spotted one!

What Michael Bay has already done to action editing and staging he has now done to character design. If Walt Disney really was a frozen head he would probably be driven out of hiding to bite Michael Bay's nose off for what he has done here. I don't think the animation is very good either, they all move too fast and seem kind of weightless and don't know how to stand still, but it's kind of pointless to even get into that when they just look so god damn ugly and confusing that even in slow motion they disgrace the many talented artists who were roped into working on this shit. If you're gonna make us wait two hours for a big dumb robot fight at least make robots that we can tell apart or can distinguish what they are doing or which part of their body is the head. In a Godzilla movie I can tell which one is Godzilla and which one is Mothra without studying it frame by frame and comparing it to charts and diagrams.

In the interest of balance, I will say some nice things about the movie. There's a part where the Transformers are in car form and they are driving around, they are all brand new and shiny stupid looking vehicles and it's shot like a car commercial. That was pretty funny. Also, it was nice that the horrible rock music only came on about four or five times, not constantly like in the cartoon version. The military stuff, sometimes that reminded me of the old '80s action movies, all this military hardware they were showing. The constant ludicrousness of every single aspect of the movie makes it less boring than many bad movies, like a *Ghost Rider* or a *National Treasure*. And, the, uh— I guess I haven't seen a side wheelie in a movie in a while. I don't know. I'm sure there are other positive aspects.

I can't remember the last time I saw a movie that left me this befuddled that it actually existed. Now I know how your parents felt when they took you to see *Transformers The Movie*. "Well, I guess this is what kids like now. Huh." I mean look, Moriarty's main argument was that the movie "delivers" and you can't argue with a movie "delivering." But fuck man, I guess I don't know what "delivery" is then. To me, this was an awe-inspiringly awful mess from start to finish, with no good characters, no sense of tension or drama, an asinine plot, badly told, full of constant, annoying attempts at humor, muddled action sequences and effects that hurt your brain trying to look at them. If you people are complaining about something like *Spider-Man 3* being too silly and then giving this one a pass, I don't know what the fuck is going on. The best "characters" in the movie are the robots during the five or ten minutes when they're trying to be serious, and those scenes come off campier than *Showgirls*. I haven't seen *Fantastic Four 2* but I can't imagine it could be *that* much more moronic, poorly executed and groan-inducing than this one. I mean this one really is off the charts, it's a record breaker. It probably required alien technology to make it like this.

I know it's not fair to drop the B&R bomb, it's like comparing people to Hitler in political discussion. But *Transformers* is honestly approaching *Batman and Robin* proportions of horribleness. You can't say it's as bad, because the lighting is nice and nobody's wearing rubber fetish costumes or pink gorilla suits, but it's a similar type of mind-numbing machine gun barrage of moronic, inept garbage. And it goes on for almost two and a half hours, longer than some interrogations.

So in a way, that does explain to me why some people might enjoy this.

Some people like to be whipped and peed on. And it's an instant camp classic. I know people who get a good laugh out of shitty movies like *Independence Day*, and I will definitely demand that they see this shit on video, because it makes *Independence Day* look like *2001*. It's so full of quick cuts and preposterousness I'm sure I missed all kinds of things. They were already onto the next scene by the time my brain processed the fact that I had just seen a Mountain Dew machine transform into a bad guy robot. Hopefully he will be the main villain in the sequel. But he'll be defeated by a good guy Nike truck. I can't see enjoying this on anything other than an ironic or anthropological "human beings really made this!" type level. No matter how it plays this summer, this movie is so full of bad taste and "what the fuck?" moments that I do believe it will live on. Ten or fifteen years from now, when some theater in a college town plays it as a double feature with *Roadhouse*, it will absolutely kill.

Did the movie work on my crowd? I'm not sure. Some of the lame jokes got laughs. Some got none. There were parts obviously meant to be crowdpleasers where you would hear one person clap or laugh in the back somewhere. There was definitely a lot of sarcastic wooing and clapping. But there was also some applause at the end, which I'm gonna assume was sincere. We have already seen enough reviews to know that some people can enjoy this. I talked to a guy who loved it, said it was the best movie he's seen this year, that it knew what it was and was supposed to be tongue-in-cheek and *what do you expect, it's The Transformers, it's a summer blockbuster movie, it's awesome*. I'm glad he enjoyed it, but none of those arguments hold water with me, and I can't help but be sad that this is what we are willing to accept as entertainment. *Batman and Robin* knew what it was and was supposed to be tongue-in-cheek and what did we expect. And if just because it's *Transformers* it's allowed to be inept, moronic garbage, then why are we going to see a movie based on *Transformers* in the first place? I know *Daddy Day Camp* is gonna be awful but I don't expect these same people running out saying that was awesome because what do you expect, it's *Daddy Day Camp*.

And I know I made this point in talkbacks, and so have others, but it bears repeating. *Die Hard* was a blockbuster/popcorn/summer/event movie. So was *Aliens*. And *Terminator 2*. *Raiders of the Lost Ark*. *Star Wars*. *Jaws*. *Road Warrior*. *Predator*. *Robocop*. *Total Recall*. *The Matrix*. *Lord of the Rings*. You people who like your *Batman* and *Spider-Man* and *X-Men* and *Superman* and James Bond and *Lethal Weapon*... these are all big event movies, many of them timeless, many of them clever, well-crafted, some of them masterpieces. I am not being pretentious, I am not expecting too much, these are mainstream, crowd-pleasing movies and they are what you used to hope for when you went to a summer movie. You can't realistically expect a movie as good as *Aliens* every time, but that's better than resigning to the idea that "summer movie" equals "horribly made infantile disposable pap" and being excited about it anyway. If a summer movie is meant to be like *Transformers*, then why the fuck aren't you people embarrassed to be going to see summer movies? At least have the decency to admit that it's a strange, possibly deviant hobby.

Everyone expects this movie to be a huge runaway hit, a moneymaking juggernaut. It happened with *Armageddon* and *Independence Day* and I lived through election 2004, so certainly I can see that happening. But man oh man do I not get it. Women, especially, I have respect for, and I cannot understand them getting any sort of enjoyment out of these goofy cartoon junkpiles wrestling each other and saying things like "One shall stand and one shall fall!" If this is accepted as good entertainment then we're another step closer to the world of *Idiocracy* and the hit movie *Ass*.

If America loves this movie, I want a fuckin recount.

But what about my Michael Bay loving buddy? Did he like it? I wasn't sitting near him at the screening and as the movie went on I started to get concerned about what I was gonna say to him afterwards. I hoped he was having a good time, and I mean, I cannot comprehend his love for the other Bay movies. So I couldn't predict what he would think. But at the same time I could not actually picture him walking up to me with a straight face and saying "That was awesome!" And I couldn't guarantee that if that happened I wouldn't shake my head sadly, turn and walk away, our friendship forever weakened by a feeling that we just weren't from the same planet.

The credits roll. I find Mr. Armageddon. He smiles and says, "That was a piece of shit! That was fucking garbage! Terrible!"

So thank you Michael Bay for bringing the world closer together. We can have peace some day. We just can't have good robot movies.

Check out Negative Nancy over here. VERN!
by Orionsangels

Get over yourself Verny. If you expected so much more out of what you got from the Transformers movie. You're insane! Maybe if you internet geeks didn't build up your bloated nerdy ass expectations so much. You'd see pass all your nitpicking comments and relize this is just a fun popcorn that has to accommodate the simple mentality of most moviegoers these days. [*from the aintitcool talkback*]

I also got an email from 'drummerkid88', who told me "your an absolute moron" for expecting Transformers *to be an Oscar-winner. The kid was right. I expected it to win the Oscar for visual effects, but it lost to* The Golden Compass.

THE TERMINATOR

Summer, 2007. 1:52 AM. Mindless, soul-less, visually indecipherable and crassly commercial garbage such as Transformers *has invaded America's movie screens disguised as "good ol' summer popcorn entertainment." Labeled a madman[29] for his harsh condemnation of* Transformers, *Vern began to search for proof that a better, more powerful type of summer blockbuster once existed...*

I'm obviously a zealot when it comes to this *Transformers* shit. Most people either like the movie or aren't as offended by it as I am. But my contention that they used to make actual smart/good versions of this type of moronic horse shit has met with some sympathy. I was happy that even the morning radio guy Adam Corolla brought up *Terminator 2* when discussing *Transformers* on his show. He agreed with his staff that the movie was "fun" but said, "Still... it's no *Terminator*."

T2 was one of many classic "popcorn movies" I brought up in my *Transformers* review, and it occurred to me that I haven't actually watched that movie in years. It's been even longer since I saw *The Terminator* and

---

29 and "absolute moron"

I've never seen part 3 at all. At the time our country's values were being terminated by Republicans and I was not in the mood for a movie starring Governor Schwarzenegger.

So I started by watching *The Terminator*, aka *T1* or *The T*. This of course is not a big summer blockbuster like *Transformers*, this is the low budget b-movie breakthrough, the calling card that got James Cameron the job on *Aliens*. So I guess the equivalent in Michael Bay's career would be that classic early work, 1990's *Playboy Video Centerfold: Kerri Kendall*.

If you haven't seen *The T* or don't remember, this is basically the story of two naked guys from the future fighting in Los Angeles. They arrive with a blast of lightning and a flash of male nudity. It's pretty much like being born, except instead of a mother there is electricity and instead of a hospital or a manger there is an alley or truck depot and there is no umbilical cord and they are adults. Upon further review I guess it's not like being born, it's more like being a pervert in reverse — instead of opening up an overcoat to reveal their sausage, they steal overcoats to cover it.

Representing evil and technology we have Schwarzenegger as the Terminator (R-CA) and on the other side we have human Michael Biehn (*Planet Terror*). The Terminator is a super-robot with human skin sent from the future to assassinate Sarah Connor (Linda Hamilton) before she gives birth to the leader of the post-apocalyptic human resistance against machines.

The role of the Terminator almost went to the great Lance Henriksen (*Hard Target*), which could've been great, but giving it to Schwarzenegger was of course a stroke of genius. His ridiculous muscles are some machine's idea of the ultimate man, and his stiff talking is in line with being a robot. He actually does a very good physical performance, limiting his movements and expressions to seem more machine-like and cold. Like it or not you gotta give him credit as an actor in this one. There are plenty of musclemen who couldn't have done it as well. That said, he is basically Jason Voorhees in this movie. Except he has to make his face into a mask instead of wearing one.

It's nice to watch these two pull themselves up by their bootstraps. They show up with nothing but their swingin dicks so they gotta find clothes, then weapons, then the target. I wonder if maybe this was a mistake, maybe the Terminator should've skipped the clothing part to get that extra jumpstart on Michael Biehn. I mean, he doesn't give a shit what people think of him, he's a Terminator. Of course, a public nudity rap could've slowed him down more than having to steal clothes. I'm sure he was programmed with all the relevant information and chose the most prudent approach. I shouldn't second guess the computer.

The Terminator of course doesn't believe in gun control, so he goes into a pawn shop and protests the fifteen day waiting period on the handguns by blowing the clerk away. (Pretty rude, man. I'm sure he could've managed with the shotgun and uzi.) He doesn't know for sure what Sarah Connor looks like so he goes through the phone book and starts murdering everybody with that name. So it's a good "oh shit" moment when our Sarah Connor sees on the news that two people with her name have been killed. I mean even if that was a coincidence you'd still have to feel jinxed if your name was Sarah Connor.

Of course now days when you think of James Cameron you think of giant budgets, "I'm the king of the world!" hubris, digital 3-D technology and obsessive deep sea diving. But in those days he was just some dude who did effects for Roger Corman. This was his second movie as a director (first was *Piranha II*, or *P2*) and it still had a b-movie feel. He even had Dick Miller as the pawn shop clerk. But you also see the beginning of a lot of James Cameron trademarks, like the way the movie keeps seeming like it's over and then some more shit happens. (In this case the Terminator gets blown up but then returns as a clunky stop motion metal skeleton.) And there's all kinds of James Cameron Players in here. Bill Paxton (Hudson in *Aliens*, guy who pisses himself in *True Lies*, submarine explorer in *Titanic* and *Ghosts of the Abyss*) is a punk rocker killed in the beginning. Lance Henriksen (Bishop in *Aliens*) is one of the officers investigating the murders. Michael Biehn (Hicks in *Aliens*) is the hero. Linda Hamilton (Cameron's future ex-wife) is the heroine.

This is a good movie that still works, but to me it doesn't work like it used to. It's a good story and has some tension and does well with its low budget, especially in those post-apocalyptic battle scenes, which seem like something out of a nightmare even if they are obviously crammed into one little sound stage. But part of that enjoyment comes from nostalgia and from knowing what these characters and concepts grew into. If I could travel back to 1984 first I would find some clothes and then I would enjoy the movie but I'm not sure I could convince my 1984 self that Cameron would go on to become a legendary action director. The movie showed potential but it didn't prove anything. If this was all he'd made it would be a good movie but I don't think anybody would think he was a great director.

(THE) T(ERMINATOR) 2(: JUDGMENT DAY)

But holy jesus *T2* ups the ante. I think *Aliens* is even better but still, this is one of the all time great sequels. By the time of this movie John Connor, the future resistance leader, is a juvenile delinquent in a foster home. Sarah Connor is in a mental hospital (same thing Cameron tried to do to Rambo in his script for *First Blood Part 2*). The machines of the future have sent another Terminator back to kill John, but this time it's a more advanced model that can change form and the twist is that the original Schwarzenegger model of Terminator has been reprogrammed to protect John. They say it's the same T-101 model, but I figure it's a T-101.1 because this time it has eyebrows.

I feel kind of stupid explaining what this movie is about, as if somebody doesn't know, but I've got to assume a lot of people these days haven't seen it. Otherwise how do we explain this consensus that big sci-fi movies are supposed to be muddled and stupid? If you would like more details about the plot email me. Arnold Schwarzenegger plays the Terminator, a type of robot, or "cybernetic organism." Don't worry, I'll explain in the email.

Visually the sequel is less gloomy than the original, there's more sunlight and of course it's less confined because they have a big ass budget. Instead of a chase through a small dance club they have chases all over Los Angeles with just about every wheeled vehicle other than a unicycle or a 3-wheeled ice cream truck.

And since the Terminator is a good guy this time they get some humor and sweetness out of him. But I think the T-1000 is an even scarier villain than the OG Terminator was. Robert Patrick's dead eyes convince you completely that he has no sympathy or even understanding of the evil he's doing. To him killing a human is a casual activity like shutting a door or buttoning a shirt. In the scene where he's disguised as John Connor's stepmother and talking to him on the phone he could've thought of a more peaceful way to deal with the stepfather than to impale him through the mouth while he's drinking milk, but why would he bother? He's the T-1000.

And this time the future nuclear war feels like more of a threat. By 1991 we weren't really as scared of that shit as we used to be, but *T2* illustrated it better than *The Day After* or any movie like that. The opening credits roll out over the surreal image of a burning playground. Later Sarah Connor has a dream where we see kids on a playground burned alive by the bombs.

A weird thing that never occurred to me before about this movie is that it's basically a more violent and paranoid version of *E.T.* Instead of a kid who plays with *Star Wars* dolls and gets in trouble at school for rescuing frogs from dissection you got a kid who hacks into ATM machines and has a criminal record. Instead of befriending a lovable alien from space this kid befriends a deadly killing machine from the future. The kid in *E.T.* is troubled because his parents are divorced, but the kid in *T2* is troubled because his dad hasn't been born yet and his mom tried to blow up a computer factory, got shot and arrested and put in a mental hospital. In both they teach the alien/killing machine how to act more human and the friendship helps fill the hole left by their shattered family life.

In *E.T.* they ride bikes over the moon, in *T2* they ride motorcycles in the L.A. storm drains and get chased by a semi. E.T.'s finger lights up and he heals Elliot's cuts, Terminator cuts the skin off his hand and pulls the bullets out of mom. In *E.T.* Spielberg later made the movie non-violent by replacing the guns with walkie-talkies, in *T2* the Terminator obeys his command not to kill by shooting hundreds of cops in the legs. E.T. dies, but the power of a little boy's dream or some shit helps him to come back. The Terminator dies, but the LED light in his eye starts blinking again, his CPU kicks in long enough to find an alternate power source and start going again. Instead of saying "I'll be right here" and pointing at the boy's head, the Terminator says "there's another chip" and points at his own head. Instead of flying off to space, he is lowered into molten metal.

Hell, even the titles are almost the same if they only would've left "The" in the title like in the original "*The Terminator*." It would be 9 syllables: *The Terminator 2: Judgment Day* = *E.T. the Extra-Terrestrial*, and then both are abbreviated to two syllables, two characters: *T2* = *E.T.*

They are the same. *T2* is *E.T.* And *E.T.* is the New Testament. So *T2* is the New Testament.

Okay, the New Testament is arguably more influential in western culture than *T2* is. But let's stick with the *E.T.* comparison. What struck me most watching this movie again after all these years was that, like *E.T.*, it had heart. Maybe not glowing quite as bright as that little alien bastard's did, but it's there. It's got tension and suspense, it's got spectacle and groundbreaking special effects, it's got tons of great action scenes, it's got a whole ensemble of iconic badass characters. A lot of "summer event movies" these days can't pull off a single one of those things, let alone having the genuine sweetness you get by the end of this movie. Schwarzenegger is great at moving like a robot, fighting like a robot, and struggling to understand like a robot. And by the end I believed that he really did learn why people cry. Sarah Connnor's narration about the Terminator being better than any of the father figures John had had is too corny, I could do without that. But the friendship between the kid and the robot seems genuine. Maybe it's because I grew attached to him myself, rooting for his dead machinery to kick back into gear, feeling elated when he comes up on the conveyor belt ready to fire an explosive into the ol' mercury man. And then sad again when he points out that all traces of him have to be destroyed in order to prevent Skynet from ever existing. It's like when your dog dies or something. Fun's over, time to face mortality.

But an even more effective emotional part of the movie is the sad reality of John's relationship with his mother. After he and the Terminator successfully rescue her from the mental hospital she scolds him for taking the risk, angrily saying that she doesn't need his help. She doesn't even throw in a "but thank you" or anything like that, and he's crushed. Near the end his mom seems to be calling out to him for help, but then another version of his mom sneaks up behind with a shotgun. It could very well be that the one with the gun is the T-1000 trying to trick him, but he assumes it's not. Because he knows his mom would never ask for help, would never reach out to him or show her emotions. It's easier for him to picture her as the one with the shotgun. It never really struck me before how god damn tragic that moment is.

In the end Sarah Connor gains faith because if a machine can learn the value of human life then maybe we can too. And what are today's heartless, soul-less blockbusters like *The Transformers* if not machines? Maybe they too will some day learn the value of human life.

One complaint: at the end, when the Terminator is all smashed up and bloodied, he says "I need a vacation." I thought maybe I missed something where somebody else said that phrase and the Terminator learned it from them. But then I looked it up and it turns out it was an ad-libbed reference to fucking *Kindergarten Cop*. Come on fellas, it makes no sense for the robot to make up his own jokes. Show some discipline.

But the fact that that joke seems so out of place shows one of the things that's great about the movie: it has conviction. It really means it. It has some humor in it but it takes its story and characters seriously. When Sarah Connor tries to explain the coming nuclear war and the robots from the future to her doctors it's chilling because we know it's true and we also understand why it convinces them that she's insane.

But think about it. If they never made a sequel to *The Terminator* until 2007 would they have had that same seriousness? I don't think so, I think they'd have some jokes about her explaining that a robot came from the future and everybody laughs. "Oh yeah and what about Bigfoot, where does he fit in?" And I would complain about all the lame jokes and everybody would say "what did you expect prickface, it's about robots from the future, it's a sequel to an '80s Arnold Schwarzenegger movie, it's not supposed to be *HENRY V*!"

Also I'm glad they didn't have a flashback to the roommate who always listens to headphones rocking out to a band called "Tryanglz". That was one part in the first one that was corny so I'm glad they just left that in the past.

E.T.: THE EXTRA-TERRESTRIAL: THE SPECIAL EDITION: FOR THE 20TH ANNIVERSARY: THE MOVIE

This is one of those things where they take an old movie that was very popular, and then they change it, because they think the only way anybody would want to see a movie they loved on the big screen again would be if somebody just completely fucked with it and tried to ruin it.

They did the same thing with the *Star Trek*[30] pictures, and *The Exorcist* and *Night of the Living Dead* on video (I'm still staying away from that one).

This goes into the *Star Trek* category where the individual who made it (Steve Spielberg) gets old, forgets everything that made him vital when he was young, and decides to change things, but claims it's actually perfectionism. The most infamous thing here is that he wanted no guns in the movie at all. Which is kind of weird for a movie where the main characters get chased by a mob of cops. So there they are, a bunch of fuckin cops and government spooks, running around all holding a walkie-talkie with their trigger fingers poised to, I don't know, hit the little beeper button that you use for Morse code.

What they didn't pussy out on was the language, because there is a bit of cussing from out of babe's mouths and shit. The famous one is the little boy, Elliot, yells "SHUT UP, PENIS BREATH!" to his brother. Congratulations to Steve Spielberg for leaving that in, although I would have liked him to update it to the more common "COCKSUCKER!"

I don't know what it is about the mentality of these hollywood people that they think something that is already universally loved by parents and children needs to be toned down for their sensibilities. According to my Nerd Issues Correspondent, the same thing was done with the *Henry Porter* movie. They followed the book very faithfully on a scene-by-scene basis, but not in its spirit. They removed almost all references to rule breaking and illegalities (like in the book, I guess owning a dragon was a crime, in the movie owning a dragon was really cute). They also took out a joke about a kid being nailed real hard in the face, then cheering for Henry while blood sprays out of his nose.

I mean what are they thinking — ten billion kids read these books obsessively, all parents who are not some kind of Christian nut love the books and are so happy to have something to capture the imagination of their little crumb crushers, etc. etc. BUT, we gotta tone it down for the children. Same thing with *E.T.* The kids all loved it, the parents cried — *they'll never see it again unless we clean it up!* I'm surprised they didn't put pants on the little fucker.

---

30 Yeah yeah, I know, I was thinking of *Star Wars*. Sorry nerds.

To be honest though all that shit wasn't that distracting. I never memorized the movie anyway, I probably wouldn'ta noticed if I hadn't read about it. But touching up the effects using computers was just a bad idea. The effects in the movie ALREADY LOOKED REAL. When you see the new shit, you see what is obviously computer animation. What's the difference? It doesn't look more real, it doesn't look like it should be there. It's just a waste of money.

Those were great effects before. The only parts that look phoney are the parts they left in, where E.T. is a midget (or emperor penguin?) in a rubber suit instead of a puppet, and he looks really bloated. All the stuff they changed was the stuff that already looked perfect. Why would you want to take out such great effects just to make something look more modern, and not as good? Would you do that to *King Kong*, you hollywood fuckwipes[31]?

I got an idea for you little shits. Why don't you make a special edition of *Plan 9 From Outer Space*. Use digital technology to fix those little imperfections that they didn't have the money or technology to avoid. Make it stop switching from day to night randomly, to capture Ed Wood's true vision from the time. Make the space ships and aliens really spectacular. Clean up the shots of the cemetery, so the tombstones don't wobble. Create a *Final Fantasy* style computer double of Bela Lugosi and dig up Mr. Wood's handwritten notes to piece together the performance he might have given had he not passed away.

Finally, *Plan 9 From Outer Space* can be seen the way it was meant to be seen: the way it never was!

Otherwise the E.T. movie is pretty okay. It's about this little kid that finds a weird alien dude in his yard. He keeps it as his dog and then it drinks beer. Later they have some kind of weird psychical connection, as if they were twins. So the boy kisses Erika Eleniak, and lets the frogs go. Then the government sends a bunch of astronauts to his house, the alien dies and comes back to the life, and ascends to the sky. This story is very

---

31 I have to apologize for that one. I get caught up in some of this name-calling, where everything is a compound word involving "ass" or "fuck" and usually doesn't make sense. For example I still haven't figured out what the hell an "asshat" is, but I read that word all the time. As for this one, I don't know what exactly a "fuckwipe" is. Come to think of it, if anything it sounds more like a useful cleaning product than an insult.

similar to the New Testament as well as the end of Michael Jackson's *Moonwalker*.

At the end the boy's dog Harvey almost runs onto the spaceship. I thought that woulda been a pretty good ending.

Also I mean what would happen? Have you ever tried to take a dog on a car ride before? I mean Harvey probably woulda gone ape shit and started shitting all over the place. And that was not a big spaceship. Can you imagine how far they probably had to fly? And there'd be this dog shit in there the whole time. Or who knows even if he didn't shit all over the place, that dog could just start trying to eat the E.T.s or something. I mean they do it to babies sometimes, who knows. I don't think E.T.s carry laser guns. Jesus this shit is just freakin me out man, some dog takin a big bite out of an E.T., and what the fuck are they gonna do about it? Except keep healing each other, and the dog keeps eating them again and again, all the way back to their planet.

Man now that I think about it those E.T.s really lucked out that the dog didn't get on the ship.

Anyway what works in this picture is the kids, they are real little but they're good. Elliot and Gertie act more like real kids than like movie kids. Like when Elliot shows off his toys to E.T., or Gertie says "I don't like his feet." Drew Barrymore is really good and she seems almost the same now. Man Drew Barrymore must be pretty young. I'm gonna feel guilty if I think she's hot next time I watch *Charlie's Angels*.

That said there is a lot of magical shit that doesn't make any damn sense. I mean how come E.T. has to run away from guys that are trying to catch him but when he's trying to impress Elliot he can make bikes fly? It's ridiculous. I believe in the magic of a young boy's dream as much as the next guy but jesus, Spielberg, give us a fuckin break.

Also, with the new computer animated chase at the beginning, E.T. hops like a limber bunny, but at the end when he's gettin back on the ship he still waddles like an elderly penguin. Maybe it's all that beer and candy he's been living off of.

But enough of that review bullshit. The real reason I wanted to write about this movie was to tell you about this dude that was sitting in front of me at the theater. He kept talking to himself, but then would turn around and shush the kids that were whispering in the back. He would clap during any famous scene in the movie. When the music swelled, he started to wave his arms around pretending that he was conducting. Then he calmed down a little for the sad part and I heard him blowing a wad of snot out. I mean he really had an attachment to E.T., but he hated kids. He perked up for the ending, applauded, loudly hummed along and pretended to conduct the orchestra for the entire end credits, with the exception of a small break to put on his jacket. This is the type of dude you usually see on the bus, but apparently they also like *E.T.*

MISSION: IMPOSSIBLE: PART 3

I like this *"Mission Impossible"* series. The first one, by Brian De Palma, is the best, a real tight and stylish twisty thriller with amazingly tense suspense scenes and cinematic tricks and surprises. And the occasional show offy special effects action scene. The perfect combination of Brian De Palma and summer event movie.

The second one, by John Woo, is a horrible piece of shit that finally made America realize what they had done to John Woo. But if you don't hold it to the standards of "being a good movie" it's pretty fucking funny. The amazing motorcycle chest bump scene comes to mind. In the John Woo filmography I consider this in the same dumb-action category as *Hard Target* and *Blackjack*.

And it was cool that they seemed to be going for an auteur approach like the *Alien* series before the fucking Predators decided to come in and ruin everything. Each installment has a new approach and feel from a different talented director. Even if hiring John Woo turned out to be a big bust they were gonna go for another beloved director with a solid vision, Mr. Dave Fincher of *Alien 3* and *Fight Club 1* fame. He worked on it for a long time and then left to pursue his other hobby of developing movies that never get made.

Then they tried some other plans and it's been kind of laying around somewhere and now it finally makes it to the theaters with the directing and co-writing prowess of none other than J.J. FUCKING ABRAMS. Which is some guy from TV, apparently. If you look him up he doesn't exactly have a John Woo or Brian De Palma type track record. He never directed for real movies before and he's written a lot of worthless horrible garbage including but not limited to *Armageddon, Gone Fishin'* starring Joe Pesci and Danny Glover, some Jim Belushi movie, and worst of all, *Armageddon.*

But it was the TV that got him the job because he created that show called *Alias* that I never watched but got sick of hearing about long ago, as well as another show called *Lost* that I also never watched but also got sick of hearing about long ago. For some reason I got a subscription to *Entertainment Weekly* and I have noticed a pattern that if fucking *Lost* isn't on the cover then it's gonna be fuckin *American Idol.* Okay, I get it. You guys are twenty-two and get a good salary for writing little wiseass blurbs so all you do is watch TV all day.

But I am willing to give J.J. Abrams a chance for ONE and only one reason. That reason is NOT that he created *Felicity* and gave its star Keri Russell an important role in this movie as well as a cameo for supporting player Greg Grunberg who played Felicity's crazy friend Sean, the inventor of Smoothaise. That is the kind of thing that might be exciting for someone who watched *Felicity* but as I've explained several times over the years I really barely even heard of that show, don't know much about it. No, the one reason I'm willing to give him a chance is because I'm a nice guy.

(Begin actual review here.)

Right from the bell you can see that this Abrams is trying some new tricks for the series, not just copying the other two as you might expect some TV chump to do. To show you what the stakes are, the movie starts at the most "oh shit, he's totally fucked" moment in the story, where you really can't imagine how Tom Cruise's character Ethan Hunt is going to get out of this mess. The villain played by Academy Award Winner P.S. Hoffman has both Ethan and his wife kidnapped and extensively strapped to chairs, and he's about to execute the wife if Ethan doesn't give him what he wants. And Ethan doesn't seem to have any way of giving him what he wants. And also Ethan apparently has "an explosive charge" in his head. An unnecessary touch but one I can get behind.

Then, of course, it skips back to show us how he got painted into this corner, and also why it matters. We see him at his engagement party with friends and family, and see how much he loves this girl played by Michelle Monaghan (a Liv Tyler elfin supermodel type). Apparently he's semi-retired, he doesn't go on Impossible Missions anymore, he just does Impossible Training. And keeps that stuff completely secret even from his special lady friend.

But then Billy Crudup (in a rare non-'70s-greaseball role) convinces him to go on just this one last Impossible Mission because his best student, Agent Felicity, has been captured. There's a funny joke where he shows up at the airport on a motorcycle wearing the same kind of corny leather and sunglasses getup from part 2. In that movie it was supposed to make him awesome, in this one it's just what he wears when commuting.

For the mission he works with a team that includes Ving Rhames as Luther (computer expert from the other two), Jonathan Rhys Meyers (the prick from *Match Point*) and some lady.[32] This is one thing I really liked about the movie, all of the missions involve teamwork, and his team sticks with him the whole time. I mean they definitely have teams in the other two but since Tom Cruise is the star and producer the story always ends up being about him and especially in part 2 it became *The Tom Cruise Show*. Tom Cruise with his sunglasses climbing a cliff and swinging on a rope and riding a motorcycle. That's fine, but the TV show was all about a team of specialists working together to trick some motherfucker. These aren't the greatest tricks ever but I'm glad they're at least leaning a little more on that concept for part 3.

Anyway when they rescue Agent Felicity of course they find out about bad things and there's hints of other bad things and eventually they're going after this weapons dealer played by P.S. Hoffman, who is after something called "The Rabbit's Foot" which we remember as what he asked Ethan for in the opening scene that happens later. So that's a little of the old De Palma spirit there, letting us know what's gonna happen but then we have to wait for it in slooooooooow fucking mooooootion. Even when he's making a plan for how to steal the Rabbit's Foot we know that whatever he's gonna steal does not seem to satisfy P.S. Hoffman by the

32 That would be Maggie Q, later thrown down an elevator shaft by John McClane in *Live Free Or Die Hard*.

time he gets it to him. People are always so proud if they get ahead of a movie, so this one just gives part of it to you in the opening scene. *There you go, assholes. A scene from later on in the movie. Take it.*

But slow motion is not the best way to describe the movie as a whole because if anything it's too fast paced. The story is always turning in different directions and leading to big faceoffs and action moments. You probably saw that great shot in the trailer where a missile goes off and Ethan bounces off the side of a car. That's from a pretty awesome paramilitary attack on a bridge. There's definitely some big stuff in here that Abrams never could've done in his TV shows. Especially *Felicity* because that kind of thing just doesn't happen to a young girl coming of age in college. I guess Roger Ebert said it's one of those movies where the action is so constant that it gets boring, but I didn't feel that way at all. My only problem was that I had to piss and I had trouble finding a quiet dialogue scene to leave during. So take that into consideration if you are one of these people who drinks liquids.

Anyway let's get to the point. Abrams did a good job. He is not on the level of DePalma in any way, but he sort of has the same basic philosophy: Squeeze as much excitement and tension as possible out of traditional suspense thriller techniques, then at the same time pull some clever little twists and tricks playing off of people's expectations for this type of suspense thriller. For example, you don't see the villain on screen as much as you see most action movie villains. For a major break-in that they lead up to for a long time, the camera stays outside of the building and waits for Ethan to come back out instead of showing you what happens inside. The Rabbit's Foot is a McMuffin or a *Pulp Fiction* Briefcase, you never find out what it is. This way we get to avoid yet another big speech about all the horrible destruction that it would cause if the bad guys won, even though you know they won't. Do we really need a guy making a dramatic speech in front of a big screen with a computer simulation? Most directors of this type of movie say yes, Abrams says no. (The closest thing to a speech like that is Simon Pegg from *Shaun of the Dead* explaining what he hopes it's not, based on no evidence, sort of played for laughs.)

Already I've seen people online complaining that you don't find out what The Rabbit Foot is and you don't see how Ethan steals it. As if it was some kind of mistake. They just ran out of budget and couldn't film the scene. Or they forgot to film it. I just can't relate to these people who get upset and confused every time a movie tries some small thing to be a tiny bit different. Their movie watching licenses should probably be suspended.

Okay if it's such a problem here you go. Imagine this little speech is in the movie, it will straighten things out.

                    TOM CRUISE
What the hell are we dealing with here? This
isn't an actual rabbit is it?

                LAURENCE FISHBURNE
I'm afraid it's not an actual rabbit's foot,
and it sure as hell doesn't bring good luck.
The Rabbit's Foot is a biological weapon, the
baddest of the bad. You want to know how bad
this thing is? So bad nobody will take credit
for it. IMF, CIA, NSA, KGB, WWE... the deepest,
darkest, black bag, black ops, off the record
undercover top secret spooks in the world
won't even put their names on this. Because
some day they'll have to face God.

                    TOM CRUISE
What does it do?

                LAURENCE FISHBURNE
I'll tell you what it does. It makes your worst
nightmares look like a day at the circus, or a
dog show. The Easter bunny brings you eggs,
this one brings you torment and horror. It
wipes out the planet in less time than it takes
to zip up your pants. Or unzip. Either one.
Even diluted times a thousand, one drop of this
stuff could turn an entire ocean into acid. On
land, one thimbleful, or an amount the size of

a baby kangaroo, could wipe out an area twice the size of Antarctica.

TOM CRUISE
But Antarctica is the largest continent, there isn't an area twice the size of Antarctica.

LAURENCE FISHBURNE
And there especially won't be if Davian gets the Rabbit's Foot. Millions will die. Their lungs will melt inside their chests and start dripping out their assholes. They'll start puking up shit that looks like marshmallow creme. Their skin will fall off their bodies in one piece and their muscles will start to shrivel and when they look in the mirror and see skeletons they'll still be alive and screaming for 5-10 more minutes.

Birds and deer will go crazy and start attacking cars. Swarms of ants will be attracted to anything metal. Bees will gather at the northernmost point of every city and start stinging each other. World leaders will rip off each other's clothes and start fucking in the streets. A nightmare that will make World War 2 look like a particularly tame bat mitzvah or maybe a church picnic of some kind, on a really nice day with good sandwiches and everything. Something like that. What I'm saying is this thing is bad.

TOM CRUISE
Thank you. Now that I understand specifically what it does instead of leaving it up to my imagination, this situation is much more dramatic in my opinion.

                    LAURENCE FISHBURNE
Ethan, wait. There's one more thing.

TOM CRUISE
What?

                    LAURENCE FISHBURNE
Good luck. You're gonna need it.

                    TOM CRUISE
Thanks

                    LAURENCE FISHBURNE
Also I've always loved you, but we can talk
about that later I guess.

                    TOM CRUISE
Later dude.

See, insert this scene into the movie and maybe you guys can enjoy it a little more, but personally I don't think it's necessary to know what it does. Because you got a good idea it's gonna kill people. It's not gonna provide anti-aging, full-spectrum sun protection while conditioning your skin with rich emollients.

P.S. Hoffman is a great villain. He's obviously one of our best actors (we own actors so they are "ours") and I have no doubt that he could be a good scenery chewing overacting super villain in an *Under Siege 3* or something like that. But what he does is more novel, he's actually pretty scary. He could be like a notorious terrorist leader or something, it doesn't really matter if he can do karate or knows how to use a gun, the important thing is his position in the organization. He's secure in the knowledge that he's one of the most powerful and dangerous people in the world. Even when he's captured he just looks at Ethan with utter contempt and disgust, like he's a little kid in Insane Clown Posse makeup who he caught writing "fart" on the side of his car. Completely immobile, he still threatens Ethan and his family and makes it not seem hollow. He could squash him like a bug but he'd rather pull his legs and wings off. Then drag him to his own family reunion and cut his dick off in front of all his great aunts and second cousins.

Laurence Fishburne is also pretty intimidating in a supporting role as one of the bosses at IMF. Michelle Monaghan doesn't have a whole lot to do but she makes lovey dovey eyes at Tom Cruise that are incredibly convincing, and that goes a long way to making the stakes more personal. All the supporting cast is at least pretty good.

And Tom Cruise is fine in his usual Tom Cruise way. Now, you might have heard one or two things on TV about how Tom Cruise is part of some weird scientist club and he 'kidnapped'[33] a teenage girl from TV and started jumping on the couch, waving a sonar machine around, or whatever. If you are interested in that kind of craziness you gotta drop it in order to watch this movie, because this is not a freak show. It's a mission impossible picture. I would love it if he just went fuckin Dr. Moreau nuts, but this is not that guy, this is just old Movie Hero Tom Cruise.

For direction, I would give Abrams a B or B-, but with a 1 for effort and full marks for attendance. I'm not surprised he's a TV director because he's got a lot of this disorienting shaky cam and at times (not all times) the action scenes are hard to follow in that way that many modern action movies are hard to follow. For example there's a frenzied scene in a helicopter where I can understand a little disorientation but I at least oughta be able to figure out which character it is who almost fell out. For the most part though the action is pretty exciting. He does better than a lot of veteran big screen filmatists do these days, including one of the guys who made Tom Cruise such a big star (yes Tony Scott I'm looking your way motherfucker).

If I have one major complaint for Mr. Abrams it's dude, why you gotta torture Agent Felicity like that? What did she ever do to you? Obviously this does not affect a guy like me who has not watched *Felicity* or even heard of it but I'm sure a lot of people who did watch that show will be

---

33 Allegedly.

pretty upset when you put her in the movie and then fuckin kill the shit out of her before she gets the chance to even really walk. When they first show her she's tied to a chair, so sick she looks like a zombie. She gets an adrenaline shot that allows her to catch a gun and bust off a bunch of shots with a badass look on her face. A great moment. But soon after she gets dizzy and dies and we even see her dead body laying there with the eyes all rotted and rolling back into her head. Couldn't she have gone on an Impossible Mission first? A couple flashback shots of her spinning a stick don't count.

I mean I know the show got less popular after she cut her hair but that's AMERICA'S fucking problem, not Felicity's. At the time, slavery seemed okay to a lot of white people, but we see things differently now. The same will happen with Felicity's haircut. So don't take it out on her.

Also, looking back on the whole story after you get to the end, I'm not sure if it makes any god damn sense. I'm not sure when certain affiliations were made or why certain people would allow certain things to happen if they were in on it with the bad guys. Then again these Impossible Mission people are really into complicated plans so maybe it makes sense and it's just over my head. You can't comprehend what the Impossible Mission Force is thinking if you're in a Possible Mission Force type of mindframe.

Other than that though this is an accomplished Hollywood summer event type picture. Maybe not a transcendent one like De Palma's but at least a real well made and fun one, which is probably more than anybody should expect from a part 3. Especially when the part 2 wasn't too hot.

NOTE: The end credits have a really horrible song by Kanye West where he keeps rappin and singin about "impossible" stuff. He was still right about George Bush, though. Anyway if you can make it through that song he also has a pretty cool remix of the classic Lalo (*Abominable*) Schifrin theme song.

All those debates about Transformers *made me start to worry that the crowdpleasing-but-not-dumb summer movie was a forgotten art. Even though everybody and their mama must've known about* T2 *and* Star Wars and all those other movies I listed above they would still keep saying shit like "What did you expect? Wuthering Heights? It's a summer movie, it's just supposed to take your money and move around in front of your eyes for two hours."

I didn't get it, and it bothered me so much I started to plan a book. Steven Spielberg had created many of the greatest summer event movies of all time — in fact, Jaws turned that previously dead movie season into the home of expensive commercial entertainment — and now he was putting his name as executive producer on this feature length commercial compilation. How had we devolved from the perfect killing machine of Jaws to the clunky comedian junkpiles in Transformers, and why did everybody think that was okay? I tried to figure out how to realistically take enough time off work to watch and analyze the highest grossing movies of each summer since 1975, in chronological order, to find out if standards had really lowered or if it was just my imagination.

I figured maybe the book would be called something like It's Not Supposed To Be Hamlet and I would also compare the summer popcorn movie in modern society to Shakespeare's plays during his era. Wasn't he kind of the Steven Spielberg of his time, the less pretentious but extremely talented guy who knew how to entertain people from all walks of life? Shakespeare wasn't as revered in his lifetime as Spielberg is. But fellow playwright Ben Johnson wrote that Shakespeare was a real crowd-pleaser: "Soul of the age, the applause, delight, the wonder of our stage." So shouldn't every "event movie" aspire to sort of be Shakespeare, unless it's trying to fuck with our expectations like Ang Lee's weird Hulk movie?

Well, luckily then the summer of 2008 came along and put out the fire, so I wouldn't have to write that book anymore. I can take a Transformers summer if it means the next year we get Dark Knight, Wall-E and Iron Man. Cynics like to say that most people are stupid, but these movies prove that we the people are capable of beating the Shit From Shinola Challenge. These were not just so-called eye candy but truly great filmmaking — movies full of the fun and the explosions but also emotions and ideas. They fulfill what the audience wants while also challenging them by pushing the boundaries of their genres. And these were huge hits. Yeah, Dark Knight wasn't supposed to be Shakespeare either. But I don't watch that much Shakespeare anyway.

THE DARK KNIGHT

I got an email from Scott L. requesting a review of *The Dark Knight*, because he's seen all these HYPERBOLIC!!!!!!!! reviews that have been springing up on all the websites and thought I might be a good outsider perspective to temper his expectations. I was happy to oblige because I liked the *Batman Begins* movie so I was already planning to see this one at a midnight show with a bunch of kids dressed up as the Joker and jacked up on Monster and Mountain Dew High Voltage.

This story is about Batman, the caped vigilante of Gotham City, who is trying to stop some crime. There are many other characters such as Bruce Wayne, etc. I won't give away who is Batman because I'm gonna try not to have spoilers. Also if you were a little confused because "Batman" is not in the title you are not alone. I kept wondering "is this a Batman movie?" Pretty weird.

Okay, disregard that last paragraph, that was just typing practice. Scott L., I have failed you. Although I haven't read too many of the other reviews, I'm guessing I loved it at least as much as those weiners. *The Dark Knight* is a hell of a movie. It's not so much a comic book movie as a super hero procedural. They took Batman and the Joker and put them in an epic crime drama — I thought Michael Mann more than I thought Tim Burton. Hell, Batman even talks like Clint Eastwood. It's only slightly about people in funny costumes punching each other — mostly it's about a cooperative effort between the well-funded vigilante, the head of the Major Crimes Unit of the police department, the district attorney's office and the mayor, with the goal of breaking the back of organized crime and giving hope to the citizens of Gotham, showing them that not everything is corrupt and broken.

Even *Batman Begins*, which was so smart about being a reality-based character drama, turned a little "comic booky" as it got to the end and had a big special effects based monorail/bomb-to-destroy-the-city thing going on. For this one they got out the mops and scrubbed clean every last drop of that "comic book atmosphere" that Tim Burton did so well back in '89ish or whenever it was that Batdance came out. The opening is like a '70s caper movie, the city is always shot like a real city, no gothic exaggerations. Lots of epic overhead shots of the buildings and most of it even takes place during the daytime (which is when the mafia comes out because they're afraid of Batman).

In *Begins* I thought Bruce Wayne was a great character but I was a little less into it whenever he actually turned into Batman, partly because that armored costume (as great of a job as they did explaining it) looks kinda stupid. So although the little tag at the end left me excited for the next chapter there was also part of me thinking maybe a second one wouldn't be as good because he'd have to be Batman more. Well, luckily this Batman has stepped up his game. The costume is still goofy but you almost don't notice because what he's doing is so exciting.

(Keep bustin'.)

All super heroes have one weakness. Superman is allergic to Kryptonite, Captain America is afraid of mice, Wonder Woman has horrible B.O., Popeye once got E Coli from spinach and Blade alienates friends and loved ones by being too awesome. Oh yeah, and Spider-Man will start dancing if you put a chair near him. In *Batman Begins* Batman's weakness was not-good-enough staging and photographing of action. I mean there was that great car chase, but I didn't like how the fights were close-up and handheld, you couldn't really tell what was going on, plus they committed the all time number one movie sin of having a scene where the hero betrays an entire clan of ninjas on top of a mountain in a burning temple and then not going into an awesome martial arts battle royale. I mean come on, who *does* that?

For this one the style is similar and occasionally confused me but they upped the ante so much that it almost didn't matter. Sometimes the disorientation is intentional, because Batman is this force that appears out of nowhere behind a guy or all the sudden comes through the window like a man-sized brick and the note attached is a serious ass-whooping. He glides on his wings, he jumps off of skyscrapers, he goes to Hong Kong to kidnap a guy, he takes a guy's rifle and dismantles it as he continues down the hall. (That seems like a good approach to gun control.) And the car chase scene in this movie is jawdropping. I'm not sure the one in the last movie will seem as cool anymore, this one is so good.

I've seen a bunch of reviews saying Batman's not in it enough or is overshadowed by the other characters, but I don't agree with that at all. This is by far the smartest and most capable Batman I can remember seeing. He does detective work, he does cutting edge forensics, he uses his business deals as undercover missions to ferret out crooked companies, he plans and executes complex operations with soon-to-be-commissioner Gordon.

He also goes over the line, beating the Joker in a police interrogation room, illegally wiretapping the whole city (whole world?). Usually Batman has these batplanes and shit but you don't really question the ethics of how far he should go. This one intends to make you wonder where he should draw the line with the technology he creates. But the movie is so awesome the relevance doesn't set in until later.

I have one major complaint, and that is the character of Two Face, the half-scarred villain that Aaron Eckhart's district attorney Harvey Dent turns into. Unfortunately this new version is not very faithful to the original version played by Tommy Lee Jones in *Batman Part 3*. For some reason this one is half normal and half burned, half good and half vengeful. That is not at all true to Tommy Lee's version which was half normal, half purple-zebra striped. He would flip a coin and if it landed on the bad side he would turn into a totally outrageous party animal. But if it landed on the good side he would re-flip it. That was way better.

Nah, just fuckin with you. Actually he's one of many great characters in this movie, even (maybe especially) before he turns super. You've already heard how amazing and scary poor Heath Ledger is in it, and they ain't lying. Such a great twist on this type of villain too. It used to be cool that they would have some tragic backstory, but now it's such a part of the formula that they were smart to avoid it. This Joker tells more than one story about his origin, so you realize he's lying and you'll never know where the fuck he actually came from. And he's real smart and devious but his schemes don't seem like your usual super villain scheme. Even Liam Neeson in the last one had some silly machine involved in his plan. The Joker is more like a terrorist or a serial killer. He made me think more of the Zodiac killer, or at least Scorpio in *Dirty Harry*, or the threat to blow up schools in *Die Hard With a Vengeance*.

The city is in a total panic, complete post 9-11 bedlam, and the beauty of it is that it's kind of Batman's fault. At the end of *Begins* Gordon talked to Batman about "escalation," and it seemed like a clever way to explain the use of cartoony characters like The Joker. But it turned out to mean a lot more than that. There are numerous copycat Batmen in home made suits trying to help, and when the real Batman tries to stop them they question why he should be allowed to do it and not them. The various gangs have to team up and follow the Joker's plan in order to stay in the game with Batman on the scene. Cops and loved ones get killed, lives get ruined, buildings get destroyed. He's rich enough to create all these weapons, and smart enough to use them well, but is he really just fanning the flames? The movie seems to lean in that direction. Poor bastard is trying to make things better but he's making them worse. But he's still a beginner. Stick at it, Batman. I had to write reviews for years before most people stopped calling me illiterate.

I want to mention the score. It's perfect, even more minimalistic than the first movie. Sometimes it's just simple keyboard riffs or drones, sometimes a violin squeal that goes on uncomfortably long. About as different from Danny Elfman as you could get, so it's not what you expect in a movie about a guy in a cape.

I would also like to point out that this is a $180 million movie that features Michael Jai White, Tommy "Tiny" Lister, Eric Roberts and Anthony Michael Hall, and all of them do a good job! So there's hope for Dolph Lundgren in my opinion.

My colleague at The Ain't It Cool News Mr. Beaks described the movie as "devoid of hope." He meant it as a compliment, but I gotta disagree. There's a very important scene showing that the Joker is wrong and that people are not inherently cruel. And unlike many movies (including *Hellboy II*) where the people turn on the hero for no reason, Batman makes a conscious decision to not be seen in a good light by them. (Hard to explain without spoiler.) The movie is all about giving people hope even if it's not by believing in Batman. And if the text of the movie isn't enough, how about the fact that it only took eleven years for this character to go from literally one of the worst movies ever made, to a triumph like this that people are seriously talking about as a Best Picture contender? Doesn't that give you some hope, Mr. Gloomypants?

This is a movie I think most people would like — except maybe not kids.[34] It's kind of a miracle that they even got to make this movie. Not so much because it's disturbing and scary but because it just never seems like it even occurred to them to make a movie that a kid might watch. This is squarely aimed at adults who don't mind if the one guy happens to have bat ears. It never feels like they're following a marketing plan or even a comic book movie formula. It honestly feels like it's a story that's about something, that happens to have a Batman in it, and not the other way around.

When the movie ended I had fuckin goosebumps. The guy sitting next to me told me it was "a triumph," so I re-used his word in this review. As I was leaving the theater I did hear one guy listing off the things he was disappointed in, such as "the appearance of the Joker." Man, I get nitpicking but this is minutes after the movie ended and he's already in talkback whiny mode. I should've told him to give it up because, sorry dude, a movie this good is one in a million. If that direct shot to the heart doesn't get you high then you are immune. The movie you want will never be made. Time to head to the mountains or somethin. Forget about comics and movies and learn to grow organic fruit and vegetables to sell at the farmer's market.

In my expert opinion this is probably the best comic strip movie ever made. Yes, better than *Popeye*. Yes, better than *Barbarella*, although if I was stranded on a desert island please forgive me for choosing *Barbarella*, for personal reasons. And yes, there is a vague possibility that it is even better than the *Blade* movies, although that has not been proven in clinical trials and probably is better left unexplored. Anyway, the point is I never expected a movie this good. I don't care what anybody says, this is the best movie summer in fuckin forever. I don't know what we did to deserve it, but I accept.

---

34 When I was walking away from seeing the movie again (after this review) I heard a sound above me. I looked up and there was a little kid maybe 7 or 8 years old scurrying along the top of a wall. He hauled ass across the ledge which curved down until it was low enough that he could jump down to the pavement and take off running across the street. It took me a second to realize that in his head he wasn't some kid, he was Batman. That's when I figured I was wrong, kids would not be bored by this movie.

We'll close the chapter out with what may be the greatest summer genre movie ever. It's a sequel to a perfect movie and it's about evil space aliens and it has a sitcom actor and a director who'd only done b-movies. And yet it's a bonafide masterpiece. I guess nobody told James Cameron he was supposed to hold back.

ALIENS

I've seen this movie many times over many years, and I'm sure you have too. I don't think I need to try to convince anybody to like *Aliens*. Asking somebody if they like *Aliens* is like asking them if they like pizza or ice cream. You can assume the answer is "yes" and if not it's just some weird quirk that person has, you can't really make much of it.

But having noticed signs that the BIG FUCKIN SUMMER BLOCKBUSTER POPCORN MOVIE may be ailing here in 2007 I decided to get nostalgic and watch *T2* (theatrical cut, back to '91) and I had such a good time with that I thought, jesus, where do I go from here? Is there anything that big and yet at the same time that good? I wasn't sure but I did know of one other James Cameron part 2 that I like even better and that of course is *Aliens*. So I watched the theatrical cut of that too.

Aliens is the perfect sequel to a perfect original. I always say I like *Alien* better, but that's just a matter of personal taste and maybe the unavoidable fact that it came first. But I don't really think one is better or worse than the other. Both are as good as they ever made 'em.

Looking at it just as a sequel it's incredible, one of the best ever, so much so that references to *Aliens* are the number one shorthand for a sequel that builds on everything that was great about the original and takes it to a new level. Every director of a part 2 nowadays seems to say he's trying to make *Aliens* to the first movie's *Alien*. Here is a movie that takes the main character, the world and the premise of the original and expands on them, takes them in new directions, elaborates on them, even puts them in a different genre. Ripley becomes a warrior but also a mother. Her working class job is over so she gets another one using a robot to load crates. We see the same planet again but also the boring space station where people live, and what life is like for the military (now part of a corporation). Instead of repeating the same horror movie structure it goes into an action movie structure. Before it was one alien sneaking around a ship, now it's a platoon trapped in hostile territory. Instead of just using the same monster — or just multiplying it into a group of monsters — they also expand on the life cycle of the monsters and introduce the Alien Queen.

Time for an ode to the Alien Queen. There have been many bigger and more powerful monsters on screen, and ones with more personality by human standards, but few as primally scary as the Alien Queen. What I love about the Queen is that she seems like a real animal, a dangerous fucking animal whose cave you would never want to walk past. Like the other aliens she has no eyes and her mouth isn't expressive and you're not sure she has emotions anyway other than anger. So you can relate to her as much as you can relate to a wasp. All you really know about her is she wants you the fuck away from her eggs. Unless you're cocooned in slime. If you were Ripley and accidentally bumped into the Queen I think you would feel a combination of the terror of running into an angry mama bear and the "how is that possible?" I-can't-believe-what-I'm-seeing awe of seeing a spider as big as your fist crawl across the living room floor.

I actually saw the Alien Queen once, but not alive. It turns out it is all a special effect and the puppet/suit/whatever is on loan at a museum here in Seattle. Even without the lighting and editing it looks amazing. I stared at it for a good five minutes before I noticed the velcro straps on the chest where people apparently climbed inside to control the thing.

But as great a villain as the Queen is, this movie is all about Ripley. She's a great character in all the movies but in this one she shines by far the brightest. Here for the first time she plays the only person who really understands the danger and can't convince anyone else to take it seriously. We know she's vulnerable because we've seen her nightmares and we can hear the emotion in her voice, but she's still tough enough to convincingly command the attention of a platoon of macho space marines. And she cuts through the machismo without having to use a word — check out that expression on her face in the cafeteria when she hears them talking about "poontang." Also, watch and see who survives longer — the tough talking warriors or Ripley. We don't need some scene where she insults them. She wants to save their lives even though they're assholes.

And why does she willingly go back there? They got spaceships, it's a big universe, why not go as far away as she can and not look back? The movie's answer is that she's worried about those colonists, and about the aliens getting to other planets, and her experiences haunt her and she can't just keep running. But I think the corporation's original idea for how to get her to go is convincing too. They offer to get her flight officer license back so she can continue her career. And you've seen that space station. That would not be a good life loading crates all day and then going back to your little room. I'd want to get on a space ship too.

Watching it this time I was thinking that I can't imagine anybody pulling it off as good as Sigourney Weaver did. Some of that dialogue might come across corny with somebody else. But Sigourney really believes it. That is a great god damn performance. I know they say you're not supposed to have great acting in a sci-fi action movie, but nobody told them that when they were making this, so they fucked up.

I also gotta mention sitcom actor Paul Reiser (*My Two Dads*[35]) who does an amazingly subtle version of the sleazy corporate bad guy. Almost always in movies this kind of villain either seems to know that he's evil or at least revels in being a total asshole. This guy seems to believe his own bullshit. I don't think he knows he's a bad guy.

And the movie just has so many clever ideas in it. For example when the marines start exploring the colony they have this gimmick of the helmets having cameras attached so the people back in the ship can see what's going on. This was before COPS was even on TV, long before reality TV and webcams and *Blair Witch*. So you can see it was an accurate prediction of future technology and a clever way to stage the

---

35 I don't trust this prick raising a daughter. You saw what he did to Ripley. I think that girl would probably be better off with just her one dad.

scenes. We are anticipating seeing one of these aliens, and from those camera feeds we start imagining aliens in every little abstract squiggle. We share Ripley's helpless perspective of not quite seeing what's going on and being at a distance where she cannot help anyway. They keep us in suspense with those ambiguous images but then they show us a clearer view. This helmetcam thing has been tried in many bad movies since and never executed nearly as well.

A classic badass moment for the record books is when the door opens up and Ripley is standing there in the power loader ready to kick the Queen's boney black ass. She wouldn't even have to have that great line ("Get away from her you bitch!") for this to be unforgettable. In fact, if this power loader just showed up out of nowhere and she used it to fight the Queen, I think people would laugh and it would be silly, but it would work. But the way they set it up is perfect. It's that old trick of doing it three times. First they mention that she has that job, tying it in with the working class "truckers in space" thing from *Alien*. Then later they show her using the power loader to help moving crates around, impressing the Sarge and making him laugh. So then when it turns up as a weapon it's perfectly organic, we know she knows how to use it, we know why, and we believe it. And it's gonna be better for fighting Alien Queens than for moving boxes.

After this and especially *T2* there was a trend of making so-called feminist characters in movies, and it just meant to give a girl a gun. If she kills some guys it counts as feminism. But I think Ripley is the real deal. She uses a gun and a blowtorch, she kills some aliens, she kicks the queen's ass. She's tough as hell. But her femininity is still intact. In fact, the whole reason for the asskicking is her maternal instincts. The Queen protects her eggs, Ripley protects her Newt.

It's too bad, Ripley sort of gets a daughter but she never gets reunited with her cat, does she? Poor Jonesy. Maybe instead of resurrecting Ripley they should've done part 4 all about Jonesy, starting on that space station and he tries to go rescue Ripley but never finds her and faces some aliens of his own. And maybe they have breeded from some cats so they are more cat-like and closer to his size so he can take them on using cat methods. By the way, you ever notice that cats are afraid of aliens and dogs are afraid of terminators? It's true. And I believe fish are afraid of robocops.

I could probably write a whole book about all the things I love about this movie, but even *I* would never read that crappy book, so instead I will leave it at this review and cut it off with one last observation. This is a sequel, a "franchise" movie, a July release, sci-fi with action, special effects, from one of the A-List blockbuster directors, the guy who later made the highest grossing movie of all time. So I'm lumping it in with all these big loud summer movies, but one thing I like is that it begins and ends quietly. In the opening Ripley drifts through space asleep in her pod. And we see her sleeping face superimposed with the Earth (a place she hasn't seen in, what, more than sixty years? I forget how long she'd been in space at the beginning of *Alien*, but it's been fifty-seven years since then).

Then at the end she returns to sleep and this time when her profile is superimposed with the Earth we also see the profile of Newt, the little girl she rescued. This is what she's gained. She went through all that shit, but she's not back to square one. The first time she went to sleep with nothing but her cat and her underwear. This time she goes to sleep and she has a family. I didn't see *Alien 3* until long after everyone said it was trash, so when I finally saw it I kind of liked it and the ballsiness of killing these characters offscreen during the opening credits. Almost as if it should say "a film by David Fincher" over a picture of him holding up two middle fingers. But watching *Aliens* again now and really thinking about what Ripley has gained in this movie I finally understand why people were so pissed. She earned that new family. She should get to keep it in a movie, not just in the between movies hibernation period. She was asleep, they didn't even get to go on any family picnics or power loader races or anything.

Anyway, it's a great ending, and then the music during the end credits lets you sit there and contemplate it. It doesn't hammer you over the head with some thrilling adventure theme as a lot of movies would've done then, or drill a hole into your brain with some horrible fucking garbage rock song by whichever shitty band the corporation that owns the studio is trying to promote, as they would do now. It's a movie confident that it can kick your ass and then leave you peacefully to consider what has just happened.

SUMMER BLOCKBUSTER SCORECARD:

ORIGINAL RELEASE DATE July 18th
IT'S NOT MADE TO GET OSCARS but it did win best visual effects and best sound effects editing. Sigourney Weaver also got a well-deserved nomination for best actress, but lost to Marlee Matlin in Children of a Lesser God.
BRAIN CHECK REQUIRED? no
STANDARDS THAT NEED TO BE LOWERED TO ENJOY: none

CHAPTER SEVEN
THE ISSUES

And now we get to the smart shit. The movies in this chapter have a lot to say about economics, class, race, violence, prejudice and love. They prove that while movies work well for escapism they also have a great potential for spreading ideas, making points and giving people things to think about and discuss.

Oh yeah, and there's no reason they can't do both. The best movies in this chapter are the ones that work as topnotch genre entertainment, but that also happen to work on other levels. Nobody expects them to do anything more than entertain, and you can appreciate them solely on that level. But if you want to you can also go under the surface and see that the filmatists have something to say about the world we live in. Those are what I call "Red Pill" movies, for reasons that will be explained in the first review.

Some of the others might not be as fun or as slick, but they talk about racism or some shit so they fit into this chapter too. I gotta organize these things somehow. Cut me some slack here, pal.

BLACK BOOK (ZWARTBOEK)

Paul Verhoeven is a true original. Even making a studio movie about a cyborg he manages to tell a story with a strong point of view about the state of the world. Throughout his years in Hollywood, Verhoeven made many great popcorn movies that outrageously pushed the envelope of violence and sex and sneakily snuck in some subversive politics. And that's pretty much my favorite type of movie in the world is one that does that. It's like some poor sucker buys a box of Mike and Ike's and doesn't realize somebody tossed a couple *Matrix* red pills in there.

But hot damn, I didn't expect a movie this good out of him at this date. I'm a *Robocop* man, I'm a *Starship Troopers* man, a *Total Recall* man, even to a certain extent the world's only *Hollow Man* man.[36] But I'm ignorant of his pre-robots and spaceships period in his native Netherlands, I've never even seen *Soldier of Orange* (which this is I guess a companion piece to). So I didn't know what to expect when Verhoeven packed his bags and went back to the motherland for an expensive-by-their-standards thriller set in the last throes of World War II. The movie he made came out officially in 2006, but since it's a new release here it's an early favorite for my BEST GOD DAMN MOVIE OF 2007.

Black Book is the story of Rachel Stein, a fictional Jewish singer in the Netherlands trying to cross over into the safety of Allied territory. Her plan goes south, but she ends up joining the Resistance and changing her name to Ellis. Throughout the movie she is involved in many adventures and ordeals, but her primary mission involves going undercover as an employee and lover of a Gestapo leader she met on a train, a guy named Muntze. Her friend tells her what a bastard this guy is, but on the train he had seemed kind of charming, and showed her his stamp collection. "And such a man collects stamps," she says, curiously.

And most of the characters in the movie are filled with those kinds of contradictions. The main theme of the movie is that even in a situation like this, The Last Great War, nobody is 100% good guy or bad guy. Even the most appalling character in the movie, the bastard who killed Rachel's family, is shown to be human in a disgusting sort of way (we see him drunk and naked after sex, taking a piss and then trying to grope Rachel without washing his hands). And it becomes clear that you shouldn't trust most of the people even on your own side. Some of them really try to follow their own code and not lose their humanity in fighting the Nazis,

---

36 Actually I bet Christian Slater is into *Hollow Man* too. He knows it's a lot better than the straight–to-video sequel he starred in.

but they screw up. Others appear to have those same morals, but are really traitors. Rachel's SS boss and lover sometimes does the right thing by trying to "negotiate with terrorists," so his side turns on him. Rachel's side misunderstands what she does and turns on her. After the war, many of the victims, understandably and disappointingly, start doing appalling shit to people, just like their enemies.

All this we see through the eyes of Rachel, a perfect performance by the gorgeous Verhoevien beauty Carice van Houten. She starts out looking almost regular by Verhoeven standards, but once she has to bleach her hair (yes, including her pubic hair, way to go Verhoeven) and cleans up she turns into a tough as hell version of a Naomi Watts type. Let's be honest, she is sort of a James Bond type super hero. She performs this dangerous mission fearlessly, almost seeming to enjoy it. She knows how to use her sexuality as a weapon and still seem ladylike. Plus, van Houten really does the singing, in both German and English. One scene that sums up her super powers is the one where she has to sing German songs at an Adolf Hitler birthday party. While she's singing this fat Nazi asshole who she despises comes up behind her and starts doing a whistling solo. But she doesn't flinch, she plays her part and smiles at this ugly fucker like he's Cary Grant. Which would be hard to do even if she hadn't just busted open a passage to the boiler room so her comrades could, at that very moment, break into the headquarters and rescue the hostages locked up downstairs.

It's interesting because supposedly Verhoeven and his co-writer worked on this for fifteen years, but never could get it to work until they realized they should switch their hero to a heroine. I don't get it because I can't imagine how this story could've been told with a dude. And that dude sure wouldn't have been as good of a character as Rachel.

This isn't gonna be a huge mainstream hit in the US. For that it would have to be really bad and star Will Ferrell or Nicolas Cage[37], which I would be against for this particular movie. This one's mostly not in English and it's almost two and a half hours long. If you're one of these people who gets mad every time a movie has the audacity to take the time

---

37 Nothing against either of those guys, I like them, but I guess they were the first mainstream movie stars that came to mind.

to tell a big story then by all means, stay home and flip the channels around while checking your phone messages. But still, this is a lot like Verhoeven's best Hollywood movies because it's always exciting, never boring, and the substance part of it sneaks up on you like a ninja. It's a thriller, an old fashioned adventure, with a classic score that sounds like Bernard Hermann or somebody. This movie didn't remind me of *The Pianist* or something like that as much as it reminded me of those old great adventures that happened to be set during wars, like *The Great Escape* or *The Dirty Dozen*. You're with the Resistance and you're rooting for them to pull off their capers, plant their bugs, rescue their friends. It was only at the end that all the atrocities and double crosses and ironic twists of fate accumulated enough to really get me at a deeper level. There's an ironic note at the end of the movie that manages to be quick and almost subtle. Things end up fairly happy for Rachel on a personal level, but at the same time profoundly sad for all of humanity.

The opening says it's inspired by true events, which refers to some of the things going on in the movie like Nazis pretending to help Jews escape, then killing them and stealing their money. That point of view I mentioned from *Robocop* and *Starship Troopers* was always said to be shaped by Verhoeven's childhood living in the Hague near the German headquarters, where he witnessed all kinds of violence and had neighbors bombed by the Allies trying to get the Germans. Now here he is making a movie that takes place right there. A WWII movie from the perspective of someone who saw people victimized by both sides.

Yes, he was there, but this is his movied-up version of the war. Rachel's friend compares her to Greta Garbo in *Mata Hari*. At one point Rachel gets thrown in a filthy prison cell, but she's still wearing a party dress and has a big red flower in her hair. The only time this type of thing got silly in my opinion was when Rachel was a prisoner of war and still had an amazing hairdo. Historically, the movie is probably bullshit. But hey, it's closer to actual historic events than *Robocop* or *Starship Troopers*. Like those movies, but moreso, the surface is not the real world, but underneath it definitely is, there's a truth to it.

Remember I started this review with a metaphor seamlessly connecting Mike and Ikes candy to the subtext of a popular science fiction movie of the '90s. That was a pretty fuckin good move in my opinion, I will accept your congratulations on that one. Although Mike and Ikes did exist in the 1940s (and are certified kosher) they do not appear in *Black Book*. However, a lot of Cadbury chocolate is eaten in this movie (at one point it saves her life), so I apologize if that makes another candy metaphor too on-the-nose. *Black Book* is a chocolate bar. A delicious Cadbury chocolate bar with a creamy filling of essential truth.

WHITE DOG

White Dog is the story of a racist German shepherd. Fuckin Germans. (Just kidding.) The story here is about Julie (Kristy McNicol), a small time actress who runs over a white German shepherd in the Hollywood Hills one night. She brings the dog (who never gets a name, so we'll call him White Dog) to the vet and pays for his treatment, then takes him in while she tries to find the owner.

Before long, some Ernest Borgnine-looking rapist breaks in and attacks her. White Dog not only takes care of the fucker, he does it in style. He even manages to jump right through a closed window to catch him. Everybody's making a big deal about the guy in *Ong-Bak* being the next big action hero, well what about White Dog. This dog jumps and climbs over all kinds of crap. This is a great dog.

Okay so now Julie's real attached to White Dog. You could say *well she saved his life and he saved her, now they're even*. But remember, she's the one who ran over him, that means she's still in debt to White Dog. So that explains why she doesn't turn on him when she finds out that he is an attack dog. The way this comes out, he viciously attacks one of her co-stars for no apparent reason while they're filming a bit part for a movie. An uncomfortable day on the set to say the least.

So she takes White Dog to a Hollywood animal trainer (Burl Ives) who has a personal vendetta against R2-D2 (long story). She wants Burl Ives to undo the dog's attack dog training, which he says is impossible. And then she finds out that it's worse. He's not just an attack dog, but a "white dog" — a dog trained by sicko bigots to attack and kill black people. That's where Paul Winfield comes in. In one of his most badass roles, he plays a trainer driven by obsession to try to cure white dogs. He doesn't even know if it's possible but, "If I don't break him, I'll shoot him."

So the movie works on a couple different levels. First is the *Cujo* dog thriller type level. There are many tense scenes where this scary looking fucker runs in slow motion, flapping his huge Gene Simmons tongue left and right, opening his freako jowls like those weird monsters in *Blade II*. But more tense than the scenes where he attacks people are the scenes where Paul Winfield is trying to train him not to attack. He slowly puts his hand in front of White Dog's wailing choppers, and you really don't know what's gonna happen. In fact, you gotta wonder how they even knew for sure they could film these scenes safely. Sometimes he's in there wearing the protective gear and you assume it's a stunt double, but then he takes the fencing mask off in the same shot and it's really him. (I read on IMDb that Paul Winfield bred pugs, but somehow I don't think that's as hard as taming vicious German shepherds).

To add more tension you got the guilt aspect. The dog gets out and kills a guy, but they bring him back and keep training him secretly. So Julie, Paul Winfield and Burl Ives are stuck with the knowledge that they could get busted, the guilt that maybe they should've put the dog down before he got out, and the uncertainty of whether this thing will ever even work.

Then the other level of course is a story about racism, about how hard it is to erase our racist past. People and dogs learn racism from the time they are young, from their parents or trainers or from bad experiences. And even if they learn how to eat a hamburger out of Paul Winfield's hand does that really mean it won't come out again? It's also about guilt, with a great uncomfortable scene where Julie visits her black friend who was attacked by the dog, and pretends she doesn't know what set him off. Because we don't even want to talk about that shit.

This movie is top fucking notch as both a b-movie thriller and grade-A allegory. It's a great mix of pulpy exploitation coating and high-minded serious movie center. In fact one of the producers is a guy called Jon Davison who later produced *Robocop* and *Starship Troopers*, so this seems to be his kind of thing. Representing exploitation you got Paul Bartel and Dick Miller in bit parts, representing high class you got an eerie, tense score by Ennio Morricone. And of course it's all very well constructed by the daring director Mr. Sam Fuller.

Not long ago, I'd heard enough about Sam Fuller to know it was time to take a look. I started with his three movies with Criterion Editions: *Shock Corridor, Pickup On South Street* and *Naked Kiss*. I liked all three of these, especially *Naked Kiss* which is probably the least political/satirical and the most pulpy. The opening scene alone makes this one a keeper (it starts with a hooker and a john in a knock down drag out fight in an apartment; the woman gets her wig ripped off, then pours a big swig of perfume down the fucker's throat). But of the ones I've seen so far I've got to say *White Dog* is my favorite. Completely absorbing, horrifying, thought provoking and original.

This is the best movie I've seen in a long god damn time. So it's not surprising that it was shelved for years by the studio and has little or no video release in this country. Apparently there's no legit DVD and the VHS I watched was an old Japanese tape with a *Friday the 13th Part 2* trailer on the beginning. Hopefully somebody will get a clue and put this one out. (Wouldn't you know just a couple days after they announce *Point Blank* is coming on DVD, I gotta discover another one to yearn for.)[38]

CRASH (2005)

Unfortunately this is not the pervy Cronenberg movie I've never gotten around to seeing about the people getting off on car crashes. This is the race relations movie directed by Paul Haggis, writer of Clint's *Million Dollar Baby*. I gotta be honest, my reason for seeing this was not that I thought I would like it, but that I was just real damn curious. Because it got so many rave reviews, and Roger Ebert chose it as the best of the year, but every single person I knew who had seen it said it was corny, overwrought bullshit.

I hate to be a centrist but I think it falls somewhere in the middle. It seems well intentioned. It's trying to point out different kinds of subconscious racism, it's trying to show that people are complicated, racists maybe have a chance of being redeemed, people who don't think

---

38 Happy ending: in 2008 the Criterion Company gave *White Dog* its first legitimate American release.

they are racists might end up shooting a black dude, etc. It's one of those movies where there's a bunch of different characters tangentially connected by coincidence and you find out as the story unfolds what they have to do with each other, which can be fun. And there's some good little moments and whatnot. One of the best scenes actually involves a cop trying to save somebody from a flipped car before it blows up. In other words, a scene you can see in every single episode of *CHiPs*. But this is better directed so it's pretty intense. Also Tony Danza has a cameo.

Other than Tony Danza there's a good cast and lots of good acting. Terrence Howard is always good, Thandie Newton is good, Don Cheadle is real good which is getting kind of old in my opinion. Come on Don, let's see one movie where your acting sucks. You're repeating yourself too much. Larenz Tate from *Menace II Society* is in there, I like him. The biggest surprise is Ludacris. I didn't think he was all that great in the much better *Hustle & Flow*, but here he really impressed me. Also his character is pretty funny. In his first scene he does a long monologue about racism and how the white woman (Sandra Bullock) that he passed on the street was obviously scared of him and why do white people fear black men and etc., then he pulls out a gun and carjacks Sandra Bullock. And he continues to preach throughout the movie while committing crimes.

So I guess I can see what people like about the movie but it really didn't work for me. Some people can't get into *King Kong* because they say the dinosaurs look fake. This is the same thing, it's hard to get involved in the characters when they live in this silly alternate universe where every single encounter you have in your day will lead to people openly expressing their racism. I mean okay, I believe that if you work with Tony Danza, he's gonna be a racist asshole. Come on Tony Danza, I don't care if you wrote letters to Tupac while he was in the can, you need to cool it dude.[39]

The thing is, a lot of racism is subtle. But *Crash* doesn't have room for subtle. It's not enough to be a racist cop who pulls over black people for no reason and molests them, you also gotta bring up affirmative action and use

---

39 Just to be clear I'm talking about Tony Danza's character. I have no evidence that the actor Tony Danza is a racist. I don't feel like I have to clarify that kind of thing on my website but a book is different. I picture the poor guy flipping through this thing at a book store or library and getting really bummed out. Sorry Tony Danza, no offense intended.

the term "you people" while dealing with health care troubles. And rich white ladies have to yell racist things in front of their Hispanic maids and repairmen. An argument between a white guy and a Persian guy takes thirty seconds to escalate into yelling about 9-11. And Ludacris keeps using the word "Chinaman." That's only a few of the incidents. Most of these things have a basis in reality but when you pile them all up it becomes laughable. I mean *Do the Right Thing* works because the shit is boiling up all day long before it explodes. *Crash* is one of those long ass strings of firecrackers.

So you gotta wonder. I'm sure Paul Haggis hopes that, in a best case scenario, his movie will make people think about their own prejudices and try to change. But who the fuck is gonna relate to Sandra Bullock's horrible bitch character? Nobody is gonna watch her and think, "Oh geez, I yelled the exact same thing about Mexicans in front of my Latin American help! Could it be that I too am a racist and don't know it? I must mend my ways."

And the situations just get more and more preposterous. I don't think it's supposed to be funny when Ludacris opens the back of the stolen van he's been driving around and discovers it's full of smuggled Asian slaves. Not only is it, uh, ludicrous that he didn't notice this before, but it's just such an outlandish situation to find yourself in that the movie oughta have an "oh shit, is this really happening?" kind of humor about it. Maybe that's the problem, the movie is so deadly serious most of the time. That horrible new age score doesn't help.

Not all of it is that bad though. I kind of like the storyline of the Persian guy. He gets in a big argument with the guy repairing his lock, who says he needs to replace the door but he thinks the guy's trying to rip him off. The next day his whole store is wrecked with "RAG HEAD" spraypainted on the wall and the insurance won't cover it because he should've fixed the fucking door. He was the one being an asshole in the first place but the punishment is so harsh you have to feel bad for him. And one of the stories that intersects with that one made me laugh out loud (maybe on purpose) with its ridiculously obvious foreshadowing. Let's just say that a little girl believes she is wearing an invisible bulletproof cloak. Completely ridiculous, but her dad is a likable enough character that it creates some dread and suspense there.

One of the threads in the movie is about a road rage incident where a long-haired white cop shoots a black man that turns out to also be a cop. It looks like the black cop was a criminal and started the incident in a coke rage, but the DA wants to blame the white guy to avoid controversy. This is clearly based on the real life incident that sparked off the whole mess that became the Rampart police corruption scandal in L.A. That story kicked off the epic *Rolling Stone* story "Who Killed Biggie Smalls?" which later became the book *LAbyrinth*. I remember reading it and thinking "This should be a movie, it would be like a modern day, true life *L.A. Confidential*." When I thought that though, just to be clear, I did not intend for the cast to include Brendan Fraser, Sandra Bullock and Tony Danza. So maybe we could do another one, please.

The only way to really end this review is with a list. But don't study it unless you either have seen the movie already or don't give either 2 (two) shits or 1 (one) flying fuck.

VERN'S INCOMPLETE CRASH RACISM / REDEMPTION SCORE CARD

DON CHEADLE — Seems cool but calls his El Salvadoran girlfriend Mexican, then makes admittedly clever racist joke. Not redeemed, his mom blames him for his brother's death and doesn't give him the respect he deserves.

MATT DILLON — Blatantly racist/perverted cop who likes to bring up affirmative action, pull over black people for no reason and molest Thandie Newton. Then he saves Thandie from an exploding car and stares thoughtfully into the distance during a musical montage.

SANDRA BULLOCK — Horrible yuppie bitch who treats her Hispanic maid like shit, calls the repairman a gangbanger and is upset that she didn't follow her anti-black instincts before getting carjacked by Ludacris. She believes her prejudices are actually a type of Spidey Sense. Then she slips on her ass and this teaches her to love Hispanics.

BRENDAN FRASER — D.A. who only cares about seeming non-racist to black voters. Not a very good actor by the way, is one thing I've noticed over the years.

LUDACRIS — Very conscious of racism against blacks, but uses the term "Chinaman" about seventy-five times. I don't know if this is an L.A. thing or what. Who the fuck says "Chinaman"? Fortunately the Asian guy he ran over and dumped on the sidewalk turns out to be a human trafficker, so Ludacris redeems himself by deciding not to sell them to a guy that wants to buy them from him for fifty bucks each. This same exact thing happened in *The Toxic Avenger* only it was an old lady that he dry cleaned to death and she turned out to run a white slavery ring.

TERRENCE HOWARD — Not really a racist but a black man who puts up with too much shit from racist white people. So then at the end he flips out and won't even be nice to the one non-racist white person.

LARENZ TATE — Makes fun of country music.

RYAN PHILIPPE — Seems like the nicest guy in the movie, then shoots an unarmed black man. (Sure he was a carjacker but he doesn't find that out during the movie so it doesn't count. If he found out the truth like Ludacris did he would be off the hook.)

PERSIAN GUY — Incorrectly blames Hispanic guy for his problems, but is redeemed when he almost kills a little girl but doesn't and decides she's an angel. You know, the kind of thing we can all relate to.

HISPANIC GUY — I think maybe you were supposed to think he was racist in his dealings with the Persian guy, but I gotta disagree. He was just trying to fix the lock. This guy gets the rawest deal of anybody who is not killed in the movie. He never hurts anybody, never steals a car, never crashes a car, and is ridiculously nice to his little daughter. And what does he get? An angry customer stalking him and almost killing his daughter. The lock company oughta be paying this guy a lot more.

TONY DANZA — This fucker still thinks he's the fucking boss, so he wants the black actors to "talk black" in his movie. You never see him again so there's no chance for him to be redeemed or to die. Maybe he slipped on his ass in a deleted scene, it's hard to say.

RACIALLY QUESTIONABLE DOUBLE FEATURE: JOHN FORD'S PRISONER OF SHARK ISLAND AND KARL ARMSTRONG'S NINJA VENGEANCE (BEAR WITH ME HERE)

After my recent Lincoln assassination phase (which mostly just consisted of reading *Manhunt* by James L. Swanson) I found out about this *Prisoner of Shark Island* movie. It's about Samuel Mudd, the doctor who treated the leg John Wilkes Booth broke by jumping out of the balcony after shooting Lincoln (fuckin ham). Mudd was convicted as part of the conspiracy but instead of being hung he was sent to Fort Jefferson in the Dry Tortugas. He tried to escape once, but failed, and had to stay in a dungeon for a while. But when a brutal yellow fever outbreak killed the prison doctor, Mudd agreed to take over and won the approval of 300 soldiers in the fort, who signed a petition for him to be pardoned. Sure enough he was later pardoned by Andrew Johnson.

The movie tells all those aspects of the story, but laces them so full of bullshit I really could not enjoy this movie. It should be called *Liar of Horse Shit Island*. The main premise of the movie is that Mudd was just a random doctor following the Hippocratic oath when an injured stranger showed up at his door. Then he was railroaded by mean, crazy Northerners. The movie starts out by saying that Mudd's name has since been cleared, but unfortunately after the movie was made his name was uncleared. He may not have known about the assassination but he did know Booth and in fact was waiting to help out in a conspiracy to kidnap Lincoln. That's why he lied and pretended he didn't know who Booth was. In the movie he really doesn't know him personally or recognize him, and even makes small talk about how much he likes Lincoln.

Of course, the reason the real Mudd hated Lincoln is because he liked slavery. He was a racist. In the movie he's a slave owner, but a real nice *Song of the South* style slave owner. His slaves take his side when a mean, crazy anti-slavery zealot comes on their property. One of the slaves likes Dr. Mudd so much he helps try to bust him out of prison. None of the actors who play the slaves are listed in the end credits, because it was 1936.

In the prison John Carradine plays a mean, crazy Yankee soldier who beats the shit out of Mudd. Representing Southerners there is one character that is equally or maybe even more cartoonish, Mudd's Confederate veteran father-in-law. He's really over-the-top but it's played for laughs like it's kind of cute and lovable. He also explains that the Civil War had nothing to do with slavery and in fact was about state's rights. (You know, rights to do things, not slavery necessarily, but, you know... whatever, let's not talk specifics, it's just about state's rights is all.) The music swells in admiration of the crazy old man's bravery when he commands a warship to try to rescue his innocent son-in-law.

In reality this most likely did not happen, because his son-in-law was not innocent and because he himself was dead.

The thing is, this really is an interesting story. Despite Mudd being a racist liar and everything, he really did his doctor thing in that fort so in a sense he became a hero. In fact the real version is kind of more dramatic than the fake version because of that contradiction. The movie also points out that the government abandoned our system of justice to deal with the conspirators. They suspended habeas corpus, had a military tribunal instead of a jury, they even executed a woman for the first time in American history. Pretty cold-blooded. It's an important thing to think about. I don't disagree with what they did all that much but I got a problem with how they did it when I think about it in modern terms.

Obviously I agree with the message that we need to keep our system of justice in place even (especially) in the face of overwhelming tragedy, otherwise innocent people can get hurt. It's a message that's more relevant now than when the movie was made. But the movie stacks the deck as much as the military tribunal did, pretending Mudd was just an unlucky innocent, making everybody involved make hammy, evil or unfair speeches and then Mudd gives an eloquent plea for justice and they strike it from the record.

I'm sure some film historians can set aside history and modern values to enjoy what I'm sure is a well made fairy tale, but it was too much for me. I watched the whole thing, but I couldn't get into it. Afterwards I needed an antidote, and luckily (I thought) I had the perfect one: *Ninja Vengeance*.

Okay, you may think that sounds like a weird choice, but you'd change your mind if you saw this fuckin cover. In the foreground, of course, is a ninja. In the background is a Klansman. What more needs to be said? I was at the video store and I saw that. I wasn't really looking for a crappy 1990 ninja movie on VHS. But it doesn't matter what you're looking for, when you come across a concept so perfect and so "why the fuck didn't anybody do this before?" as ninjas vs. Klansmen, you really don't have a choice but to rent it. You don't even have to read the back of the box. But you do have to read the tagline:

You can't fight the evil forces of power without the power of force.

Word. True dat. You took the words right out of my mouth.

Let's take a moment to think about this ninjas vs. Klansmen concept. I mean when you think about it, they have a lot in common. Both cover themselves in cloth covering everything but their eyes and maybe hands. Both are mean bastards who kill people. Both like to set things on fire. Both base their lives on outmoded ideas that the rest of society has long since moved past.

But in other ways they are perfect opposites. Klansmen wear white, ninjas wear black. Klansmen have pointy hoods, ninjas have unpointy hoods. I'm not sure if ninjas ride horses or not, I'm gonna say they don't, which is the opposite of riding a horse, which is what the Klan do. Ninjas are highly trained masters of martial arts and multiple forms of weaponry and stealth, Klansmen are a bunch of semi-retarded yahoos with shotguns. It's no wonder they don't get along. Plus you gotta figure a ninja is probably gonna be Asian, the Klan is gonna be against them due to bigotry. Also the Klan are so dumb they might be going after ninjas for wearing black, the color of the race they hate the most. Even the word "ninja" sounds kind of similar to a racial slur the Klan like to use. So this is the best idea since *Snakes On a Plane*!

But similarly underwhelming. Tragically there is not a lot of ninja-on-Klan violence in this movie. Those two people you see on the cover I'm pretty sure are not the same people in the movie. The ninja definitely is not in the movie, because the only time you see a ninja costume is when the dude is unpacking his suitcase. He never puts it on! What the fuck is going on here? Didn't these filmatists ever see *Ninja*? You at least gotta put it on at the end when you go to war.

It does start out with some of that clueless home-made charm you get when first timer independents outside of Hollywood try to make a movie.

The dialogue and the delivery of said dialogue are endearingly terrible. There's lots of ridiculous *On Deadly Ground* style looped dialogue. ("Remember that game where you got the winning touchdown?" "That wasn't the *only* game I won that night!") The situations and behaviors are humorously ludicrous. The ninjitsu-practicing hero (a white guy, of course) is passing through town on his way to a ninja conference when his motorcycle breaks down, *Doc Hollywood* or *Cool As Ice* style. His motorcycle, I am happy to say, is a Kawasaki Ninja, and yes there is a long close-up of the logo to make sure you know this.

I'm not sure how good this guy Craig Boyett is at ninjitsu. He does seem to know a few moves. But somebody must've decided he was best at somersaults, because he's always doing fucking somersaults. Whenever someone comes at him, or surprises him, or even when he almost bumps into somebody on the street, his response is to do a somersault.

He never uses a sword like on the cover. He practices nunchakas in the park but never uses them on anybody. He has throwing stars but they're only thrown dismissively by racist cops. I don't think he owns a blow gun. They show his suitcase full of weapons more than once, that is proper action movie grammar, but then to never use them is improper, and should probably be illegal. It at least demands vengeance.

Speaking of which, there's very little vengeance in the movie. He spends most of the movie running through the woods hiding. He gets in a few scuffles in self defense and then repeatedly whines about how he's supposed to avoid violence. To be fair there is a part where a Klansman does karate, that's pretty funny. And a Klansman catches on fire. But the only real ninja shit this guy does besides the somersaults is one smoke bomb and a sort of clever scene where he picks the lock on his jail cell and you only see it on a security monitor over the heads of the female lead and racist lead having a conversation.

The female lead is kind of cute and shows her boobs. Her best friend has just been murdered in a hate crime by racists including her own dad, but she likes this white ninja so they fuck in the woods. You keep expecting Jason Voorhees to show up, but I guess that would only end up being another wasted opportunity when the ninja and Jason don't end up fighting.

One surprise is that the opening credits are negative images of ninjas sparring and I thought "Hey, that looks like that white guy from that ninja book I got at the used book store." Sure enough the lead character's mentor (shown in flashback) is Stephen K. Hayes, author of *Ninja: Spirit of the Shadow Warrior* and I'm sure many other books.[40] Our hero has some ninja instructional book in his suitcase, I'm not sure how good that one is but I wish he had *Spirit of the Shadow Warrior* because it has some pretty good advice in there that would've helped him be more badass. For example there is one action movie style scenario given where "a couple of obnoxious tough guys" get in your face at a roadside diner. Some of the options for how to respond include:

"Water — You joke around with them and make laughing wisecracks as though you were one of their buddies... ask them about their cars or motorcycles. You sound naively sincere and you seem to be convinced that they will not really hurt you. You laugh it off when they make direct reference to injuring you. You suddenly tell them you will be right back and take off for the restroom. When they amble in to find you, you surprise attack with a trash can bettering ram to the face..."

or

"Fire — When it is obvious that they are about to make their move, you dramatically lift the pepper shaker to a position about two feet above the table top. You stare them in the eye and then shift your vision to the raised pepper shaker, taking their eyes with you. With their attention on your hands, you slowly and deliberately remove the shaker cap. While they are watching your show, you inconspicuously raise one foot beneath the table and position the heel in front of the crotch of the man across from you. With the cap off the pepper shaker, you suddenly roar with an explosive shout and fling the pepper into the second man's face, and immediately shove the heel of your poised foot into the crotch of the thug across from you. You dump the table over on them both, while kicking and beating

---

40 Hayes has written over 15 ninja related manuals and novels and also appeared in the mini-series *Shogun*.

them into submission. You disappear before any shocked witnesses can react or call the police."

Of course, this guy in the movie might try the lame Wind method:

"You begin acting crazier than they are. You twitch around and make incoherent references to keeping a low profile for awhile so the police will not find you. You giggle a lot... you go into some sort of fit or seizure..."

Fuck that shit. I guess at least he doesn't do *that*. But he would probably choose the Earth method which is basically to stay cool and calm them down and hopefully they won't want to fight anymore. A good thing to do in real life but not in a ninja movie. Especially when you're not even wearing a ninja costume! Where is the ninja in this ninja movie, I ask?

So it doesn't deliver as a ninja movie, but the other sad thing is it doesn't even have that broad anti-racist spirit I needed to counteract the pro, uh, states rights spirit of *Shark Island*. Because for a so-called ninja getting so-called vengeance on some asshole bigots who murdered an innocent kid there sure is a weird lack of righteous indignation. At the beginning of the movie the white ninja is in a diner and witnesses a group of African-Americans getting bullied and then forced to leave by a group of racists, one of them a cop. Not only does he not say or do anything about it, when he tries to leave and his motorcycle doesn't start he doesn't hesitate to accept help from the racist cop. Later he's coming into the motorcycle shop and has to do a somersault to dodge the young black man being physically thrown out the door. He still doesn't seem bothered by this and cluelessly says to the girl, "Your friend seemed pretty upset." It's not until he sees a circle of bigots in hoods beating the guy to death that he finally seems offended by all this.

And in true *Shark Island* fashion the girl's dad is treated way too sympathetically by the movie. At the end he looks at a picture of his deceased wife and has a change of heart and he and his daughter get along again. He tries to humbly play down his heroism by saying that "it's getting out of hand, somebody has to stop it." When it was just a guy being murdered that was one thing, but lately with all this chasing it's getting out of hand. If I'm not mistaken this guy participated in beating his daughter's friend to death because he was black! With a sheet on his head! And we're supposed to be touched that he makes up with his daughter. Let bygones be bygones. Earth response.

I mean, I understand things are different in the south, but this isn't Jim Crow era, or even the '60s. This is fucking 1990! Shit, *Billy Jack* is a pacifist too, he was interfering with these types of incidents almost twenty years earlier. So this guy is already hard to sympathize with before you know he's a poor excuse for a ninja.

Unlike *Shark Island*, the black actors do get listed on the credits. Of course, most of them are just in a list under the word "BLACKS."

So, damn, I guess I struck out with that double feature there. Of the two I would say *Prisoner of Shark Island* has the better production values and acting, *Ninja Vengeance* has more unintentional laughs. So if you have to decide between the two, I don't know, maybe go with *Ninja Vengeance*. Or maybe just look at the cover.

BROKEBACK MOUNTAIN

For God's sake man, when I go to see a western there are certain things I expect to see, and certain things I *don't* expect to see, and one of the things I *don't* expect to see—

Nah, I'm just fuckin with you. Everybody knows that *Brokeback Mountain* is "the gay cowboy movie." Or that's the hype anyway. So first thing's first, I gotta tell you that the "gay cowboy" description is utter bullshit and if that's what you wanna see you're gonna be just as disappointed as I woulda been if I went in expecting *The Outlaw Josey Wales*. Because this is not about gay cowboys. It's about gay shepherds. They herd sheep. They shepherd. They are gay shepherds. Get it straight, America. Cowboys are dealing with cows and cattle and whatnot. If they herd sheep, they are shepherds. In this case, gay shepherds.

Second thing to say is, this really is a good movie, they are not lying. Ang Lee knows his shit when it comes to gay shepherds in 1963 Wyoming, or giant green radioactive mutants contemplating lichen in the desert, or some guys in a tree fighting over the green sword of destiny, or whatever the fuck he wants to make a movie about. Ang Lee is a guy, you could just toss movie ideas at him and he would hit them out of the park with his eyes closed. Mafia epic. Opera based on the life of Malcolm-Jamal Warner. Pee-wee football tragedy. *Hamlet* acted out by raccoons. If you can describe it, this motherfucker can make a good movie out of it. Don't even try it. You can't beat him. It's like fighting gravity.

Now, I don't want to be one of those chumps that emphasizes "ALTHOUGH I AM STRAIGHT, I liked this movie, BUT I AM NOT GAY THOUGH" or that type of shit. So sorry if you think I'm a chump for saying this. But the simple fact of the matter is, I like vaginas. I don't like buttholes. The protruding butt area on a woman is an excellent area, I am not so interested in the actual hole, male or female. That's just the way I do things around here. And I'm not all that hot on romance movies anyway, or cowboys for that matter, let alone shepherds. (Although Joseph, Jesus's dad, was probably a good guy, and a good shepherd.) What I'm saying is, I did not necessarily expect to like this movie on more than an intellectual level, even if it is Ang Lee.

But I did. This is a real effective movie with beautiful atmosphere and relatable human type emotions. It's a tragic love story between two dudes in cowboy hats. But in a good way. When they're alone up in the mountains it makes sense to be in love, but they're soon gonna have to face the fact that it's 1963, it's Wyoming, they are working with sheep and riding bulls and crap. Nobody's gonna let them just be themselves. In trying to live their lives the way they're supposed to, they both end up with wives and kids. But they can't help but two or three times a year get together for, uh, you know, fishing trips.

I'm man enough not to squirm during a gay love scene but I'm sissy enough that it sometimes makes me uncomfortable. That said, this is one of the least gay gay love stories you're gonna see. Sure you got your buttfucking, you got your men kissing and cuddling. But not all that much. You would have to be a real fuckin wuss to get "grossed out" by the love scenes in this movie. I only mention this because I checked out some of the talkbacks over on The Ain't It Cool and not only was the anti-gay squad in full force but you also had your "I'm not homophobic but I would never watch a movie about gay faggot cowboys." Well I am one straight man that had no problem watching these dudes fall in love. Also there was a whole lot of lesbians in the theater and they didn't seem to have a problem. (They also provided some applause for the boobs of the gal who I guess is from *Princess Diaries*. Not Julie Andrews, the other gal.)

Heath Ledger is the main character and the best performance. I had no idea this kid was such an actor. His voice, his posture, his whole demeanor are completely different from what I've seen him do before. Gyllenhaal does fine, although just adding a mustache and some gray streaks doesn't make him seem twenty years older. But at least he looks older than *Princess Diaries*. So good job on that at least Jake, you showed her up. You at least looked like you could've been within fifteen years of the age you were playing by the end.

Is this some kind of gay issue movie? Kind of, kind of not. I mean obviously the issues here are specific to being gay and in the closet. The tragedy is not just that these guys can't be together. You feel at least as bad for Heath's wife Michelle Williams (*Halloween H20*). The movie could have a long drawn out secret but instead she finds out at the first possible second what's going on with her husband and this "old fishing buddy" of his. So a lot of the movie is about her pain knowing that this is going on. They can't be together, their wives are fucked over, they can't connect with their kids or their parents because of their secret lives, they lose work, they always gotta look out so they don't get killed by bigots, they gotta waste their lives and gas money driving back and forth to fuckin Brokeback Mountain, and they can't even completely connect with each other because they can't agree on how to approach their doomed situation. There's a lot of tragedy in here to go around.

But of course you don't have to be gay to be interested in this story. Some asshole newsie was saying that 2% of people are gay but movies try to make it seem like it's common. Well first of all that number has got to be lowballin it like civilian casualty rates, but it doesn't even matter. How many fuckin hitmen do you know, man? How many undercover cops? How many ninjas, or vampires? I mean jesus, I think it would be okay to every once in a while have a movie about gay people. There's gotta be way more gay people in this country than there are sheep herders, but I don't hear your bitch ass complaining about the sheep herding. In fact I can say for sure, in Seattle at least, there are lots of gay people, and not very many shepherds. So if you're just going on percentages I think the gays are in good shape for earning an Ang Lee movie.

Hell, how many percent do you think care if Grito shot the ewoks first or what Spider-Man uses to shoot his magic spiderwebs from? I'm betting there are more gay people in the US than there are people who can name all of the main characters in *Lord of the Rings*. To this talkbacker guy it's okay to glamorize the Nerd Agenda online but acknowledging a really well made love story between two men is "rubbing it in his face." I mean, think through these things and you'll realize all these arguments you're making, you're just running around in circles trying to make excuses for something that's your own god damn problem that you just need to get over. You know what I did, I used to be against "fags" and "fruits" and "fairies" and what not, because that's the way I was raised. But it's fuckin 2005 now, almost 2006. Civilization is on the march. You gotta come to a point where you actually think the thing through and realize it doesn't make any god damn sense. How does it hurt anybody if some male shepherds are doing each other in a tent somewhere, or if there's a movie about it? I shouldn't care. Hey guys, come down from the mountains, we don't care if you're in love. Love is good. And it's okay if you don't really like to fish.

You know, I wonder if Ang Lee has a real sad love life. *Brokeback Mountain*, they can't be together. *Crouching Tiger*, they can't be together. *Hulk*, if I remember right, they can't be together. *Raccoon Hamlet*, if he made it, there would probably be some raccoons that can't be together, and I believe a ghost in one part. Man Raccoon Lady Macbeth is such a fuckin ice queen. I love *Raccoon Hamlet*.

But back to *Brokeback*. When you point out that this is a universal forbidden love type story, people will say "well then why should we care, if it wasn't gay guys the critics wouldn't be making such a big deal about it." Well, first of all the movie is so well made that I think in that magical world where you can create an exact non-gay equivalent to this movie, the critics *would* like it. More importantly though, a lot of times we go to movies to see things we don't get to see that often. For example, *Snakes On a Plane*. Everybody wants to see that movie because they never seen snakes on a plane before. Same thing here. If you can name another gay shepherd movie, good job. But I can't. And how many GREAT or even

REALLY GOOD gay love stories can you think of in the films of cinema? I guess I'm not an expert, I'm sure there are many of them but I don't know of one other than *Boys Don't Cry*. (Don't fucking say *Bound*, that was made for us straight guys and you know it.)

But this really is a universal story. It could be two gay guys, it could be Naomi Watts and a giant gorilla, it could be a cat that falls in love with a mouse. The important thing is the dramatic angle that this cannot possibly work in this time and place, but what are they gonna do, just forget about each other? That's not working out. It's not as dark as *Boys Don't Cry*, it doesn't feel like it's mostly about hatred. It's more about societal pressure than straight up bigotry. It shows how not letting these two shepherds just be themselves we're just making it more difficult for everybody.

Including the sheep. The first night they sleep together, a sheep gets killed because they weren't paying enough attention. This scene could even work as an anti-gay argument, you could use it as an argument against gays in the military or in the shepherding industry. Or at least, against any stripe of horsin' around on the job. So homophobes, come see *Brokeback Mountain*, you will love it as much as anybody. It's a good movie for anyone interested in love, sheep, mountains, etc.

ANG LEE SUBJECT MATTER CHECKLIST

[X] Family comedy
[X] Jane Austen adaptation
[X] '70s American family dysfunction
[X] American civil war
[X] Mandarin-language historical martial arts epic
[ ] Elderly werewolf
[X] Marvel Comics
[X] Gay shepherds in 1963 Wyoming
[ ] Live action Yogi Bear
[ ] Dolph Lundgren vehicle
[ ] Motorcycle racing and/or competitive diving

THEY LIVE

They Live is one of my favorite movies ever. It is probably the very best version of a rare type of movie I love: the badass action movie that also works as a political statement. *Billy Jack* may be more political, but it seems so self important and it has no sense of humor. *They Live* is kind of saying the same thing *The Matrix* is saying about a society brainwashed by media and advertising, but it's saying more than that. It's about the America of the Reagan years, when everything was geared to help the rich at the expense of the working class. Which for some reason seems awfully familiar today. Huh. Weird.

"Rowdy" Roddy Piper plays Nada, a drifter who walks into town with tools and a sleeping bag on his back. (Hey, what happens to that sleeping bag? I think it disappears.) This is a hero who not only doesn't drive a sports car, but doesn't have a car at all. Or a house. Or a job, at first. The plants are closing, the jobs are drying up, that's why he's on the move. But he happens to get a construction job, where he meets Frank (Keith motherfuckin David from *The Thing*) and finds out about a homeless encampment near a church where some nice people serve food for the homeless.

The first section of the movie doesn't have a lot of dialogue. It's all about watching. Nada watches people watching TV — an old lady in an apartment, a dude standing outside an electronics shop, even homeless people who have a TV set up outside. We can see that Nada is a little creeped out by the vapid commercials and their hypnotic effect on people. And then they get pissed off when, every once in a while, some weird old man cuts into the broadcast desperately telling people to "wake up." And then everybody gets a headache.

Nada also starts watching the church, because he notices something odd going on. He watches a helicopter watching the church. He sneaks in and sees that it's not a real church. The choir he hears from outside is a reel-to-reel tape and there's some kind of rebels hatching a plan in there. He even bumps into a secret panel in the wall and sees a box inside, but he gets found out by an elderly blind priest, so he leaves.

All this watching is actually very cinematic. I like the good ol' non-verbal storytelling. And of course the director is John Carpenter and he knows how to pull this shit off. It's got a bluesy take on the usual John Carpenter driving electronic score, so it creates a real powerful mood. The movie's actually a little stiff when they have dialogue explaining things, but the story is so perfect that I don't care.

One night an army of riot cops come raid the church. Not just that, they bulldoze the entire homeless camp and beat everybody up, including the elderly, blind priest. This might seem over-the-top to some people, but not to me. If you've been around WTO or any big police riot like that you know this movie is accurate. Except there is less chanting in the movie version. It might make you lose respect for Keith David's character if he kept chanting, "This is what democracy looks like! This is what democracy looks like!"

The next day, Nada goes into the church, opens up the secret panel, steals the box, brings it to an alley... and finds out it's just a box of sunglasses. Shit.

But you guys know what happens next. It turns out that the sunglasses were created by the rebels, they somehow break through a hypnotic signal that has brainwashed the world. So as Nada walks around he sees the truth: billboards and magazines that say things like "OBEY" and "CONSUME" and "MARRY AND REPRODUCE" in plain black letters on plain white backgrounds. Money that says "THIS IS YOUR GOD." And some people, many of them coincidentally with ties or fur coats, have ugly skeletal alien faces. Because the ruling class are aliens, keeping us "asleep" with our competition and greed so we won't notice they're infiltrating our world and slowly changing our climate to theirs. (I wonder if Al Gore likes *They Live*? Maybe if he said that in 2000 he would've won by enough to stay president.)

The section of the movie where Nada walks around with his sunglasses and sees what's going on is undeniably classic. Especially when he tells off some rich alien ladies in a high end grocery store, and all the aliens start talking into their Rolexes. "I've got one that can see." Nada ends up killing two alien cops, stealing their shotgun and shooting up a bank, which is where he says his most famous line, "I have come here to chew bubble gum and kick ass. And I'm all out of bubble gum." Apparently John Carpenter gave Piper free reign to ad lib dialogue, and he made that one up. There's lots of funny lines like that. My favorite line actually I always remembered completely wrong. I thought he said, "It fuckin figures" when he saw all the rich people were aliens. But he actually says the equally perfect, "It figures it would be something like this."

It's perfect because it's true, it *does* figure. The details of the alien takeover all fit the world as we know it. A lot of rich people are our alien controllers. We see two guys talking, the alien got a big promotion and the human didn't. Who's an alien and who's not always seems to fall along class lines. The assistants aren't aliens, the waiters aren't, the people of color aren't. Some cops are aliens but most of them aren't, they just work for the man anyway. A lot of humans benefit from the takeover too — as they sellout, they find themselves getting raises and promotions. There are even humans who know about the aliens and still sellout, and in addition to getting money and power they're honored at a fancy banquet in the aliens' underground tunnel system.

And you know one giveaway that they're not on our side? They got these fancy watches that work as walkie talkies and as teleporters. You always thought *why can't I have one of those fancy rich people watches? Because I can't afford it.* But actually it's because you're not a they live. In the '80s those watches were a big thing for yuppies and shit, now in the 2000s it's mostly rappers that are they lives, such as P-Diddy is definitely a they live and he hands out watches to people at awards shows to secretly honor their collaboration with the they lives.

Once Nada finds out the secret, the movie is less about watching and more about shooting. There's a lot of shooting in this movie. But the greatest and most distinctive action scene in the movie is the famous alley fight between Nada and Frank. Nada wants Frank to put on the sunglasses to see the truth, but Frank doesn't want to. He has a wife and kid, he just wants to mind his own business, stay out of it. So the result is an amazing five-and-a-half-minute wrestling match on concrete. There is some bodyslamming, a lot of punching, a whole lot of kicking and kneeing in the balls. I mean they just beat the shit out of each other, and these are our heroes. This scene is both legendary and infamous because it goes on for so long, and most people (including people who like it) seem to think it is completely gratuitous. I disagree. I think it's a perfect symbol for the distance somebody will go to not see the trouble in the world. I don't like politics. I just mind my own business. All Frank has to do is look, but he must know instinctively that it is a seditious act, it will change his life. Once Nada gets those glasses on him, Frank can't look away. He's on the team, and the two of them set out to see what they can do to take the planet back.

Actually first they limp to a hotel room, all bloody, and check in together. I wonder what the hell the hotel clerk thinks is going on?

I mean, *They Live* has everything. The brilliant *Twilight Zone* type premise. The dead-on social/political satire. The catchy soundtrack. The hilarious tough guy oneliners. The wrestling. The shooting. The cool alien monsters in ties, making speeches. The violent rebellion against the oppressors. The badass kamikaze conclusion. Keith David. Roddy Piper. Everything. That right there was a list of everything.

Piper is clearly not as good of an actor as Kurt Russell, but he's perfect as this particular John Carpenter hero. He seems believable as a homeless construction worker. And even though I think he has a bit of a Canadian accent, you believe him when he says he believes in America. When he puts the glasses on and finds out what's happening to America, he knows he has to fix it. This is a movie about real patriotism.

Unfortunately for patriotism though, the Americans really fucked up on releasing *They Live* on DVD. There's a German version with a commentary track by Carpenter and Piper (in English, of course). The region 1 version went out of print for a while so I assumed they'd put the commentary on when it came out again. But when the "special edition" finally came out there was nothing extra. (It figures it would be something like that.) If you can get a hold of it, and if you enjoy Carpenter's commentaries as much as I do, this is as good as the other ones.

The most interesting thing to me is when Piper explains the effect this movie had on his wrestling career. He was at the WWF of course, where he was the Joker to Hulk Hogan's Batman. But he wanted to do this movie. Vince McMahon didn't want him to do it because he always wanted to control all aspects of his wrestlers' careers, and this was an offer coming from the outside. Apparently they told Piper just to forget about it, don't do the movie, and the WWF will find a bigger movie for him to do instead. But Piper said yeah, you can get me a bigger movie, but it won't be directed by John Carpenter. He quit the WWF to work with John

Carpenter.[41] So I like the guy! Just for that, I might try watching *Hell Comes to Frogtown* again. I haven't seen that since the days of *USA Up All Night*.

My only complaint about *They Live*: the title is not so hot. I know, it comes from the graffiti that says "They live, we sleep." They're living their real lives, which is to fuck with us and put us in a dreamworld. Just like those god damn machines in *The Matrix*. So it makes sense, but it just sounds kind of awkward. I mean you can't really make a *They Live 2* or a *They Live Again*, it just sounds bad.[42]

Oh well. Still one of the best movies ever. And every time I watch it it's better than I remember it being. And I like to think it's just because it's a great movie, not because it's getting more and more relevant by the day.

---

41 Or so he claims on the commentary track. He tells the story pretty differently in his autobiography. I like the commentary track version of the story though, I prefer to believe that one.

42 What about *They Live 2 Screw Us Over* or something like that? *Step Up 2 the Streets* really opened up a lot of doors for sequel-titling in my opinion.

CHAPTER EIGHT
THE ARTS

I don't like to brag, but it just so happens that I am a man with many interests and passions. While it is true that I am mainly interested in the lowbrow topics (the history of the American ninja movie, the unspoken backstory of Predator) I also have another brow that is higher. You are gonna be so surprised by all the shit I know. What I am about to do is tell you all about a wide range of artistic subjects. I will touch on surrealism, Indonesian puppet theater, J.M. Barrie, and, uh, folk art or something. True, the name "Jean-Claude Van Damme" may come up more than once, and I may have originally talked about wrestling in this chapter before I realized the book was too long. Still, I think this will show a different side to my works that is gonna blow your god damn mind. Read at your own risk. Vern and Titan Books are not liable for any hardship or inconvenience caused by blown minds.

THE DISCREET CHARM OF THE BOURGEOISIE

A lot of you know that I am a big fan of the surrealist movement. Well actually I do not know a whole lot about the history of the movement, but among respected film Writers I'm pretty damn sure I am the biggest supporter of Jean Claude Van Damme's surrealist period, which is best represented by his collaboration with Tsui Hark and Dennis Rodman, *Double Team*. Well someone pointed me towards Louie Buñuel the famous surrealist and I was able to catch one of his later works, *The Discreet Charm blah blah blah*, on the Bravo network.[43]

Most of you sickos probaly know Louie from that old porno *The Andalusian Dog* where some sick fuck cuts a lady right in the eyeball (but it's actually a cow's eyeball which is almost as bad, I mean jesus). He did that one with Salvador Dali and in his later solo work he still loved the dream logic of the surrealism but he used it to make comedies making fun of dumb rich people. And this, my friends, is a good fucking use for a movie.

Discreet Charm, aside from some gunplay, isn't as action packed as *Double Team*. But it is almost as weird and freaky assed. The "plot" is about a bunch of uptight ambassadors and ambassador's wives who are always inviting each other over for dinner, and a bunch of weird shit happens before they ever get to eat anything.

My friend that recommended this picture to me explained it like this: "There is a scene where this ambassador is having a meeting, and he sees a woman out his window walking a mechanical dog. He says, 'Don't worry, I know just what to do,' then he pulls out a rifle and shoots the dog."

There are many great cinemanic moments like this and what makes it so funny is how unimpressed these characters are by all the weird shit that happens around them. They are so wrapped up in inviting and entertaining and choosing a good wine that they never think to question bizarre behavior or bombs going off outside their house. There is one scene where some soldier they've never met comes to the table and says that he would like to tell them the tragic story of his childhood. He does, then immediately gets up and leaves, and they don't even seem to think it's weird.

My favorite scene though is when a Bishop comes to the house to see this family. The maid (who is said to be elderly but looks about nineteen) tells him they're not home, and he decides to wait for them to come back. He sneaks off to a shed and changes into the clothes of

---

43 Obviously I wrote this one in the late '90s. At that time, believe it or not, Bravo mostly showed arty movies. They were letterboxed and without commercials. A&E was the same kind of thing. No one could've ever predicted *Dog the Bounty Hunter*.

the recently fired gardener. When the couple comes home, the Bishop comes back in wearing overalls and a straw hat and announces himself — they don't believe he's the Bishop and throw his ass out. A minute later he comes back, wearing the Bishop's robes again, and they let him in. And that's when he tells them that he would like to be their gardener.

You may be asking, what the fuck? Well I don't know either. And that is the beauty of it. This movie illustrates the absurdities of a shallow rich fuck lifestyle but without being bitter about it. It just makes it funny as hell. It also makes fun of movies themselves by imitating them up to a point and then senselessly dropping out. The story starts to go one way and as soon as you might be on the edge of your seat it completely abandons that plotline or says that it's a dream or a dream within a dream.

It's all played real poker-faced and that makes it a lot funnier. And there are so many little details. There is this one scene where a couple is about to get it on, and the dude keeps turning the gal around and putting her ass on his lap. She'll turn back around and start kissing but every time he'll figure some way to get back around to the doggystyle. I thought ha ha ha it's funny cause it's true, I know so many guys like that. Always wanting to do her up the butt and only because she doesn't want it. You know what I'm talkin about fellas. Well let me tell ya, spend a few years in the can and you wouldn't ever want to do that kind of vile shit to your lady you bunch of fucknuts. Grow up.

The character most of us will relate to is the lady with the mechanical dog, some kind of anarchist revolutionary who tries to spout off her beliefs but they always get drowned out by low flying airplanes or loud typewriters. One of these bourgeoisie motherfuckers tries to tell her what's what while he's feeling her thighs and every time he pauses to get her input, she breaks something in his house. That is my kind of lady in my opinion.

Anyway some of you may be misled by the title, you may think wait a minute, I HATE the fucking bourgeoisie, I don't want to hear about their charm no matter how god damned discreet it is. Well don't worry bud it's sarcasm, it's making fun of them in my opinion. Don't worry about it man thanks.

ACROSS THE UNIVERSE

Look man, I'm pro gay rights, pro gay marriage. I'm all for gays from A-Z, Alan Cumming to Ziggy. So don't take it the wrong way when I say I'm not the type of dude who intentionally watches a musical. It just ain't me. If I'm gonna make an exception to that policy it's gonna take a hell of an extenuating circumstance, something air tight. I haven't even watched that one with Clint Eastwood and Lee Marvin, that's how strict I am. But for Julie Taymor I went out and got a waiver.

Now, I have been accused of being sweet on Julie Taymor, but nothing could be further from the truth. Actually I've seen interviews with her and I'm afraid of her. If I had a chance to hang out with her I don't think I would do it. About the only scenario where I would feel safe and comfortable would be some sort of puppetry workshop in a neutral public place, but I'm not into puppets so that's out. Despite these feelings, I also think Taymor is a genius. This is based on *Titus* and on a book I read about her. She's an opera-directing, puppet-carving, globetrotting, volcano-climbing, secret-forest-ritual-witnessing, visionary genius. So even though *Frida* was a mixed bag, and even though this is a musical, and especially even though it's a musical where the actors sing Beatles songs and are named after Beatles lyrics and their story illustrates the turbulent political climate and cultural shifts of the 1960s (oh for cryin out loud), I decided to give it a try.

I'm not gonna paint myself as brave though. I hesitated. I kind of put it off and since it was a low profile movie it very well could've left theaters before I got a chance to see it and then I could've waited for video and then kind of forgot about it for a while before I got to it. And I would've gotten away with it if it wasn't for those young girls who made it kind of a cult hit and caused it to stick around longer than movies usually do these days. I realize that this will lose me that feminism award I was about to get for praising Julie Taymor's artistic vision regardless of gender, but *Across the Universe* is definitely a girl movie. I mean, it opens with a doey-eyed, shaggy-haired, *English-accented* dreamboat on a beach, singing about a girl! Let's face it, only young girls are gonna be accepting of that type of behavior. A guy might get hot watching a woman sing some sultry tune in a night club, but not on a beach or a rooftop, or a street. There are limits. There are rules.

So because of the singing, and because of this '60s/Beatles thing, you gotta accept right away that this movie is gonna be as corny as Hell during Autumn. You know how the movie *Tron* takes place inside a computer, this is kind of like that if it took place inside somebody's collection of Beatles records. So the characters have names like Jude, Lucy, Prudence, Jojo, Dr. Robert, Mr. Kite, Dr. Octopus I believe, I forget what else. Luckily no Eleanor Rigby and thank Christ no Sergeant Pepper. I actually read on IMDb trivia that they had a Sergeant Pepper in an earlier draft but then I believe they changed it to Dr. Pepper and then finally they took it out. I'm glad they backed down but if it was me actually my compromise would be to have a sergeant in it and have him played by Barry Pepper, but not ever say his name.

Early in the movie there are signs of rough waters ahead. The opening scene has a bunch of animated newspaper headlines superimposed over breaking waves as a deep-voiced woman (who later turns out to be the Janis Joplin type character Sadie) butchers 'Helter Skelter.' It's ironic that the Manson Family painted 'Helter Skelter' on the wall in blood after one of their crimes, because that's exactly what she does to this song, she stabs it to death and writes on the wall with its blood. That combination of imagery and sound pretty much exemplifies everything you feared about a movie like this being corny and about using Beatles songs but not the original recordings. Also there's a scene early on where a guy says something about what's gonna happen "when I'm sixty-four" and you think *oh jesus, that's what we're in for here?* Luckily most of the other lyric references I didn't notice, so they must not have been too intrusive.

One thing I was glad about, they live in an apartment in the Village. They do not all live in a yellow submarine.

Actually I think you don't have to be as forgiving of the Beatles stuff as you do the sixties stuff. I mean, you could pretty much make a list of what's gonna be in this movie, you would be right on most counts. You got the young goodie two shoes with a military boyfriend, he dies in Vietnam and she joins the student protest movement (she's played by Evan Rachel Wood of Skander Halim's *Pretty Persuasion* fame). You got a guy who gets drafted, thinks about dodging, goes to 'Nam. You got the Weather Underground making bombs. Cops beating protesters. People traveling on a rainbow-colored hippie bus. A Jimi Hendrix type. A Janis Joplin type. A Timothy Leary type and accompanying drug freakout scene. Race riots. Watching a TV finding out about the assassination of Martin Luther King. Square parents that don't understand your hippie lifestyle.

On the other hand, they don't waste a lot of time with an experimenting-with-drugs plot (Taymor's visuals get psychedelic even when there's no drugs involved). When the character Max is in the veteran's ward, five sexy nurses all played by Salma Hayek dance for him and shoot him up with a syringe that contains a bright blue liquid and a miniature naked dancing Salma Hayek. I bet you naked Salma Hayek juice is even harder to kick than morphine but fortunately they don't waste our time with a plot about that.

And maybe the use of the Beatles songs has an advantage too because that way all the songs are Beatles songs, they don't have a *Forrest Gump*-type Greatest Hits of the 1960s soundtrack. Also I was happy that Daniel Stern wasn't narrating it from the future, that would've been lame.

I guess I wouldn't know, but if you're somebody who digs musicals I'm gonna guess this is a pretty decent one. It's got all the musical shit but it's cinematic, putting the people into real locations, giving it a visual reality before it spins off into fantasyland. And I'm not completely sure why but for me anyway this one was easier to stomach than most musicals. Yes, you got dudes with big smiles on their faces hopping around and dancing and singing to each other. But many times a giant puppet can and will show up. Or a crazy animated circus show. If a guy is reporting to the draft office then the painting of Uncle Sam is gonna reach out of the poster, point at him and sing to him. Then he's gonna get strapped into a big metal machine that does medical tests on him and next thing you know the draftees are gonna be in their boxers carrying the Statue of Liberty across a miniature model of Vietnam. I bet they didn't have that in *Chicago*.

Also, even if they're often bad versions of the songs, at least they are good songs. To me a lot of this type of shit they're singing songs that weren't even good in the first place. So that gives this one an advantage.

I don't know, man. Everything about the movie screams lame, but I gotta admit, I somehow enjoyed watching it, it kept my interest, I did not groan too much. But every once in a while you do get a little chuckle like when Evan Rachel Wood is upset with the British guy, she says "I can't believe you would do that!" and what he did was he went into her protest committee office and had a musical number.

It's nice that some of the main emotional scenes of the movie don't really have to do with the '60s clichés. For example the main character is dealing with immigration issues and with meeting the father who abandoned his mother before he was born. So you can get involved in that, or if not there's something cool to look at like when a cheerleader walks through a football practice singing and the players keep flying and flipping past her violently but she never flinches or gets hit.

There were some dance numbers in here that with their rhythmic sound effects made me think of the good old days when Michael Jackson was an actual guy who made incredible videos and not just a spooky ghost story from the past who the young singers all try to dance like. I mean, no offense to Justin Timberlake, Usher, Chris Brown and whoever else they got now, but part of the reason it was cool when Michael Jackson danced like that was because HE WAS MICHAEL JACKSON. So it made sense for him to dance like Michael Jackson. He was Michael Jackson, you're some dipshit from the school talent show who, because of low standards, Bush, etc., got millions of dollars and some blowjobs and treated as a celebrity because you could copy those moves better than the average person. But you're still a dipshit in a talent show and you know it. It is your secret shame. Every time you slant your hat you feel it like a needle in your heart.

Anyway the reason I bring this up is that *Across the Universe* made me think of Michael Jackson videos, *Titus* made me think of Michael Jackson videos... I think it's obvious what needs to be done here. Julie Taymor needs a subject that can truly suit her, Michael Jackson needs a kick in his freaky ass to get him in gear again. These two need to hole up in a haunted temple on some mountain somewhere with a live band, a team of dancers, some painters and storyboard artists, a green screen, some digital cameras, Rick Baker's makeup team, two shamans, a couple giraffes and a documentary crew and they need to plan out the epic Imax 3-D musical that they ABSOLUTELY MUST make together.

Fuck *The Lion King*. Fuck 'Thriller.' After this nobody will even talk about those anymore, except as early works by great artists. This is the movie where Michael declares *I Don't Give A Fuck* and waves his freak flag so high it pokes out of Earth's atmosphere. And Taymor announces — in images, not words — that *Titus* was not a fluke and she really was here to flip cinema over like a rock and reveal all the possibilities squirming around beneath it. Michael will play a dancing, singing Phantom of the Opera, an iconic screen legend somewhere between Vincent Price, Gene Kelly, James Brown, Jodorowsky, E.T. and the Elephant Man. With Taymor's help Michael will dip a quill straight into his pyramid shaped alien brain and paint right onto the screen with it. Dance numbers like 'Thriller' and 'Smooth Criminal' covered in acid, dipped in chocolate and fed to one of those psychedelic toads.

I mean seriously. You can't tell me this wouldn't be a cult classic for the ages. I am using The Secret now. I am visualizing it. Shooting those white thought beams out there in the world to make this happen. Julie Taymor, Michael Jackson, coming next summer. Imax people, get working on new 3-D goggles that have a lens for the third eye.

Anyway, I almost forgot I was talking about *Across the Universe*, which shall forever be known as that one Beatles movie Julie Taymor made before she changed the world forever with the Michael Jackson movie. Here's the thing about these '60s nostalgia movies. For younger generations, the '60s doesn't have all that much meaning. They can't feel the anger with the Vietnam War, the civil rights struggle, the assassinations. They just know the symbols, the visuals, the soundtrack. It might as well be the old west or the pirate age, it's not something they can imagine being a part of their world. It's a Halloween costume. And the more we use those images and sounds as shorthand for life in the '60s, the more their meaning blows away and dissipates like smoke.

I'm sure part of Taymor's goal was to show young people what was going on in the '60s so they could draw parallels to today. To show them that they can fight against the war, incite a revolution, sing Beatles songs to each other. But sadly I doubt this connects with most young people on any level deeper than *Grease* or *Hairspray* (Travolta in a drag fat suit version). Young people in general do not have a personal connection to the war. They don't know anybody that's in it and they know there's no chance of being sent themselves. They don't see it on TV because nobody's watching anymore and nobody's showing it anymore, it's old news. They don't know the excitement of music because, see above, re: Justin Timberlake. The kids that are passionate about real music are mostly listening to a bunch of mopers in sweaters pouting through their guitars. I'm not gonna say there's no great music right now, because I'm sure there is some hidden somewhere in a vault deep beneath the earth where human ears can't hear it. But 95% of kids today will never experience music like what The Beatles were then, or what Hendrix was. If there is a modern equivalent — and sorry, there isn't — it's not gonna be on TV or radio or their ringtones so they'll never know. You say you want a revolution, well, you know — actually you never said that, because you don't give a shit, and are not actually totally clear on what a revolution is anyway. Wasn't that the civil war or something? one of the like, way long time ago wars, maybe world war one.

And the thing is, we don't need to relive the '60s. Those good parts of the '60s that the movie celebrates, those are like the first Michael Jackson. You can't have a second Michael Jackson or a second '60s. I've been to more war protests than I can count, and I've seen first hand people trying to direct lightning to strike in the same place again. And it ain't working. We need to blaze new trails, crack open a new world. Stop trying to walk backwards in footprints that are already there.

So, nice try Taymor. I hope this works as more than nostalgia for the old and a period piece for the young. But I'm not convinced it does. But it's not too shabby. Seriously though think about this Michael Jackson idea.

FINDING NEVERLAND

Finding Neverland is one of those movies that feels kind of like a remedial imagination class they force you to take on Saturdays because you fucked up. You may not know this, it tells you, but it turns out imagination is important and magical and all that kind of crap. Johnny Depp plays J.M. Barrie, the writer of *Peter Pan*. The movie starts the same as *Ed Wood*, he's the writer of some flop play that the audience already hates literally about two seconds after it starts. It's the first line of dialogue and a dude is already asleep.

So J.M. needs to imagination up his life somehow to inspire him to write *Peter Pan*, and luckily he runs into a widow (Kate Winslet) and her spunky kids (a bunch of kids) while he's walking his novelty oversized dog. Next thing you know he's hanging out with the kids, dressing up in silly costumes and imagining stuff with them. They're still pretty bummed about their dad dying so he has to teach them to have a childlike sense of wonder, etc.

I mean it's a good sentiment but I think the whole thing is too broad. It's one of those movies where it's supposed to be real life but they got Darth Vader style villains. Both J.M. and his new surrogate family have to deal with a crusty old bitch who just doesn't understand the power of imagination, et al. J.M.'s always gotta put up with his social climbing wife, and Kate Winslet's gotta deal with her rich old bitch of a mother bossing her around. There's no need to argue, parents just don't understand.

When J.M. imagines stuff it appears on screen, but usually in play form, since he's a playwright. I got pretty confused at first because he's dancing with his dog and telling the kids it's a bear. Suddenly he's in the middle of a fake circus with a painted audience, dancing with a guy in a fake looking bear costume. So the kids are imagining that the dog is really a guy in a bear costume? What kind of a fantasy is that?

For a movie about the power of fantasy, most of the fantasy sequences are pretty light on the visual imagination. One exception is a scene on a pirate ship that has some pretty nice looking theatrical waves and sharks around it.

Maybe this will illustrate what's wrong with this movie. There's one part where J.M. and his wife both walk through doors at the same time, and the wife's door leads into a room, while J.M.'s leads into an imaginary beautiful outdoors. They oughta just leave it at that and it would work, but the movie doesn't trust you to understand how magical it is. So they put an orchestral *twinklety-twinklety-twee* on the soundtrack for you. *Listen up class, it's magical imagination and dreams and everything, that's what's through that door, that's what it means.*

Also there's a scene where Kate Winslet coughs, and I thought oh shit, it's gonna be that kind of movie. Why is it that nobody ever just has a cold in a movie? If you cough even once, you're dead meat. I wonder if anybody knows of movies that have coughing in them where the person who coughs doesn't turn out to have cancer or pneumonia or some other horrible disease? Let me know if you can think of any.[44]

This isn't a terrible movie. It has its moments. All the main actors are real good, and especially the kids. This kid Freddie Highmore plays Peter (not Peter Pan, but the kid Peter Pan is named after) and he gives the best performance, very believable as a smart and angry kid dealing with the loss of parents and the fear that the adults are hiding things from him. He also has an interesting goofy looking face with big ears, he's not some little Hollywood test tube baby. Next he's gonna play Charlie of *Charlie and the Chocolate Factory* fame, so it might turn out this movie was worth Johnny Depp's time just as a scouting mission for that one.

And it's an interesting story if this is really what inspired that play. You want to like it. It's not that bad.

What I'm saying is, I can understand why people would like this movie, but it ain't even close to one of the top five movies of the year. No way this would be nominated for best picture if somebody besides Miramax released it. I mean it's pretty mediocre in most respects. How do you even make a movie like this without having beautiful photography? They even got this awkward part after the opening credits, it tells us "London, 1903" so we think we're into the actual story now, but after that, "inspired by true events." This is not a masterfully crafted movie.

I gotta be fair though. I can't fault the movie for getting Oscar nominations it doesn't deserve. But I still want to because for Johnny Depp to get a Best Actor nomination for this almost proves the movie wrong. If imagination and following your dreams were so damn important and powerful then Depp wouldn't get a nomination for a square role like this. Not that he's bad — he'll probably never be bad in his life. But when he's been so original and spectacular in so many movies without a peep from the awards people... I mean think about *Fear and Loathing in Las Vegas, Ed Wood, Edward Scissorhands,* even *Once Upon a Time in Mexico* and *Sleepy Hollow.* It was huge for him to get a nomination for *Pirates of the Caribbean,* a movie based on a Disneyland ride, a movie made popular

---

44 One answer is *Inside Man,* in which Denzel Washington stops to cough between lines at least twice, but never has a fatal disease.

because he followed his weird brilliance even while the executives were telling him he was ruining the movie. But now that he broke that ground, he's being rewarded for settling down and doing a normal role. In most of his roles, he is living it, in this one he's just talking about it. Go out there and live your dreams, but preferably with a nice suit and Irish accent.

I mean I agree with the pro-imagination message of this movie. I'm for it. But that's what everybody would say. I can't help but picture people watching this movie and siding with the weirdo, wanting to stick it to the man Miramax style and take the starch out of the collars of those old rich ladies always bossing us around and telling us not to imagine stuff. Then the credits roll and the second the lights turn on, they don't believe that shit anymore. They work in an office and they know for sure Michael Jackson is a pervert, because why would he be so weird if he wasn't molesting children? They drive by some people holding up signs about something they believe in — first they lock the doors, then they crack the window and yell "Get a job!"

Like that *Chocolat* movie (a bigger waste of Johnny Depp's talents) this is the grown up equivalent of those movies where kids paint the principal blue. Remember in the *Police Academy* movies they would trick the commander into super-gluing his hand to his dick or something, and you're suppose to go *ha ha ha, take that you crusty old asshole*, but the real pleasure is not in his humiliation but in watching his reaction. Because he's so uptight. Ha ha ha, get it? This and *Chocolat* are kind of the same thing, where you watch the reaction of the grandma to J.M. coming into the house wearing an Indian headdress, or the wife when he hangs a spoon on his nose during a formal dinner. *Ha ha ha J.M., you showed those old uptight broads.*

And then at the end the grandma watches *Peter Pan* and is magically and instantly transformed, and she claps the fastest and hardest to bring Tinkerbell back to life. She is the ballbusting sergeant who plays mean before he breaks into a smile and gives the maverick cop an unexpected break. She's the old white lady that starts to use hip hop slang, or the mean old dean who pulls the stick out of his ass, puts a pair of panties on his head and parties down at the wet t-shirt contest.

So anyway, if you're too bland to figure out where Neverland is at on your own, this movie will give you detailed instructions.

RAIDERS OF THE LOST ARK: THE ADAPTATION

If you're on the internet (which you would be if you weren't reading this book), maybe you heard legends about it. Or if you know how to read (which in my opinion you do), maybe you saw the article in *Vanity Fair* a while back. The story is these kids who, from ages eleven to seventeen, took upon themselves the monumental task of remaking that movie *Raiders of the Lost Ark*, which was popular at the time.

Their movie has all the same dialogue, and they pretty much faithfully re-created the whole god damn thing, with the one exception being the scene where the big bald guy gets chopped up in the propeller blade, because they decided it was too dangerous. They're just kids, man, cut them some fucking slack. But they have everything else: jungles, caves, deserts, the giant boulder, real live snakes, a teenage Indiana dragged from a truck. And most of this was filmed in their basement, garage or backyard. A few times they had to be clever to be able to pull it off, so one plane chase was changed to a boat chase, and instead of a traitorous Nazi monkey on his shoulder, he carries a sieg-heiling weiner dog. But as the years went on and they got more on tape, they convinced more and more people they weren't fucking around and they were able to shoot on a real boat and submarine.

I was lucky enough to see this movie at a rare public screening last month (with the guy who played Indiana Jones in attendance) and I gotta say I was pretty impressed. It looks like shit of course, all shot on Betamax cameras and dubbed onto other tapes in the editing process. But here is this movie that we all know, the Steven Spielberg movie, and we are reliving the whole thing as a no budget camcorder epic with kids playing adults. It's kind of like that weird deja vu feeling you get watching Gus Van Sant's shot-for-shot remake of *Psycho*, except way weirder. Because you know they weren't conscious of anything, they weren't trying to say anything or get a reaction out of anyone, they just love Indiana Jones and they wanted to remake the movie. Because that's the type of shit that kids want to do. Either go on adventures, build a spaceship, feel up Daisy Duke from *the Dukes of Hazzard*, or remake *Raiders of the Lost Ark*. All of these are unachievable dreams for most kids, but this is the one time, the one group of kids that actually pulled one off.

Throughout the movie, the kids change ages and sizes. They go from pre-teen to teen and back. Their hair grows long and gets short again within one love scene. Their voices change. These kids were obsessive about the movie. According to the article they studied the comic book, made a tape recording of the movie (this was before the age of home video), made a script and painstakingly storyboarded every shot of the movie. So they didn't just do the fun parts, they did the boring parts too. The long scenes of dialogue at the college, where Professor Indiana Jones talks to a bunch of dudes about archaeology or whatever it is, I don't know, I don't pay attention to that shit. Well in *The Adaptation* these kids did those scenes, word for word, boring minute for boring minute, but they got kids saying the lines. This nine-year-old kid wearing a tie and horn rimmed glasses, his hair painted grey — I don't know man, that shit cracks me up.

But they do the fun parts too. They got the boulder. They got kids getting lit on fire. They got the bar burning down by setting the kid's basement on fire! You see this shit and you start getting excited thinking *holy shit, how did they do that*, and *oh man, how are they gonna do the guy getting chopped up in the propeller?* (Uh, sorry, not at all.) *Or everybody melting at the end?* (They actually made dummies and melted them!)

Now, I am not the world's biggest fan of Steven Spielberg, or of *Raiders of the Lost Ark*, or home made videos, or obsessive nerdy fan films[46]. Although I do kind of like the first two on the list, and the third one if you are talking only about porn. But this movie is amazing because it *exists*. If this was a TV show or movie (and they are trying to make a movie about it, with a script by Dan Clowes of *Ghost World* fame) you would never believe that kids (or adults, for that matter) would have the resources, or the energy, or the attention span to even finish half of this fucking thing. And these kids did the whole thing.

(You know I was thinking, it's lucky that it was *Raiders of the Lost Ark* that they were obsessed with, because it turned out to be pretty timeless. Everybody's seen this movie, everybody remembers this movie and most people like it. So it's still relevant. Plus, it was a movie good and not corny enough that they could still be into it when they were seventeen. I mean what if it was *Mac and Me* or something? Or *Romancing the Stone*? They would never have stuck with it for so long, and if they did you couldn't show that shit now. Nobody would watch it. So they picked their subject well.)

But this is not just some funny fan video, this is actually very inspiring. Because you think about how much shit these kids got. How many times in those seven years do you think they had to explain to somebody, "Yeah, we're doing an exact remake of *Raiders of the Lost Ark*." I mean at that age it's hard enough to explain why you have a ponytail or got your ear pierced or some shit like that. They gotta explain why they've spent seven years of their lives dressing up in hats and building paper mache caves and memorizing one god damn archaeology movie. How are you ever gonna achieve your life long goal of getting a handjob if that's your whole life? This is an important question for a young man growing up.

I mean I doubt anybody really believed in it other than this director and this Indy guy. I bet their parents didn't believe it, their classmates didn't believe it, their neighbors didn't believe it. And what were they gonna do with it when they were done? They couldn't sell it, they couldn't project it, there was no internet. I mean anybody besides them must've thought they were complete retards. And they still did it. They *had* to do it.

Now, I'm not trying to encourage people to go out there and do *Star Trek* movies or some shit like that (see *Trekkies* for more information). But sometimes you get an idea, and it's such a stupid idea that you know you should do it. You know that most people won't understand it, they might even make fun of you, but it is something you have to do. And if you have the nerves of a samurai or of these kids, you will do it, even if it takes seven years.

I mean there are things I don't understand. I don't understand those dudes that waited four months in a parking lot to see the last *Star Wars* movie. (And I have to take points away because they tried to call it an art project and especially because they didn't stay there after the corny human interest interview opportunities dried up, they just left a tent there and pretended they were inside). But those guys had an impossible idea and they sort of did it.

Sometimes I get those kind of ideas. Not as ambitious as *The Adaptation*, but sometimes you get an idea that makes you laugh and it's so stupid and would take so much effort and would maybe only amuse you. But that means you should do it! I got an idea for a book a while back, a book that would require watching and analyzing a lot of bad movies, in chronological order. I've invested a lot of time into the book and sometimes I feel good about how it's going and sometimes I don't. I go through phases where I work on it obsessively and then end up taking a long hiatus and then start to wonder if it's good enough that anybody will ever even want to read it. And then I watched this adaptation here and I thought *shit, if these kids can finish this movie then I can definitely finish my stupid book.*[45]

And you can too. Go out there everybody, reach for your dreams, strive for excellence, and all that kind of crap. GO FOR IT!

---

45 I did finish the book, but it did not turn out to be stupid. Instead it was the acclaimed film studies classic *Seagalogy: A Study of the Ass-Kicking Films of Steven Seagal*, available from Titan Books

CHAPTER NINE
MISCELLANEOUS

For some reason the otherwise respectable Titan Books is not interested in releasing a 1000 page collection of movie reviews by some internet boob most people never heard of. But they were okay with doing one of a reasonable length. After I cut out thirty-some reviews from my manuscript some of the sections didn't really make sense anymore. So here is what remains of what would've been the chapters "Ones That Pissed Me Off" and "Science, Fantasy and Space Shit." Nomoretimetoexplaindon'twanttorunupmywordcount.

DOMINO

I probably never woulda known this if there wasn't a movie, but it turns out Laurence Harvey, who is a guy in *The Manchurian Candidate* (but not Frank Sinatra), had a daughter named Domino. But wait, there's more. This daughter supposedly tried to follow in the footsteps of her supermodel mother, but then got bored and became a bounty hunter. Rich girl model becomes bounty hunter — sounds like a good story, and apparently director Tony Scott was friends with Domino and spent twelve years trying to bring "her story" to the screen. Tragically, she died of a drug overdose last summer having only seen parts of the unfinished movie. I just watched the whole god damn thing so believe me, I can relate.

Okay, that was low and unfair and in poor taste. In the spirit of the movie. They say the real Domino liked what she saw of the movie and was real excited. She was a DJ and recorded a song for the opening credits. And her death was ruled an accident, unlike my paying $9 in good faith for a movie I hoped would be entertaining. You gotta wonder if the best way to honor your dead friend is to put her name on a horrible movie that has nothing to do with her. Whatever happened to pouring one on the curb? I guess maybe they had a weird friendship.

[Confidential to Skander Halim: if I die tragically before your option runs out, FOR GOD'S SAKE don't let Tony Scott direct. Or produce. Or watch. Life is too precious.]

The movie *Domino* is most like is *Natural Born Killers*. I always figured Oliver Stone was trying to make some prophetic warning about the media's exploitation of violence, not realizing that everybody already figured that one out before he did. But in retrospect it turns out maybe he *was* prophetic: he was trying to warn us of the incoming tide of the Michael Bay style, the Bruckheimerization of the cinematic language, and/or Tony Scott's big screen mid-life crisis. Oliver Stone was whacking us over the head, cutting the soundtrack into 750 pieces, torturing us with electric guitars, jarring edits, uncomfortable closeups, senseless switches from super 8 to regular to vhs to black and white to cartoon network. As obnoxious and pretentious as it was, at least we knew what he was going for, I think. Some kind of impression of an oversaturated media culture is my guess.

What Tony Scott does now in movies like *Domino* and *Man On Fire* is torture us with that same beating-you-to-death-with-a-movie style, minus the purpose. He just does it because he mistakenly, foolishly, embarrassingly assumes that it is cool. This time he does bother to come up with an excuse: she gets dosed with mescaline at one point. So therefore it's supposed to make sense that at whatever point in the future when she is narrating the story of her telling Lucy Liu the story of her life, she tells it like she just blazed ten turkey sized crack rocks.

There is not a scene where they are on peyote and go out into the desert to get mystical advice from a Native American guru. There *is* a scene where they are on mescaline and go out into the desert to get mystical advice from Tom Waits.

I am not going to say one way or another, but I want you to guess whether or not this is one of those movies where every time they introduce a new character they freeze frame and write the character's name on the screen. And if so, do you think you will remember those names at the end, or feel that you have learned much more about them other than their names? I think you will be able to guess correctly but who knows.

Any random thirty second sampling of this movie would contain every symptom of the Bruckheimer plague: Avid farts, whooshy camera move sound effects, flying subtitles, Michael Bay energy drink edits, disorienting extreme closeups, overexposed/digitally saturated photography on any shot, no matter what it is, from a big ass shootout to a closeup of a fish to an interview in a police station. There is no sense of rhythm or momentum or build because EVERY. GOD. DAMN. SCENE. MIGHT. ASWELLBEABIGEXPLOSION. BOOOM.

JUST GUESSING HERE BUT I BET IF I WAS GONNA WRITE A WHOLE REVIEW IN ALL CAPS THAT NOBODY WOULD WANT TO READ IT. WHAT IF I JUST STARTED REPEATING STUFF FOR NO REASON JUST STARTED REPEATING STUFF FOR NO REASON NO REASON AND WHO NEEDS PUNCTUATION ANYWAY WHO NEEDS PUNCTUATIONOKAY HERE IS SOME PUNCTUATION FOR YOU YOU BIG ASSHOLE.......?!!!

WHAT TONY SCOTT TONY SCOTT DOES NOT UNDERSTAND IS THAT CINEMA IS A LANGUAGE LANGUAGE LANGUAGE. TONY SCOTT. THERE IS A CHARACTER IN THIS MOVIE WHO'S ALWAYS SPEAKING SPANISH TO ENGLISH SPEAKERS, NOT CARING THAT THEY DON'T KNOW WHAT THE FUCK HE'S TALKING ABOUT. THAT'S TONY SC0TT RIGHT THERE. NO RESPECT FOR COMMUNICATING A STORY OR CHARACTERS. IF I JUST START THROWING IN WACKY COLORS AND FONTS FOR NO GOD DAMN REASON IT IS GOING TO *START* DISTRACTING FROM from **THE** MEANING THE MEAN_ING_ THE MEANING I'M (allegedly) TRYING TO COMMUNICATE. HOW THE FUCK IS ANYBODY GONNA UNDERSTAND WHAT I AM TRYING *TO* SAY ABOUT THIS MOVIE IF I BURY THE WHOLE GOD DAMN TH*I*NG *I*N A PILE *OF* RANDOMLY SELECTED, ANNOY*I*NG STYL*IS*TIC FLOR*IS*HESQUESTION MARK

**************xxx##############

Or to put it another way, if a guy is telling you a joke, but at the same time he's pissing on your leg, you're probably not gonna catch the punchline. In my opinion.

And this is not a well-told joke, because Tony Scott is putting all his effort into pissing on your leg. I don't expect this to be a true story. I like that they openly don't care about the facts and got the *Donnie Darko* guy to write the script. But the whole thing is muddled. Somehow they manage to make it feel like it has no plot and at the same time has way too much plot. Because you're never involved in any character or event, and yet you can't keep up with who is trying to do what to who or why.

If you have any interest in a goofy movie about a bounty hunter, watch *The Hunter* starring Steve McQueen. I am not sure this one is even about a bounty hunter. If kids, martians or the Amish watched this movie, not knowing what a bounty hunter was, I am betting they would come out still not knowing what it was. Although she does say "My name is Domino Harvey, and I am a bounty hunter" many times throughout the movie, there is only evidence to support the first part. The actual bounty hunting in the movie is minimal. Even when she first meets her bounty hunter team (Delroy Lindo, Mickey Rourke, one other guy) they are not actual bounty hunters. They're pulling a scam, taking money for a "bounty hunting seminar" and then taking off out the bathroom window. I think there is one scene after that where they go to collect a bounty, but instead of asskicking she gives the guy a lap dance. (Seriously.) "My name is Domino Harvey, and I am a stripper." The main plot has something to do with an armored car robbery, the mafia, the FBI, etc. Not bounty hunting. There's a shootout or two but for me there wasn't a single frame of film that seemed like an action movie. Because it goes out of its way to make everything so visceral that nothing is visceral at all. You can't have Christmas three times a day.

WHHHHHHOOOOOOOOOOSSSSSSSSSSHHHHH. (lights cigarette.) sizzzzzzllllllllee. BOOM! SHHHOooooPP! boom bip boom bip. (repeat until movie ends)

We get it, Tony Scott. You're not old. You're young. You're hip. You probably have an earring. You got your tips frosted! Maybe a soul patch. Only one problem asshole: your act is about as convincing as Vin Diesel in *xXx*. The truth is, you're sixty-one years old. You remember when your fictional Domino character was saying she didn't like Hollywood bullshit? Did you ever wonder who she might be talking about there? Let me point out a few facts. You directed *Top Gun*. You directed *Beverly Hills Cop 2*. You introduced Tom to Nicole. This is all documented. Your character hates Hollywood bullshit, and you directed *Top Gun*. I will let you draw your own conclusions.

And of course, this movie *is* Hollywood bullshit. For a guy trying to be so hip Tony Scott you sure are out of touch. For example, this story centers around a reality show. You really thought that was virgin territory for satire, huh? Jesus, Tony Scott, *Ron Howard* did a movie about reality TV six years ago. I saw it on cable. RON FUCKING HOWARD beat you to this. The guy with the baseball hats that likes astronauts. The guy who did *Splash*. There's a rule of thumb for you: if Ron Howard beats you to a topic by more than half a decade, you are officially for sure a bonafide Square with a capital S. Motherfucker, you can't deny that you watch *Jay Leno*. No, you tape *Jay Leno* every night because it's too late to stay up. If you can figure out how to program your VCR.

I mean, one of the big "laugh" scenes in *Domino* is an episode of *The Jerry Springer Show*. Damn, how did they get Jerry Springer to play himself? He hardly ever does that, unless you count *Meet Wally Sparks, Killer Sex Queens From Cyberspace, Kissing a Fool, The 24 Hour Woman, Austin Powers 2, Sugar & Spice,* or *Pauly Shore Is Dead*. Other than those seven movies and the one he starred in and a few others, it is very rare to see Jerry Springer parodying himself in a movie, so that was quite a coup there for *Domino*.

This is a movie that really leaves a lot of questions for you to ponder. Like, is there really still a *Jerry Springer Show*?

Roger Ebert, who somehow performed the feat of enjoying this movie, talked on his show about a scene where an arm gets cut off because it has the combination to a safe tattooed on it. (Believe me, not as exciting as it sounds.) He thought this was funny because it would be easier to just write down the number. That means Ebert didn't pick up on one of the few jokes in the movie that made me chuckle slightly. After we already know the arm is chopped off, we find out that the arm was chopped off due to poor cell phone reception (the boss told them to take his arm out of the jacket and look at it, but his phone kept cutting out and there was a wacky misunderstanding). I don't blame Ebert for not catching this, it's hard to make any sense out of this big screaming mess of holy hell. It's like watching *True Romance* while jumping on a trampoline and people keep taking turns banging you on the head with pans.

I only compare it to *True Romance* because Tony Scott directed that one also and I guess that would have to be considered his best movie. I don't think it's a great movie but it's a good one and they got a lot of similarities: single parented white kid fascinated by the dark side plays movie anti-hero, gets in over his or her head with mafia and FBI but soldiers on to bloody conclusion. *True Romance* was also written by a hipper, younger writer and remember it had some goofy pop culture touches like getting advice from an Elvis apparition in the bathroom and his friend auditioning for *TJ Hooker*. I saw it a few years ago, and saw *Domino* last night, but I remember *True Romance* better. I remember specific characters with personalities (Brad Pitt as the stoner roommate, the douchebag from *Perfect Strangers*, the movie producer/coke dealer, Drexl the white pimp). I remember specific scenes with actual tension or suspense (the Dennis Hopper/Christopher Walken showdown, the shootout in the hotel). For *Domino* I don't remember anything like that, but I remember that two guys from *90210* were in it.

I guess when you have goofy touches like the ghost of Elvis in a studio crime movie like that, it almost seems subversive. But when you do it in a movie that's clearly trying to wave its ass in your face 24-7, it doesn't mean shit. This movie is a sullen teenage girl with a giant blue mohawk and a 666 tattoo on her forehead, wearing a shirt that says "SUCK MY DICK." You know she's just trying to get a rise out of you so the shirt has no meaning. If Condoleeza Rice wore it though you might raise an eyebrow. This movie spends its whole afternoon poking the mohawk at you saying "Hey look mister, look at my mohawk, I have a blue mohawk, did you notice my mohawk?"

There was a line I liked at the end of *Domino*, something like "If you're wondering what parts are true, too bad. It's none of your fucking business." The problem is I assumed none of it was true since there's not a note in the whole symphony that rings true. It has all the soul of a

BMW commercial. In fact, there is an actual BMW commercial also directed by Tony Scott that has the exact same feel as this movie. If you ever saw *The Hire*, the series of short films/BMW commercials starring Clive Owen as an underworld driver, maybe you saw this. It was called *Beat the Devil* and it was a story about how James Brown (playing himself) made a deal with the devil, played by Gary Oldman. And Clive Owen has to take him to the devil's apartment to try to renegotiate his contract. I know, it's a crazy idea, it sounds good on paper and you would think there would be no director on earth who could make a concept like that dull. Ladies and gentlemen, meet Tony Scott. This asshole makes eight minutes seem feature length. It goes beyond self-indulgence. Tony Scott's movies have figured out how to suck their own dicks. They invite you over to the apartment, tell you to make yourself at home, and you look over and suddenly they're sucking their own dick right in front of you. I don't know about you but I think that is rude.

The only enjoyment you get out of *Beat the Devil* at all is you keep telling yourself, "But James Brown. And Gary Oldman is the devil. Ha ha, and James Brown." You keep telling yourself there is no way you don't like it and yet, in reality, you don't like it. Same thing here. How could Christopher Walken be in this movie as a crazy TV producer and add nothing? Ask Tony Scott. Want to see Lucy Liu do nothing? Here's your movie. There are two guys from *90210* playing themselves (as hosts of the reality show). They're there for almost the entire movie and they only get one good joke at the end. They are actually more successful than most of the rest of the cast though because they are better when they have nothing to do. Like, there's a scene where the self-proclaimed bounty hunters are being hunted by the mafia, etc. and they are stranded out in the desert and even though he hasn't added anything to the plot in about half an hour, Brian Austin Green is still in their entourage, sitting there all bandaged and bloody. Just there, for no reason. That was kind of a funny idea, I thought, in my brain. Here, hold on, let me write this down. Yep, sure enough, it looks good on paper.

Now because I am a gentleman I will say a couple nice things. Do unto others as you would have them do unto you even if they just tormented you for two hours and made you pay money for it. First of all, Mickey Rourke is good. He might have the closest to a full character, coming in at almost one half of an actual movie character. Keira Knightley has gotten some shit in reviews but I don't think she was that bad in this movie. She is not believable as a tough girl but she is not as bad as you might think. The real Domino didn't look that tough either at least in the couple of pictures I've seen. Although she had more meat on her bones. Anyway, if the movie bothered to give her a personality or motivations instead of just phony poses — hell, if it just gave her some better poses — I think there is a possibility that Knightley would've pulled it off okay. I don't know if there is a trophy for that or not but that's all I got for her.

There is a good crazy idea here and there, thanks to *Donnie Darko* guy. He probably was trying. I might forgive him for this one. I can't say the same for fucking Tony god damn pain in the ass fuck you Scott, though. Last year he had Denzel Washington in a pure, simple, badass revenge story with the screenwriter of *Payback*, and he fucked that up bad. Now he has the *Donnie Darko* guy doing a crazy story about a bounty hunter, he fucks that up even worse. There is definitely, for sure, no redeeming this motherfucker. These are movies that any competent director would've at least made watchable. Not Tony Scott. He has other plans. Looks good on paper + Tony Scott = run for the hills. In my opinion.

In fact, before I saw this movie I was not too pleased about Tony Scott remaking *The Warriors*.[46] And then I read somewhere that he wants his remake to be "*Kingdom of Heaven* meets *The Warriors*" and that instead of say thirty guys in a big knife fight he's gonna have armies of 3,000 running through the LA river basin. And I thought well actually, that sounds good, as long as he doesn't try to make them realistic gangs, and it doesn't sound like that's the plan. I mean, imagine one of those big *Lord of the Rings* battles but with Baseball Furies! That sounds good, I thought. On paper. Uh oh.

Tony Scott, you have long since used up your get out of jail free card. Your time is up. You're 86ed. I'm sorry sir, I'm going to have to ask you to leave. Your garbage is no longer welcome on our screens.

---

46 As has been threatened, but has not happened yet as of this writing.

M. NIGHT SHYAMALAN'S LADY IN THE WATER

a bedtime story by M. Night Shyamalan
directed by M. Night Shyamalan
produced by M. N. Shyamalan
written by M. Night Shyamalan
co-starring M. Night Shyamalan
inspired by the true adventures of M. Night Shyamalan
dedicated to M. Night

The movie I really wanted to watch this week was *Wassup Rockers*, but for some reason it went straight to the second run theater in Seattle. That theater's a little out of the way for me and today I just wanted somewhere nearby with some air conditioning, so instead of seeing Larry Clark ogle Hispanic skateboarders from Compton I got to see M. Night Shyamalan ogling Ron Howard's daughter. I'm not sure which one's freakier.

The advertisements say that *Lady In the Water* is "a bedtime story by M. Night Shyamalan" which is a nicer way of saying "he made this shit up as he went along so it doesn't make any god damn sense and it doesn't matter because the whole point of it is to put you to sleep." And now that I think about it there actually was a dude snoring in front of me (no lie) so Shyamalan must know what he's doing.

I actually think Shyamalan is a real good director, at least when he's working with Bruce. *Signs* was a little too goofy for me, and I didn't see that last one (maybe that's why I still like him). But I like his filmatism — his pacing, his deliberate camera moves, etc. On most of his movies he has this very serious tone and you feel like he's in total control of what's on screen, showing you the best angle to watch things from, making the right part of the screen be bright red or whatever, getting good quiet acting performances out of Bruce and that little Haley Joel Osment dude. But those movies were directed by the old "guy who got lucky and got to work with Bruce" Shyamalan, this is the new Shyamalan who thinks he's a fuckin rock star, makes credit card commercials about his brilliant imagination and casts himself in this movie in a major role as the savior of humanity, wearing a hip shirt. Rock Star Shyamalan doesn't seem to have the same control over the movie, he's too busy making googly eyes trying to look sensitive to give as much of a shit about a story and characters and where to put the camera as he used to.

The characters are all wacky gimmicks or bordering on racist stereotypes. Paul Giamatti, as the hero/building superintendent, is the only one with any kind of humanity to him, but it's all Giamatti doing his best with a formulaic character. Even the backstory that's supposed to give him depth kind of pissed me off. At the beginning the movie seems to be saying, "Look at this schlubby, lonely, stuttering apartment manager... now watch as he helps do something extraordinary!" But then later the movie says, "actually he used to be a respected doctor with a family but they were murdered so now he's sad and he doesn't give a shit about being an apartment manager because it's a loser job that anybody could do." And then at the same time they keep saying that "everybody has a purpose." (As long as they are a doctor or brilliant writer.)

That shit pissed me off because WHY CAN'T he just be a schlubby apartment manager who lives by himself and still be a hero? We have to find out that he used to be upper class in order to truly accept him? Shouldn't we acknowledge that going around fixing people's toilets and light bulbs might be a pain in the ass job and a perfectly acceptable purpose in life because somebody's gotta do it? Seems kind of insulting, Shyamalan.

By the way, please note that I am spelling Shyamalan's name correctly. None of that "Sham-a-long-a-ding-dong" or "Shymalawhateverthefuckitis what a CRAZY name it's not American!" xenophobic bullshit. I'm not one of those type of jokers. I am treating the man with dignity and respect. However in the next paragraph I might accuse him of falling for a girl spawned by the dude who directed *The Grinch*.

Probably the most distracting element for most people is gonna be Shyamalan's appearance in the movie as a Writer who is writing "some thoughts about society" which it turns out are destined to inspire a child who will go on to become president and make the world a better place but the writer won't be able to see it because his ideas are so dangerous he's gonna get assassinated like Dr. King. Shyamalan's acting is passable but you can't help but be distracted because there is a large ego that keeps blocking the view of the camera. People were bothered when Spike Lee cast himself as Malcolm X's buddy, this is kind of like if he had played Malcolm X himself. Or at least Elijah Muhammad. And because this is a Shyamalan movie, a lot of his role involves long shots of him staring meaningfully or with awe. And by far the most uncomfortable scene for me is when he talks emotionally to Story the Sea Nymph about how they have a connection and she inspired him and changed his life, and I couldn't help but start to wonder if this movie is actually about how he fell in love with Bryce Dallas Howard while filming *The Village* but he doesn't want to admit it because he's married and that's Ron Howard's daughter so instead he rationalizes her as being a Muse sent to him by the destiny of the universe to inspire him to make a movie about her walking around with no pants on.

I don't mean to be judgmental. If Shyamalan really does think she's his muse and made a whole movie about it, it's not a crime against society, only against moviegoers.

The part of the movie that actually made me lose respect for Shyamalan, though, was this whole subplot about a movie critic played by Bob Balaban, the director of *Parents*. I'm not stupid, I know what Shyamalan's doing, he's criticizing the critics for not liking his last movie and at the same time making an excuse to say why critics won't like this one. Well played, Shyamalan, well played. To me this comes off as petty and childish, but more importantly, the guy doesn't know what he's talking about. This character is not an intelligent criticism of criticism. He's just an asshole who makes speeches about the different formulas for movies, and they turn out to be wrong (because get it, this movie is SO UNPREDICTABLE! because he MADE IT UP AS HE WENT ALONG!) This character would've been a good guy in *Scream* but here you're supposed to hate him (in fact, he even states that he is the character you are supposed to hate, in case you don't get it) and he is the only character who gets killed, and nobody even finds out that it happened or cares.

You guys know me so you know I'm not getting defensive on account of being some kind of critic. I actually agree that a lot of critics are stupid. In fact because I've spent these years striving for excellence in reviewing I've thought this shit out a hundred times more than Shyamalan and I probably hate some of those critics more than he ever could dream of hating them. Obviously you got your Gene Shalit types with the puns and shit. Hell, you got all kinds of punsters out there who are more respected than Shalit but they still think if they review *Pirates of the Caribbean* they gotta work in a thousand boat and grog and bottle of rum and yo ho ho references. Then you got your "quote whores" or your Peter Travers with his "EXPLOSIVE! The summer's best whiteknuckle thrill ride!" hyperbole. You got Larry King (if that counts) saying that every other movie he sees is "FINALLY a movie to get excited about!" or "THE FUNNIEST MOVIE I'VE EVER SEEN!"

That shit's obvious, but for me it gets deeper, the actual writing style pisses me off. You write these things over and over again, you start to find yourself using the same phrases and words to describe movie after movie. So then either you settle into a predictable formula and you're boring, or you start coming up with the corniest shit to describe movies, words nobody would ever use to describe a movie unless they were writing a review. I got hearing like a dog for this shit so I see phrases that probably wouldn't bother a normal person but for me I wince when I see these magazine writers with the corny phrases like "whizbang" and "crackerjack" and "hangdog" and using "meta" whenever possible and talking about whether or not a movie has "crackle" or "verve" or whether it "pops" and then they have to work in some reference to *The Sopranos* or *Lost* or whatever TV show they are currently obsessed with.

"Like the island inhabitants of *Lost,* these apartment dwellers are trapped in their own world while mystical beasties creep and crawl in the shadows just beyond the cabana room. But alas, *Lady In the Water* doesn't have the crackerjack sparkle or verve of J.J. Abrams. It's as flat as the carnivorous 'scrunts' become when they camouflage themselves in the courtyard foliage."

And yes there are more pretentious critics who look down on "entertainment" which I guess is what this character is supposed to be, but in modern society those type of critics are few and far between, they have almost no power over who goes to see Shyamalan's movie and they are marginalized members of society who are only respected (or even known of) in an insulated subculture of film buffs that 99.99999% of all earthlings will never even know about, let alone encounter. So who the fuck cares?

What I'm saying is, Shyamalan takes cheap shots when I thought he was a guy who could take dead aim between the eyes. Back when he made *Unbreakable* I woulda figured he was a really smart guy, if he chose to go after critics he would have a smart way to do it. But this movie is telling me that the guy is not actually that smart.

If you're around movie discussions for long you eventually run into these chuckleheads who claim "I listen to what the critics say and then I do the OPPOSITE — ha ha ha that's how cynical I am I blew the lid off this whole thing with my unique iconoclastic stance." I always wonder what those people do when they read the reviews for, say, almost any movie ever made, and discover that critics disagree with each other. Or do they just wait until the cases where the critics are unanimous, and then show those fuckers by going out and enjoying *Catwoman* and *Christmas With the Kranks* and shit? There's this idea that critics don't know how to enjoy "a good popcorn flick." But you look on that silly "Rotten Tomatoes" site you see a 93% for *Die Hard*, a 92% for *Face/Off*, a 100% for *Aliens*. Hell, you can see that about half the critics will even go for a shitty one like fucking *Independence Day*.

There are so many deeper, more accurate points to make about a critic than "they think they know everything about movie formulas." So if that's all you got and then you kill the guy you look like a fuckin whiney baby, especially when you're a filmatist who's had a better track record with critics than most. And by the way, Joe Dante did it better when he killed the real Leonard Maltin sixteen years ago in *Gremlins 2*. But only a critic would say that.

I guess maybe the critic part is supposed to be funny. Stranger things have happened. But that's another problem, Shyamalan knows how to do deadly serious melodrama but when he starts trying to make you laugh he's out of his element. This one is so cartoony that you figure it must be supposed to be funny, but if there was a good joke in there I must have missed it. There's a character who works out only the right side of his body as "a scientific experiment" which I thought was a really funny idea. And then that's where he left it. A funny idea, nothing happens with it. And that's the best he's got in the whole movie.

So that's a lot of complaints there but I honestly think he could get away with all that if he had a really good dramatic story here. Which he doesn't. It all comes back to this bedtime story gimmick and the fact that bedtime stories are something you make up on the spot to put a kid to sleep. They are not something you spend a hundred million dollars on and make a person pay money to watch for two hours. I know Shyamalan is into this idea of the magic of storytelling and storytellers and he even has the lady in the water be named "Story." But bedtime stories, by definition, are half-assed bullshit with no effort involved, that are considered more successful if they are boring. So the idea of a feature length bedtime story is an insult. They don't make feature length versions of the sketches on that "*Whose Line Is It Anyway?*" show, do they? I mean it's kind of like if Walt Disney Studios made an animated movie about bathroom graffiti. "You don't get it. The drawing is bad because IT'S BATHROOM GRAFFITI. It's not SUPPOSED to look good. It's a shape scratched into linoleum, possibly a dick. You snob critics don't understand the magic of a dick carved in a door."

Look here Shyamalan, you wanna tell us a bedtime story, then come to our house and tell us a bedtime story. We'll be thinking, "Oh shit, I can't believe M. Night Shyamalan, the famous movie star, came to my house and told me a story!" We won't hold it to a high standard of entertainment and storytelling. We'll think "that's cool that he would do that." When we pay money to see it on a big screen, though, we'll expect you to put a little god damn elbow grease into it. Please.

This is the story: Giamatti's whimsically named character Cleveland Heep spots somebody in the pool at night, but he slips and hits his head. He wakes up and Story the Pantsless Sea Nymph has rescued him. She wants to go home (the pool?) but when he tries to carry her out there he gets chased by a wolf made out of grass. Instead of asking her "what's up with that?" he goes and asks one of his tenants, whose mother knows a bedtime story about the world of the Sea Nymphs but she only speaks Korean. So throughout the movie she keeps translating to him the rules of the magical sea world: the nymph appears to inspire a writer to change the world, then she has to go back and get picked up by a giant eagle but there's a wolf that tries to eat her but also there's three evil monkeys who try to stop the wolf. Various apartment tenants have parts in bringing her to the pool to get picked up by the giant eagle, he just has to figure out who's who for it to work. Then he figures it out and a giant eagle picks her up and BAM! WRITTEN, PRODUCED, AND DIRECTED BY M. NIGHT SHYAMALAN, GENIUS.

I don't know why Cleveland doesn't ask her to explain what's going on until halfway through the movie. Then when he finally does she says she's not allowed to talk about it so instead she answers questions in sign language. Then later she starts telling him stuff without sign language and nobody seems relieved or surprised at this development. I also don't know why, if she comes from the magic world of the sea in the swimming pool, the way to get home is to fly into the sky with a giant eagle. Shouldn't she just jump back in the swimming pool?

Maybe that's the big M. Night Shyamalan twist ending. She needs to get home to the swimming pool... BY FLYING AWAY FROM THE SWIMMING POOL. Look at that man, M. Night just blew your mind like a fuckin balloon.

The last time I saw a giant eagle in a movie it was *Lord of the Rings Part 1* I believe. And that was a movie where you could tell they weren't making it up as they went along. They planned out the world in intricate detail. They knew what this world was and it all made sense and seemed like reality and sure as fuck didn't use half-assed fantasy creature names like "narf". I mean come on man, "narf?" That's really the best name you could up with for magic pantsless sea nymphs? I had faith in you Shyamalan. I think you're due for a Bruce intervention.

You know what this is, this is one of those half-assed fantasy movies they had in the '80s, like, I don't know, *Ladyhawke* or some shit like that. I'm sure some kids will see it and kind of like it because it's corny as hell and talks about magic. And then years later they'll remember it fondly because of the wolf and the monkeys. But then they'll catch it on TV and realize that's about five minutes of the movie and the rest is about people explaining things to Paul Giamatti. And they'll say, "Huh, I remembered that being a lot better. Oh well," and then they'll never think about it again. It is possible that one of these people will then go on to become president and change the world. But if so it would probably be a coincidence.

STAR WARS PART 3: REVENGE OF THE SITHS

Here's a couple topics I never want to hear about ever again: *Star Wars* started the era of the blockbuster. *Star Wars* was the first movie I ever saw and made me fall in love with the films of Cinema. I camped in line for thirty-two days to see *Star Wars*. *Empire Strikes Back* is the greatest sequel ever made, and also better than any non-sequel ever made. George Lucas earned ten billion dollars on merchandise. I hate Ewoks. I love Jawas. (Or is it the other way around.) Originally there was a part where Hans Solo shot Jabba the Hutt with a harpoon but now they changed it so a robot bit Luke Skywalker on the leg. George Lucas ruined my life. I have a tattoo of Hans Solo. I had all the *Star Wars* dolls now they are worth one hundred and sixty-two dollars on E-bay if somebody would buy them, which they wouldn't. The first time I ever jerked off was to Princess Leah in a metal bikini. I have nightmares about the part where Jar Jar stepped in space shit. George Lucas touched my childhood in the bathing suit area.

For years there's been a cliché about trekkies who like *Star Trek*, how they're obsessed nerds and they gotta get a life and etc. And I agree but somehow I think the trekkies for *Star Wars* are worse. Because at least the *Star Trek* trekkies are obsessed with something they LOVE. Now days the *Star Wars* trekkies seem to be defined by hating ewoks, hating jar jars, hating computer effects, hating George Lucas's neck, hating the prequels, the Anakins, the special editions, some of the originals, themselves, their parents, and orphans. I mean there's six *Star Wars* movies and if you're a REAL fan it's only socially acceptable to like 2 of them. But that 1/3 of *Star Wars* (or more often the other 2/3) is their whole god damn life. Go over there on the ain't it cool news talkbacks, and every god damn topic turns into how they been wronged by George Lucas. *Lord of the Rings is good, take THAT George Lucas. I enjoyed such and such movie, which is more than I can say for GEORGE LUCAS MOVIES, are you listening to me George Lucas?* The article could be about the translation of Kinji Fukasaku's *Battles Without Honor and Humanity* series, it would still come back to how George Lucas would've screwed up the translation if he was a guy who translated classic Yakuza movies instead of a guy who directed space movies every once in a while. And there is a 300% chance there'd be an ass-rape metaphor in the discussion. Even in real life these fuckers are crawling all over the place. Just the other day I heard a guy announce emphatically, "*Phantom Menace* is quite possibly THE worst piece of crap that George Lucas has EVER made." You could tell he got really worked up about it — I thought the dude was gonna start crying.

Well luckily, this *Revenge of the Siths* is the last puzzle piece for *Star Warse*s so give it a seven or eight year cool down period and maybe the nightmare will be over, and these ponytailed assholes will fixate on some other god damn thing, like the *Lord of the Rings* prequels or something. What we got here is the best of the newer *Star Warse*s in my opinion, one where you only gotta forgive a couple scenes and you actually get to enjoy the rest. This one has a better, more emotional story, the main guy Anakin is a better actor, and they got Darth Vader in there. I mean facts is facts, Americans love a picture with a Yoda or a Chewbacca or a Darth Vader in it, and this one's got both.

I admit, I was soft on the other two. I realize there are some real howlers in there, but who gives a fuck. There's enough detail and imagination in this spaceland, and the whole feel of the thing is different enough from any other movies that exist that I was willing to give it a whirl. I'm not saying you gotta enjoy it too or that I don't feel dirty in the morning but they really didn't bother me the way they did to anyone who ever wrote anything on the Internet. This new one though, honestly, it's a lot better. Except for one part where Darth Vader, in the full iconic costume, looks up to the sky in anguish and yells "NNNOOOOOO!!!" which will probably be the butt of nerd jokes for generations to come.

One thing I liked: they actually made Anakin into kind of a cool dude here. Before he was a whiny kid who talked in bad love poems but now he's got cool '70s hair and a scar, he does some dashing derring-do or whatever it's called, and he's got a dark streak. A pretty big one where he ends up murdering children. Which I'm against. The exact moment of the switch from good guy to bad guy is a little bit iffy but the story is surprisingly convincing. There's a lot of different complicated motives for it that tie into the events of the other movies. I guess what made me realize it was working was when I caught myself rooting for this guy to figure out what's going on and make the right decision. I mean I had a pretty good idea it was gonna turn out bad. (There's other movies that take place later where he's Darth Vader, for those who don't know.)

Also, I liked his relationship with Obi Won. I mean there's a little scene early on where the robot R2 fucks up and almost gets them killed. And Obi is about to complain about it but Anakin gets in his face and defends his boy R2. Because these two go WAY back to the days of bowlcuts and podraces and he's got R2's fuckin back. They're like brothers. Same goes for Obi and Anakin, but they're a little more like the brothers in *Gummo*, they fight sometimes. But they're still brothers so you gotta feel bad when they end up trying to kill each other and one of them (I won't give it away) ends up face first in the mud, on fire, with both legs chopped off, gargling "I

HATE YOU!!" in anguish just before being turned into Darth Vader. This is a tragedy by the way. Kind of a bummer, even in space.

You can never underestimate the whining and negativity of people who like movies, but my guess is some of the trekkies will actually like this one. This is the first movie I've ever seen where the audience applauded a hallway. There was a hallway that I believe was also seen in the original *Star Wars part 1*, now called *Star Wars part 4*. So everybody clapped. A real crowdpleaser as far as hallways go. There's one big opportunity that Mr. Lucas missed out on though, and that is to kill Jar Jar. I think we all know that if Jar Jar died in this movie, it would create joy and thunderous applause in every theatrical screening. Of course, it could've ended up Jar Jar dies heroically saving babies. Maybe it's better you don't make a god damn martyr out of the guy. I was also kind of afraid he'd be there for the birth of Luke and Leia (note: they are the main characters from the original *Star Wars*). Jar Jar would be saying: "Pusha! Pusha!" and then maybe "Looksie! Yousa has twinsies!" Instead, Lucas pretty much abandoned Jar Jar, showing him in a couple scenes but no lines. So it turns out Jar Jar lives which means that in the later movies, when a battle is waged to save the universe from Jar Jar's fuckup in the senate in part 2, he doesn't bother to help out. Fuckin figures.

I only seen this movie once but as far as I could see there was only two scenes to really be embarrassed of. One was the "NNOOOO!!!" scene I mentioned before and the other one had Anakin and Podmay in an apartment together talking that kind of forced soap opera dialogue that part 2 is renowned for. But otherwise this one is a lot stronger and faster paced than the last two. There's a ridiculous amount of detail in these battles like some kind of where's Waldo come to life. But at the same time they make you care about what's happening with the individual characters, even the robots. And they got some smartass dialogue going between them for a while, before children are being massacred and amputees are being burned alive. Before all that mess it's the kind of feel that fans love the *Star Warses* for. So they're probably gonna hate this one.

I gotta say though as a movie watcher, you fuckin *Star Wars* trekkies should be grateful for getting a part 3 this good. Who ever heard of a part 3 that's better than part 1 and 2? Not fans of *Blade, Alien, The Godfather, Halloween, Scream, Superman, Batman, Texas Chain Saw Massacre, Friday,*

Night of the Living Dead, Hellraiser, Wild Things, Cruel Intentions, Jurassic Park, Naked Gun, Beverly Hills Cop, Rambo, Robocop, The Terminator, Tremors, Vampires, The Crow, etc. *Friday the 13th 3-D* was probably my favorite though, 'cause it was in 3-D and has the best theme song. So I guess *Revenge of the Siths* is the *Friday the 13th 3-D* of science fictional movies.

Well shit, you know me, I gotta talk about the politics for a minute. When I reviewed the last one I talked about how nobody was acknowledging how much the political events of the movie reflected what was going on on Earth. Well this one obviously has to continue with the story of the end of democracy in skywalkerville. The pervy chancellor who announced "I love democracy!" in volume 2 is now being even more blatant about his power grab. When he makes a crazy speech to the senate about how he's gonna make the republic into an empire and kill everybody that's allegedly after him, what happens? Everybody claps! Sound familiar?

Of course it does (hint: space story = exactly what is happening in America, except with robots.) I honestly believe that this is not based on what's going on in our country right now. I think it just happens to be what's going on in our country. The story is based on the cycle of how all democracies tend to end. It follows inevitably from the stories in the other new Star Warses and to what happens in the older Star Warses. I'm sure most of this aspect of the story was probably made up in the '70s or '80s. But a funny thing is happening: this time people besides me noticed. There was even early word that this was a "Bush bashing movie" and I saw a couple right-wingers complaining about it on their "blogs" (or websites as I call them, because "blog" is a stupid god damn word that will hopefully die quickly like "dotcoms" and "webzines" and other "buzzwords"[47]). I like that some of these guys are noticing. Our government does the same things as the evil empire in *Star Wars*, but it's the *movie* that's bad. Not the evil empire. The movie is unfair to evil space villains.

Obviously a lot of people in the US aren't gonna be able to watch this movie without catching on to that parallel of a scared republic losing track of the values they once stood for, letting them be perverted. But maybe

---

47 Still waiting on that one. It could happen.

there's a *Star Wars* trekkie out there somewhere cursed with a poetic soul who will see it as a symbol of Lucas losing track of what made the original trilogy good. I don't know but I got a question for you *Star Wars* trekkies that I can't figure out. The question is what the fuck is your problem with ewoks. More specifically, why do you hate ewoks but not other lovable furry creatures such as chewbaccas.

This movie has some scenes on the planet of Chewbaccia where the chewbaccas live. Chewbaccas are like a far more lovable version of ewoks. They live in trees and have cartoony primitive tools just like ewoks, but they are much taller for hugging and they love people instead of growling at them and trying to cook them on a spit. Also chewbaccas do not bash people to death with rocks and logs and do not play drums on the severed heads of storm troopers. Chewbaccas are basically the kiddie version of the ewoks, for little babies who are afraid of ewoks just because they are cannibals. What I'm saying is you guys are a bunch of fuckin bigots. This is 2005 man, lay off the damn ewoks.

By the way I got a theory here about part 1 or 2 or whichever it was, when they got the E.T.s in it. As all trekkies know there is a scene in one of the Star Warses where they're in the senate, and in the corner of the screen you look closely using the pause technology and what you got is a delegation of the E.T. aliens from the movie *E.T.* Well at the time I thought this was sort of an "in" type joke but now that I've had five or six years to really seriously contemplate this scene I realized what's REALLY going on here in my opinion. You see E.T. — not just any E.T. but the specific character of E.T. we all know and love from the movie *E.T.* — he used to be a space senator. But that was a long time ago in a galaxy really, really far away or what have you. And the senate was dissolved when the empire was created. So now it's years later, 1982 or whenever, and the poor glowing bastard is flying around picking god damn flowers for a job. It's pathetic. So what I figure is, E.T. is always complaining about it. "I used to be Senator E.T. We flew around on platforms. I knew chewbaccas and everybody. I was like a god to girl E.T.s. And now this is my life, sneaking around at night picking flowers. I'm a fuckin migrant worker." Eventually these other flower pickers are gonna be sick of the senator's bullshit and take matters into their own long alien glowing fingers. What I'm saying here friends, is that the beginning of *E.T.* was no god damn accident. What I'm saying is, they left that fucker there for a reason. They WANTED Senator E.T. to be stranded on Earth. Because otherwise they had to fly back with him. And you know what happened though, my man learned his lesson by going through one of them inner journeys. He hit rock bottom. He learned how to party, getting drunk, dressing up like a girl, etc. He flew on a bike, he died and came back, he turned on his heart light, all because of the magic of a young boy's dream. And now hopefully he's gonna be a little bit less of a prick. It's like Scrooge in space. Only on Earth.

Anyway E.T.'s not in this one that I noticed so fuck him. The point is, *Star Wars 3* is a pretty good space movie in my opinion.

2001: A SPACE ODYSSEY

Lately I've only been reviewing current movies, but as you know, *The Hollywood Reporter* had a story the other day that MGM has hired a first time director to do a "re-imagining" of *2001* with "modern pacing and music" that will "take full advantage of state-of-the-art digital effects." The director is not someone I'm familiar with, but they say he is perfect for the job because he's done a lot of music videos and won a couple of Miss Clio awards for his commercials. So before they ruin it I thought I would revisit Kubrick's masterpiece of space ballet and shit.

No, don't worry, I'm just fucking with you. They're not doing a remake, as far as I know. But you almost believed it, right? Because it's so awful, so wrong, so undeniably vile, that someone is definitely going to have to do it eventually. They came for Hitchcock and Hooper and Romero and Carpenter and *Walking Tall* and *Amityville Horror* and *House of Wax* and they even tried *Billy Jack*. They already got *Charade* and *Planet of the Apes* and Dr. Seuss. They burrowed into the brains of Lucas and Spielberg and Friedkin and Scott and made them second-guess their younger, better selves. And now they've got their greedy bastard eyes on Kubrick. You fucking *know* they do. They'll wait until his assistant is dead and his assistant's grandchildren or whatever it takes, but the day it becomes possible, they dig out the contracts and they sign them in blood and they will swallow one end of *2001* and suck it down like one of those threads the yogis use and pull the entire movie out through the ass and into a paper shredder. You already know this, but I'm telling you this, because we need to get this out in the open, for our own good. We need to face the inevitable.

Actually I just saw the movie in 70mm at the 2nd Annual Cinerama "Reel" Film Festival here in Seattle and that's why I finally decided to review it. Sorry to bum you out. Actually it was a very positive experience. Imagine that opening with the eclipse and the mighty dun... dun... dun... *DUH-DUN!!!* as the curtains open... and open... and *open*, revealing the giant curved Cinerama screen that is way w i d e r than you expected. The movie is huge and the screen is huge. It gave the hairs goosebumps standing up on my balls or whatever the saying is.

What this picture is about is there are these monkeys during the dawn of man. There are also warthogs and they are all scavengers who eat the meat of the dead. But there is a cheetah who kills them sometimes and eats them. Also there is a baby monkey. Later on they wake up and there's a big rectangle that they touch. So then it occurs to one of the monkeys, what about tools. And he starts to hit a bone against other bones. You know, tools. So then I guess he kills a warthog and they all eat the meat and I bet it's more fresh than usual. All because of tools.

Well I fell asleep so I never found out how these monkeys get into space, but I guess you could pretty much see where it would go from there. There is the moon and Jupiter, for example, and a space baby that looks like Gollum. Dave gets locked out of the ship, and HAL won't open the door. It's like when the kids locked Bernie Mac out of the house for the whole episode and kept spraying him with the hose.

No, I'm just yankin your chain again, actually I didn't fall asleep but I trust my readers to know what *2001* is without me having to explain it to them like a bunch of fuckin space babies. What I will do here instead is try to talk a little bit about what makes this picture so god damn amazing. And I think the best way to illustrate it is to try to picture some alternate dimension where Stanley Kubrick is a living filmatist without a lot of clout, trying to release this movie today. Can't you just hear what the executives would say?

Mr. Kubrick, we think you have a great picture here. The special effects are dazzling and groundbreaking. You will be taking sci-fi fans to places they have not seen before. However, we also feel that there are a few changes that could be made to tighten the pace and to make the story more absorbing.

We know you are very close to the material so it is hard to see, but there is a lot of unnecessary and repetitive information which slows down the story and takes out the sense of adventure necessary to attract today's audiences. One of the basic rules of filmmaking is this: if a character walks all the way across the room after a scene, you don't have to show the entire walk. Just show him begin to walk, then cut away. Cut out anything that is not absolutely necessary to the plot.

With that in mind, we would like to show you our new improved cut of *2001: A Space Odyssey*, which clocks in at 102 minutes, a running time that worked very well for us on *Agent Cody Banks*. The picture opens with a short prologue about Dr. Floyd arriving at the space station, going to the moon and investigating the monolith. (We cut the Dawn of Man sequence, which we found confusing and unnecessary to the plot.) The editing is tightened but we were able to leave in some of the dialogue-free shots that you enjoy. We also improved the "monolith" scene with an evil cackle and eyes to show that it is evil. Also we cut to a quick clip of the cheetah jumping on the monkey from the dawn of man sequence.

We did not understand the tangents about classical music but if they are important to you we would be happy to include them as deleted scenes on the DVD. Also we are very close to signing Seal and Beyonce for a duet on the end credits. We'll send you a demo soon.

The movie is really about Frank and Dave and HAL 9000, so that's the section of the movie we have focused on. This section is very strong and we have been able to spruce up the sound effects and music (we felt some scenes were too quiet). Also we tightened the pace for more tension.

The psychedelic sequence has been trimmed for brevity and retimed to a song by Crystal Method. We have also taken the liberty of hiring Renny Harlin to direct a new ending which ties all the threads together. Frank wakes up from his "star child" nightmare to realize that he has been rescued by Dr. Floyd and his team. They explain how they discovered just in time that the monoliths were an alien device which was being used to control HAL 9000. This leads into the thrilling climax where the star fighters destroy the monoliths in a high-speed intergalactic battle!

Okay, I think you are bored with my point by now but you have to admit that it's true. Everything that makes this picture so great is also everything that studios say you can't do in a movie. You can't make long scenes where nothing happens except movement and classical music. (It's like *Fantasia* in space!) You can't make the movie about monkeys at first and then about space. You can't make an ambiguous ending that people will still wonder about decades later.

Yes, I would like to go on record as saying that this *2001* is a movie that I think is good in my opinion.

CHAPTER TEN
FILTH AND SLEAZE

Okay listen up. This particular chapter is not for squares or the weak of heart. It is not for youngsters, the elderly or old timey gentlemen with monocles. If you sometimes use phrases such as "Well, I never!" or "My goodness!" or have ever filed a complaint to the FCC, or considered filing a complaint to the FCC, or if you feel that it would be justified for somebody to file a complaint to the FCC, I want you to skip this chapter. Especially if you are a relative, neighbor or co-worker who's just reading this to be nice so you can say "hey Vern, good job on your book," then I beg you to skip to the next chapter. This is not something you want to read. You will lose respect for me.

The fact is that I'm proud of these reviews, I got a couple in here that I think are some of my best. But the movies they describe necessitated the use of, you know, some salty language. Some disturbing imagery. Some adult situations and scenes of sensuality. Some crude bodily function humor and non-humor. I mean these are mostly documentaries, but they're not documentaries about penguins or Amelia Earhart or something like that. This first one, Zoo, I don't want you to even know what the movie is about, let alone read my review of it. I think I've already said too much.

Or the second one, The Aristocrats, that is not the cartoon about the cats. It's a documentary about a long obscene joke. I had to explain the joke for it to make any sense and I had to go to extraordinary lengths to make my version more tasteless than the ones in the movie. So it's just all-out disgusting, inappropriate horribleness.

Seriously, some of these movies talk about things you don't know even exist, and you don't want to know they exist. I don't want you to know they exist. Me, I passed through that threshold a long time ago, so I can watch and discuss filth like this. But you are still free and you should keep it that way.

I know it sounds like I'm trying to brag or be funny here, but I'm not. Do not read this chapter. Forget it exists. Thank you.

ZOO

Seriously though, do not read. Turn back now.

Zoo, directed by Robinson Devor, is a movie you might've heard of when it played Sundance last January. For some reason it had a very limited theatrical run, it was not really given the same chance a *Spider-Man* or a *Shrek* would get to catch on with the public, but fortunately THINKFilm releases the DVD September 18th.

I really liked Devor's first movie *The Woman Chaser*. That one, *Cockfighter* and *Miami Blues* are the only movie adaptations of my favorite writer, Charles Willeford. Patrick Warburton is so good playing a bored used car salesman turned desperate embezzler/nihilistic independent filmmaker that I have a hard time not picturing him as the lead in other Willeford books as I'm reading them. I can't recommend that movie enough, but unfortunately it's never been released on DVD, and good luck finding the VHS.

What I didn't know when I saw that one was that the director was somewhat local. He apparently splits his time between L.A. and Seattle, where with local writer Charles Mudede he filmed his second and third movies, *Police Beat* and now *Zoo*. Based on a true incident in the small town of Enumclaw, *Zoo* is mostly set in the outlying rural areas of the Puget Sound region, the camera floating dreamily through barren farms, glimmery blackberry bushes and beneath ominous cloudy skies. But the central character, called "Mr. Hands," works as an engineer for Boeing, so there is some footage of him on a balcony looking out on Seattle proper, the home of John Wayne's McQ, Bruce Lee's grave, me, and I guess Frasier. The cinematography by a guy named Sean Kirby is excellent, and he shows Seattle not as a postcard of the Space Needle, but as a menacing explosion of buildings springing from the earth between water and mountains. This is my Seattle, this is how the city should be shown.

Oh— except for one thing. I forgot to mention. (SPOILER.) This is a movie about horsefuckers. Or I guess horsefuckees, if you want to get technical. The plight of the horsefucked. Requiem For a Guy Fucked To Death By a Horse, pardon my French. I'm trying to be a gentleman here but if there's a polite way to say "fucked to death by a horse" they never taught me that one in school.

You know, when a daddy and a special horse love each other very much— No, sorry, I just don't know how to do it.

So in that sense, no, it is not the most positive portrayal of the region. Speaking for myself only I would say that the guy getting fucked to death by the horse was not one of the prouder moments in local history. Your mileage may vary. I don't know what the governor's stance is on it or anything but that's just me, I'm against horsefucking.

You know how they have those different quarter designs they're doing for each of the fifty states? I thought it would've been pretty badass if Washington State had had the balls to put Bruce Lee and Jimi Hendrix on our quarter. It would've been EASILY the coolest quarter and all the other states would've been jealous. Instead we just did a picture of a fish jumping out of water, which kind of bummed me out.[48] But in retrospect I should be happy we didn't go with a guy being fucked to death by a horse. That would've been an embarrassing quarter.

Anyway, maybe they should've lied and set *Zoo* in Chicago or San Diego or somewhere. I've lived in Seattle for years and the only horses I've seen were ridden by cops. I have never ONCE seen a horsefucker. So don't get the wrong idea. This is not representative of Seattle. It's all on Enumclaw. Horsefucking capital of the west.

---

48 I mean, I get why it's a fish. People love our seafood and everything, so we're a fish. But then Alaska came out with their quarter and guess what it shows? A bear *eating* a god damn fish. Can you believe that? Alaska's quarter eats our quarter. They never would've tried something like that if it was Bruce Lee instead of a fish. Sonny Chiba defeated a bear in a movie one time and I have no question in my mind that Bruce Lee could defeat Sonny Chiba. Logically it follows that Bruce could defeat a bear and therefore would be impervious to being chomped on by some other state's quarter. If you ask me Washington DC has the best quarter of anybody, theirs just has Duke Ellington on it. That was smart because no other state is gonna have a bear eating Duke Ellington on their quarter. Maybe Duke Ellington *riding* a bear. But then it would not be an attack on the Washington DC quarter, it would be more of a companion piece. They wouldn't look like chumps like we do, getting eaten by Alaska.

Zoo is an unusual centaur type hybrid of documentary and re-enactment. The entire movie is narrated by audio interviews of the actual people involved in the incident, the horsefucked as well as the horse rescuer who was called in to figure out what the hell to do with a horse that fucked a guy to death. She loves horses too, but in a platonic way. There was another recent documentary narrated by tapes of Kurt Cobain, but they had to do that because he died. In this case they had to do it because nobody's gonna invite cameras to follow them around talking about having sex with animals. Well, probably for a VH-1 reality show but not for an independent film.

The filmatists cleverly avoid going in the obvious directions. It's not really a freak show or a shockumentary. They even tastefully avoid the goldmine of uncomfortable black humor that faces, say, the hospital workers who have to slowly piece together why this patient has a perforated colon and why the guy who brought him there took off in such a hurry. I read an interview with Mudede where he mentions some pretty funny things that were left out of the movie, such as the horsefuckers talking about rejecting a potential new horsefucker because he was "a total freak," and also them complaining about the low quality of their home farm sex videos. So there is some real restraint here. Anybody can make jokes about horsefucking (see: this review) so it's actually more shocking for the filmatists to go the other way. I honestly think they're trying to get a rise out of you by being tasteful.

Like anybody (I hope), when I heard this story I could not even imagine what the hell kind of person does that shit. It's hard to even picture them as human beings, let alone regular people you might encounter in your daily life. Some weird scary Michael Berryman-looking redneck out there in Enumclaw, maybe. But the movie depicts Mr. Hands, the dead guy, as a city boy. He's a successful engineer in Seattle, the re-enactor is fairly handsome and usually shown wearing a tie. He's divorced, but has stayed close with his ex-wife and is very proud of his son. In fact, he's trying to bring the family together, and his ex-wife and kid are in town visiting at the time of his death. Which is pretty befuddling — he's entertaining guests but he finds time to slip over to Enumclaw for a poke from the ol' giant animal schlong? It's weird how the more details you fill in the more mysterious it becomes.

But the animal molesters are humanized, and the photography even makes them kind of glamorous. The camera slowly pans around, focusing on the poetic imagery of the setting, often shrouding their faces in shadow like characters in a film noir. They meet at a diner and go by their Internet handles like "H" and "The Happy Horseman." They could almost be *Reservoir Dogs*, except their crime is a little less understood by society than stealing diamonds and shooting people. They point out that bestiality was not a crime in the state of Washington until after this incident. I think they saw that more as progressive legislation than as an "oh come on, nobody's gonna do that" type loophole. They just see themselves as a bunch of guys who like to hang out together on a farm, make some drinks, talk about their lives, and then maybe on a good night go out and, uh, let the livestock mount them.

It's so non-judgmental, in fact, that one guy, "Coyote," was willing to play himself in the re-enactments. (The horse rescuer and some of the other non-animalfuckers do the same.)

I'm not sure if I can say I *liked* this movie, but I thought it was very well made and morbidly fascinating. I thought there were only two real fuckups, really. At one dramatic point in the movie they suddenly cut to a dude sitting on a stool in front of a white background, telling a story directly into the camera. You think "Holy shit, is this one of the actual guys? Who is this guy? Why is he willing to be on camera?" He turns out to be the actor who plays "Cop #1" in the movie, and he talks about getting the part and then tells an unrelated story about seeing a kid die. I appreciate trying out a weird idea like that, but it doesn't work, they should've cut it. Worse is a short burst of pretentiousness at the end of the movie where they throw in some quick shots of explosions and some guy whispering about math as Mr. Hands wanders naked into the horse field. That's kind of the pretentious bullshit I expected when I read reviews of how "poetic" this movie is, but really that was the only part where it was too much for me. (I even liked the opening psychedelic light show that turns out to be somebody's flashlight or something.)

You ever see that *Onion* article about Marilyn Manson going door-to-door trying to shock people? That's sometimes how I feel about Charles Mudede, who is credited with "story and research" for *Zoo*. Mudede has written for *The Stranger* (the less corporate of Seattle's two free weekly tabloids) since 1999, where he reviews movies and does the Police Beat column that inspired his movie of the same name. I've read a few pieces I really liked by him, but a lot more that I hated. His main interest seems to be to provoke people by coming up with some completely preposterous angle on the subject that would never occur to any other human being. In his reviews he makes any legitimate insights useless by tying them to some historical, philosophical or literary context seemingly picked out of a hat or by rolling Dungeons and Dragons dice. In movie reviews you never have to agree with the reviewer, but you probably do have to see where they're coming from. If we can understand horsefuckers in a movie we should be able to understand the writer of a review. When friends of mine first started noticing and complaining about Mudede I honestly believed that his reviews were a put-on, that they could not possibly be serious. His thoughts on almost any topic would somehow be related to the traditions of ancient societies, a line from the communist manifesto, Russian literature or some other topic he studied in college.

Take for example his review of Takeshi Kitano's *Brother*, where he dismisses it as "Kitano's weakest film yet," then launches into what appears to be a comical parody of New York film critic jerkoffery: "The next gem worth noting is the matter of Kitano's Hegelianism. Hegel was a 19th-century German philosopher who believed that human history had basically three stages: primitive (African societies), despotic (Asian societies), and democratic (Europe). *Brother* presents this order of history, but now in the form of a gangster class order..." etc. etc.

Over the years Mudede has toned down some of those "hey everybody, look at me!" tendencies. But that doesn't stop him from semi-regular reviews like the one where he pretends to find meaning in *Bratz*.

It can't be denied that *Zoo* is in some ways an extension of that kind of obnoxious college-professor-meets-Tom-Green approach to expression. What could be more "you gotta be shitting me" than a movie that hints at being pro-bestiality from behind the hypnotic drone of a haunting arthouse documentary? Fortunately, the movie is put together really well and there is a bit of a switch up near the end, where we move from the perspective of the horsefucked to that of the horse rescuer. When she shows up at the ranch with the dead man's brother she describes meeting one of our narrators who was "very obviously deeply involved" and who she saw as a "creepy child molester type." Then we hear the guy she's talking about bitterly complain that the rescuer "doesn't know her ass from a hole in the ground when it comes to horses." (Oh for God's sake, use the hole in the ground this time. Please, horsey, fuck the hole in the ground.) But it's kind of a relief to be violently yanked from the lull of the poetical horse lovers' POV and back into the world of the poor suckers who had to suddenly find out what had been going on on this ranch. (One scene depicts the grey-haired owners of the horse throwing up after sitting with police watching a video of the incident.) And I'm sure audiences must've gasped when the miniature pony ran in and... well, you'll have to see it.

What is the value of exploring the guy who was fucked to death by a horse? I'm not sure. It is probably more of an, uh, interesting story than an important one. They show how the Internet brought together a community of freakos that never could've existed in the old days. Reminds me of the time I accidentally found out about adults who wear diapers and pretend to be babies. Or the guy that gets off on photoshopping the gals that dress up as Pocahontas and Cinderella at Disneyland to make them look giant. I don't care if you like to make out with lobsters or suck on jump ropes, whatever sicko garbage gets you hard you can make a club for it on the Internet. For these guys it's all those popular sex with cattle blogs that brought them together. And once they are no longer alone in their secret shame, but are part of a secret shame club on Yahoo, they start getting big ideas. I don't think they ever specifically mention gay rights, but they try to paint their plight as similar. They argue that they have a pure, simple, primal love with these animals, one that we who have chosen to keep our assholes free of horsecock cannot possibly understand.

(Incidentally that reminds me, shoulda mentioned this earlier but no kids should be reading this review. Go to bed kids this is grownup talk.)

So it brings to mind that old anti-gay rights argument "if you allow people of the same sex to get married then some dude will want to marry his dog/horse/box turtle." I always thought this was a funny comparison. Number one, two men — let's say Dolph Lundgren's character in *Blackjack* and his faithful assistant — happen to be of the same species, and they can communicate with each other. That is not true of the fictional guy (we'll call him "Turner") that is gonna make an honest woman out of his dog ("Hooch"). Number two, you REALLY honestly think some guy is gonna try to marry his dog? Or, say, a gorilla who knows sign language, if society demands that they must be able to communicate? He's gonna bring his ape into the courthouse and apply for a marriage license? This, in your mind, is a likely scenario? Well, okay then dude. How bout we cross that bridge when we come to it?

I am tempted to delete that last paragraph just to avoid the worst talkback of all time, but that would be dishonest. This is definitely a topic the movie directs you toward. I'm guessing at least 60-70% of you are with me, and are against horsefucking. But the movie forces you to ask yourself why, question your instincts. Which is uncomfortable but it's not a bad thing.

And one conclusion I came to is that, despite what they say in the movie, these guys don't really believe they made a soulful love connection with these animals. They just like to have giant horsecocks in their butts. The reason I know this: they literally have buckets full of homemade bestiality videos. You even (horrifyingly) see a tiny glimpse of what I assume is the real video of the fateful incident. And we're not talking Andrew Blake here. We're not even talking *One Night In Paris*. They just shine a light on a guy's ass and do a closeup as he's being slain by a giant horse dick. They are not in love, they get off on it, they like watching it, they know other guys who will watch it on the Internet. That is not a mature relationship there, fellas. Blackjack would never do that. So their argument is pretty phony, it's a rationalization. In my opinion.

That was pretty brave, wasn't it, how I took a stance against horsefucking just now. That's just what I do man, I make the tough calls.

One diabolical thing they do in the movie, they play some talk radio clips over some of the footage, and one of the clips is of Rush Limbaugh disagreeing with the animal rights activists who said the horse didn't consent. So Limbaugh becomes the voice of the pro-horsefucking movement. I think they should use that in the advertising and turn it into a political issue:

"No matter which side you are on, you gotta see *Zoo* for yourself. It's the movie everyone is talking about. See it for yourself and make up your own mind on being fucked by a horse!"

Zoo is about the furthest thing from what you imagined when you first heard about this incident. It shows the whole thing from a completely fresh angle. But there is one thing I thought when I first heard the news story that this movie only reinforced: I am not going within ten miles of any horse, ever. Get the fucking things away from me. I don't care if it's Seabiscuit or Mr. Ed or a heroic horse who saved orphans and piloted the first manned (or horsed) mission to Mars. I don't even care if it's a girl horse or a eunuch horse. All horses are bad news. I might even stay away from glue and dog food for a while.

If any horses are reading this: NO means NO.[49, 49a]

That review was posted on The Ain't It Cool News and spawned one of my more notorious talkbacks. Of course there was lots of horse puns and joking around but then a guy calling himself "Equinas" showed up to "post a few enlightenments" about "the zoo community." He gave a brief history of pre-Internet bestiality and railed against the "douchebags" making sex with animals a felony in Washington state. I tried to make polite conversation:

ME: Equinas — Thanks for all the info, I didn't want to know that. Er, I mean I didn't know that. I wonder what the secret codes were in the back of magazines? I'd hate if some poor bastard tried to order some *Mr. Ed* videos and wound up in over his head.

Did you happen to catch *Zoo* yet? I'm curious what you thought of it. Because it sounds like you are more familiar with the horsecock topic than most people. I'm assuming you did a report for school or something?

EQUINAS: Vern, you could say I've done a lot of "research"', but it wasn't for report-writing purposes. ;)

ME: Oh, for scientific research or something. I get it.

EQUINAS: Something like that!

Equinas came back for days, responding to many points, debating anyone who

---

49 A lot of people asked me why I said "NO means NO" and didn't go for the more appropriate horse pun, "NEIGH means NEIGH." The reason I didn't use that is because I'm not Gene Shalit. This is a serious review and I didn't want to cheapen it by ending on some silly pun.

49a Okay, I'm totally lying. Actually I just didn't think of that for some reason, and will always regret it.

came after him. He admitted to looking down on chickenfuckers, but only because he believes it hurts the animals. What made it disturbing was the same as the handsome Boeing engineer in the movie: this guy apparently had sex with animals, yet was obviously intelligent and eloquent (if not necessarily convincing) in his arguments. People like you and me, our brains are not prepared to process the existence of a person like this. It messes with our perceptions. It doesn't fit with our stereotypes — in fact, he himself made derogatory statements about "inbred hillbillies"! In response to accusations of mental illness he said, "I'm happy, successful, and have an active social and professional life." And I believe him.

There's no way to know, but I'm convinced this was a real bestiality-practicing individual defending his lifestyle. I was worried by mentioning a gay rights parallel in the review that I would bring out some frustrating homophobic arguments, but I never suspected there'd be a one-man–against-the-world debate about the ethics of sex with animals. I guess that just emphasizes the movie's point about the internet making this sort of thing more likely. It's amazing what they can do with computers these days.

Also one talkbacker named "GimpInMyPants" criticized me for writing a long review that discusses the setting and author of the movie, so I rewrote it Entertainment Weekly blurb style just for him:

ZOO (THINKFilm, $29.95, available September 18th). Talk about a horse of a different color! Director Robinson Devor combines poetic imagery of the Pacific Northwest with taped interviews to discuss a notorious incident involving horses. Is it for the squeamish? Neigh! Also it has no setting or writer so don't worry. I love that show *Lost* it's so great! What about that new Kanye single!

THE ARISTOCRATS

This is a whole documentary about one single joke, so let me tell you what the joke is. I am not a good joke teller but this is the joke.

Some guy walks into a talent agency, says look mister can I please have a moment of your time, I got an act here and I think you will agree it's gonna knock your fuckin socks right off of your ass. It's a family act, I got my wife and my kids involved and what not, real fancy, etc. So the talent guy says okay, you know I got a couple minutes before I have to meet somebody, you got two minutes to give me your pitch there asswipe.

So the guy says well you know we come out, my wife is playing piano real soft, we got these matching uniforms — I got some glossies in my billfold here if you want to see em, they got sequins and everything. And I come out and I balance on one toe on top of the piano while she's playing, right? And she's real good, kind of a ragtime style but she puts her own spin on it you know? Then my kids come out, they're teenagers but they're wearing diapers right, and this homeless guy has them on a leash, and they're carrying magazines in their mouths, like *Motor Trend, The Economist*, stuff like that. I got subscriptions to these magazines already by the way, I don't expect you to provide anything, we have all the equipment already. Just so you know. Anyway they put the magazines down in front of me and I look at the pictures and I just start jerking off all over my wife's hair. So then my wife stands up and just takes a shit all over the keys of the piano and smears it all over, and smears the cum all over it with her hair, and then the kids start playing a duet of the theme from *Rocky*. Not 'Eye of the Tiger,' the actual theme by Bill Conti. Then the homeless guy pulls out this mason jar full of brown recluse spiders and lets them loose, and they're trained to crawl all over us, right. And we all start pissing all over each other, and shaving each other, and smearing the spiders and hair around. And then you know, I don't know if you've seen that movie *My Neighbor Totoro*. Well my wife has a costume of the neighbor Totoro, but it has an asshole on it, and this Shetland pony comes in from stage right, there's kind of a real classy sort of reddish orange lighting at this part, very moody and atmospheric you know, so anyway the pony starts just fucking away at the Totoro. And in the movie there's these little girls that are trying to visit their mother in the hospital, well my kids make little sculptures of the girls from the movie out of all the shit and hair and dead spiders and everything. They're good sculptures too, I mean my daughter is better at it, my son's actually looks kinda like a snowman or something but he's getting better at it. Anyway we got the shit dolls on sticks and then they act out the end of the movie except in this version the pony is fucking the Totoro up the ass. I mean don't worry, it's only a small pony, we're not talking no Enumclaw shit. Well I guess medium sized because actually, I mean the pony's name is Maximus, he's pretty large for a pony but, you know. Not as big as a horse, it's not that bad. Anyway, point is we got it timed so exactly as the pony cums, these red white and blue fireworks go off, and we dedicate the whole thing to the victims of 9-11.

So there's kind of a pause there and the talent agent looks at the guy, says, "Wow. I mean I never— I mean, what do you call an act like that?"

And the guy says, "The Aristocrats!"

I know, I don't get it either, but that's the joke the movie's about. Some of the people in the movie make it funny, some of them admit it's not a very good joke. Everybody has a different variation on it. Only the setup and the punchline are the same, but everybody makes up their own filthy, offensive act, usually involving shitting, incest and dogfucking. Because you're not supposed to talk about that stuff, so obviously that means it's hilariously funny. Ha ha ha the guy from *Full House* is being naughty. The premise of the movie is that different joke tellers "riff" on this joke like a jazz musician or one of those new hippies they got that noodle on a fuckin guitar all day at some outdoor campout musical festival. "It's the singer, not the song" the movie argues. And nobody argues back, because who the fuck cares. It's an interesting topic though and there's a lot of funny variations on this horrible joke, lots of laughs during this documentary.

I don't think this is as good of a movie as people will tell you it is, though. Although the laughs eventually win out, the movie did get on my nerves at times. For example, the opening five or ten minutes are an extension of the obnoxious "Get in on the joke!" advertising campaign. "There's this joke... the first time I heard the joke... every comedian knows the joke... nobody has ever told the joke to an audience... the first time Phyllis Diller heard the joke she fainted.... the joke the joke the joke jokety jokety aristocrats aristocrats aristocrats aristocrats look at us we know it you don't know the joke the aristocrats aristocrats aristo—

So if you were at a screening where some crazy guy yelled out FOR THE LOVE OF CHRIST JUST TELL THE FUCKING GOD DAMN JOKE then, well I never talk during movies but I wouldn't be surprised if somebody did that. And the movie keeps that smarmy, insidery tone throughout. Acting like they are doing us a big favor, letting us in on the elite top secret comedian shit they learned from the Aztecs. And it has this reverential tone toward any semi-recognizable comedian, from Robin Williams to Drew Carey to that bureaucrat that almost gets Ripley killed in *Aliens*. They get Chris Rock on there for about twenty seconds but he doesn't comment on the actual joke, he seems to be saying that only white people care about a stupid joke like that. I think Whoopi Goldberg is the only other black person in the movie, which is too bad because I bet Rudy Ray Moore could've told the joke better than any of these motherfuckers.

Don't get me wrong, there's a lot of laughs in the picture and I'm being extra hard on it just because I heard so much about it ever since it's been playing film festivals. But at the same time, they do got a guy that makes wacky faces. They do got a ventriloquist that says racial slurs and calls you a cocksucker — *there's* an act with a lot of dimension.

interlude

"So you said you were a performer?"

"Yeah, yeah, I'm a ventriloquist."

"Oh, a ventriloquist. Hm."

"Oh no, don't worry, I know what you're thinking. But I'm not like those regular ventriloquists, like a magician or something. I'm an underground ventriloquist. I'm part of the alternative ventriloquist scene."

"What's— how does that work? Is that still with puppets?"

"Well, not puppets. We call them dummies. But yeah, I mean it's totally different though. See, my dummy is an asshole and says fuck and cunt and stuff like that."

"OH! Okay, ha that's funny. Cunt. I thought it was some lame vaudeville thing."

"Oh no no no, not at all. Don't worry, I get that all the time."

"Ha, 'cunt.' But a puppet says it. That's hilarious. Let's go have sex now."

Anyway, so Sarah Silverman is pretty funny, and George Carlin's in there, but it's not exactly a perfect comedical pedigree in my opinion. I mean they end with fuckin Tim Conway. I'm not joking. Emo Phillips also. Carrot Top. All the top guys. Yakov Smirnoff is missing but I bet he'll be on the DVD. Him and Weird Al maybe do a commentary track.

The most interesting part of the movie takes place at a Comedy Central roast for Hugh Hefner. I think I remember seeing this thing but what you see in the movie is the parts they cut out. It was in New York, less than a month after 9-11, when people still weren't sure what to laugh at or what to joke about. Gilbert Goddfried makes a couple 9-11 jokes and the audience is pissed, they're apparently booing and yelling "too soon" (we only hear a description of this part, I guess the cameras must've been turned off) so suddenly he shifts gears and decides to push it in a different way. He tells the aristocrats joke to the audience, something that the movie previously said had never been done because it was such super freemason secret higher echelon top secret black ops stuff that only Drew Carey and the ventriloquist who says cocksucker know about. And the guy from *Full House*.[50] But strictly those guys, backroom top secret off the record meetings in the basement of Giggles. And make sure you weren't followed.

Anyway it's interesting to watch Gilbert Goddfried win over this audience by speaking horrible obscenity at a television taping. The movie kind of ruins it though by having an overly reverential interview with some guy from the *New York Observer* or something talking about watching the faces of the comedians who are in on this unbreakable universal bond of comedian brotherhood. And for some reason, even though Gilbert Goddfried is interviewed for the movie, I don't think they have him talking about telling the joke. They treat it like it's the Beatles on Ed Sullivan or the discovery of penicillin but they don't bother to ask the guy who did it. (Unless I'm forgetting. Correct me if I'm wrong.)

At the beginning of the movie somebody compares the telling of the

---

50 I should be clear here, when I say "the guy from *Full House*" I'm talking about the dad, Bob Saget, who played a real square on that show but is also a standup comic who is overly proud of freaking people out by being obscene even though he's the guy from *Full House*. I am absolutely not talking about the other comedian on the show, Dave Coulier, who did the Popeye and Bullwinkle voices all the time. That guy would never tell this joke because he is the founder of the cleanguys.tv website and his gig posters promise "100% of your daily allowance of clean comedy!"

joke to jazz musicians, and specifically to John Coltrane. And not too much later, somebody else mentions Coltrane.

And I thought okay, that's interesting. I wonder, would anybody else like to draw a comparison between

a. John Coltrane burning through your soul with 'A Love Supreme' or 'My Favorite Things'

and

b. the guy from *Full House* telling a joke about shitting and fucking a dog and raping little kids

Anybody? No? Nobody wants to get to strike three? Okay, good. You know what's best for you, I guess.

So the movie didn't strike out and I would recommend this picture. Unless it sounds bad to you, in which case you shouldn't bother. I don't give a shit, man.

p.s. it is probably better with a large audience. I was at a sparsely attended matinee where one guy was laughing his ass off and kept clapping, making me uncomfortable. Is it just me or is it kind of weird to clap when there's nobody there? I mean it's not like the director is there, it's not like Tim Conway is there, it's not even like the ventriloquist dummy is there. And it's not some big communal experience where we have all been cold cocked by a surprisingly great movie and we spontaneously explode into applause as an expression of our shared delight.

Or maybe we did and I just missed it I don't know.

p.p.s. "What's the name of your act?"

"GG Allin and the Murder Junkies."

HATED: GG ALLIN AND THE MURDER JUNKIES

Supposedly this is the highest grossing student film of all time. It's only about fifty minutes long and it's a documentary about one of the shittiest and most unlikable rockstars who ever lived. But it's great entertainment. The film was directed by Todd Phillips, who went on to do a controversial HBO documentary called *Frat House* and then the teen comedy *Road Trip*.

In that one there was some dude who put a mouse in his mouth and that was supposed to be the ultimate grossout. Well obviously the individuals who said that haven't heard of *Hated*.

You see when I said GG Allin was the shittiest rock star who ever lived I meant that literally. One of this dude's trademarks was that he would take a shit on stage and then wipe it all over his face and ass and throw it into the audience and etc. Or one time he takes a banana and sticks it up his ass and then mushes it up and throws it out there. Basically, he is like the most mentally illest motherfuckers you ever come across in the correctional system, but with a microphone.

Now this guy had a small but very dedicated following of troubled alcoholic punks. And obviously they weren't in it for the lyrics. But he was able to tour and do small shows and live his life as an outlaw. Personally I think he gave the lifestyle a bad name but what can you do man. He kept his one pair of pants and one shirt in a paper bag and must have crashed on people's floors but god only knows how he bought food and drugs.

The documentary takes place when GG has just been released from prison and he agrees to break parole to go on tour so the film can be made. Every show he does seems to break into chaos in under ten minutes and end with this maniac pulling on his underwear and running from the cops or security guards all covered in blood and shit. Sometimes the fans jump on stage and kick the shit out of him. More often he attacks them, grabs some girl by the hair or punches some dude, then rolls around on the floor and starts shoving things up his ass. He says, "My mind is a machine gun, my body is the bullets, the audience is the target." Which means, "I throw shit on people." In his "spoken word performances" he does the same shit, he attacks people and cuts himself and then just starts calling everybody motherfuckers and robotic puppets of society.

I gotta be frank as well as honest, this great movie is not for the weak of stomach. And not just because there's a video of his birthday party where a gal pees in his mouth and then he pukes all over himself and then takes another mouth full of pee. Even if you fast-forward through that kind of garbage it is still very unpleasant to watch this dude. He is always naked and it is not a pretty sight. Even his tattoos are ugly as shit. I don't know what most people consider entertainment but it is probably not seeing a pudgy punk rocker strutting around all covered in shit, naked with his tiny little dick bopping up and down like a headbanging bumblebee.

I mean, the filthiest hippies in the world will probably hop into the shower after watching this movie. Not because they feel bad for watching it. But you don't want to take the chance that something splattered on you.

I wish I could wash the germs off from this movie but even the permanent mental damage, nightmares and emotional scarring it has caused me is probably worth it for this fascinating freak show. Phillips extensively interviews GG and his brother/bassist Merle (who is more reasonable but has a bald head with giant sideburns and a Hitler mustache) to find out what in fuck's name made GG this way. He goes back to GG's home town to play tapes of his music to his mortified high school band teacher. He even interviews a group of GG's high school buddies who are a bunch of idiot good ole boys who know a lot about guns and love jokes about wifebeating.

It is obvious that this illness came from somewhere, and you get a sense that it may have been passed on from his father, who often threatened to kill himself and his family and even started digging the graves in the backyard. GG is also able to share the madness with his fans who are not always just thrillseekers. Some of them seem to actually admire him and wish they also had "the fucking balls" to wipe shit all over themselves and eat it and threaten to kill themselves on stage on Halloween.

There are a lot of interview clips with a fan named "Unk" who is a smarmy looking guy with big black hipster glasses. At first you just think he likes GG because he's so crazy that it's entertaining. Then he tells a story about GG going to visit John Wayne Gacy in prison, and what Gacy told *him* about it the next week! And I'm really not sure whether Unk went to see Gacy because he was so fucked up he'd want to go visit Gacy, or because he was so fucked up he'd want to visit anybody that GG Allin had visited.

Jesus, the things that are popular these days!

The entertainment value is unbelievable. This is the most "HOLY SHIT!"

movie I've seen in a while. There is also a naked drummer who is as crazy, but less violent, than GG. And there is a former band member who quit not because he couldn't take GG, but because he was jealous of him. He keeps bragging about what *he* would do if he was GG (involving a mass cult suicide and/or presidential assassination) and about how it's not that big a deal to bash your head with a microphone. I would almost think it was all staged if I didn't see this fuckball shitting and then eating it in one shot.

As amazing as this documentary is, even more memorable is the "fifty minutes of bonus footage" on the DVD. This is a home video Phillips made of GG's last performance. Right after this video, GG had a drug binge and overdosed and died and then they put headphones on his bloated body and had a traditional funeral for him but the drummer was still naked when he helped carry the coffin.

I know right now it is considered cool to pretend you never liked the *Blair Witch Project*. Well I never even seen the fucking thing. But I think this video is probably more intense. There are only a couple of edits so you get to see first hand and in real time the incredible adrenaline rush caused by hanging out with this shiteating maniac.

The footage starts with the "rehearsal", where all the band members and the club owners are all swearing at each other about a soundcheck.

When the performance starts it is still daylight and they seem to be playing inside this little house. The hardcore fans and masochists are inside and there are others gathered outside looking in the door, for safety and hygiene purposes.

They only do about one and a half songs before the fighting and shitting and the tiny bumblebee dick start to be too much and there is mass chaos and apparently somebody from the club tells them they can't play. It is hard to tell exactly what's going on because the camera is shaking around, but if you listen to the conversations it sounds like the people who are there aren't exactly sure either. There is a European guy dressed in all white who at first I thought was the one kicking them out, but then I think he puts his hand up GG's ass. Not sure.

Then GG starts kicking things and whining "I wanna play, we came here to fucking play we wanna fucking play" and it's virtually indistinguishable from the part where he was playing. And there's this nutball fan who starts chanting "GG! GG! GG! GG!" At first I thought it was to be funny but it continues through the rest of the video. Turns out that former band member wasn't wrong about GG being able to be a cult leader. Something about a guy who wipes himself with shit, I guess, it makes people like you.

So then GG goes outside and this is when it really gets good. You see this concerned teenage gal who says, "GG, you gotta put your shorts on!" Not wanting him to get arrested. The fans start breaking some windows and GG is shaking his bumblebee dick in front of unfortunate passersby and you can hear Phillips behind the camera complaining that he got shit on himself, not from GG but from fans who GG threw it on. And then a cop car drives by and GG runs and hides and then his entourage starts to try to get out of there.

But a big crowd of fans follow them. They keep trying to get a cab, but what cab driver wants to help a bunch of punk rockers and a guy covered in shit escape from a small riot? And the fans are chanting "GG!" and GG goes back and forth between raising his arms in victory and telling them to fuck off.

This goes on for a long time until GG finally catches a cab and escapes to his destiny. Left behind, Phillips reconvenes with some of his buds to talk about how great the show was. There is a young gal who breathlessly repeats over and over "That was amazing! That was fucking amazing!" And for the first time you understand what the attraction is for some of these people. They know GG is a fucking nut, but when else can you experience that type of full on danger and nuttiness outside of prison, and for only seven bucks? It is similar to that thing they do in Spain or whatever, where the bull is let loose on the streets and everybody runs like hell. Same thing, only GG had no horns and a smaller dick. I think Phillips started making his documentary as a joke but when he got to know GG he experienced the rollercoaster thrills and maybe even got to convincing himself that there was something important about the way his act pushed the envelope.

Well, there probably wasn't. But they sure had fun watching that shiteater run from the cops and a hundred punk idiots while his friends say, "This is Beatlemania! This is Beatlemania!" and another guy says, "You better not get any shit on my pants GG!" and every once in a while GG starts bashing his head into a pole or something. That's what life is all about, man.

THE REAL CANCUN

Well somebody loaned me a *Run Ronnie Run* screener and it happens to have *The Real Cancun* on the same disc. Not sure what happened there but somehow accidentally I dropped the disc into the player and pressed a combination of buttons that caused it to play the movie and then also I watched the whole thing. It was weird.

What the movie is: the producers of *The Real World* TV show cast a bunch of rich kid morons in their early twenties and then paid them to go drink Jagermeister and high five each other in front of cameras. I thought it was funny that they called this a "reality movie" since they apparently are going for an audience that does not know that there is such a thing as documentaries. But after seeing it I realize that it's actually better not to call this a documentary. A documentary you find real people who are already doing something (pimping, selling bibles, living in subway tunnels, living in a house infested by raccoons, etc.) and you attempt to follow them with minimal interference in their actual life. This is the opposite where you find people and make them go do something. For example I do not believe that these kids, if they had gone to Cancun on their own, would've paid money to go bungie jumping and have a dolphin encounter and that type of crap. That was for Hollywood. The only major difference from *The Real World* is that they don't make them have a job and they use cameras that look more like film.

I wouldn't really recommend this movie but not because I'm embarrassed or appalled, just because it's not all that exciting. If you're just watching it for titties and what not I definitely would recommend many fine pornographical works over this. But it does have some interest as a horrifying cultural artifact. Not of authentic American culture as far as I can tell but of that bizarre virtual culture that only exists in the matrix of cable television.

Let me put it this way. If it weren't for MTV and the teen movies of the 1980s I don't think I would know that you're supposed to go to an exotic beach somewhere on Spring Break to try to get drunk and laid. Of course I've seen this a million times on TV but I can't think of anyone I know who has actually done this before or even considered doing it. Maybe it's a regional thing, I don't know. But that seems like something you have to be especially rich and stupid to do. When I was that age and younger everybody knew how to get ahold of cheap wine and if they didn't have a car to fuck in there was always such a thing as the bushes. Maybe if we wanted to get *real* fancy we would save up for a shitty hotel room for a night. Nobody ever dreamed of flying to another country *and* being able to afford a hotel.

But as far as this movie is concerned this is what 90% of all kids in their twenties do. Also the kids in this movie are young enough that they grew up watching *The Real World* and *Road Rules* and the various offshoots like *Real World vs. Road Rules X-treme Bungie Jump/Obstacle Course Gender Challenge Reunion — Jamaica Stylee 2*. So being somebody who tries to get laid on camera but not in porn is something they all aspire to.

My buddy Harry Knowles of The Ain't It Cool News made some good points about this picture and that "the real Cancun" is something you have to work for. You don't get free travel and hotel and unlimited drinks and bungie jumps and dolphins and assigned roommates. I mean maybe some of these kids would (there is one guy who talks about how he doesn't go to college because his mom supports him in doing what he wants to do with his life, which is shopping) but even then they would have to produce cash or credit cards sometimes and worry about if they were going to overdraw for the day and get shut off by the bank. Not these kids.

Also to my surprise that nutball from TV Richard Roeper made an interesting point that apparently this was taped at the same time the US was invading Iraq. So while these little fucks were watching wet t-shirt contests and drinking liquor out of girls' bellybuttons their peers were off being freedom fried by depleted uranium and dropping bomblets on innocent people. Now it's a couple months later, the Cancun kids are back home sad that they have to work for a living and waiting nervously for the release of the DVD. And some of those peers of theirs are still in Iraq, guarding nuclear waste, getting picked off in the night one at a time, wondering why the fuck they can't go home yet and getting more and more impatient with the growing chaos and anger around them.

The reason why this is interesting is because there is no mention of the war or the outside world in the movie. That in itself could've been an interesting subject for a documentary if there had been at some point a

TV on showing coverage of the invasion. Would the kids be interested? Would it interfere with their enjoyment of watching girls shaking their asses? Or would it not bother them? Since it's not mentioned we have no idea whether the kids even know what's going on or whether the filmatists purposely erased the deaths of thousands from their titties and Jagermeister epic, but I guess either one is pretty emblematic of something or other.

It's hard to be specific about the movie because, in the tradition of *Alien 3*, I can't tell any of these people apart. It tells their names at the beginning, but how the fuck you expect me to remember that. You don't get much about their personalities, their backgrounds or their hobbies. I know one guy plays guitar and sings wacky songs. There is a girl who says she has a boyfriend back home. That's about it.

There are attempts to discuss many issues. For example, should you be faithful to your boyfriend? What size of dick do you like? Should you wear your bandana on your head or on your wrist? They also use the term "hook up" a lot.

The closest thing to a main storyline involves the evolution of one kid, who knows what his name is so I'll call him Timmy. Timmy is the outsider to the Spring Break world, like us. Because he is from the Real Generation he is a postmodernist, and keeps referring to himself as "the good kid." He is very self-conscious of his role as the one guy who doesn't have giant muscles and a bandana. When he tells the other kids that he doesn't drink, they look at him like he just told them he masturbates to pictures of spiders. Completely bewildered. While trying to process this they don't say "Not even a beer?" or "Not even a wine cooler?" but "Not even one shot?" Because it's all about shots to them.

Of course, they immediately have bets about who can get him to drink a shot, and when they humiliate him into it, liquor suddenly becomes spinach to his Popeye. Or liquor to his Drunken Master. Literally seconds after he puts the shot glass down he announces that he needs titty. Suddenly he is more confident and has lots of fun. Women let him lick their cleavage and suck shots off their bellybuttons. When he didn't drink he got stood up and more than once punctuated a conversation with the awkward pronouncement "I want to see some booty!" Now that he's binging he's turning women down. He falls in love with a cute

French girl and even wins "the hot bod contest" despite his skinny frame.

(To be fair, it kind of seemed like he won the contest in the same sense that Carrie won prom queen. So there should be an asterisk next to that. Also, when you see how sad Timmy is to leave it's hard to not imagine a painful return to the actual real world now that he knows the excitement of hard drinking. Welcome to the club, kid.)

There's another story about a blonde gal who bungie jumps into the water and gets stung by a tourist-hating jellyfish. This was a great move on the part of the subversive jellyfish because according to the local doctor the only cure is for the girl to pee on her own leg. But she doesn't have to pee so in the most romantic moment of the picture, one of the bandana guys sees his big opening, he pees in a cup and pours it on her leg.

Well of course they become close friends and the guy obviously has ideas. I hope he at least cleaned off her leg first. Actually they are just friends because she has a boyfriend at home and she wants to be faithful. He keeps saying things like "I hope your boyfriend knows he has a great, great woman here." But on the next to last day of the vacation, she catches him fucking some chick in the shower and gets angry like she just caught him cheating. She yells "You had twenty-four hours!"

Maybe I'm just old but for me that brought up more questions than it answered. Was she testing him, and if he could go for one week with just being a friend then they would drop the boyfriend, clean off the pee and start fucking like dogs? Or was she just saying that if he had fucked a girl in the shower twenty-four hours later then it would've been okay because it would've been the last day? I don't get it.

At any rate he yelled back that he was hanging out with her all week and he couldn't wait any longer. Because god knows no kid can go more than five days without sex or their dick will explode. It happens every day.

Whenever there is fucking in this movie, it is under the covers. Whenever somebody says something, there is a high five. In one of the greatest moments in documentary film ever, a couple gets out of bed and high fives each other. Good game. Way to hustle.

You know the more I think about it maybe I actually did like this movie.

THE BROWN BUNNY

You probably heard what Vincent Gallo's *The Brown Bunny* is all about, and so did I. I'm not gonna pretend I didn't know what I was getting into. Obviously I've heard a lot about this movie since its notorious debut over there in the Cannes. Most people said it really sucked, it sucked the big one. They said Academy Award nominee Chloe Sevigny really blew it by being in this one. Doesn't matter if she did a good job, they said, because this movie really blows. They had a real hard time swallowing it. A real long, hard time. Also there is a blow job at the end I guess.

Gallo plays Bud Clay, a streetwise motorcycle racer who has just finished a fierce competition in New Hampshire. Now he has to get back to L.A. to have his bike tuned up by Renaldo (sort of his Q or Whistler), and only one thing can stop him: pining. He misses his former girlfriend Daisy (Chloe Sevigny) and he's on a mission to find her. The mystery leads him on a deadly trail from Daisy's parents house, to a pet shop, to a gas station, to a hotel, to another hotel, to Las Vegas, to another hotel, etc. Mostly down streets though. When I say "deadly," by the way, I mean "boring."

There is a lot of driving. A whole lot of driving. Don't worry though, he's in a van, not on a motorbike. The motorbike is in the back of the van. So his ass probably doesn't hurt as bad. He does have a hole in the ass of his jeans though, because that's the type of individual we're dealing with here, a guy who has a hole in the ass of his jeans. You know the type.

There's one scene where he does a little gumshoe business. Daisy's parents say they haven't seen her in years and don't know where she is, but they have her pet bunny. He throws his weight around in a pet store and finds out that a bunny can only live for four to five years. The bunny proves that Daisy has been at her parents' house within four or five years, probably less. The trail hasn't gone cold.

I guess I'm exaggerating to make it sound more Hollywood. He's not exactly pulling a Charles Bronson on this pet shop, he's just politely asking some questions about bunnies. The dumbest question: "Are these the bunnies?" I mean come on Bud, I think you can figure out whether or not these are the bunnies. There are ways of looking at different types of animals, examining their characteristics and discerning whether or not they are bunnies.

And by the way, yes, Daisy's pet bunny is brown. That's the brown bunny. It's not some shit like *he is the world's deadliest bounty hunter, on a cross country trip to the edge of the world. Those who know him call him Bud Clay, but those who cross him know him only as... THE BROWN BUNNY.*

I mean, we're not talking a situation where this guy passed out on the salt flats and discovered the brown bunny was his spirit animal. There is a pet bunny in the movie, and it's brown. (Though Mike D'Angelo of New York, USA swears that in an earlier cut of the movie he crashes his van and it blows up and a bunny hops out. No shit.)

I kind of liked Gallo's first movie as a director, *Buffalo 66*. In that one he played some asshole who just got out of the joint but has to piss real bad, and then you can imagine where it would go from there. Some of it's real pretentious and I could understand why people would hate it, because Gallo's character is such an asshole and it's a good performance because, let's face it, playing a whiny, sleazy, egomaniacal asshole is not the hugest stretch for this guy. In that movie there's a ridiculous scene where he's pissing at a urinal and some guy starts looking at his dick and freaking out saying "it's so big!" That was the most embarrassing scene in the movie and in this one Gallo takes his "I have a big dick" tendencies to the next level by actually showing his dick being sucked in the movie. (There are some theories that it's a prosthetic johnson, because he keeps his pants on and clutches onto the thing the whole time, but I think if it was fake he would've gone for more of a John Holmes size. In fact, considering who we're talking about here, he probably woulda had it three feet long with the girth of a tree trunk.)

Gallo's whole schtick could be called Asshole Chic. He's always gotta be unshaven and scraggly haired and dirty lookin with an oversized belt buckle and '70s shirts, getting in arguments and whining and shit. In fact the whole movie is made to look like the '70s except that they have modern Coke bottles and McDonalds wrappers and shit. So it doesn't take place in the '70s, it just takes place in a world where everybody likes to dress up like they're from a different era, like that dude from the Stray Cats.

In *Brown Bunny* you're probably supposed to feel sorry for him too, although in this one he loses sympathy right at the beginning when he convinces the young clerk at the corner market to drop everything and go to California with him, then ditches her while she's packing. The poor girl has already abandoned her post at the family store and left a note to her aunt and uncle explaining why she decided to run off with a stranger. Now you gotta figure she has to explain herself without even getting to go on the trip.

The movie is basically a series of awkward encounters with women like this. It is probably only a coincidence that the writer of the movie is also the actor who gets to make out with Cheryl Tiegs and get a blowjob from Chloe Sevigny. I'm sure he probably wrote it figuring some other actor would play Bud but then there was some mix-up and at the last minute he had to fill in. Anyway, in between the encounters you mostly get driving shots with an occasional hotel stop. Then he combs his hair or lays around on a hotel bed in his tighty whiteys. There's not a lot of dialogue. The only real back and forth conversation is with Chloe at the end, and half of that she has to talk with his dick in her mouth. (A cinematic first I'm pretty sure, at least for an Oscar nominee.)

At one point you're watching an extreme closeup of Gallo as he's driving, looking intense, his long bangs blowing around in his eyes. And it occurred to me, I mean just as one possible theory, that this motherfucker is pretty fond of himself.

The Asshole Chic aesthetic extends to the actual filmatism of the movie. Gallo's character spends most of the movie being sensitive and mopey, so it's the movie's duty to be an asshole to the audience. The very first shot of the movie is faded and handheld, a motorcycle race as seen from the stands. At first it seems like kind of a cool shot, and then you realize that it is gonna show you the whole damn race. Like somebody's expensive home movie. Even if it was your home movie, you would never go back and watch it. This guy actually put it in a movie released in theaters. At least half of the shots in the movie are like this, specifically designed to test your patience and taunt you. Picture a camera sitting on the dashboard of a car, filming the highway through a dirty windshield while a Gordon Lightfoot song plays. The *whole* Gordon Lightfoot song. That is a lot of this movie.

He stops to get gas and it's pretty suspenseful because you're really not sure if he's gonna squeegie the windshield or not. It turns out he doesn't, because then the driving shots wouldn't have all those bug splatters on them and it would really cut down a lot on what makes the movie so interesting. In Roger Ebert's famous review of the movie he talks about how at one point Bud pulls over and gets out of the van to change his jacket, and the audience applauded. That scene must've been cut out of this version though because I didn't notice it. Not sure why he'd cut out a real *Indiana Jones*-type crowdpleaser like that.

A reasonable person, specifically me, could also argue that *Brown Bunny* has kind of an anti-porn style. You ever see that cool '70s style movie poster they had, with the old fashioned XXX logo on it? I'd like to think some perv somewhere watched this really thinking it was an old porno. If so, that perv got Punk'd. It's got this amateurish blown out '70s look to it, and this greaseball goes around hitting on cute girls he never met and they are always into him. Every one of these scenes could lead to wah wahs and erotic moaning, but they don't. It's just one interruptus after another. At the end it finally turns into hardcore porn but as soon as he cums he calls her a whore and then rolls up into a fetal position and starts crying.

You know what it is, it's a fictional porno you'd see a poster for in a movie, but somehow it's crossed over into our world.

You might remember back when I reviewed *Last Days of Disco* I maybe had sort of a thing for young Chloe Sevigny, in some people's opinions. Of course I never figured I would see her doing hardcore sex, so, you know, Merry Christmas to me. On the other hand you gotta wonder how the poor gal got talked into doing this one. It's not like he's taking a risk. He gets one free blowjob (and you fucking know this prick insisted on lots of rehearsals) and you know, nobody's gonna blame him. The double standard is in his favor. Or at least, it's not gonna lower people's opinions of him. Put it that way. But poor Chloe, in addition to having to perform the act and put it on Superbit DVD for all eternity, was putting her career and reputation on the line for a small and purposely annoying movie. I'm not sure what she was thinking but luckily she seems to have made it through. Since then she's worked with Woody Allen, Jim Jarmusch and David Fincher. And not one hardcore sex scene was required.

I don't think the blowjob is important to the story, but it *is* important to the movie. Because it's the carrot at the end of the stick of the *Brown Bunny*. Everybody knows about The Blowjob and without its golden promise a lot of people aren't gonna sit through all this god damn driving. Without The Blowjob, we probably never would've even heard of the movie. The same critics still would've hated it but they wouldn't have been interested enough to make a big deal about it. Without The Blowjob all they can say is "It's so boring! He keeps driving!" With The Blowjob, people want to listen.

I forget which review I read where it mentioned that all the critics would've walked out, but they kept watching just to find out how bad it would get. Yep, that's the reason you kept watching. For informational purposes. Nothing to do with The Blowjob.

"Oh, this was the— BROWN BUNNY was the one with The Blowjob? Yeah, you're right, I knew there was some talk about a movie with that, I didn't make the connection that it was— I mean, ha ha, I just wanted to find out how bad it would get."

Why the fuck would a guy lie in a movie review? You're not on trial here. We don't blame you. Be honest.

On DVD the carrot at the end of the stick adds a new dimension to the endurance test. Because now you don't have to sit through the whole thing to "find out how bad it gets." There's even a handy chapter menu, you can skip to "Fidelity" and you're just about there. But if you're really tough, if you're really disciplined, you can watch the entire movie in order without even pausing. And I got no way to prove this but I swear to you, with my right hand on the Bible and my left hand on a biography of Steve McQueen that somebody gave me but I haven't read yet, that I actually passed the *Brown Bunny* gauntlet. I got all the way to the end in one sitting, without cheating. And it actually wasn't nearly as hard as I expected. Of course I am a veteran of *Garfield* but still, *Brown Bunny* is better than advertised.

I'm really not gonna recommend the movie to anybody, not as art and not as porn. But I cannot tell a lie and personally I did not think *The Brown Bunny* movie was all that bad. Sometimes egomaniacal assholes can make good movies, and this sort of in a way almost is one. It takes a unique approach, it stays completely committed to its goals, it has a blowjob scene at the end, etc. And seriously, it does come to a, uh, climax that makes some sense out of the rest of the movie, it doesn't just fizzle out. *The Brown Bunny* is an experience I will always remember. Well, mainly the part at the end, but still. I regret nothing.

Suggested alternate title: *THE LONELIEST MOTOR BIKE RACER*

SPECIAL SPOILER SECTION FOR *BROWN BUNNY* VETS: Man, I didn't expect that *Sixth Sense* style twist ending. But I gotta say it worked pretty good to tie the movie together. Of course, I got no idea why this dickhead didn't do something when he saw those junkies raping his pregnant girlfriend. But overlooking that it sort of redeems what comes before. One of those movies where you can imagine it would have a different meaning if you watched it a second time, even though you wouldn't watch it a second time. Anyway, another alternate title, considering the ending: *HEAD OF THE DEAD*. Think about it.

BAD LIEUTENANT

A guy I know told me a funny anecdote about renting this in the early '90s when he was a teenager. He said he got it at a tiny little mom and pop store in a suburb of Seattle. You don't really see stores like that now but they used to be around, especially in the '80s, before Blockbuster and Hollywood were everywhere. This one had a nice old man who ran it (the pop) and when this kid and his little sister brought up *Bad Lieutenant* the old man got excited. "My niece is in this movie!" he says.

"Really?"

"Yeah! Watch for the scene where he pulls over the two teenage girls. She's one of the girls!"

So, of course, if you've seen the movie you will remember the scene where Harvey forces one girl to show him her ass and the other one to pretend she's sucking a dick as he stands there jerking off and repeating "you ever had a guy's cock in your mouth? You ever have a guy's cock in your mouth?" over and over again. Well, don't worry, one of those actresses has a proud uncle.

That's right man, that Harvey Keitel is one bad lieutenant. I'm not talking about a baaaaad*ass* lieutenant. I'm talking about a coke snorting, crack smoking, heroin shooting, hard drinking, walking around naked, money stealing, lying, gambling addicted, n-word using, jerking off in front of some teenage girls he pulled over, spying on a naked rape victim, law enforcement sonofabitch. That would be a more accurate title but it's too long to fit on a marquee and gives away pretty much 95% of what happens in the movie.

I saw this movie years ago and thought it was a piece of shit, but after years of movie-watching training I have to admit I kind of liked it this time. At least for a while. The rawness of the acting, the minimalistic camerawork, and there's sort of a dark sense of humor to it when, for example, a cop is telling a crime victim to contact them with any details she remembers because "the sooner we get that over the radio—" and it cuts to Harvey listening to the Mets-Dodgers game that he has his life savings bet on. And we know all the cops are obsessed with this series and betting money on it. One of the central events in the movie is Keitel investigating the gang rape of a nun, but there's way more screen time spent on these playoffs.

After a while you get sick of seeing him going to different places and shooting up with different people, but especially in the early scenes it's pretty interesting to see how things unfold. I like the scene where some guy across the street is opening up the trunks of cars and Harvey's watching from across the street but he's on a payphone changing his bet. There's some obvious drug deals going on and you're not sure if he's gonna do anything or not. Then he runs over there and chases one guy into a building and up a couple flights of stairs but then the guy stops and sells him some crack and he smokes it right there. I guess this is not a lieutenant who chases drug dealers, except for show. Or looking for a bargain.

Keitel looks high out of his mind for most of the movie. He does at least fifty of those wookie-style yelps he did after Mr. Orange got shot in *Reservoir Dogs*. In one part he's naked, waddling like a penguin. Trying to settle a dispute between some young guys and a store owner who says they stole money out of the register he suddenly pulls out his gun and fires a bullet at one of the kids' heads. This guy is the biggest fuckup you've ever seen, but he has kids! In the hilarious opening he's driving them to school, yelling at them for missing the bus. They complain that their aunt hogged the bathroom and that was why they were late. Harvey says "she hogs the bathroom, come tell me I'll throw her the fuck out!"

By far my favorite scene though is near the end when he's starting to feel, you know, bad about being a coke snorting, crack smoking, heroin shooting etc. etc. and owing $120,000 to a bookie and everything. And he can't figure out why the nun says she forgives her attackers and won't tell him who they were. So he goes into the church and just starts blubbering and yelling at God for allegedly forsaking him. And he's high as usual so all the sudden he sees Jesus standing there. And he says to Jesus, "What!? You got something to say to me? Huh? You rat fucker! YOU RAT FUCKER! FUCK YOU!!!" etc. So as repetitive and as miserable of an experience this movie may be for most people, at least you are rewarded by the ridiculous sight of Harvey Keitel seeing Jesus and calling him a "rat fucker." If there is anybody out there who is in an acting class I highly recommend choosing this monologue for one of your class assignments. If not ALL of your class assignments.

As the bad lieutenant keeps piling up the bad behavior you start to wonder where the hell this could be going. Ultimately I think it's supposed to be a story about redemption. In the end he does break down and the way he ends up finding redemption is by not killing the nun-rapists when he finds them. He really wants to kill them, but he's trying to be a better person so instead he puts them on a bus out of town. So it's kind of a head-scratcher. In a way it's deep because that is true religion right there, to forgive somebody for something that seems crazy to forgive somebody for. But frankly I don't think not having an understanding of true Christian forgiveness is high on the list of Bad Lieutenant's faults. He's got bigger fish to fry in my opinion.

Man, I wish this was one of the movies they remade in *Be Kind Rewind*. Or maybe some kids somewhere grew up loving it and did their own remake. Or they could do an ill-advised stage musical of it. It lends itself better to a musical than *Grey Gardens*, that's for sure.

I probably shouldn't recommend this movie to anybody, ever, but in the irresponsible spirit of the Bad Lieutenant I recommend that every one of you see it immediately, preferably with children and grandparents in attendance. You will probably have a fun time and if not you will forgive it and put it on a bus.

CHAPTER ELEVEN
TALES FROM VERN'S BLOODY CRYPT OF PHANTASMOGORIFYING HORRORS

I don't know what it is about screen violence. In real life I'm a sweetheart, I swear, but a lot of my favorite movies have people getting beat up, shot or killed. I try to focus most of my cinematic scholarship on the action movies, because it's my favorite genre and the one I think has gotten most unfairly ignored by people who analyze movies. Horror has also gotten a bum rap at times, but always resurrects itself by going through cycles. First it completely dies out for a while, then a hugely successful movie pops up out of nowhere and inspires a whole bunch of similar ones (whodunit slashers, ghost stories, Asian remakes, '70s remakes, whatever). The pendulum tends to swing back and forth between watered down PG-13 horror (which makes everybody complain and ask why horror is for babies now) and brutal hard-R horror (which makes everybody complain and ask why horror has gone too far).

And who wants to debate porridge with Goldilocks? I think some of these arguments are pretty stupid, but overall horror in all its many incarnations has managed to inspire a lot of smart analysis and great books. I can't compete with decades of horror studies, but I can try to showcase the broad range of enjoyment I find in this genre. In this chapter I got a couple goofy sequels and lower-tier slashers, a couple serious spookfests, a widely hated video game adaptation that I thought was really good. I will also explain my "slasher movies are like the blues" theory (which I use for various action subgenres too), take a look at a couple critically respected movies that I think might be getting too much credit, and explore the morality of violent movies and derivativeness in the only review that ever got me challenged to a wrestling match.

PHANTASM II: LORD OF BALLS

There's actually not a subtitle on this one, I made that up. Anyway this is the first sequel, made eleven years later with the backing of Universal Studios. It's the year after *Evil Dead 2* but it's the same kind of thing Universal did later with *Army of Darkness*, taking a cult movie and its director, putting a little more money behind it and hoping to trick mainstream audiences into thinking they care. Nobody knows why they did it, but we're kind of glad they did.

The advantage of the Universal money is that they have some pretty good special effects. The disadvantage is that they have to ditch the original star, A. Michael Baldwin (a rogue Baldwin brother not related to Alec Baldwin), and replace him with James LeGros of *Drugstore Cowboy*. You know, for that guaranteed James LeGros demographic who will just go to any James LeGros movie over and over again, and get all of their friends to come, just to watch James LeGros. It's like the old Hollywood saying goes, don't ever make a movie that doesn't star James LeGros. Trivia: no movie has ever made a profit without James LeGros, and vice versa.

YOUNG HIP UNIVERSAL EXECUTIVE: Yeah, so it's the sequel to this low budget movie from 1979, it's a weird movie but it has kind of a following, people really were creeped out by this old man who says "BOY!" and by this metal ball. We got the old guy returning, and it's a little more action oriented than the first one, we have three different huge fiery explosions, and some really good effects, some weird monsters tearing out of people, and...

OLDER UNIVERSAL EXECUTIVE: Hmmm.

YOUNG HIP UNIVERSAL EXECUTIVE: I know it sounds weird, it sounds like a hard sell, but horror sequels are very popular right now. *Elm Street, Friday the 13th...* there is this whole subculture of people, they read *Fangoria* magazine, they idolize the guys who do the special effects, they know all about this director, Coscarelli.

OLDER UNIVERSAL EXECUTIVE: And it's about metal balls?

YOUNG HIP ONE: Yeah, flying metal balls with drills.

OLDER UNIVERSAL EXECUTIVE: I'm not sure this—

YOUNG HIP ONE: We just signed James LeGros.

OLDER GUY: Greenlit. Here is the money, I want you to drive directly to the set from here, do not slow down, begin filming immediately. *MOVE!*

No, I'm not sure why it is that they needed to replace him. LeGros does fine but I would've preferred a little continuity here. Other than the re-casting though this feels like pure Coscarelli. Remember how *A Nightmare On Elm Street* ended with a weird, reality-bending thing, it seems like everything is fine but then Freddy appears in what we thought was the waking world to yank Nancy's mom through a window? *Phantasm* has a similar ending where it turns out the whole thing was a dream, or so we think, but then the Tall Man comes out of Mike's mirror.

Unlike *Elm Street*, the *Phantasm* sequel actually continues from that ending. So I guess the first one was a dream, except the Tall Man is real. Or something. The movie starts by replaying the final scenes of part 1, Mike and Reggie talking about hitting the road, then Mike goes upstairs and has his mirror trouble. Reggie hears it and runs to get a weapon, only to get attacked by the dwarves (this time with an excellent animatronic monster face). It turns into a full-blown action sequence and somehow I didn't notice while watching it that they only show Mike from the back because it's a stunt double.

To pull the actor switch they skip forward many years. LeGros as Mike has been locked up in an institution, pretending he doesn't believe in evil morticians from another dimension turning corpses into four-foot tall monster slaves. But one day when Reggie comes to visit he finds Mike has snuck out to dig up graves. It seems like Reggie has somehow forgotten why he blew up his own house to kill evil dwarves, so Mike re-convinces him and they blow the joint, becoming a pair of badass drifters in a muscle car, following the Tall Man's trail throughout the northwest, trying to put him out of business. They're like the hunters in *Vampires* or Blade, going around with various power tools, finding weird monsters and blowtorching them. Meanwhile Mike has prophetic dreams and a telepathic connection to a blond girl having Tall Man problems of her own. When the girl gets kidnapped I thought it would be like *Dracula* (the book — I know how to read) and they'd be hot on the trail using the psychic connection like a tracking device. But they don't bother.

The Michael and Reggie scenes seem to take the story from part 1 to the next level, but the early scenes with the girl sneaking around spying kind of rehash it. When they combine forces it gets better. They build more deadly contraptions (a booby trap made out of a beer can, string, and a hand grenade) and they fight more metal spheres. There's a new one that's gold, can burn through doors and has a buzz saw on it. Mike figures out how to throw the balls as a weapon. He even captures one and uses it as a key to get into the portal room.

This is interesting because it proves the balls are just machines. If we understood how they worked we could learn to use them safely. In fact, if we knew how they worked we could really use that technology for the betterment of our civilization. Obviously some asshole would want them for the military, send them into Pakistan or some shit. But forget about the blades, this is some sort of a self-propelled flying device. It can hover. It can fly in perfectly straight lines at varied speeds with no apparent wings, jets, propellers or audible motors. Who knows what powers it? It might help our energy crisis, it might not. But surely applying this technology to vehicles would have a game-changing effect on the amount of pollution we put in the air.

If he wanted to, the Tall Man could stop global warming. He wouldn't even have to do it as an act of interdimensional kindness. He could take out the patent and become a trillionaire. And he'd be a hero. But the Tall Man will never do that because he's a zealot, a "dead ender," unable to let go of his backward, abusive way of life. The only way we can fix this is to go through that portal and change the hearts and minds of the

Phantasmiacs. We've got to show them a better way than their slave-based economy. Until we destroy the demand for dwarf slaves the Tall Man will always need our dead bodies. And if he needs dead bodies he's not gonna give a fuck about global warming. It only makes his job easier. Plus it probably reminds him of the windstorms and scarlet skies back home.

Coscarelli was friends with Sam Raimi, and *Evil Dead 1-2* definitely seem to be an influence. There's a great metal ball POV shot that chases the heroes and breaks through doors, just like the Evil Dead spirit in part 2 I believe. More importantly they sort of turn Reggie Bannister into a tongue-in-cheek badass like Ash. He's not as arrogant but he's memorable because he's a man's man but he kind of looks like Clint Howard. He's not some square-jawed hunk and he doesn't try to hide his baldness, not even by shaving the sides. The baldness doesn't stop him from getting laid, in fact it helps. The car doesn't hurt either. Or his skill with a chainsaw.

Phantasm II: The Secret Mortician's Other Ball is not a great sequel like *Evil Dead 2*. But it's a good one.

FREDDY'S DEAD: THE FINAL NIGHTMARE

So here we are. The VERY LAST time we will ever see Freddy Krueger. Dead forever. Never, ever again will he appear in a movie of any kind, because this at last is the end of him. It says it right there in the title, twice. He is dead, and this is the final one. And what a journey it's been. But thank God we have this precious last eighty-nine minutes to spend with him.

I don't know if all the New Line Cinema people were wearing funeral clothes when they made this, but behind the scenes it was kind of a family affair. Director Rachel Talalay had been working on the Freddy pictures since part 1, usually as a producer. This was her first time directing — she later did *Tank Girl*. She's also the only woman to ever direct a Freddy movie.

The writer was Michael De Luca, who was New Line's president of production for years, so you will recognize his name from all kinds of movies during the height of the company, like *S7v7n* and *Boogie Nights*. Before this he had written the god-awful movie *Lawnmower Man* as well as five episodes of *Freddy's Nightmares*.

In the beginning of the movie the crazy ticket-taker is played by DeLuca's boss Robert Shaye, who is best known for refusing to pay Peter Jackson the money he was owed for *Lord of the Rings* and then spending New Line's last dime directing *The Last Mimsy* (Mimsy's Dead: The Final Mimsy). Before turning the keys over to the landlord Shaye gave Jason and Freddy to Michael Bay's company. Too bad he doesn't get killed in the movie.

Freddy's Dead is also notable for some weird cameos: Roseanne and Tom Arnold as crazy people who try to forcibly snuggle and adopt the teen protagonists, Johnny Depp as himself (or his dead *Nightmare 1* character?) on a TV anti-drug PSA, Alice Cooper as Freddy's adopted dad, the Harlem Globetrotters as the employees of the shelter for homeless teens where some of the movie takes place. (Okay that last one is a lie, but it would've been a good idea in my opinion, I am pretty good at casting.)

In the role of "guy who gives the movie unexpected credibility" is Yaphet Kotto as the dream expert. This was only two years before he started in *Homicide: Life On the Street*. Also you got Breckin Meyer of the *Garfield* series of movies playing the stoner kid.

Now, you should probably sit down for this because it is shocking as hell, but in my opinion part 6 is not all that great. Still, I think Tank Girl and Blowjob Guy deserve a little credit for trying some weird stuff. For example they made it take place in the near future when Freddy has actually killed all of the Elm Street kids except possibly one who is rumored to still be alive. This is explained to us with an *Escape From New York* style map, and later when the teens and their social worker visit Springwood they notice that in fact there are no kids alive in the whole town, or at least at the carnival. They show a clown smoking a cigarette — at least somebody is able to take advantage of these tragic circumstances. Good for you, clown.

Also it seems to me that the physics of the dream killings has changed, so now the sleeping bodies are way more affected than they used to be. I know from part 1 on Freddy was able to carve into people's skin and there was at least one sleepwalking victim, but in this one it goes further. You see a guy getting knocked around like he's being beat up by an invisible fist. A guy who is walking up stairs in his dream walks up invisible stairs in real life. The best one is the guy who dies in a video game dream — his body bounces up and down like Mario, smashing his head into the ceiling. I'm surprised that didn't wake him up though.

Yes, there is a video game dream, and yes, Freddy does make a joke about his "power glove." He also has a line about a high score, which made me wonder how familiar he is with video games. I'm not sure when he was born exactly, and we see in some dream/flashback combos that he had a real bad childhood. But I'd like to think he had some peace playing pinball in a diner somewhere in his teens, and that's why he knows what a high score is. I think he was supposed to die in 1968 or something, way too early to be kidnapping kids playing Centipede at the local pizza parlor.

Anyway, as you can imagine the dreams all have stupid gimmicks like that. The stoner dies to the tune of 'Inna-Gada-Da-Vida,' etc.

We find out more unnecessary backstory — turns out Freddy had a wife who he killed because she found out about his murdering, and he had a daughter. Now we understand him so much more, don't we? Pretty deep. Alice Cooper, who wears a plaid shirt and holds a bottle of booze (characterization), beat Freddy when he was young, and Freddy learned to enjoy it. When he was younger he killed animals. The other kids in school were mean to him and called him "Son of 100 Maniacs." In other words, everybody's misused him, ripped him up and abused him. Another junkie plan, pushin dope for the man. You know, it turns out not all of the lyrics from 'Freddie's Dead' by Curtis Mayfield apply to this movie.

I probably mentioned this in an earlier review, but I'm not sure I agree with the biology of that "son of 100 maniacs" thing. I don't think that works out. Also I kind of wonder what the point of it is in this version of the story. He has the abusive non-biological father and the childhood pet-killing, just like Michael Meyers in the *Halloween* remake. Everything but the Kiss t-shirt. So that implies that it was a bad childhood that turned him into Freddy. But then the son of 100 maniacs thing makes it seem like it's supposed to be hereditary. He got it through genetics. Which is it?

Whatever it was that made him a psycho, we know from this one how he became a dream stalker. Turns out there are these flying stop motion worm monsters called Dream Demons who picked out the vilest most horrible human being they could ever imagine and gave him this power. Remember how Freddy was a child killer, he got off on a technicality, John Saxon and friends wanted justice so they went and burned him alive? Well, what John Saxon probably didn't know is that while they were outside making sure Freddy didn't come out he was inside talking to flying skull-headed snake things. He wasn't surprised to see them and told them "I want it all!" I wonder why they didn't mention this in any of the newspaper articles?

Toward the end Freddy comes into the real world and shows up in Yaphet Kotto's office, and Yaphet beats the shit out of him with a baseball bat. Unfortunately he didn't know to set booby traps, and a mere bat beatdown won't cut it for Freddy. But this does give Yaphet the idea to have the heroine fall asleep and dream, with a set time to wake up while holding Freddy so that they can kill him in the real world. This is also an idea he would've gotten from watching part 1. Of course, it didn't completely work in part 1 because in that last shot he seems to have outwitted them after all. But Yaphet has an idea for upping the ante — kill the fucker in 3-D FREDDYVISION!

So the big ending battle is done in eye-damaging red and blue 3-D, recreated in all its muddy glory on the DVD. It does look slightly 3-D but also looks as fuzzy as an eighth generation VHS bootleg. Nevertheless, I believe this movie proves that 3-D is the future of moviegoing. This is where James Cameron got the idea from. This will really keep the theater experience alive. Hopefully all of the Freddy movies, as well as less genre-oriented movies like *There Will Be Blood* and *Judgment at Nuremberg*, will be re-released with their final sequence in Freddyvision.

But even if Freddy's legacy lives on in the form of 3-D scenes that hurt your eyes and cause you to keep taking your glasses off to make sure it's still supposed to be in 3-D, I'm still gonna miss the deep fried old bastard. I know, I know, he was always killing people and he was just kind of annoying with all his stupid puns. So fuckin greedy about collecting souls. What was that all about? I know it's easy to just think of him as a total prick, but somewhere inside there he was also a human being. It's hard to understand there was love in this man. I'm sure all would agree that his misery was his woman and things. Things being his daughter and also the kids picking on him. You know what, now that I think about it this really is kind of based on the Curtis Mayfield song. He probably shoulda got a story credit.

CANDYMAN

This movie surprised me. Everything about it is classier than I expected. From his reputation you'd think this Candyman guy is just a B-list Jason or Freddy type. But it turns out he's more a classic movie monster like Dracula or the Phantom of the Opera. And his movie has more subtext than all of Freddy and Jason's pictures put together, including *Jason X*. Hell, throw in a couple *Child's Play*s too. And one or two *Halloween*s. And one *Silent Night Deadly Night*. No *Texas Chainsaw*s though, that would tip the scale.

You know why we have to deal with Jason? Because of some horny counselors not doing their job. Freddy, because of some overzealous parents who took the law into their own hands. Dr. Phibes because some doctors fucked up a heart operation. But we got Candyman because of a bigger reason: America's history of racist oppression. This is the only slasher/ghost movie I know of that deals with the legacy of slavery and racism (only *Blacula* comes close).

Candyman (who is never given another name) was the son of a slave who was an inventor of a machine used in the mass production of shoes (the shoe gin, I'd call it). Anyway that's Candyman's dad, but Candyman (who wears really nice shoes, come to think of it) was a talented portrait artist who fell in love with one of his rich white lady subjects, and for that he got lynched. Actually, not just lynched — they cut his hand off and rubbed honeycomb all over his face. Which explains why now, in ghost form, he has a hook jammed into his bloody stump and a beehive in his ribcage. Then they burned him and spread his ashes over what would become Cabrini Green, the notorious Chicago housing projects.

So Candyman haunts Cabrini Green, and race and class issues haunt the whole movie. The main character is some white lady (Virginia Madsen), who's working on a thesis about urban legends when she hears the story of Candyman murdering somebody in Cabrini Green. She decides it will make her thesis more interesting to go find out about this murder. And the whole movie has the tension of the upper class white woman going sticking her nose in other people's business. It makes you uncomfortable to see her bothering (and in some cases endangering) the black cleaning staff at the college, some poor single mother in the projects, and a little kid. And it seems like they're supposed to be impressed that she's working on a thesis. Good job, white lady.

The movie draws a parallel between "the bad part of town" and the haunted house from old movies. Her best friend, played by Kasi Lemmons (director of *Eve's Bayou*), says "I won't even drive past there." But together they go to the scary projects (filmed on location), walk past the gangbangers and drug dealers (played by the actual residents) and explore the abandoned, graffitied apartment where a strange murder took place. These ladies figure Candyman is an urban legend like the other ones they've studied, but Candyman begs to differ. The fact that Madsen is casting doubt on his existence forces him to "shed innocent blood." Because if people stop worrying about him existing then by some kind of supernatural technicality that means he won't exist anymore.

The famous thing is like the old "Bloody Mary" urban legend: look into the mirror and say "Candyman" 5 times and he'll appear. This isn't as big of a part of the movie as I expected. But I like how Candyman enters the world through the mirror and Virginia Madsen enters the apartments through the mirror. She discovers that one flaw in the cheap construction of the projects is that you can remove the medicine cabinet and climb into the bathroom of the apartment next to you. Writer/director Bernard Rose says that came from a real murder that happened in some projects. I don't know if it really happened or if it happened to his uncle's friend.

According to my math this movie came before the *Urban Legend* movies, making it *Urban Legend 0: Candyman*. It has the various spooky touches based on urban legends, the college professor giving a lecture on urban legends, etc. Everything except the suckiness.

There's a lot of things that make this movie stand out, like the score by Philip Glass, the creepy use of live bees, and the real fancy coat Candyman wears. But my favorite thing is that crazy shit happens that you assume has to be a dream, and then it's not. About halfway through the movie the white lady sees Candyman for the first time — he walks up to her in a parking garage, of all places. And then all the sudden she wakes up laying in a puddle of blood in the bathroom of the single mother she bothered in Cabrini Green. The mother is screaming in the other room and on the floor there's a bloody meat cleaver and the severed head of the lady's dog. Virginia picks up the meat cleaver and goes to investigate. She finds out the mother is screaming because there's blood everywhere and her baby is gone. When the mother sees Virginia obviously she assumes she killed the baby and she jumps on her. You'd think it couldn't get much worse than this but then Virginia fucks up by hitting the poor lady with the meat cleaver.

Even this far into the mayhem I was thinking this would turn out to be a dream or a delusion, but before I knew it she was at the police station covered in blood, crying and begging for a shower while she gets strip searched. Her cheating college professor husband shows up, horrified, and you have to laugh picturing some poor bastard cop having to explain to this prick how his wife ended up in jail.

So it really doesn't follow the standard formula of this type of movie at all, and it gets kind of surreal. There's some pretty brutal and gory death scenes but it doesn't have the kind of tension of a chase movie like *Texas Chain Saw* or *Halloween*. In fact Virginia Madsen never runs from him because when she sees him she gets hypnotized (they say they really hypnotized her in these scenes, no shit!) and then he does weird shit like open his mouth and bees fly out (he really put bees in his mouth!). So maybe it's a little slower than a Freddy or a Jason, but it's a good trade.

My one complaint is that you don't really know why people call him Candyman. There's one part where she finds a bunch of Halloween candy with razor blades in his lair, but if he was fucking with trick or treaters they must've cut that subplot out. We never see him carrying a bunch of candy in his pockets or anything. And I doubt he eats a lot of candy because he's pretty slim. Unless maybe he eats it but the bees in his rib cage digest it for him. Anyway, a guy with a huge bloody hook hand with a million bees crawling all over him and flying out of his mouth, I don't think anybody's gonna fixate on a subtle detail like he has a pile of candy on the floor. They're gonna call him Hookman or Hiveman or something. Candyman — that's just poor nicknaming. The only logical explanation I can think of is if his real name is Steve Candyman or something like that. But if that's the case they should've mentioned it.

THE GINGERDEAD MAN

get it, gingerDEAD instead of gingerBREAD

For hundreds of years, gingerbread has been a delicious and vibrant European treat. It was used to make soft cakes that would be drenched in hot lemon sauce and whipped cream, or for ornate candy-covered houses like the "witch's house" from the fairy tale Hansel and Gretel, or to form the shape of a small man, a reflection of its creator. As man is to God, gingerbread man is to man. And therefore also to God.

No one knows the origin of gingerbread, because how do you pin down something like that? I'm sure they could figure out who invented the McRib Sandwich, but not gingerbread. Some believe it came from the Eastern Mediterranean, and spread across Europe as soldiers came home from the Crusades. At least something good would've come out of the Crusades then. Wherever it came from, its ginger packs a powerful punch, so much so that throughout the 17th century you needed a license to bake gingerbread except at Christmas and Easter.

Perhaps the all time greatest gingerbread was found in Nuremberg in the early 1600s, where it was baked exclusively by an elite guild of master bakers known as the Lebkuchler. But even these highly trained artisans could never have foreseen *The Gingerdead Man* starring Gary Busey as the voice of the Gingerdead Man. The Lebkuchler knew that in fairy tales the gingerbread man is a little guy who runs fast, always on the move to prevent being devoured by man or beast. But there is one gingerbread man who refuses to run. This is his story.

Charles Band, who directed *The Gingerdead Man*, is the son of Albert Band, who directed *Zoltan, The Hound of Dracula*. So B (or lower) movies run in the family, but Charles has his own spin on it: he is a tinyphiliac. He's been making shitty horror movies about tiny little fuckers since *Ghoulies* in 1985. If there was a low budget movie about killer dolls or miniature vampires or some type of little guy like that then nine out of ten this weirdo had a hand in it at least as a producer. This includes but is not limited to the *Ghoulies* series, the *Troll* series, *Dolls*, the *Puppetmaster* series, the *Subspecies* series, *Dollman*, *Demonic Toys*, *Dollman vs. Demonic Toys*, the *Prehysteria!* series (tiny dinosaurs), *Shrunken Heads*, *Leapin' Leprechauns* and its sequel, *The Creeps* (midget Dracula, mummy and wolfman), *The*

Shrunken City, *Blood Dolls*, *Ragdoll*, *Doll Graveyard* and *Evil Bong*.

He didn't do the *Leprechaun* series though, or *Jack Frost*, or *Elves*. Until now he has stayed out of the holiday oriented little guys. *The Gingerdead Man* doesn't take place during the holiday season, but like its pastry namesake it is the perfect holiday treat for you and your family or church group. If they like crappy movies with funny premises.

The movie begins in turmoil as Gary Busey (not yet a cookie) is in the midst of an armed robbery at one of those charming old fashioned diners they have in small towns because they're so backwards and unsophisticated. (Or it might be a themed chain restaurant such as Johnny Rockets, who knows). Busey kills some guy, tries to kill a girl but misses, then he hears sirens, says "Oh, shit," and runs off camera in a way that makes you think he should've left a little puff of smoke.

Next we find out that he got caught and executed off camera. The girl he didn't kill, Sarah (Robin Sydney), now runs the independent Betty's Bakery, across the street from one of those Wal-Mart style corporate bakery monoliths that we all fear. A couple days after the execution a mysterious cloaked figure leaves a box that says "Grandma's Gingerbread Spices" at the back door of the bakery. This seems like an ordinary every day mysterious occurrence but actually it is an ingenious plan by Gary Busey's mother to avenge Sarah for testifying in court against her boy. The mother has surmised that if she leaves these spices, Sarah will mix them into dough, then her co-worker will accidentally cut himself and spill a bunch of blood into the dough, then she will still use the dough to make one two-foot tall gingerbread man and then while she bakes it there will be a power surge which will (as all scientists know) bring life to the bloody, ashy, gingery dough.

So the gingerdead man comes out of the oven, gets a knife, tries to kill them. It is basically a siege movie where they are trapped in this one bakery. Imagine *Assault On Precinct 13*, except instead of some cops and criminals trapped in a jail, it's some L.A. actors doing bad southern accents trapped in a bakery. And instead of a faceless army of gangsters attacking, it's one puppet (sometimes a guy in makeup) of a gingerbread man that occasionally shows up and burps or mumbles to himself in Gary Busey's voice. And then somebody makes a pun like "the Killsbury Doughboy."

There's really not much of a movie here. It's only an hour long, and that's including the long opening credits that I fast forwarded through. Gary Busey kills two people while in flesh, only one while in gingerbread. He does cover a girl in frosting (with cherries for nipples) but otherwise doesn't do much of note.

That might not matter if it felt like a real movie. Sometimes a movie with a premise this ridiculous can be fun just by treating it with (ginger)dead seriousness. But this is Full Moon Video. It seems more like an episode of some horrible children's TV show than a genuine independent horror movie. It's supposed to be in Waco but they don't even have any stock exteriors of anything that looks outside of L.A. The score is one of those awful non-stop circus music type keyboard deals they do on a lot of worthless DTV horror garbage. The characters are all annoying clichés made deadly through bad acting, the stuck up mean girl being especially difficult to watch. The one exception is actually Ms. Sydney, who seems to take the role of the heroine very seriously. She actually does a pretty good job in the scenes where her character is emotional, and when she's flirting with the thirty year-old twentysomething with the eyebrow ring, her eyes look like she's truly infatuated with him. She will probably go on to success on some TV show or something. You heard it here first.

The premise of the movie really makes no sense, and I'll tell you why. There's no such thing as "gingerbread seasoning." If you're Betty of Betty's Bakery then you fuckin know how to mix ginger and cinnamon, you don't just use some mysterious package that shows up claiming to be "gingerbread seasoning." In fact, if you type "gingerbread seasoning" into Google you won't get a bunch of gingerbread recipes, you'll get a bunch of reviews of this movie.

Other than that it's very plausible.

The funniest thing that happens is when a guy kills the gingerbread man in the most obvious way: he eats him. Or his head anyway. He really has to chew at it, and raspberry jelly gore comes out. The Gingerdead Man is surely the most delicious of all the horror movie slashers and monsters, although werewolves might not taste that bad, I'm not sure. Maybe leprechauns are good too, if they have some kind of minty shamrock milkshake type flavor.

But of course, just eating his sweet, sweet evil is not going to solve everything. The eater then becomes possessed by the Gingerdead Man.

You would think okay, this killer Gary Busey has had his soul transferred into a cookie much like the serial killer Charles Lee Ray was transferred into the Chucky doll. Now a guy eats the cookie so the Gary Busey soul is transferred into the guy, right? The whole Gingerdead thing is over and the soul moves on to a new body, right? Nope, that's not how it works. This guy's face turns all evil and his skin turns a gingerbread brown. He's possessed by a cookie! This is possibly one of the first three or four times this has happened on film so I at least give the movie credit for that.

I don't regret seeing the movie, it's short and it's funny to see them try to pass this off as a movie. But with some elbow grease it could've been a lot more fun. I would not be against a sequel, but they gotta get a better director and better production values for this to work. Even Charles Band movies, like *Puppetmaster* and shit, used to look like real movies back in the day. They were actually trying to make it work, none of this TV style *Power Rangers* bullshit. I want to see a group of soldiers on leave run into the Gingerdead Man. Or a cult of Gingerdead Men are living in the sewers of New York City. Or of course there's always the Gingerdead Man in space possibility. Just get a professional cinematographer, a composer who does not own any keyboards, and pretend you're really trying to scare me. And then we'll talk.

p.s. Thanks to Tony Tibbetts for recommending this movie multiple times. And Charles Band, you have my permission to use the first three paragraphs of this review as the opening crawl or back of the DVD box for part 2. thanks bud.[51]

HIGH TENSION (AKA HAUTE TENSION, AKA SWITCHBLADE ROMANCE)

This is another one of those heavily buzzed foreign imports that I put off watching forever. The final deciding factor, I keep seeing the trailer for a remake of *The Hills Have Eyes* which is made by these same Frenchmen.

---

51 Sadly, Band did not take up my offer to quote the review or to make a good sequel.

So I figured I oughta investigate, see what these guys are about.

High Tension is a well made throwback kind of slasher movie, but not as good as *Wolf Creek*. Similar subject matter though. Two young ladies, Marie and Alexia, go to visit Alexia's parents out in the French boonies. While everybody's in bed, some grunting redneck schlub (he looks like M. Emmett Walsh in an Ed Gein costume) drives up in a rusty truck, breaks in and starts killing everybody. Most of the movie — and the best part of the movie — involves Alexia being tied up and gagged in the back of the truck, while Marie chases the killer trying to save her.

So it's the kind of energetic, non-verbal chasing that can be fun when well directed. A cat and mouse game is what they sometimes call it. The clever thing is that for a lot of the game, the cat doesn't even know the mouse is there. She keeps sneaking around just out of his eye sight until she can find a way to save her friend.

Another twist is that these two are more than just friends, if you know what I mean. If you don't know what I mean, what I mean is Marie obviously has a crush on Alexia and Alexia doesn't know it. I like that they leave that unspoken, it seemed like a nice idea, although the way the movie ends up it seems like a pretty backward view of gay people. I don't know, maybe that's how they do it in France.

There's some pretty gruesome deaths in this one, and even a little kid dies. The first time we see the killer he's in his truck, getting a blowjob from a severed head, then he throws it out the window like a piece of litter. So you know right away that you're dealing with a classy movie. It didn't piss off critics as much as *Wolf Creek* did though, for two reasons. One, the look is pretty stylized, very nice photography but not realistic, and the killer reminds you of the killers in that disowned Sam Raimi/Coen brothers movie *Crimewave*. It's more of a cartoon. And number two, it's just not as good. You can't take it as seriously when it's not as scary. And it has a ridiculous plot twist at the end.

Some movies I might not mention that. Because sometimes just knowing that there *is* a plot twist ruins it as much as knowing what the plot twist is. But with this one, every single person who told me to watch it said "it's good, but there's a really dumb plot twist at the end." And I was glad they warned me because otherwise it would've been pretty disappointing when the fun movie went off the tracks and just became stupid. Ah hell, I'm just gonna tell you what it is since it's not that hard to guess either. Marie (who is shown in the opening to have some sort of mental problems) is actually imagining the killer, it is she herself who is killing everybody. Wow, what a mindblower, huh? There is no explanation for how or where she got this cool looking truck near her friend's house out in the middle of nowhere. Also I have to wonder about that severed head blowjob scene I mentioned before. Nobody saw this happen, and the guy who did it only exists in Marie's head. So what is this scene, exactly? A hallucination that she didn't see? I'm confused.

It's funny, because just by being simpler and more generic it would've been a way better movie. Slasher movies are a pure form, like the blues. You don't have to complicate them to make them good. Sometimes you can get away with it, like *Scream* if you like that movie, or Muddy Waters' psychedelic album *Electric Mud*. But usually what you gotta do is play the same song everybody else does, but play the hell out of it. You fuck it up when you try to get all fancy with this subjective-reality bullshit.

But before that twist it's kind of fun. Reminded me a little bit of that great section at the end of *Halloween H20* where Laurie is about to escape from Michael Meyers but decides, "Ah, fuck it," then turns around, chases him and chops his head off. Spoiler.

SLUMBER PARTY MASSACRE

This is a slasher movie about girls at a slumber party, and a dude with a portable drill. There is no pillow fights or nothing but otherwise it pretty much plays out how you would imagine.

Almost anywhere you read about this movie they say it's a feminist slasher movie. I can see a touch here or there that supports that theory, but I am positive that pretty much every one of these people would be saying it was misogynistic if it was directed by a man. In most respects it's exactly like every other slasher movie of the time, including showing lots of gratuitous female (and not male) nudity. When the girl gets up in the morning you see her take her shirt off to change into a dress. When she goes to school you see lots of nudity in the locker room, including a really funny shot (I'm not sure if it's intentionally funny or not) that pans down and just focuses on a girl's ass for a while before panning back up to where it started. Then during the slumber party they all take their clothes off to change into their night clothes and for the most part don't wear pants for the rest of the movie. The other characters, who don't get naked, wear those tight running shorts that were popular at the time.

Plus, there's a scene where the girls are in the school gym playing basketball, and they're fucking terrible. They can barely dribble, let alone shoot. I thought it was okay, they're just high school kids in gym class. But then they mention that it's not gym class, it's the actual varsity team. You call that feminism? I've seen the Seattle Storm before, I know girls can play basketball.

The alleged feminism in the movie is pretty minor. There is a shot (also used for the movie poster) that goes from between the killer's legs with the drill pointing down to look like a dick, but that's not all that different from Jason's machete or Leatherface's chainsaw (especially in part 2 where in one scene it's almost more of a prosthetic penis than a phallic symbol). At the end one of the girls hacks the drill bit off with a machete and this makes the killer helpless, so the phallic thing is obviously not a coincidence.

When the slumber party attendees first find out there's a killer after them, the two boy characters say "We have to do something to help the girls" and come up with a plan to split up and "make a run for it." Of course, they both immediately get killed. So much for that macho chivalry shit. But I don't think that's anything unusual for the genre either. As most of you know, all the males get killed in the vast majority of slasher movies.

The one and only thing I noticed that I think could be considered a feminist theme unusual to the genre is the way the killer is handled. And this is also the most successful horror aspect of the movie. He has no mask, no gimmick other than the drill, and not much to his backstory. He's just a notorious killer who, we hear on the radio, has escaped. When we see him he's just some dude in a jean jacket and boots. He doesn't make any quips or threats while chasing his victims, so he stays mysterious and you can put yourself in these girls' shoes (or bare feet) because he's just some dude you've never seen before invading the house. But then at the end he finally talks, he tells the girls that they're pretty and that he loves them, and then that they know they want it. And one of the girls says "I don't even know you." It's a pretty good illustration of a guy obsessed with girls from afar who decided because he's sexually attracted to them that he is in love with them. But I guess, like everything else in the movie, calling it feminist might be stretching it.

But since the director (Amy Holden Jones, writer of *Mystic Pizza*) and the writer (Rita Mae Brown, *Murder She Purred: A Mrs. Murphy Mystery*) are both women, people are looking for something to interpret in a different way than they would in any other slasher movie. Maybe more than the fact that they're women it's relevant to point out that Brown is in fact a feminist and gay rights activist, and her lesbian coming of age novel *Rubyfruit Jungle* can actually be seen as a set decoration in the movie. Supposedly she wrote the screenplay as a parody (under the title *Sleepless Nights*) but then it was directed as a serious movie. I'm not sure how that could be unless either it wasn't a very funny parody or they took out most of the jokes. There are at least three funny parts in the movie, though. There's one part where the younger sister keeps opening and closing the refrigerator part way trying to sneak a beer, but keeps not noticing there's a dead body inside. Another part, one of the girls decides that the way to fight a guy with a drill is with another power tool. The drill in the garage is too small, so she takes a buzzsaw and runs upstairs, but she gets to the end of the extension cord before she can use it. My favorite part though is when the killer is loading dead bodies into the trunk of a car and starts counting them. "One... two... three... four... SHIT!" I don't know if he's mad because there's no more room in the trunk or because his body count isn't high enough.

But that's the kind of humor that fits in a serious horror movie, it never feels like a parody. On the other hand, the acting is generally bad, the dialogue is often atrocious, and do girls really have slumber parties and hang out in their underwear eating pizza? Maybe Brown was saying no and that was where the parody comes in, I'm not sure. If they really wanted to make a slasher movie for women maybe they should've reversed the tables and had men as the victims and sex objects. They would have to pick a male oriented get together such as *Super Bowl Party Massacre* or *Fraternity Porn Watching Massacre* or maybe *World's Biggest Gangbang Massacre*.

I don't know, this is definitely not a classic. The title has the same amount of syllables as *Texas Chain Saw Massacre*, but the horror classic it feels most similar to is *Halloween*. It's got a lot of the same elements — high school girls and some boyfriends as the leads, a killer is loose, faceless shots of the killer driving around spying on the victims, starts out in the day and ends at night in a suburban house, scary movies on TV, making phone calls to friends, banging on the neighbors' door but getting no response, finding friends dead hidden around the house... even the keyboard score sounds a little similar. But of course, it's not shot or especially acted as well as *Halloween*, it never feels as real or as tense. It's more gorey than *Halloween*, but with lots of unbelievably easy delimbings and beheadings that make it harder to take seriously. The way limbs come off in some of these movies, you'd think we were like insects, with arms and legs designed to pop off if a predator tries to grab us. You'd think we'd be losing those things every time we trip or bump into a wall or anything.

Still, it has a certain something. I sort of enjoyed it. I think the secret is not in the fact that the writer and director are women, but that they are opposites. You see, Rita Mae Brown is the author of a series of popular mystery novels that she allegedly co-writes with her cat Sneaky Pie Brown. Apparently they involve many animals, but the lead character is a cat detective named Mrs. Murphy. Amy Holden Jones, meanwhile, is the writer of the movie *Beethoven*, not the one with Gary Oldman as Beethoven, but the one about a huge dog that does all kinds of hilarious things that dogs do, although I believe it leaves out the shitting on the floor, the eating vomit, the humping your leg, pissing on things and smelling asses. Anyway, you got a dog person director and a cat person writer, somehow they form this mystical yin and yang balance that creates the perfect vibe for a crappy but somewhat watchable slasher movie.

FUNNY GAMES

Not funny ha-ha, though. This is a very simple, solid, unsettling Austrian picture from 1997. The director is Michael Haneke, who has since become real respected due to movies like *Caché*. In this one a couple and their son arrive at their vacation home. We know they're well-to-do not only because of the vacation home, but because they listen to opera music in the car and have a boat. Right after they get there father and son are putting the boat in the water, mom is talking on the phone, cooking some steaks, and a young man shows up at the door to borrow some eggs. He dicks around for a bit but before too long there are two young visitors, eight broken eggs, one broken leg and the family held hostage.

So most of the movie is spent in the house with the family sitting helplessly as their smug home invaders talk about games and bets and pretend that they're being friendly. It is not graphically violent or shock value oriented like *Chaos* or something. The cruelty to the characters and audience is mostly psychological. The most horrible stuff happens off camera. One scene focuses on one of the tormentors walking into the kitchen and calmly making a sandwich while the horror goes on in the other room.

There's no music except during the credits. A lot of the filmatism is show-off-edly minimalistic, like the shot that lasts about ten minutes, mostly motionless, its first couple minutes looking like a still photo. I think the creepiness comes from this stark simplicity and from the Leopold-and-Loeb superior attitude of the villains. They have no motive, no backstory, and somehow that makes them seem more real. They're just some pricks that like to do this. You hate them and you can feel that in this movie they have a good chance of winning.

The weirdest part of the movie, the part that shouldn't work, is the way these pricks start to address the viewer. Me. You. During one sadistic "funny game" one of the guys turns and winks into the camera. But you're not sure, the camera could be the POV of the other guy, maybe he's not winking at us. Then later he turns to the camera again and is clearly talking to us when he asks what we think will happen, and if we're siding with the family. It's pretty uncomfortable, like when you're at a bus stop and some dude with a ferret in his coat mumbles something to you and laughs, and you give him a courtesy laugh before you realize that he was nodding toward those black dudes over there and was probably making some racial comment. *Yeah, me and you, a couple of peers, white dudes, joking together.* That's kind of what it's like, this guy is smiling at you and putting on the charm and you have no way of telling him no, dude, I'm not your pal. It's not okay for you to joke around with me. Don't involve me in this.

It's pretty weird to have a serious, disturbing movie where a character "breaks the fourth wall." You don't get that too much outside of comedies. Don't worry though, he doesn't come out during the credits like Ferris Bueller and tell us to go home.

The movie's ultimate self-reflective stunt — BIG ASS SPOILER ALERT — is right after the mom manages to grab the gun and blow away one of the dudes. The other guy freaks out and searches frantically for the TV remote. When he finds it he uses it to rewind himself, his reality, the movie itself. He backs it up so he can grab the gun before she does and his partner doesn't get shot.

Okay, this is ludicrous, how can this work? The movie has gone too far. It's magic now. It's a joke. An Adam Sandler movie. That's what I thought for a second. Then I realized that for some reason it actually worked. Haneke gave the audience a release, a hope, and then he rescinded it, retroactively removed it from the story. *Okay, here's what you've been hoping for, enjoy. Oh, wait. It seems there has been some sort of mistake. You don't get to keep that release. Please give it back. We apologize for any inconvenience this may cause.*

It works because it manipulates you, and it goes so far in manipulating you that it calls attention to itself. *Hello, director Michael Haneke here with a friendly reminder that I have complete power over this story. I can have her blow the guy away, I can have her not blow him away. I choose the one that will be less satisfying to you. But please know that this is not an accident. This is my choice. And my decision is final. Fuck you and your mother. Love, Michael Haneke. P.S. eat a dick*

And you know, as weird as the remote control thing is, it would be worse if he had a time machine that he used to stop her from getting the gun. So I am happy with the remote control.

I like the gimmick, but I believe I do have a disagreement with Haneke, and with many of the fans of this movie. If you listen to Haneke (including on the interview that was on the DVD I watched) and if you read what people write about the movie, it's all about violence in the media, and it is indicting the audience for watching violence and all that type of horse shit. In that interview Haneke talks about the remote control scene, about how people at film festivals cheered when he got shot, and then when it rewound they went dead silent, because they realized they had just cheered a murder.

But I think maybe because he's trying to be cynical he misunderstands how scare movies work, including his own. He has this carefully constructed tension and suspense here. He has designed it for us to root for the family to get away. He puts a weapon somewhere knowing we will wait for the family to find it and use it. He even has the bad guys looking directly at us and discussing with us that we are rooting for the family to survive.

And that's exactly what we're doing. I'm not saying there aren't sadistic people out there, but that's not the only thing film violence is about, or even the primary thing. The whole point of a movie like this is for the audience to not want to see violence. We root for the family to get away and honestly when she shot him I was not thrilled because *ha ha, the bastard deserves it*, I was thrilled because I thought she was gonna get away. So I think I speak on behalf of all those people clapping at the film festival when I say no, stupid, I was not clapping to prove your point about how dude, *the media is sooooo violent I just noticed*, but because you made a hell of an effective thriller. Dumbass.

He's good at making this type of movie, so what's wrong with somebody else being good at it too, and with people enjoying watching it? Does he know that the characters in these movies are fictional, and are no more hurt by a fictional bullet than they would be by the cancer they'd have if they were in a Susan Sarandon movie? Are his motives really so much more pure than anybody else making a thriller?

Also does he know that they did the same type of thing in *Jason Lives: Friday the 13th Part VI* where the guy sees that Jason's grave has been dug up, looks directly into the camera at the audience and says "Some folks sure got a strange idea of entertainment"? Does that mean that *Funny Games* and *Jason Lives* are both morally better than other violent movies?

Haneke may be against watching movies where violence happens, but I am for it, so I recommend his movie *Funny Games*. But be sure to watch some violent American action movie afterwards and mail him a creepy videotape of you watching it and tell him that you loved *Funny Games* so much that it encouraged you and all of your friends to watch more violent movies and you would like to thank him and could he do a cop movie next that would be awesome.

VERN ON THE CHAOS DVD, THE AGE-OLD TORTURE PORN DEBATE, AND WHAT HAPPENS WHEN A PRO-WRESTLER RUNS LOOSE IN THE L.A. COUNTY CORONER'S OFFICE

Well boys, there's this horror movie called *Chaos* that comes out on DVD at the end of September. I thought it would be good to review it now so that you will have forgotten about it by then. I wouldn't recommend watching the movie — in fact, if possible, I recommend not ever hearing of it. Just stop reading now, unread the first part of this paragraph, and don't think about it again. We're only encouraging them. By reviewing this movie I'm just giving the dipshits who made it the attention they're waving their dicks around begging for, but I want to review it for two reasons:

1. I'm always up for another round of that stupid "torture porn" debate.

2. For masochistic horror fans I might recommend borrowing or stealing (but not buying) the DVD just because the extras are so hilariously insane.

Chaos is a low budget, no imagination, blatant ripoff of *Last House On the Left* directed by a former pro-wrestler named David "The Demon" DeFalco. Its one and only claim to fame is that they managed to get a no-star review from Roger Ebert and then they wrote him a letter that lured him into an ongoing debate about violence in movies, as if their movie deserved to be a part of that discussion.

During the opening scene I actually thought I might like the movie. A Honeybunny-from-*Pulp-Fiction* type is hitchhiking when some rednecks pull over and imply that they will give her a ride in exchange for sexual favors. She refuses their offer, they grab her like they're gonna rape her. But these rednecks aren't the ones you gotta worry about. The girl's friends, one of them a big, bald Stone Cold Steve Austin type, come out of the trees, beat the shit out of the guys, and destroy their car with a baseball bat. The way it cuts right in the middle of the car-smashing just tosses you into the movie like a rock through a window.

But that's as good as the movie gets. The story is credited to "an original idea by David DeFalco and Steven Jay Bernheim," the original idea apparently being to remake *Last House On the Left* without paying for the rights. They are using a little known legal loophole that if you act confused and change the subject when somebody mentions it's a remake then it doesn't count as copyright violation. If you've seen *Last House* there's no reason to watch this, it's just the same god damn thing but not done as well. Two girls go to "a rave" (which is portrayed by some dudes hanging out in the woods during the day time without music. I guess they couldn't afford a stereo). They try to buy ecstasy from a random dude (Sage Stallone, *Rocky V*) who says he has some but they have to walk about twenty minutes to where his friends are. They are hesitant but decide to go.

We know Sage's friends are the crazy gang of fugitives we have been seeing since the attack on the rednecks. Their leader is the big bald guy, played by Kevin Gage (who seems like he could be good in other movies). The character's name is Chaos. I'm surprised the others aren't named Anarchy and Six Sixsix, because that's the kind of imagination and refined taste you got behind the movie. There is little suspense or tension. As soon as the girls come in the house the bad guys grab them and start menacing them, and the girls spend the rest of the movie crying and begging for their lives.

The gang takes the girls out in the woods, they let them get away, they chase them, rape them, kill them, etc. At the end the killers say their car broke down and ask if they can stay with the parents of one of the girls. The parents figure out that these people killed their girl, and try to get their revenge. But they don't do as good of a job as the parents in *Last House*. So it's a TOTALLY different movie. Remake? I don't know what you're talking about. The ending isn't as good, so how could it be a remake?

I can see how if you'd never seen *Last House* but you were open to that kind of movie, and you were in a charitable mood, you might think this movie was disturbing and raw enough to give it a mild, open-minded kind of pass. Most of it is competent as far as this kind of thing goes. There's some laughable line readings, but you're a horror fan so you're used to that. At least it's serious and somewhat realistic. Not nearly as well executed as the similarly serious and somewhat realistic *Wolf Creek*, but maybe you didn't see that either.

The trouble is, if you've seen *Last House* you gotta be wondering even more than the people who are offended by this kind of movie what the fuck is the point of making this. The original is definitely not for everybody. I hated it the first time I saw it. It's not a fun time, a lot of it is sloppy, and if you're gonna make a moral argument against a movie it's a pretty easy target. But over the years I've sort of learned to appreciate it. It was a movie that came out of the Vietnam war, it was some young angry guys trying to make a movie against violence by depicting it as horrible and messy. It makes death long and painful. It has a sadistic villain who seems like the original Mr. Blonde. And it has that muddy, dirty look of some low budget '70s movies that make them seem so spooky and almost real. In the end, when the parents try to kill the murderers using methods as vicious as those used against their daughter, Craven is hitting on one of his favorite themes of seemingly civilized people breaking down into savages when the shit hits the fan (see also *The Hills Have Eyes*).

The *Chaos* chumps try to do all the same things, except for that last one, which is probably a little over their heads. They're not interested in that stuff, they're just interested in serial killers (which DeFalco explains he has been researching for years, even before he wanted to make the movie.) They never veer from the original plot in any way that I noticed, adding only the insignificant detail that the parents are an interracial couple and the sheriff makes racist comments. YOU SEE, NOT A REMAKE. TOTALLY DIFFERENT. DO NOT SUE.

So it's *Last House*, but not as good, and less. Except — and I'm pretty sure this is how they justify it in their minds — the details of the girls' murders are even more disgusting. It's not wall-to-wall violence or anything but it's true, the two murders of the girls will be something you will wish you didn't see. Which they will take as a compliment. Way to go guys, here is a sticker for your star chart.

In an ideal world the movie would've disappeared like all the other crappy horror movies that people throw on the pile every day, and I wouldn't even be reviewing this shit. But there was that Roger Ebert thing. Somehow they got him to review the movie, unsurprisingly he thought it was shit, so they turned that into "controversy" and the ol' torture porn argument comes up again.

This time around the argument is especially stupid because it's obviously just a promotional gimmick for a shitty movie. But it also comes up every time a more legitimate movie like a *Hostel* or a *Wolf Creek* comes out, which is a lot these days. And it's generally a debate between people who don't watch horror movies and people who occasionally watch horror movies, some of both types accusing the latest horror movie of being "nothing but torture porn." Usually, they're just being ignorant of the genre. I didn't think *Hostel* was very good, and it definitely has that "dude, it's fucked up, like Miike!" corniness to it. But you are clearly supposed to sympathize with the idiot frat boy dickhead protagonists. You are supposed to root for them to escape the torturers. Just like you rooted for Laurie in *Halloween* and Sally in *Texas Chain Saw Massacre* and Nancy in *A Nightmare On Elm Street*[52] and all those other horror movies that even these critics admit are classics. You are not supposed to just get a boner because people are being tortured, like the "torture porn" label implies.

I was more impressed by *The Hills Have Eyes*, which both had more to say and was more fun to me. And I liked *Wolf Creek*, which to many critics was torture porn and to me was a good old fashioned adrenaline pumping oh-shit-let's-get-the-hell-out-of-here type of slasher movie. I thought a lot of critics punished that movie for being too good. If it had been silly and cartoony like *High Tension* they would've laughed it off but since it was believable and intense they acted like it had pissed on their shoes. I mean if you're gonna make judgments about which grueling horror experiences are acceptable, where is the line drawn? Why did some people think that escaping the mutants in *The Hills Have Eyes* remake was appalling but escaping the mutants in *The Descent* was great fun? Was *Hills* too close to reality because the mutants were wearing clothes? Or does it not count as torture porn if it's below sea level?

It's the same as the "gore vs. no gore" debate, the whole thing is based on a false premise. You know, somebody always has to bring up that old classic about "movies are only scary if the gore is off screen, like Hitchcock." And then there are the guys who are only interested in the goriest, most graphic shit available. The people who buy the *Guinea Pig*

---

52 And Clarice in best picture winner *Silence of the Lambs*, for that matter.

box set and movies with either *Cannibal* or *Holocaust* or both in the title, those types of movies that I'm not sure if Ebert even knows about. The whole issue is ridiculous, it's like saying that you only like movies with balloons in them or you only like movies *without* balloons in them. Gore could be good or it could be bad. It all depends on what the story is and how the story is told. *The Texas Chain Saw Massacre* manages to be disturbing by making you imagine there's horrible violence even though almost all of it is off screen. *Texas Chainsaw Massacre 2* is disturbing by being gory as hell — that scene where Chop Top beats L.G.'s head in with a hammer is no picnic. In some movies gore can actually be a fun rush, like when the wood splinter goes into that gal's eyeball in *Zombie*. Some people like car chases, some people like that. Or of course a lot of the newsies enjoy the over-the-top bloodiness of *Dead Alive/Braindead*.

I don't understand why people like *Faces of Death* and *Android of Notre Dame* and shit, but oh well. Life goes on. It's kind of obnoxious to moralize about it. All these people who don't like horror trying to convince me it's wrong to like *Wolf Creek* is like me trying to tell Tim McGraw how to make his albums better. It's none of my business. For me all that matters is *Wolf Creek* works as a horror movie. *Chaos* doesn't.

But there's always gonna be that bullshit "HAS HOLLYWOOD FINALLY GONE TOO FAR?" debate, so it's a handy way to add a sheen of importance to a shitty horror movie like this. At least they didn't go the First Amendment Martyr route, I guess. On the DVD extra "The Roger Ebert Controversy," director DeFalco sits mostly silent while producer Steven Jay Bernheim quotes from reviews and defends the movie. One review he talks about is by some dude named "Capone."[53]

Okay, I don't want to take away from Capone, who apparently thought the movie was pretty good. But he buys into their claim that it's "a cautionary tale," as if the producers are desperately trying to help teenage girls make better decisions that will prevent them from being attacked in the woods by roving gangs of serial killers. The movie opens with an

---

53 Capone is another writer on The Ain't It Cool News. I was just giving him some guff by pretending not to know who he was. He later clarified with me that he "almost bought into" the idea that it was a cautionary tale, but not entirely. He admitted that he had become an "apologist" for the movie but said, "If it's possible to like a film but still not recommend that anybody else see it, that's how I feel about *Chaos*."

unintentionally funny After School Special type text crawl that ends by saying, "The producers hope the film you are about to see will serve as a warning to parents and potential victims alike. It is intended to be as disturbing as the subject matter it depicts in order to educate and, perhaps, save lives."

What's great is watching Bernheim go into detail trying to support this ridiculous idea that the movie is educational. At first it just seems insulting to your intelligence, then at a certain point you start to wonder if he has actually sold himself his own bullshit. I think he now really believes that this movie was planned as a public service announcement to help teenage girls be more streetwise in the woods.

I almost don't have the heart to tell him that very few teenage girls watch movies like this. The people who watch these movies are the dudes I mentioned before who are always looking for the most "fucked up" thing available. They might enjoy the two sicko rape/mutilation scenes in this movie. After all, on the commentary track they explain that they are exactly based on the mutilations that a real serial killer did. They keep dropping the killer's name like it's an old blues singer they're fond of, and Bernheim says that depicting the mutilations he did "gives legitimacy to the movie." If that's not classy enough for you he also explains that one of the actresses had been raped in real life and was creating a cathartic experience for other victims of violent crime by playing a character who spends most of her screen time being raped and killed. Hopefully these selfless humanitarians will get some kind of award for their great compassion toward victims of sexual assault. I mean I don't like to throw around words and phrases like "hero" or "the new Gandhi" or "makes Jesus seem like kind of a dick in comparison," but Steven Jay Bernheim has earned all those labels with his work on this film, it sounds like, the way he tells it.

Anyway, some *Faces of Death* types may enjoy that shit, but they probably won't agree with DeFalco's description of this as "the most brutal film of all time" (repeated dozens of times throughout all the extras as well as on the front cover, the back cover and the disc itself) since they've jerked off to *Cannibal Holocaust* since they were thirteen, and the "brutality" in this is mostly confined to two scenes. It's weird because they are the only audience for this movie but they're gonna be bored during most of it.

Unless they're parents and they're busy learning, because it is after all gonna "serve as a warning to parents and potential victims alike." I'd love to see the family meeting where mom and dad sit down little Susie and Taylor to watch *Chaos*.

"Honey, as you get older, you're starting to notice changes in your body. You're not a little girl anymore. So stay at the party, don't leave with someone you don't know. As you can see here, a guy might cut off your nipple and stick it in your mouth and you'll puke, and then he'll stab you in the back a bunch of times and then buttfuck your corpse and then peer pressure his buddy into doing the same. I know it's tough to watch but it is intended to be as disturbing as the subject matter it depicts in order to educate and, perhaps, save lives."

You know how the fake controversy goes. Decide for yourself. You gotta watch it so you can make up your own mind about some dudes buttfucking a corpse. Listen to the commentary track, watch the "Roger Ebert Controversy" extra. Maybe you'll disagree with me. Maybe you'll think they seem like reasonable people and that they make an intelligent argument.

Then I want you to click on the next extra, "Inside the Coroner's Office: A Tour of the L.A. Coroner's Crypt." This is a little featurette following L.A. county forensic technician Michael A. Cormier, who talks about his job while showing off actual rotting corpses in his "crypt." And it keeps cutting to footage of director DeFalco in the same place, with no shirt on and a chain around his neck, flexing his muscles and yelling pro-wrestling type commentary such as "10,000 bodies a year baby, go right through these doors and THE DEMON... the Demon's playground — ARRGHH!! (flexes muscles) — is here, now!"

I'm not kidding. This very serious filmmaker, who has a strong educational message about the nature of violence, stands among real life murder victims declaring that he is "the Demon" and "the director of the most brutal film of all time."

"First time, baby! First time IN CINEMA HISTORY! A director has EVER been interviewed in this... crypt... of homicides, su-i-cides, car wrecks, and every other horrific faTALity in Los Angeles, California."

And I swear to God that in this featurette he starts calling out Roger Ebert as if he was Macho Man Randy Savage calling out whoever it was that Macho Man Randy Savage used to fight.

"Well Roger Ebert, as I stand here surrounded by homicides, suicides, and all the brutal fatalities in Los Angeles, I ask you, jack... THIS is reality! This is why I have the outlook on life that I have. Because this is where it all ends up. They end up in pieces, head exploded, extremities torn off. This is what it's all about. This is what *Chaos* is all about. The horrific part of life, the part that you don't see in movies. The part that they don't tell you about in books. Because this is the reality, this is MY reality, Roger Ebert."

THIS JUST IN: THERE ARE MURDERS. COURAGEOUS NEW MOVIE WILL REVEAL SHOCKING TRUTH. BOOKS ARE LIARS.

Before this insanity gets boring there is a crazy plot twist where DeFalco ends up in the same shot as Cormier. He shakes his hand and talks about being his close friend. At first I thought this poor coroner guy really didn't know "The Demon" very well and was starting to wonder what he had gotten himself into by letting the cameras in here. But then you find out that they really are friends and are developing a movie together which DeFalco keeps calling "the next step in the succession of evil" as well as "the next step in the progression of evil."

That's when Cormier starts talking about his theory ("we'll call it a theory for now") that when people use methamphetamines it opens up a "doorway" to another dimension that allows "demonic beings" access to "this realm" so they can possess them and commit brutal crimes. You may think this sounds far-fetched, even asinine, perhaps even fucking embarrassing. But Cormier explains, "I've been documenting it for several years, and it's undeniable. People who use methamphetamines are opening themselves up to demonic possession..."

Later DeFalco says, "You are looking at the future of horror," he flexes his muscles and the camera zooms in on his bicep.

The whole thing is so crazy I started to wonder if maybe this Cormier guy was an actor, and it was just another gimmick to promote DeFalco's next crappy movie. Googling technology failed to bring up a real coroner named Cormier. But an email to the L.A. Coroner's Office Media-Public Information Officer proved that it wasn't a hoax. The Chief Coroner Investigator and Chief of Operations confirmed Cormier's employment, adding, "I believe that he was offering his own opinion/theory regarding the subject matter he was speaking to and not the official position of the Department of Coroner or the County of Los Angeles."

Which is good to know. But still, I have a message for those of you who live in L.A.: try not to get killed. You don't want that guy cutting on your body, in my opinion.

Anyway, probably the most insane DVD extra I've ever seen.

I should correct something that Quint said in his introduction to Capone's review, that "having Sage Stallone in it is almost a stamp of approval" because of Stallone's involvement in restoring and releasing gory Italian movies. By now Quint has probably heard that when Stallone signed up it was to work with his friend David Hess (from *Last House On the Left*... what an incredible coincidence!) who was playing the sheriff. When Hess was fired a few days into production Stallone tried to quit but couldn't get out of his contract. And this has apparently led to at least one humorously tense panel discussion at a horror convention. It's not clear to me whether or not the cast really signed on thinking it was an official remake, but whatever happened, you can't deny it's a brazen daylight robbery.

To me that's the biggest strike against the movie, that it's an unnecessary and not very good remake of *Last House On the Left*, and that they won't even admit it. The only big difference is that they dumped the booby traps the parents made in the original and changed the ending. In their version the cops try to get the dad to put down the gun he has to Chaos's head. For no reason, the sheriff shoots the dad in the forehead! Then the mom shoots the sheriff, Chaos shoots the other cop, then shoots the mom and cackles as we fade to black.

The ending is actually kind of a relief because after so much sadism you get to laugh at these idiots and their attempts to be shocking. Craven was pretentious when he made his movie but that's better than this moronic Insane Clown Posse type "dark" bullshit. OOOOOH! He's laughing! Because he's EVIL. And not only that, he's CHAOS. EVIL CHAOS. Zip-a-dee-doo-dah. You can probably be an idiot and get away with making a "fun" type of horror movie, but you gotta have a little bit of intelligence behind this grim nihilistic stuff if you don't want it to be laughable and sad.

I guess because of that dumbass change to the ending they have convinced themselves that their movie is not a rip-off. In fact, nowhere on any of the extras do they ever mention *Last House On the Left*. It's almost as if some sort of lawyer had advised them not to mention it. They do mention being inspired by "all those '70s drive-in movies" but they're careful to always specify that this means *Texas Chain Saw Massacre*. *Texas Chain Saw* is of course named as the inspiration for the chain saw fight at the end, even though it happens to be exactly like the chain saw fight in *Last House On the Left*, which came first. The closest they ever come to mentioning *Last House* is on the commentary track when Bernheim gets defensive about the parents' revenge at the end:

SJB: "And this is a theme that dates back to mythology, to folklore."

DD: "Yeah, it's a public domain story."

SJB: "it's a theme that, that, you know, a revenge theme. It's not the principle focus of the movie."

Of course, all of us remember that old folk tale about the father whose daughter and her friend get raped and killed in the woods by a gang of fugitives (one female, the rest male) and there's the two wacky cops looking for the girls and then the fugitives come ask to stay at the father's house and he notices that they have an article of his daughter's clothing and they must've killed her so he attacks them with a chain saw. I think it was called "Anansi the Spider" or something, I forget, but it was a good folk tale. And public domain. Don't worry about it.

On the commentary track they go on and on about how they were trying to make a movie that depicted violence as ugly and not glamorous, as if they had no idea that Craven was going for the same thing with his movie almost thirty-five years ago, or that he described his goals similarly on his commentary track. It's like they live in some alternate universe where *Last House On the Left* doesn't even exist.

That must be it because how else do you explain an extended debate with Roger Ebert about violence in horror movies that never mentions his 3 1/2 star review of *Last House On the Left*? He called it "a tough, bitter little sleeper of a movie that's about four times as good as you'd expect," and compared it to *Wait Until Dark* and *Straw Dogs*. If DeFalco and Bernheim lived in a world where *Last House On the Left* existed, they could bring up this review and say, "Hey, you liked the exact same thing when Wes Craven did it, you're such a hypocrite." But then they'd have to wonder if that meant it wasn't just the gruesomeness of the movie that was bad. It was the movie itself. Craven did it better, smarter, and three decades earlier.

But Craven's biceps are much smaller than DeFalco's, he always wears a shirt, and he never went into a morgue and flexed his muscles, yelling shit about demons. So you guys can be proud about that one. Way to go fellas.

If you must watch this movie — and believe me, you mustn't — just find somewhere to download it. Then if they get mad because you downloaded their movie just say "What? This isn't your movie. It's totally different. And besides, I'm watching it to, perhaps, save lives."

I ALMOST didn't send that review to Ain't It Cool, because it was not a movie most people had heard of and I didn't really want to promote it. But I did think those DVD extras were pretty spectacular, and I'd been itching for a fight on the so-called "torture porn" issue, which had been pissing me off because I kept hearing about from people who didn't like horror movies anyway. So I used this as an excuse to write about those things and get the talkbackers discussing them.

The discussion was going about as expected, a little talk of violence in horror, a side-argument about me not mentioning that Last House *lifted its plot from Ingmar Bergman's* The Virgin Spring, *and as usual some scandalous accusations that my review was really long. But the talkback became legendary that night at 1:28 when director David "The Demon" DeFalco unexpectedly posted a response.*

DeFalco brought up the Virgin Spring *issue and said that his movie was an "homage" to* Last House, *not a rip-off. He claimed that Sage Stallone had not wanted to quit, as had been reported. But most of all he objected to me calling him a "dipshit" and a "chump" and making fun of what he said "in the coroner's crypt." And then it turned weird:*

"You're a fuckin' critic and are entitled to your opinion about the fuckin' movie but that's where it ends. You are not going to talk shit and make fun of me and get away with it. Why don't you get into the ring and do it to my face? The thing I hate the most about the internet is that a pussy like you can talk shit about a guy like me and not have to answer to it. I dare you to do it to my face, Vern. In fact, if you can survive in the ring for more that 60 seconds with me, I will never direct another movie again. If you can't, then you can stick the review up your ass."

Of course DeFalco (posting as "Demon Dave") was immediately mocked and told to fuck off by various talkbackers, who quickly had my back. But he had put me in a spot. Unlike Roger Ebert I do try to be a tough guy, and can imagine the hilarity and sweet justice of a guy in my situation taking up the offer and actually defeating him. But of course I'm not a wrestler, I really did not want to get beat up over not liking a movie, and plus I don't know where you go to get a good lucha libre mask to conceal your identity. Seems like kind of a hassle. So I responded:

Dear Dave,

I regret to inform you that I will not be attending your wrestling challenge that would have proven that *Chaos* is not a ripoff of *Last House On the Left*. I think I have to wash my hair that day or something. Seriously bud, welcome to the talkbacks and thanks for your response. That was actually a good move challenging me to wrestle. Moriarty says it's a remake of Uwe Boll's boxing challenge, but I think both have their roots in folklore and legends.

Anyway, I can't say I'm interested in getting beat up by a muscleman (even if I get a good nose bite in or something). It would set a precedent where all critics now have to wrestle somebody every time they write a harsh review. I don't want to see Michael Bay suplexing Roger Ebert knowing it's my fault. So I gotta turn you down like you knew I would and shave some points off my precious tough guy reputation, as well as crush the illusions of any readers who for some reason assumed I was good at wrestling. So you got me bud, touché. Now I wish you would apply some of that cunning to your movies.

Speaking of which, let me respond to your non-wrestling related points. First of all, come on bud. I'm not retarded. Am I supposed to believe that you actually based *Chaos* on a Swedish folk tale, and coincidentally it came out exactly like *Last House On the Left* but with different rapes and a corny ending? OF COURSE it's based on *Last House On the Left*. If you had said that from the beginning you wouldn't have had such a harsh reaction I don't think. As you said, Wes Craven openly talks about *Last House* being based on *Virgin Spring*. And maybe somebody here could verify but I'm betting it's not a scene-for-scene remake. If you honestly just intended *Chaos* as an homage and somehow don't realize how closely you copied your inspiration, maybe you could explain how you go through the entire commentary and those extra features without even once mentioning *Last House* or Craven? Was it just a brain fart like when whatsername forgot to thank her husband at the Oscars?

As for me getting the facts wrong, if that's true then I sincerely apologize. The thing about Sage Stallone quitting came from IMDb and from the letter that Ebert published about you threatening the audience at a screening. Since you make fun of Stallone on the commentary (claiming that he was rejected from *Rocky Balboa* and therefore "available") and apparently at the panel in Chicago (where you chanted "Adrian!" as he came to the stage) I believed those sources. But you were there, I just read about it so if the public record is wrong, by all means, set the record straight. I tried to be accurate (I really did contact the LA County Coroner's Office) and if I got anything wrong then I apologize.

Also, as far as me calling you a chump and a dipshit — fair enough. I made these judgments based on your various defenses of the movie, and honestly I was talking more about Bernheim than you. (I hope that doesn't set me up for a bass fishing or crossword puzzle challenge or something.) But it's true, I don't know you personally. Although you just challenged me to a fight over the internet, I'm open to the idea that you're a cool guy and I was too harsh. The truth is, I don't want to stop you from directing. I just think you need some brains in your movies to go with the brawn. I guess since I turned down your crazy challenge I haven't earned the right to offer you one. But that's what it would be: make an original movie. The minimalism, the rawness, the seriousness, the lack of a score — those are all good things about *Chaos*. The casting wasn't too bad either. I've seen alot of DTV shit and I don't agree with Bloody Disgusting that *Chaos* is "one of the worst films in the history of cinema." It's just that it exactly copies a movie we've all seen but takes out the intelligence, leaving empty shock value.

Meanwhile, that coroner's office extra is fucking INSANE, I liked it better than the movie. If you applied that kind of creativity and madness to a movie you might have something. If you ever make a movie I really like and THEN do crazy shit like standing among dead bodies flexing your muscles and calling out Roger Ebert, you will be my fucking hero. I really mean that.

Next, producer Steven Jay Bernheim showed up to play the part of the good cop, congratulating me on a well-written review. It seemed like peace could be achieved. But then from out of nowhere comes a talkbacker called "JuggFuckler":

"My name is Jason 'Juggfuckler' Stevens. I think that you are a pussy, a shitty director, and a shitty human being. Your mother is a whore and your father is a closet homosexual. I am now calling you out the way that you called out Vern. What do you say? One minute in the ring with the JuggFuckler. You don't even have to quit directing (you have already effectively destroyed your 'career' all by yourself). I just want the privilege of kicking the shit out of a no-talent plagiarist."

Bernheim responded by offering to promote and referee the fight as well as put up a $250 purse, but DeFalco never accepted. The talkback continued for a full month, with Juggfuckler and the Demon eventually offering each other words of begrudging respect as warriors. DeFalco admitted the influence of Last House *while trying to shift some of the blame to his producer and co-writer, saying they were better educated than him and should've known if it was a rip-off. He felt that any similarities were insignificant, but "What is significant is that we captured real EVIL on film." He also teased us with various cliffhangers and hints about his next movie. "I think this one you will definitely find very interesting and very original," he wrote. "But, right now the Demon is going to bed. Goodnight."*

THE VIRGIN SPRING
or Max Von Sydow's Badass Revenge

Recently on The Ain't It Cool News I reviewed this movie *Chaos*, which is a rip-off of *Last House On the Left* (not on purpose, I am assured by the filmatists) which itself was an update of *The Virgin Spring*. One of the talkbackers, Readingwriter, was annoyed that I didn't mention *The Virgin Spring* in the review. He had a good point that it would've been interesting to compare all three of them, not just those two, and I'm sure I would've done that if I had actually seen *The Virgin Spring*. But I hadn't.

Until now. Today, I return to the topic armed with a new, more Swedish perspective of the classic revenge tale.

I would have to say Ingmar Bergman's take is the best of the three, and one of the nicest slasher pics you'll ever see. His is less graphic, but more medieval, more religious, and more Swedish. Instead of those faded, muddy '70s colors his has crisp black and white photography. Must've looked weird playing in those grindhouses. Maybe that's why it has been banned in over 5,000 countries or whatever. Or I might be thinking of a different movie.

It is a pretty disturbing movie actually, just not rubbing-a-dog's-nose-in-his-shit-hard-to-watch like the subgenre it accidentally spawned. The story is pretty similar to the other two in its basic outline. There are two girls, Karin and Ingeri, but instead of both of them getting raped and killed, Ingeri survives and blames herself because 1) she was jealous of the other girl and 2) she may have prayed to Odin to fuck up the other girl's life. Just a little bit. Anyway, it's a good thing this girl survives because she's pregnant. That would be too much. (Oh jesus, I can only imagine what Demon Dave would've had happen to poor Ingeri and Ingeri Jr.)

Instead of going through the woods to get to a rock concert or a rave, these girls are going to church. Instead of going off to get pot or ecstasy, they stop to eat sandwiches. Karin hangs out with three brothers she meets in the woods, some weird goat herders. "Thin Herdsman" is sort of the leader, "Mute Herdsman" has his tongue cut out and seems a little pervy (this guy has a great villain face, by the way), "Boy" is a little kid. That makes it creepier because when they attack and Karin tries to escape, the kid runs after her. I don't know what the hell was going on out there in the 14th century Swedish woods, but that's not how we raise our kids in America. That kid needs some discipline.

Anyway, after hanging out with Karin for a little bit they turn on her. They rape her and beat her to death with a club. Ingeri watches from the woods and actually picks up a rock to throw at them in Karin's defense, but stops herself from doing it. And she's so horrified and torn up by the whole thing that she bites the rock. This reminded me of the ridiculous scene in the movie 8MM where Nic Cage watched a snuff film and was so horrified that he bit his fist. And now that I've mentioned that I would like to apologize to the world for comparing an Ingmar Bergman film to a Joel Schumacher. Sorry world, sorry Ingmar. My thoughts are with all of you.

Anyway, I knew she shouldn't trust those herdsmen. I hate to make generalizations, but you know how those herdsmen can be. I'm not talking about shepherds. John Brown was a shepherd. Jesus was a shepherd. Babe was a shepherd. Even *Brokeback Mountain* was a shepherd. But that's sheep, these guys are dealing with goats and people who deal with goats are a whole different pack of Kools, or at least they were back then in the woods of Sweden. It's like I always say, "Fuckin herdsmen, man."

Okay, I take it back, that is an unfair generalization. But there is kind of a class tension thing going on in this movie, I think. Karin naively trusts the herdsmen, trying to be open to meeting new friends and shit. They oughta respect her for that. But she has that fancy silk dress, and she tells them fantasy stories about the amazing lifestyle she supposedly lives, and you're not entirely sure if they understand that she's joking. I think to some hungry, lonely, crazy herdsmen out in the woods she's just some dumb rich bitch, that's how they justify it in their minds, I bet.

After they've killed her, of course, the herdsmen end up staying with Karin's parents. This is one thing that makes a lot more sense in the original story than in the remakes. Sure, it's a coincidence that they would take the same path and end up at Karin's place, but it was probably more common back then for poor travelers to take shelter with charitable strangers. And these people are very religious so it makes sense that they would want to help the poor. Because of the way things are today you might expect a very religious family to be uptight and judgmental about these unkempt goat workers, but they're not. They follow what Jesus said. At first.

It would all just be cruel irony (remember, this takes place before 9-11, so there was still irony) if Thin Herdsman wasn't stupid enough to try to sell Karin's fancy silk dress to her mom. And there's blood on it. Even before DNA testing, this is a pretty solid tip-off for mom and dad as to why Karin hasn't come home from church yet. So at this point dad, played by Max Von Sydow, takes his badass revenge. As I suspected, there are no boobie traps like in *Last House*, and no chain saws like in both *Last House* and *Chaos*.

Although many (like me) know *The Virgin Spring* as the inspiration for Wes Craven and Dave "The Demon" DeFalco's works, it is also considered a beloved arthouse type of classic, so the Criterion DVD has an introduction from Ang Lee talking about how it was the first art movie he saw and was a huge inspiration to him and etc. And it's real quiet and pretty and all but what surprised me is that it actually has some genuinely badass moments. My favorite is when mom sees Karin's dress and realizes that these fuckin herdsmen killed her daughter. But they have no idea. Her voice gets cold as hell and she says something like, "I have to ask my husband what he would give to someone for something like this," and you know that what he would give is some god damn REVENGE. Keep the change, herdsmen. And by the way, you smell like goat piss.

Max has an even colder reaction to the news. He doesn't stop to cry or nothing. He just fumes. He talks to Ingeri, tears down a birch tree, takes a bath while beating himself with the branches (must be a Swede thing), then gets his sword and goes after the herdsmen. It reminded me of the great *Rolling Thunder*, that silent, single-minded, sort of ritualistic pursuit of revenge. He immediately knows what he must do, takes a bit to prepare himself mentally, then does it. No discussion, no hedging. After he's stabbed the two older herdsmen to death he actually picks up the boy and throws him against a shelf, which kills him (not on purpose). I'm not even sure how they shot that — maybe the age limit for stuntmen is lower in Sweden.

The big difference from the Craven/Demon Dave takes on the story is that this version is all about religion. The family are very religious, they say prayers before all meals, they send their daughter to church, and she says her prayers when she stops to share bread with the perverts of the woods. Ingeri fears for herself because she knows she's blasphemous. She makes evil prayers to Odin, an unlicensed god. The herdsmen are not religious and keep forgetting to say grace before eating when they're with

Karin and her family. So the question is, how does God let this happen? Is it because Karin was backsliding and overslept, missing church? Is it because Odin interfered? Or because God was pissed about this girl praying to Odin? But isn't that bullshit if this family is so dedicated to God and just a couple fuckups causes them to have their daughter taken from them violently? This movie pretty much runs the whole gamut of "why did God let this happen?" questions.

Some people I read interpret the movie to be pretty harsh, they think Karin's charm and beauty is actually bad for the family, that the parents are too liberal with her, that their love for her makes them focus on her when they should dedicate their whole life to worshiping God and not, like, having a relationship with their daughter. If that's your interpretation though then it seems like it is God's will to get rid of Karin. And I hope that's not what my man Ingmar was going for. Because if so he's making God out to be a real asshole. Anyway, it leaves you with plenty to ponder and interpret for yourself.

Virgin Spring itself is based on an old Swedish ballad (which was probably itself based on an old comic book or TV show). In the ballad, the girl actually gets her head cut off and then a spring comes out: "From her body they cut her golden head / A spring welled forth where the girl lay dead." Maybe it's just the translation but I'm thinking that actually means a geyser of samurai style blood spraying out of the neck stump. Bergman takes it literally, he has a spring of water appear. The head stays intact but when they lift up the body a spring is behind where the head was and the water comes out and I guess because the water is a virgin, everybody cleanses themselves in it. It is God water, very refreshing, offers hope for atonement, probably works on vampires. Good shit, and not a bad idea as far as miracles from God go.

But still, I gotta say, the samurai neck geyser would've been cool too, and I'm sure fans of the original ballad were pretty fuckin pissed that Ingmar changed it. The same way those guys were mad at *X-Men Part 3*. So what I have done here is I have compared an Ingmar Bergman film to a Brett Ratner joint.

YOU HEAR ME INGMAR? I'M CALLING YOU OUT. THE SPRING IS THE BLOOD, NOT WATER. YOU'RE THINKING TOO LITERALLY, MOTHERFUCKER. LET'S TAKE IT TO THE RING.

Update: Ingmar emailed me and apologized, so I am calling off the wrestling challenge and changing it to a Steven Seagal trivia challenge. However I have been told that Ingmar knows his shit in that particular area and that I may in fact be venturing into dark territory here. Well, whoever wins, *The Virgin Spring* is actually real good, I highly recommend it.

So here is my ranking for this particular rape-revenge tale:

1. THE VIRGIN SPRING
2. LAST HOUSE ON THE LEFT
3. The 13th century ballad TORE'S DAUGHTER IN VANGE
4. "INSIDE THE CORONER'S OFFICE" extra on CHAOS DVD
5. Upcoming LAST HOUSE ON THE LEFT remake, maybe, I don't know[54]
6. CHAOS
7. The uncredited remake of CHAOS that some freako will make twenty years from now

---

54 Actually, the remake turned out pretty good. Like *Chaos* it has a changed ending that sort of invalidates the meaning of the ballad, the Bergman and the Craven. But otherwise it's a smart and well-executed film so I'd like to move it up to #3. I mean, nothing against the ballad, I'm sure it was real good at the time, but it just doesn't hold up that well in my opinion, it is not as timeless as I would like it to be.

CHAPTER TWELVE
THE MANY FACETS
OF BADASS CINEMA

When you talk about Badass Cinema there's a pretty obvious pantheon. If it was up to me Clint Eastwood, Charles Bronson, Lee Marvin and Steve McQueen would be the guys carved on the Mount Rushmore (Mount Punchmore? Mount Crushmore? I don't got a good name for it. Please disregard this parenthetical comment). Those guys are my favorites but that doesn't come close to covering the broad range of Badass cinema. That's four guys, all white Americans, roughly of the same generation. It ignores the people who came became before and after, the Asian martial arts, samurai and heroic bloodshed genres, the Schwarzenegger/Stallone types of the '80s, the women, the American martial arts movies starring the Van Dammes and Seagals, all the great blaxploitation icons of the '70s, the lesser known actors who made some good ones but just never became legendary, the more "respectable" type movies that happen to be very badass…

What I'm getting at is that my idea of a Mount Rushmore for Badass Cinema is a stupid idea. I apologize for that idea. No mountain carving could ever represent all the many sides to Badass Cinema, and neither could one chapter in a book. But I'll do what I can.

For this one I tried to pick mostly reviews shining light on the shadowy corners of this artform. I got some lesser known movies, some guys who are pretty well known but still not appreciated enough in the U.S., some guys who are thought of more as serious actors than as tough guys, but that deserve *tough guy status. I got* Enter the Dragon *in here which is an obvious one, but I use that as a lead-in to focus on one of the supporting actors. I also have Clint in here but I'm using him as an example (along with Takeshi Kitano) of the badass-turned-director, a career trajectory that has not been studied enough. And what the hell, I threw in a Charles Bronson too, just because what kind of an asshole would buy a book that didn't mention Charles Bronson in it? Not you. I respect you too much to think you would do something stupid like that.*

Then we wrap up with three of the great Badass icons starring in three movies that are all telling the same story, and two of them are among the greatest Badass movies ever made. .

ROLLING THUNDER

This great overlooked revenge movie was one of if not *the* first movie to deal with the effects of the Vietnam War. With a script by Paul Schrader (rewritten by another dude) it works on two levels, as a raw exploitation picture and as a depressing statement about the mess our country was in at the time. Fortunately we never repeated those mistakes ever again so this movie is completely irrelevant now and only good as a curiosity.

The picture opens with corny music as heroic Vietnam POWs arrive home at an airport, among them William Devane and Tommy Lee Jones. Mr. Devane will be our protagonist this evening, and as he pretends to enjoy the ceremony honoring him as a great American hero, you can tell right off the bat that he's not quite there. He's got a wife and kid waiting for him, and the kid doesn't even remember him he's been gone so long. Some guy named Cliff is there to give them a ride home. "You remember Cliff?" the wife says innocently, and you fuckin know what that means.

The wife left the house exactly how it was, to make the return more comfortable for him. And that makes you think how fucked up it would be to be locked up for years and all you want to do is come home, but then when you get there you don't even recognize it. That would suck, and he didn't get this. But what also sucks that he did get is his wife immediately tells him she's been fuckin Cliff and they're gonna have to get a divorce. There is a great scene where Cliff tries to have a man-to-man talk with him, and brings him a beer. You expect the major to chew Cliff out but he's just real nice about it, which makes it so much creepier. Instead of beating up Cliff he makes him uncomfortable by pressuring him into pulling up his arms behind his back like his torturers did to him in 'Nam. And the major almost seems to enjoy it. Making Cliff uncomfortable. Then all he does is tell him, "I'd appreciate it if you don't call my son a runt."

Now I already mentioned there's gonna be some revenge involved in this picture, but it's actually not against Cliff. Instead, there is a ceremony where a department store awards the major with a silver dollar for every day he was locked up — somewhere around $2500. Afterwards, a bunch of rednecks (including Roscoe P. Coltrane from *The Dukes of Hazzard*) show up at his house to try to force him to give them the coins.

Now look, I know I'm one to talk, but these here are some dumb fuckin criminals. I mean no offense to the handicapped but this is one retarded fucking crime. The *Radio* of home invasions. These guys are stealing $2,500, but they bring like five guys. If they're splitting it five ways, that's only $500 each, right? And the way they choose to go about getting this $500? By torturing a man who is famous for being tortured for years on end. The exact guy that you should probably not want to torture information out of. Because obviously the guy knows what he's doing when it comes to getting tortured.

Worse, they end up killing his wife and kid, and stuffing his hand in the garbage disposal. So it's double murder plus, for 500 fucking silver dollars. If they can even carry them. Nice fucking plan, fellas.

Anyway, soon after our guy gets out of the hospital with a hook on his hand he starts tracking the motherfuckers that did this to him, trying to find their whereabouts, so that the revenge can take place. Once he catches their scent he goes out to visit his old war buddy Tommy Lee Jones. This is another great scene because the whole family is there (including brother-in-law Paul Partain, who played the obnoxious Franklin in *Texas Chain Saw Massacre*), nobody knows what's up and they're all gonna have dinner together. But Devane takes Tommy Lee aside and says, "I found him." "Found who?" "The sonofabitch that killed my son."

Tommy Lee doesn't even hesitate, he says, "I'll go get some equipment," and starts getting ready to go kill the motherfucker. And as they're about to start supper the family is kind of confused because William and Tommy suddenly leave, completely suited up in their uniforms.

It's a simple movie but it's a good one. So much tension and so much that is obviously going on that the characters never talk about. It's a little bit *Taxi Driver*, a little bit *First Blood*. I guess Schrader said that in his version there was no family, the guy was just a maniac because he was so damaged by the war. He seems to think the family was Hollywood bullshit, but I disagree. It creates so much great tension, and if you read up on the divorce rates, domestic violence etc. that happens in military families (not even POW) it is clear that this has a basis in reality. I mean coming home to find out your wife fell in love with somebody else was a common experience after Vietnam, and it will be now. I just read today about a soldier here in Washington State who they think killed his wife and left her in the bathtub. His dad said, "That's not my son. My son is still in Iraq, and for that you can thank George W. Bush." I think the major's dad could've said the same thing about his son, although you probably should thank his captors and various other factions. Bush was playing all day water volleyball at that time and obviously cannot be blamed for these problems.

The director, John Flynn, also did the pretty good *The Outfit* (with Robert Duvall as Richard Stark's Parker character, who you know and love from *Point Blank* and *Payback*). And he did *Out For Justice*, which for my money is Steven Seagal's grittiest and best-directed movie, even if Seagal does a bad Italian-American accent for the whole thing. Apparently his first movie *The Sergeant* had Rod Steiger as a drill sergeant who hides his attraction to new recruit John Phillip Law by treating him like shit. Unfortunately other than that the rest of his filmography is pretty uninteresting.

Anyway, this is a real good one and highly recommended for all those trying to catch up on the '70s badass classics.[55]

---

55 As of this writing, *Rolling Thunder* and *The Outfit* still haven't made it to DVD, but if a traumatized, one-armed man can track down his son's murderers then surely you can track down a couple old VHS tapes.

SORCERER

If you're a never-give-up Rocky Balboa type of dude, a real achiever, or if you have to carry heavy objects a lot as part of a job or strongman competition, then you know this feeling: your body is exhausted, bruised, broken, covered in sweat, maybe some blood, your task seems impossible, but you're too stubborn to give up. You keep going until you're done, powered by the sheer force of will. That's what the second half of *Sorcerer* is about. Four guys, two trucks, a bunch of nitroglycerin, and miles of untamed South American jungle. They gotta drive the nitro without blowing up, because it's needed to put out an oil fire, *On Deadly Ground* style. The job is ridiculously dangerous so it pays well, and they're doing it for the pay day. They're all fugitives hiding out here for a wide selection of crimes and the money they'll get represents a chance to start over somewhere nicer. (The first half sets all this up.)

So there they are, in a couple of fucked up trucks, rolling over craggy roads, along the edges of cliffs, through swamps and across the shakiest bridges you've ever seen. And who better to lead the charge than Roy Scheider?[56] I think he's the right man for the job, and if you disagree I think you will change your mind pretty quick when you watch the movie. In one harrowing scene they come to a broken rope bridge in the middle of a storm. It seems logical to give up at this point, but Roy refuses. He has his partner crawl across the bridge guiding him inch by inch all the way across. It's a terrifying ordeal that seems to take forever and then the second they're safely across the movie cuts to the other truck getting to the bridge and having to do the same damn thing. No time to catch your breath.

Another great scene has them come to a redwood-sized tree in the road, and Roy still can't give up. He flips out, gets his machete and starts whacking, ranting about carving a path around the tree, how he'll only have to cut down eight other trees. The other guys just look at him like

---

56 Actually there's one person that might've been better, that's Steve McQueen, who almost starred in the movie. But he was having trouble with his marriage to Ali MacGraw and wanted Friedkin to make her a producer so she could be on location with him, Friedkin said no and the rest is Scheidermania. That's too bad but just try to forget I told you that and appreciate that Scheider was a good second choice.

they feel sorry for him. We always liked Roy Scheider's damn fool mind, too bad he lost it. But one of these guys was a bomber in Jerusalem. Not one of the more admirable trades, in my opinion, but one that comes in handy for this particular situation. He's examining the tree and he says, "I think I can do it." And then you get to see him try.

Friedkin's filmatism is smokin in this one. More of that confidence to tell a story the way he wants to instead of the way you expect. The beginning of the movie introduces each of the characters at the tail ends of their criminal endeavors. It doesn't coddle you with context or explaining that these characters will connect later. It skips between four different countries. And it takes its sweet time. But then when it finally does cut to the next scene it's WHOOMF, right into the action. Good editing.

It's a remake of *Wages of Fear,* and maybe that's why it doesn't feel like an American movie. I haven't seen the original but from what I gather the only huge departure here is that sorcerer that comes out at the end and starts shooting magical wizard rays at everybody. That was a little airbrushed-on-the-side-of-a-van for my tastes, but— nah, I'm just fuckin with you, there's no sorcerer in the movie at all. Supposed to be some kind of a metaphor. Oh well, even a sorcerer knows you win some, you lose some.

An artsy fartsy idea that does pay off is getting The Tangerine Dreams to do the score. It doesn't pop up much but when it does it's John Carpentery, a little Gobliny, adds to the drive of the journey.

This is kind of a sad turning point in Friedkin's filmography because it was after *The Exorcist* and *The French Connection* but then it went over budget, his behavior on set pissed people off and it was a huge flop competing against *Star Wars*.[57] It didn't totally Cimino his career, but it took away his right to do whatever the fuck he wants with his movies. It wasted his get out of jail free card. Still, looking back now I don't think there's much doubt that it's one of his best.

Long story short: *SORCERER* is MAGIC!

---

57 Which must've been a huge shock to them. There was every reason to believe this would catch on with the kids, sell a lot of Roy Scheider pajamas and tree-bombing playsets.

KIKIJURO

This work from the great Takeshi Kitano is not his most popular. Apparently there are a lot of individuals out there who hated this movie. Because this time Takeshi is not playing a violent cop or a gangster. He's just some dude. And the movie is about how he has to take care of an adorable little boy.

Now I know what you're thinkin. *Cop and a Half. Three Men and a Baby.* The one where Chuck Norris is a cop and his partner is a dog. All this type of garbage. And it's true, that is the type of basic storyline we're talking about here. But that is what is so important about this work, is that it shows you can take the tough guy and little kid formula, and do it Takeshi style, and it comes out as a great comedy. Not as crap.

Takeshi is, like our own Mr. Clint Eastwood, one of the great Badass Laureates. He has a stoic type personality and he is a master of the deadpan expression. He plays characters who go way overboard and convinces you with his eyes that he doesn't see anything wrong with it. And what brings him into the Laureate category is that he directs his own pictures, and that his directifying style happens to be exactly the best one to showcase his Badass persona.

In a typical tough guy and kid picture, there might be a similar scene to the one where Takeshi goes back and beats the living shit out of a trucker for not giving him and the kid a ride. MAYBE. But there would be wacky music playing or 'Bad to the Bone' or some shit like that. The trucker would start screaming like a baby and wiggling around goin "Oh no!" and eventually "Mommy!" and maybe he'd piss his pants and you'd think, "He's not gonna be hurt that bad but boy is it fun to watch this fella squirm! Ha ha!"

Not here. Takeshi does it in one uninterrupted shot, no music, from across the street. Like a police video or something. And he just starts beating on the dude with a stick. The sheer brutality of it is where the laffs come in.

But the movie's not all that violent. Takeshi's character is basically a juvenile delinquent in an adult body. His wife convinces him to take her friend's grand kid on a trip to see his mother. So he takes the kid to bet on bicycle races. This doesn't work out so instead of trying to come up with a legitimate plan for traveling, he comes up with a bunch of dumb schemes. Like, *what if we pop somebody's tire, then we could help them change their tire, and they would offer us a ride.*

The key to Takeshi is that he'll do stupid shit like this, or blatantly stealing right in front of somebody, or assfucking some dude out of the blue in *Boiling Point*, and then you'll look at him and he just sits there with this blank expression on his face that says, "What?"

The Takeshi approach could pump some new blood into any number of dumb comedy premises. Think of any one of these comedies that Arnold Schwarzenegger does every couple of years. Like he is pregnant or he has a short twin brother or he has to train an ostrich to defuse a bomb and etc. etc. Arnold has no fucking clue how to make that funny. Takeshi can do it in his sleep. And then wake up with a new idea for a gangster movie that came to him in a dream.

Please my young friends out there who have not yet seen the pictures of Beat Takeshi. I promise you. You will fall in love with the Takeshi style if you give it a chance. It is a very understated style, very slow and quiet. And that's why it works so well. It's not flashy or action packed and there's not a lot of talking. It's all in the air. His persona never gets old and his directation is only getting better. There is no one else like Takeshi. But let's leave this guy in Japan, all right Americans. He's doin good over there.

EASTERN PROMISES

Viggo Mortensen is a damn contortionist of the face. He stretches and twists that motherfucker from regular Viggo face into badass Russian gangster face. His eyebrows and the lines on his forehead turn into an arch. His mouth twists and curls into an arrogant smirk. The slash-like lines on his cheekbones suck extra deep into his skull. I could've sworn the motherfucker even created a dimple on his chin somehow, like through some weird breathing technique, but I checked photos and it turns out he already had that. But it fits his character well. That's just the chin dimple a Russian gangster like that would have.

After all those years of great supporting performances, and then hitting the lottery by being the king that returned in *Return of the King*, now he is getting the roles he was born for. *A History of Violence* is my favorite of his movies so far, so I'm glad he's reteaming with Dave Cronenberg here. Hopefully they will continue to collaborate for at least one more movie, it could be known as "the Viggronenberg Gangster Trilogy."

I think this is a really good, smart and original movie. But I don't want to talk it up too much. Part of the appeal is the subtlety. It leaves a lot of things unsaid, it's pretty short and it's small in scope. It deals with a family of Russian gangsters, but it doesn't feel like an empire — they live in London, after all, and all the activity is centralized at one restaurant.

In fact I'm a little surprised that the reactions aren't more divided. I heard nothing but good things from all the people I talked to who saw it before me, so I bet you'll like it too. But still, you can't go in expecting *The Godfather*, which is what the critic's quotes in some of the ads ask you to do. I heard a radio ad with a quote that was something like "Francis Ford Coppola. Martin Scorsese. And now David Cronenberg can be added to the list of directors of the greatest gangster movies of all time." That's kind of a cheating quote because it might be literally true but you fucking know it sounds like you're saying this movie is as good as *The Godfather* and *Goodfellas*. So you get to go into the hyperbole and then say you didn't mean it.

So I was hoping maybe to do a quote like "*Eastern Promises* makes *The Godfather* look like the fucking *Boondock Saints*." Or maybe "*Eastern Promises* makes *Goodfellas* look like *Corky Romano* or *Jane Austen's Mafia*." But one of my buddies told me I should just leave people scratching their heads with "*Eastern Promises* makes *The Godfather* look like *Goodfellas*." So that's my quote for the DVD cover, Focus Features. Please use a large font.

Anyway, the movie stars Naomi Watts as a London midwife whose father was Russian, who happens to be there when a young prostitute dies during childbirth. She finds the girl's diary, in Russian, and wants to get it translated so she can find out who the girl's family is before the baby goes to an orphanage. But of course there are secrets in that diary that Russian gangsters don't want her to know, and she gets into trouble.

I love Naomi Watts, she does a fine job and she looks cute in her motorcycle gear. But at least on my initial viewing I felt like this wasn't her movie, this was stolen by the men. You got Armin Mueller-Stahl as the owner of the Russian restaurant. Somehow he plays it entirely as a kindly old man on the surface while being completely menacing. There are perfectly uncomfortable scenes where he keeps trying to get her to give him the diary while trying to seem like he's not threatening her, and she either doesn't pick up on it or knows how to play it cool like she doesn't pick up on it.

Then there is his son Kirill played by Vincent Cassel. I think this is one of the best performances I've seen by that guy. He does an amazing combination of jolly, crazed, hurt, jealous, cruel, in love, and repressed. And his face is so weird looking. Great performance + weird looking face = classic.

But of course the guy everybody is gonna remember is Viggo as Nikolai. He's Kirill's driver/mortician, and at first it seems like the type of supporting role that Viggo did for so many years before *Lord of the Rings*. But he becomes more central to the movie the more it goes along. You sort of think of him as the main character ultimately but a lot of what's going on with his character is never spelled out. I have plenty of ideas about what he wants but it's sort of up to interpretation, or at least they purposely leave it unexplained.

There's one particularly memorable scene that would just about be a shoo-in for some kind of Outlaw Award if they happen to occur this year. I wouldn't want to give it away but it's been mentioned in every review I've seen in the movie so I already knew about it going in and you probably do too. This is not an action movie, but it's kind of like Takeshi Kitano where it occasionally explodes into bursts of brutal violence. And there's one amazing fight scene in a bathhouse. Roger Ebert and others have declared it a landmark scene, and I was worried I would have to be the asshole pointing out that 50 Cent already did an amazingly realistic prison shower fight scene in his otherwise pretty crappy *Get Rich Or Die Tryin'* movie. Fortunately the *Eastern Promises* scene doesn't have the same feel at all. What it does have is the dude from *Lord of the Rings* fighting two guys while butt ass naked. And there's not any Austin Powers type tricks here, he's got the balls swingin the whole time. I hate to say "no pun intended" but it took balls to do this scene. Holy shit.

I think Viggo has a real good shot at an Oscar nomination for this, I hope he gets it.[58] There's all the surface reasons, the fact that he speaks Russian, does a Siberian accent and accurate broken English, the way he physically transforms himself with his expressions and the way he carries himself. Then there's the more interior reasons, the way he plays this scary guy but then shows his other side, the way he implies other secrets. It's a hell of a performance, with so many dimensions to it, but hopefully the Oscar clip will be him naked stabbing a dude in the eye.

It's a movie that's hard to peg. It's not weird like you expect from Cronenberg, but it's not a traditional thriller either. It has a plot twist that I suspected long ahead of time, but I wasn't sure if I was ahead of the movie or right where it wanted me to be. A lot of people have told me the ending was abrupt, but I thought it was perfect. For one character it's happy, for another it's victorious, but also ironic and sad. And it does kind of feel like the end of chapter one. They could definitely do another movie, and I would be excited to see it. But I also have to wonder if maybe the continuing story should just be implied. Sort of like how the end of *The Matrix* leaves you wanting to see the revolution, but most people now probably realize they should've left it to their own imaginations.

One thing for sure though, I keep thinking about this movie and will have to see it again. I think it has a lot of things that seem small and unimportant that looking back are very significant. Here's an example. I'll be kind of vague so it won't give too much away, but if you've seen it you'll know what I'm talking about. There's a quick little part where Anna's uncle makes a horribly offensive comment, she gets upset and storms out. It completely works as just a moment, a weird uncomfortable thing that happens and makes the uncle flawed. But then if you go back and think about it, it accomplishes a whole lot of storytelling in that one moment. Most important is that it gives us a piece of Anna's history that makes us understand why she is so attached

---

58 He did.

to this baby. At the same time it establishes the relationships between Anna, her uncle and her mom. And it gives her a reason to trust the other Russian family when she should stick with her own. And not only that, it sets up this theme of the "old school" Russian ways, that they can be backwards and prejudiced, so that also pretty much explains Kirill's entire character and why he does everything he does throughout the movie. Think about it. So that one little goofy part that seems almost random is actually a crucial piece of the machinery.

But it leaves a lot for you to puzzle over. For example, what the hell does the title mean? Okay, I get the *Eastern* part, but what about the *Promises*? In the sense that it's hard to figure out, the title fits the movie well.

So I guess this is more of a critic's movie or an arthouse movie than a mainstream crowdpleaser. But I suspect it will make at least a small dent in pop culture thanks to rappers and their fascination with gangsters. It's not gonna be *Godfather* or *Scareface* popular but maybe in that area a little below *Carlton's Way*. If I'm right that's kind of interesting because Russians have never been considered cool in America. Their image took a beating during the Cold War, especially in the '80s when they were called "commies" or "Russkies" and were the go-to bad guys in action movies. They were evil and mostly faceless, personality-less. With the possible exception of Ivan Drago there wasn't even a bad guy Russian that it was cool to like, like a Darth Vader. I don't think Drago even counts, I don't know who was rooting for him. Even today Russian gangsters are just cheesy villains in DTV action movies.

As far as good guy Russians all we had was Yakov Smirnoff. And I don't know about you but I never realized that guy was really Russian, I thought it was a character like Father Guido Sarducci.

This movie not only has a great badass Russian, it has a fascination with this whole world of Russian gangster traditions, in particular the symbolism of their prison tattoos. So there will finally be something about Russians that Americans will think is cool.

Wait, maybe Nikolai Volkoff from the WWF, he was a Russian bad guy character that people liked. But he's gonna be surpassed by this new Nikolai, I guarantee it.

DOLEMITE

Josef von Sternberg was an Austrian-American director whose first film, 1925's *The Salvation Hunters*, is considered by some to be the first American independent film. He worked with Charlie Chaplin and Howard Hughes, he discovered and bedded Marlene Dietrich, Robert Mitchum threatened to throw him off a pier, he directed twenty-five movies including *The Last Command, The Blue Angel,* and *The Devil is a Woman,* and his influential films and stubborn dedication to directorial vision made him a hero to proponents of the auteur theory. Also he had a son named Nicholas Josef von Sternberg who was the cinematographer for *Dolemite.*

While *Dolemite* is arguably not as accomplished a picture as *The Scarlet Empress,* it does follow in von Sternberg's spirit of independence, and that's part of what appeals to me so much about the works of my man, the legendary Rudy Ray Moore, who passed away in October 08.

I don't know about other places but in these past ten or fifteen years young white people in Seattle have picked up the adjective "ghetto" to mean low rent or shoddy. It kind of bugs me because I don't know how the "ghetto Safeway" that doesn't have the best selection of organic foods is comparable to the actual experience of living in poverty and segregation. But I think "ghetto" is a pretty good adjective for the life works of Rudy Ray Moore, because he seemed to maintain the same ethic from beginning to end, the ethic of a club singer who learned a poem from a homeless man, reworked it into a standup act, started pressing his own comedy records and selling them out of the trunk of his car, made a cottage industry of underground XXX comedy records like *Eat Out More Often* and used those profits to make a series of scrappy low budget movies shot in his house, at a night club where he performed and in the parking lot of Ralph's.

I think he would've been great as somebody's hilarious uncle or grandpa in a mainstream comedy, but he never went that studio route. He was independent to the end. To the age of eighty-one he was touring tiny clubs (I saw him perform with a broken hip on his eightieth birthday) and making crazy no budget kung fu movies like *Shaolin Dolemite* and the please-God-release-this-on-DVD-soon *Dolemite Explosion!*

His merchandising empire was definitely "ghetto" in the white people meaning of the word. The absolutely awesome *Dolemite* soundtrack CD reissue sounds like it was transferred straight from the record, and some of the songs don't fade out, they just stop like somebody hit eject on a tape deck. The *Dolemite* DVD I own, if you go into the chapter selections, the titles for the chapters are all referring to what happens in a totally different movie, *Petey Wheatstraw* ("Petey's back," "magic cane," etc). At his shows Moore sold chintzy wooden backscratchers tied into a song he was singing for a while. So yes, I do own an autographed Dolemite backscratcher.

When I heard about Rudy Ray Moore's passing I thought about that DIYFS (do it your fuckin self) ethic of his and how it inspired me in the stupid shit I do. And I realized that although I wrote about that eightieth birthday show and reviewed a couple of his movies I never officially reviewed *Dolemite*. So I got out my Dolemite box set ("Officially Disapproved By the Man" it says on the box) and here is my belated tribute.

Usually when I think of Rudy Ray Moore my image of him comes mostly from those comedy shows and from what I consider his two best movies, *Petey Wheatstraw* and *The Human Tornado*. Those two are exaggerated, comedic takes on the blaxploitation genre. But I forgot that this first one is pretty serious. Moore portrays Dolemite as a version of himself, a comedian famous on the streets for his toasting and his comedy records, but he puts himself in a typical blaxploitation plot. I guess that's what you do when you're trying your first home made movie, you take your character and put him in a plot you've seen before. In that great "Let's put on a show!" tradition Moore got together friends and connections to pool their talents to make this thing. Some of his comedian and singer friends perform in the movie, director D'Urville Martin also plays the villain Willie Green, screenwriter Jerry Jones also plays Detective Blakely. Moore himself is credited as set decorator, and he found a local karate champion and a swordfighting expert to do the fight scenes. It was a lot of hard work decorating those sets and shit so forgive him for not getting the Dolemite tone perfect the first time around. (Or you could argue this is the best one because it seems the least aware of how ridiculous it is.)

Dolemite just got released from jail and now that he's back on the scene he pays Willie Green's stooges the fifty grand he owed him and considers himself once again the owner of Dolemite's Total Experience night club. Willie Green disagrees, because he thinks he should get 100 grand in interest, or if not should be co-owner with Dolemite. So it's a story about business disagreements that end mostly in karate.

From the opening scenes, despite Mr. von Sternberg's efforts, you can see that the filmatism is crude. But then the theme song fires like an arrow right between your eyes and injects you with six tons of funk so you know this movie means business. It's like the riff from 'Inner City Blues' has been hanging around with a bunch of wah wah pedals and drinking too much caffeine, very fast and hard blaxploitation funk that would make the Pope strut like a pimp. The theme song is important because the lyrics impart ten crucial facts about Dolemite:

1. He's bad
2. The man is outta sight
3. He's a tough son of a gun, y'all
4. His name is Dolemite (maybe this one is self-evident)
5. Ben Taylor (the singer of the song) heard of Dolemite's coming even before his time
6. He ain't lyin' about number 5
7. On the day that he was born his pappy wore a sign saying "Dolemite is here and this bad little brother is mine."
8. In addition to being outta sight Dolemite also is all right
9. He's gonna let the whole world know how bad a man is he
10. It is recommended that you stop, look and listen due to the fact that Dolemite is here for y'all to see.

(By the way, I highly recommend that soundtrack CD. Not only is this song a must-own, the thing is loaded with ridiculously funky instrumentals that I never even knew were in the movie because they play quietly in the background, you can't really make some of them out. Also it has some radio spots at the end where Rudy Ray says under eighteens won't be admitted without a parent or a note from their jailer.)

The Dolemite we see onscreen is not quite the mythic figure of the

Dolemite toast, who went eight years without eating food, has an uncle who killed a dozen men with the smell of his breath, caused the Rocky Mountains to part and, uh, fucked an elephant until she broke out in tears. Also he can look up a bull's ass and tell you the price of butter, that's one of his abilities. It's like Rambo being able to eat things that would make a billygoat puke, though — you're just never gonna see Dolemite using the butter pricing thing on film, unfortunately. So the movie Dolemite isn't as super-powered, but he has the same kind of foul-mouthed insults and boasts. His character is established pretty quickly when he comes out of the joint, gets picked up by a limo full of hot chicks, strips off his clothes, throws them back to the prison and tells the guard to wipe his ass with them. That's a good one — many movies could benefit from these types of dramatic gestures. And to be honest I would rather see that than him fucking the elephant.

Everything about the plot is generic: released from prison, framed for a crime he didn't commit, racist white cops trying to bust him, sympathetic black cop sees what's going on, etc. If you just read a plot description it wouldn't sound like it stood out from other blaxploitation movies in any way. But it does, because Dolemite is unlike any other movie character. He's not suave like Shaft or Superfly, he's not physically impressive like the Hammer or Jim Kelly. But he's more sure of himself than any of them, and has a bigger mouth. He brags that "When I see a ghost, I cut the mutha fucka," that "Dolemite is my name, and fuckin up mothafuckas is my game." He calls somebody a "rat-soup eatin, insecure, honky motha FUCKA!"

One thing people like about the blaxploitation pictures is the ridiculous outfits. The '70s was the best time for an audacious motherfucker to really go overboard on a white bellbottom suit or a fur coat. Dolemite took advantage of that window, and wears a lot of silly shit in this movie. After performing part of his "Signifying Monkey" toast at the Total Experience we see Dolemite in a dressing room, wearing a silver sequined cape and powdering up. When he goes back into the club to confront Willie Green he's wearing a white tux with a huge plaid bow tie.

But the thing that really makes Dolemite stand out from other movie heroes is his rhyming. He gets to perform his toasts, and not just in the club. One of my favorite parts is a long scene in a parking lot where he performs the "Shine on the Great Titanic" toast for some dudes who recognize him. He kind of gets self-conscious that they don't want to hear the whole thing, asks "Is that enough?" but they're into it and he has to keep going. It's a good story (the black guy working his ass off in steerage who shows those silly rich people up by surviving), Dolemite tells it well, and this is the one scene in the movie that feels like reality. I imagine this is exactly what would happen to him every once in a while when people approached him on the street.

Dolemite is not a good movie in any of the traditional ways, but the over-the-topness of the character combines with the crappiness of the filmatism and the funkiness of the music and clothes, causing a chemical reaction that can burn through metal. It's a crappy movie that's awesome enough that we hold it on a pedestal more than thirty years later. We're protective of it.

When they were talking about remaking this with LL Cool J, the prestigious cracked.com complained that "some clever devil at Dimension Films... decided that Dolemite would be a much better character if he wasn't a pimp, and if he was framed for a crime he didn't commit." But I gotta point out that neither of these would be changes from the original movie. Dolemite was in prison because the corrupt cops Mitchell and White planted coke and stolen fur coats in the trunk of his car. Although he seems like a pimp when he gets out and is met by what appears to be his stable of hoes, Queen Bee explains that while he was gone things got so desperate that his girls had to sell themselves on the street. In fact they are the employees of his club, and he never pimps them. He does call one of them a bitch for bringing him cotton drawers, which he says she should know he never wears. That's disrespectful but it doesn't really count as pimping in my opinion.

So I can't really be outraged by that. Like with many things I think a pretty good remake could happen, but wouldn't. The passing of Rudy Ray may or may not push along the development on that thing. Last I heard it was some nobody production company trying to do it with Snoop Dogg. I still think Busta Rhymes would be better, with his gravelly voice. Snoop is too tall and lanky, too smooth and soft-spoken. He's more of a Superfly than a Dolemite. Him and Busta both had Dolemite on their album intros though. Maybe he passed one of them the torch. Good luck holding onto that thing, fellas. Not gonna be easy. I'd rather they not try, but if they do they better not fuck up.

What will a post-Dolemite world be like? It's too bad, Rudy pretended to run for president so many times, but he didn't quite live to see President Obama. Probably would've been disappointed that legalizing prostitution wasn't on the agenda. As far as an artistic output, the guy was eighty-one, he had enough time there. I'm dying to see *Dolemite Explosion!*, but I didn't expect him to do another one. He was actually moved into a retirement home and had to be carried around. Even if he could walk the main thing he was doing in those later years was cameos in crappy low budget movies most of us weren't gonna track down. I don't care how big your posse is, I will not watch a movie made by Insane Clowns. It's not my thing.

Will that remake still happen? With Dolemite gone will some studio take it over? Would that maybe be better?

What happens to the cottage industry anyway, when the boss isn't here? Does his son take over? Or Queen Bee and the girls? Does it just disappear, since there are no shows to sell t-shirts at? Or does Dolemite become the registered intellectual property of some corporation? A license, a franchise, a property, a brand. House of Blues Presents The Dolemite Total Experience™ Resort with your host Dolemite™.

Whatever happens, the legacy will live on. *Dolemite* isn't even his best movie, but it alone is enough to make him legendary in my mind. The power of *Dolemite* in your DVD player will overcome whatever some stupid motherfucker tries to do to make money off the name.

ENTER THE DRAGON

Breaking news: *Enter the Dragon* is a classic and it's mainly because of Bruce Lee's performance. More on this story as it develops.

Okay maybe that's old news. He'd been trying for years to become a superstar in the US (he only went back to Hong Kong after being dissed one too many times by the white man). So it was a big deal for him to have his big American co-production. And in the movie he has so much screen presence that they had to build a special type of camera to film him, after going through six different regular cameras that broke because of his power.

Actually that's complete bullshit, I just made that up. That woulda been cool though. Anyway anything you need to know about why Bruce Lee is such an icon is in this movie: the arrogant persona (his character is actually kind of a dick), the perfect physique, the powerful moves, the cool nunchucks, the occasional philosophy, the greatest theme song of all time (thank you Lalo Schifrin).[59] But everybody knows that. I'm not telling you anything you don't know if I talk about that. So let's give some credit to the rest of the movie. For example, co-star John Saxon.

Now right now I gotta apologize to John Saxon. More than once in other reviews I used him as an example of a certain type of action direction. I said that in this movie, they pulled the camera back to show everything Bruce was doing, and pushed it in to hide what John was not doing. Maybe I imagined it, maybe it just looks that way on the pan and scan TV version. But seeing the widescreen version I see that John Saxon (or stunt double) does do some good kicks and punches and crap. What I said was true to a certain extent but not as bad as I remembered it. And most of all I should acknowledge that Mr. Saxon did fine and apparently has a blackbelt in karate even though he was hired for his acting, which he has a brown belt in.

Even not counting Bruce there's a real good cast. Sammo Hung is in there (fighting Bruce in the opening scene and doing amazing fat man handsprings), Bolo "Chinese Hercules" Yeung is in there as the imaginatively named henchman character Bolo, and of course you got Jim "Black Belt Jones" Kelly and John Saxon as Bruce's fellow good guy competitors. Jim and John both get flashbacks to explain why they're on this island, and that makes me root for them. John owes a bunch of money to some mafia types, he's only got sixty-three bucks in the bank and he needs to win the competition to get the money. Jim was about to go anyway but some fuckin pigs started harassing him, so he beat the shit out of them and stole their car. So it's probably best he's on an island

---

59 This is an error. Although *Enter the Dragon* does have an excellent theme song, the greatest of all time is actually *Shaft In Africa* by Johnny Pate. I regret the error.

somewhere for a while. (Although he ends up staying there longer than you would wish. Spoiler.)

Bruce tops them all though because he has a landmark *three* motives for this movie. I can't think of another kung fu movie that has to give three different motives. #1, he is sent on a mission to restore the honor of the Shaolin Temple, because this former Shaolin monk Han is going around being an asshole, giving the Temple a bad name. #2, some British dudes want to send him there on a secret agent type mission to prove that Han is responsible for all these girls who keep turning up dead. It seems like Bruce lucked out getting sent on a secret agent mission to do something he was about to do anyway. And then he finds out #3, Han's henchmen killed his sister. Or at least cornered her so she killed herself.

At the beginning we see that Bruce is from Shaolin, which I figure means he's a monk. But he doesn't seem like a monk because he wears a suit and tie sometimes, he goes on secret agent missions, he suggests killing the villain with a gun, and he even gambles. (It's cool gambling though, he wins a hundred bucks on a praying mantis fight.) In comparison to Han though, he's pretty straight laced. That fucker is no monk. He has a self-sufficient island fortress with its own harem, heroin production plant, grape-feeding, and more. He not only wears a suit like Bruce does, he also has a collection of metal prosthetic hands. Some are like regular hands but one of them has fur on it and another one is like a bird talon. And one like Wolverine from the x-man movies. I figure if he was a monk he wouldn't even get one prosthetic hand because you're supposed to be humble and not own stuff, aren't you? And definitely not a variety of styles.

The writer of the movie (some gwilo named Michael Allin who later wrote *Truck Turner*) admits he didn't know shit about martial arts or kung fu movies, but that helps I think because it's weird seeing a kung fu movie that thinks it's supposed to be a James Bond or a Flint movie. You got this crazy island and a weird villain ("straight out of a comic book" says Jim Kelly) and a bunch of deadly killer babes and a gimmicky end scene. Bruce sneaks around a secret fortress at night, but he's so good at it that he gets bored and yawns. This movie also takes the one-man-against-many cliché to the highest possible level. There are literally dozens of dudes swarming down the hallway toward Bruce and for him dispatching them is about as hard as swatting a bunch of ping pong balls with a tennis racket.

I mentioned Flint a minute ago and that reminds me, James Coburn was one of Bruce Lee's celebrity students. He tried to help Bruce develop American projects like *Kung Fu* and the one that became *Circle of Iron*. There's a documentary on the *Enter the Dragon* DVD that has footage from Bruce's funeral here in Seattle. And James Coburn and Steve McQueen were two of the pallbearers. Can you imagine that? James Coburn and Steven McQueen were both learning kung fu from this guy. Of course it's a real bummer he had such a young death by misadventure but especially if you figure he coulda made a kung fu movie with him, Coburn and Steve McfuckingQueen. *The Great Escape 2*, maybe.

One of these days I'm gonna do a thorough study of the works of Robert Clouse. This guy directed all across the spectrum of martial arts because he did everything from this to *Black Belt Jones* to *Gymkata* and *China O'Brien*. Also *The Big Brawl* with Jackie Chan, which a lot of people say is bad but I liked it years ago. Partly due to Lalo Schifrin's funky theme song though.

In the end though I gotta wonder, what the fuck happened to John Saxon's character, Roper? He gives Bruce a thumbs up but here he is with no tournament and no money. Did he get killed when he came back? Did he just stay on the island? Maybe he stole some of Han's artifacts, sold them on '70s eBay, and paid the guys back. I don't know but I hope some day they make a sequel to explain it. *Dear America, we plan to make a sequel to Enter the Dragon, but since Bruce Lee is dead it will be only about John Saxon's character. Thank you for your understanding. It is mainly for Vern, he requested this. Your friend, international co-production.* I'm sure that would go over well.

THE GLOVE

I'm on the mailing list for this Dark Sky DVD label. So I get all these nicely packaged Italian horror obscurities and what not, and to be honest I haven't watched most of them yet. I loan them to my horror watcher friends and hope they'll tell me I got a must-see there. But that doesn't usually happen.

For this batch though I found time to watch them and I was impressed. The one I had the highest hopes for was *Who Can Kill a Child?* which is a creepy sun-drenched Spanish horror movie in the vein of *Village of the Damned*. But I already heard that one was good before, so a more impressive find is *The Glove*, the b-picture in their latest "DRIVE-IN DOUBLE FEATURE" along with *Search and Destroy*.

They've been doing this series for a while with basically the same concept as *Grindhouse*, they put two old drive-in appropriate movies together as a double feature and they include vintage theater promos and trailers. *Search and Destroy* seemed pretty cool, I didn't really get into it but I'll have to go back and pay more attention next time. *The Glove*, though — this one is a winner.

The movie opens with a black on red graphic of the titular glove, accompanied by a theme song all about this glove and how fearsome it is. Then we see a sleazy prison guard leaving work with his mistress. Suddenly he's ambushed by The Glove, which happens to be worn by Rosey Grier.

I'd never talked to anybody who knew of this movie before, but I'd admired the VHS cover. If you've seen that you sort of know what the Glove looks like, but the cover exaggerates it. On there he looks like some comic book super villain, a guy who could beat Darth Vader in a bar brawl. And he's got two gloves — in the movie he only has one, like Michael. In that painting it has spikes on it, his chest guard looks like samurai armor and the helmet makes him look like a robot. In the movie it's riot gear, it's not from outer space. But it is Rosey Grier wearing it, so it's pretty menacing.[60]

We learn later that The Glove was designed to replace billy clubs for mean riot squad cops in the '60s, but later it was outlawed. It's "five pounds of lead and steel" but I guess there must be something else in there because the hero jokes that it takes two people to lift it. Whatever the deal is, the combined forces of The Glove and big tough Rosey Grier equals something like super powers. He not only beats the hell out of this prison guard, he literally tears his fuckin car apart, knocking dents into it

---

60 If you're not familiar with Grier, he's a big dude known for playing American football for 12 years on the New York Giants and the Los Angeles Rams, starring in *The Thing With Two Heads* and taking the gun away from Sirhan Sirhan after the assassination of Robert F. Kennedy. But he's also a pioneer in badass juxtaposition: he sang 'It's All Right To Cry' on the children's album *Free to Be… You and Me* and authored the book *Rosey Grier's Needlepoint For Men*.

and pulling pieces off of it. You don't want to fuck with The Glove.

Next we meet our hero, down on his luck bounty hunter Sam Kellog, played by John Saxon. This is exciting because I've always liked John Saxon when I see him in movies like *Enter the Dragon, Black Christmas* and *A Nightmare On Elm Street*, but I'm pretty sure this is the first time I've seen him as the lead. The movie is actually much more about his bad luck than it's about The Glove, which is only one of the bounties he's after. It's kind of like an old private eye story so he even gets to do voiceover narration. The guy is divorced and broke. He's only happy when his daughter visits, but he's behind on his child support so that could come to an end if he doesn't dig up some cash quick.

You don't see too many guys like John Saxon in movies anymore. He's a tough guy but more of an everyday tough guy than Steve McQueen or somebody. You can see why he plays cops all the time. He looks like a real life cop or a football coach or maybe a fire fighter. Even at this time (he was in his mid '40s) he had a combover, but because of the way he carries himself he can still be kind of a ladies man, and he almost manages to steal Joanna Cassidy away from her rich husband. But she's scared off by his dangerous life. On one hand, he lost the girl, on the other hand he's dangerous. So it's not too bad a loss.

Sam finds out about this Glove case. Turns out the guy is called Victor Hale, he's an ex-con who's been beating down a series of prison guards. And he stole The Glove and the riot gear from the first guard he went after. There's a $20,000 bounty put on the guy by the prison guard union. Kellog needs that money and that feather in his cap, so he investigates. When he talks to Hale's grandmother it sounds like Victor's not all that bad — the reason he went to prison was for getting revenge on the pimp who mutilated his little sister. And then the sadistic screws in the prison tortured him with The Glove. So there's more revenge in the works.

Meanwhile Sam goes after other smaller bounties to keep afloat moneywise, gets involved in some gambling and in Joanna Cassidy. There are several major scuffles, all worthwhile. The fights are a little slow and stiff but they make up for it with clever moves like when he hooks a guy's head with a swimming pool net, or when he swings on a meat hook to kick a guy in a meat packing plant, or in the same fight when he and the other guy are beating each other with cow bones. The occasional Glove attacks are good too. When Victor beats up a screw in his bathroom he ends up smashing the toilet, the sink, the shower, and the guy.

The other thing that makes the movie a surprise is the human touches. Kellog is a tough guy and he does some bad things, but his main goal is to be able to visit his daughter (Theory of Badass Juxtaposition). His first bounty turns out to be a gay man, but he doesn't seem too put off by that and barely comments on it. Later he has to go after an old lady who stole petty cash from her boss. He feels sorry for her so he takes the money and lets her go, then tells the boss she "escaped." Right after we've seen this soft side the movie gives us our first look at Victor Hale's life outside of attacking prison guards. Up until this point he might as well be a monster. He's had no dialogue, he's worn this menacing outfit and he's been going on a rampage. Most movies of this era would be happy to leave him as that type of villain. But *The Glove* surprises us by revealing that this guy's a genuine sweetheart, and not just because he killed that pimp. He finds a little kid vandalizing the stairwell in his apartments. He wants to give the kid a positive influence so he brings him in and gives him a lesson at playing blues guitar. You see that? Not only does he care about kids, he plays pretty music! (Theory of Badass Juxtaposition again.)

So now we as viewers have a problem. We love both these guys. We want them both to win. We sure as hell don't want Victor to get caught, but we also need Sam to get the money. Victor is a no-nonsense guy so when he finds out this bounty hunter has been tracking him he just calls him up and tells him to back off. Sam explains that he needs to do it for the money. "It's nothing personal. You understand that?"

So when they finally do come face-to-face it's that perfect intersection between action climax and emotional climax. Earlier Sam got to test out one of those Gloves and seemed to like it. Now Victor actually lets him borrow his to make up for the size difference and have a fair fight. You get a lot of fighting in this scene but an equal amount of bonding.

This is a real entertaining and unusual movie. Lots of funny lines, weird uses of music and quirky touches. I like how Kellog bets his friend ten bucks he can smash through a table with the glove in one swing. So when he wins his buddy not only has to give him ten bucks, but he has a broken table and all his shit scattered everywhere. And he just kind of frowns like, *fuck, shoulda thought this one through.*

The director was a rookie named Ross Hagen. Before directing this he had acted in TV westerns and written a cockfighting movie called *Supercock*, aka *A Fistful of Feathers*. His other directorial efforts after this have mostly been savaged on IMDb. He's directed as recently as 2005 but he seems to spend most of his time as a character actor in low budget movies like *Alienator, Midnight Tease II, Illicit Dreams 2* and *The Escort III*.

Anyway, *The Glove* will grab hold of you. It's a perfect fit. Five fingers of quality cinema. You gotta hand it to *The Glove*. If the glove don't smash, John Saxon got his cash. etc.

DEATH WISH II

For the first *Death Wish* sequel we trade down from Dino DiLaurentiis to Golan and Globus producing. Apparently Menahem Golan almost directed, but Bronson wouldn't do it unless they got Michael Winner back. I bet he said "why get a loser when you can get a Winner?" Anyway we caught a lucky break there. I guess Winner must've broken up with Maria from *Sesame Street* by this time so Herbie Hancock was out.[61] Instead he got one of his neighbors to score, a neighbor who happened to be Jimmy Page. I was worried but there's only guitar soloing on the beginning and end credits, the rest is standard old school score, not cheesy '80s keyboards and rockin guitars and shit. So I'm not gonna complain.

It's 1982 now, eight years later, but they say it's four years later. (The magic of cinema.) Paul Kersey lives in L.A. now. His adventures in Chicago (portrayed in the book *Death Sentence*) are ignored. He's still an architect, he has a new girlfriend (Jill Ireland) and he's moved his daughter to a hospital in California. She's still so traumatized she doesn't speak.

His life seems happy but then he has a run-in with some weirdos in the park. They steal his wallet so he chases one of them down and beats him

---

61 She had played the *Headhunters* album for Winner, inspiring him to hire Hancock to score the first *Death Wish* movie.

up in an alley. Very satisfying, but too bad his driver's license was up to date. They go to his house, rape his housekeeper, hit him over the head with a crowbar, kidnap his daughter, then rape his daughter until she kills herself.

One time a guy at the DMV scolded me for not updating my address after I moved, and he said if the police were looking for me they'd go to the old address. I said that was a pretty good case for not updating your address, and *Death Wish II* is another one. If Paul was still carrying around his Illinois driver's license his daughter and maid would still be alive. And those thugs would be wandering around Chicago trying to find him.

This story raises a few questions. In *Death Wish*, Kersey's vigilantism was said to lower the crime rate in New York City. And it inspired other people to stand up for themselves and fight off muggers. But did that last? And is he gonna hafta travel the world to lower crime rates everywhere else, because L.A. of 1982 seems way worse than New York of '74. How's he ever gonna keep up? He's not Santa Claus. The hoodlums here are even less human and more violent than Jeff Goldblum's crowd. They just run around grabbing people. They giggle and stick their tongues out and swing around like monkeys. Then occasionally they just set up a boombox and dance badly to shitty guitar rock.

A word of warning: the rape scenes in this one are much longer and more graphic, almost headed toward *I Spit On Your Grave* territory. In the Jeff Goldblum future-respected-actor-playing-rapist slot we have Laurence Fishburne as "Cutter", wearing sunglasses like LeVar Burton on *Star Trek*. I read that the U.K. cut has some of that stuff censored but I wouldn't mind. I get the idea.

I always wondered why in *Death Wish* all he needed was a gun. Wasn't he ever gonna get mugged by somebody with more than a switchblade? In *II* that escalation has taken place, so he does get in shootouts. These guys are pretty pickpockets and crazy rapists, but they trade a bag of coke for machine guns from the mob. Shit is getting crazy out there.

The simplistic approach to issues continues. People Kersey helps call him a hero and refuse to give a description to angry cops who seems to care more about busting him than other criminals. A lot of sticking it to the man goes on in these movies. Jill Ireland's character is very interested in criminal rehabilitation, Kersey kind of plays along and you're probably supposed to think "isn't it cute, women don't know what they're talking about." An anti-death penalty senator is made to look naive by only giving him one weak sentence to explain his stance.

But since Kersey's tracking down the specific guys who did the crime this time it's hard to get too mad at him. And his methods are extra badass — he calls himself Kimball, wears a knit cap and rents a rathole to use as his headquarters, his hall of urban justice. Meanwhile he's trying to act normal whenever his lady shows up. He keeps having to hide guns or hope she doesn't notice the blood pouring out of his sleeve. For his last kill he has to use her connections and a fake doctor ID to get into a mental hospital where the guy gets locked up for rehabilitation. The craziest part is Kersey proposes to her and plans it so that running off to Acapulco will also be his post-murder-spree getaway. Not too romantic. That's kind of in the same category as Homer Simpson buying Marge a bowling ball with his name on it for her birthday.

There's some pretty good violence. Laurence Fishburne has the best death — he tries to hold up his precious boombox to shield himself from bullets — it gets shot in half in time to see the bullet hit him in the face. But actually my favorite part of the movie is earlier, when Kersey is not yet on the warpath because he's only had his wallet stolen. He doesn't have a gun but he beats the guy up. The guy tries to stab him, he catches the blade in a cardboard box and disarms him. He gives him a few pounds but the guy turns out not to have his wallet, so he tosses his knife over a tall fence. Schmuck.

Then when he goes back to the ladies he doesn't even tell them what happened. He just claims he can't buy ice cream because he forgot his wallet. That's Paul Kersey for you.

SUDDEN IMPACT

I'm not sure what the title means on this one, but if it were up to me it would be called *A Dirty Harry Salute to Death Wish II*. The three before this all felt like *"Dirty Harry"* but in this one he goes to San Paolo and all of the sudden he's in Charles Bronson's jurisdiction.

Let me point out a few connections: The score is by Lalo Schifrin, but the opening credits are still *Death Wish* sequel style cheeseball drum machine and keyboard rockafire explosion over establishing shot of the city (Lalo's revenge for not getting to score part 3, I bet). Kevyn Major Howard, the gang rapist Stomper in *Death Wish II*, plays a criminal who gets off due to improper police work by Callahan. And like most *Death Wish* movies the lead villains are maniacally overacting gang rapists. In *Death Wish* and *Death Wish II* Bronson is getting revenge after (among other things) his daughter was gang-raped into a state of catatonia. In this one Sondra Locke is getting revenge because she and her sister were gang raped and her sister is in a state of catatonia. Speaking of which, Bronson's wife Jill Ireland was in *Death Wish II*, and here we have Clint's live-in lady friend at the time starring in this one. It ends a little more like the first *Death Wish* with the police (in this case Harry) knowing about the vigilante actions and letting it go because they sympathize.

This is the only *Dirty Harry* directed by Clint, and although it's not the best one it's got some of his thoughtfulness in it. In the *Death Wish* series there was always a little sense of some kind of patriarchal shit where it's always the women in his life getting hurt and he's getting revenge, it's like they keyed his car or something. Here it's the actual victim of the crime getting the revenge, and evening the score by shooting off their balls. (I wonder if this is the first review where I tried to describe a movie as thoughtful because of guys getting their balls shot off? Probably not.) *The Enforcer* explored gender equality and this one still seems down with this idea (although still not enlightened about the gays — check out the small town cop casually referring to one of the villains as "the dyke").

It further explores the "where do you draw the line?" question of *Magnum Force* but this time comes out on the side of vigilantism, at least in this case when it's not done by a cop. Harry seems a little less sure about what's right and what's wrong. This lady is saying shit that he could've said. "What about *my* rights?"

Even the climax of the movie is reminiscent of a *Death Wish* because it takes place in an amusement park (Santa Cruz boardwalk I think) and uses some western-showdown-meets-horror movie type imagery when Harry appears down the boardwalk completely covered in shadow and holding his gun. It's weird having Harry so out of his element — even out of San Francisco — so it seems like the least Dirty Harry *Dirty Harry* movie. And yet it's the one that used the line always associated with the character: "Go ahead, make my day." They probably couldn't have known how much that line would catch on, but they knew it was a good one because they use it twice. They do not have a scene where he foils a crime while eating, but they do have a scene where he criticizes a colleague for putting ketchup on his hot dog, which is a good point. Also Albert Popwell returns, this time promoted to partner. Kind of a mixed blessing — he's graduated from punk to partner, but of course both categories of characters are doomed in a *Death Wish* movie. So what's the point? Also he gives Harry a dog named Meathead.

Sondra's character is an artist — she funnels her troubled psyche into spooky paintings, but clearly she doesn't do enough of them to get it all out. She mentions that she's in town to restore the horses on a carousel, but somehow I didn't see the PERFECT VILLAIN DEATH coming. The lead rapist falls off the top of a rollercoaster, breaks through the top of the carousel and is impaled on a unicorn horn. I mean that would be a cool death no matter what but in this case you can read it as his victim raping him with her art — pretty fuckin amazing. I mean I enjoy a good impalement regardless and I'm not a big fan of looking for phallic imagery in everything, but in this case it works. That's right, a unicorn horn is actually a big dick. Keep them out of your daughter's room.

Sudden Impact is not as good as *The Enforcer*, which is not as good as *Magnum Force*, which is not as good as *Dirty Harry*. But it's better than most *Dirty Harry* and *Death Wish* rip-offs. Between "make my day" and the villain being fucked to death by a unicorn I think it's safe to say this is a worthwhile artistic venture.

UNFORGIVEN

I saw this movie years ago and like anybody I loved it. But watching it again recently I was surprised to find that it was better than I remembered. *Unforgiven* is a GFM (Great Fucking Movie) for many different reasons, most of them you know, but I'll try to point out a few of them.

For one thing it's a story that you never quite know where it's going. Supposedly it's designed so you think Little Bill (Gene Hackman) is the good guy, since he's the sheriff. I didn't get that though because the first time you see him he comes in to settle this dispute in the brothel where some assholes cut up a prostitute because she gave a giggle at his "teeny pecker". Little Bill isn't evil but he obviously makes a poor decision by not punishing these guys but just fining them a couple ponies. Not even horses, he specifically says ponies.

At best Little Bill seems like a Dirty Harry sub–villain, an ineffectual bureaucrat in the police department who is not tough enough on crime in the movie's opinion. But that turns out to be just in this one scenario, because he happens to not be too enlightened when it comes to gender issues. In fact he is very tough on crime (Eastwood apparently asked Hackman to base his performance on LAPD Chief Darryl Gates) and beats one of the protagonists to death during an interrogation.

That isn't surprising. What is surprising is that he's not entirely a bad guy either. There's a long section of the movie where we actually do side with him. He knows the prostitutes have put out a bounty on the creeps who slashed them, and that killers may be headed into the town. So each time a stranger comes into town he and his deputies confront them and take their weapons away. This doesn't come across like some anti-gun control message — it seems like a smart way to do his job. (And a challenge for Clint as hired killer William Munny to overcome.)

One of the many classic scenes in the movie is when Little Bill has English Bob (Richard Harris) in jail and has a long conversation with his "biographer" W.W. Beauchamp (Saul Rubinek, the cokehead producer in *True Romance*). This scene is part of why the movie is known as a revisionist western. Beauchamp has written up all these tall tales that English Bob told him, believing them to be true. But Little Bill joyfully pisses on his parade. He was there when one of the stories took place and says that actually Bob was just drunk and shot an innocent man.

It kind of blows Beauchamp's mind, you can see him lose respect for Bob and you can see Bob getting sad, knowing that his fan club is switching sides. But he does have some loyalty, so it really fucks with his head when Little Bill hands him the keys to the cell and a loaded gun and dares him to shoot.

It's a test and a lesson. He doesn't think W.W. will shoot him and is trying to show him that murder is not the fun he makes it out to be in his books. Rubinek is great in this scene. He goes through shock, terror, fascination, temptation and deviousness. The second before he could escape the uncomfortable situation unscathed he pulls back and challenges Little Bill, asking what would've happened if he had just given the gun to English Bob. Then he could help him escape without having to pull the trigger himself. He thinks he's outsmarted Little Bill by suggesting this, but then Bill dares him to go through with the plan. W.W. can't figure out what this maniac cop wants him to do. He doesn't really want me to do that, does he?

During all this English Bob is in the cell watching, wondering what the fuck is gonna happen here. He's the audience. He's as tense as we are.

It's a funny scene too though, the way Bill taunts Bob, pretending to misread the book title *Duke of Death* as *Duck of Death*. And Bill is the subject of taunting himself in a scene where his deputies make fun of the house he built. That's one thing I forgot about the movie — it's pretty fuckin funny. The overall tone is dark and sad but there's a lot of humor mixed in there too. There's a big scene where Munny gets his first target and instead of being glamorous it's a slow and awkward death, and everybody clearly feels awful about it. But even in this scene there's some good laughs when Munny is so bothered by his dying victim's cries for water that he yells at his friends to bring it to him and promises not to shoot at them.

And oh yeah, I haven't even gotten to Clint yet. This was a groundbreaking role because he is the greatest icon of westerns and here he is turning that persona on its head. William Munny could be the future of some character like The Man With No Name or Josey Wales. Years later he fell in love, his wife got him to stop drinking and killing, he has kids and a humble pig farm. But his wife dies and without that positive influence he's tormented by memories of his murderous past. When the young, tough-talking Schofield Kid (James Woolvet) tries to get him to come kill the whore-slashers you know he'll accept the offer but you don't know if it really is for the money or if he's jonesing to kill again. He's definitely ashamed of that past, but who knows what's going on in that head?

It seems like the main reason he's doing it is to try to provide a future for his kids. He's falling in hog shit and that's yet another way he doesn't want his kids to follow in his footsteps. He seems like a good father the way he talks to them, demanding hard work but not expecting the impossible, telling them to do the best they can with separating the hogs and then clean up. On the other hand when he tells them to kill a chicken if they get hungry and he'll be back in a week or two, that doesn't seem like that good of a father. But things were probably different back then. Kids were tougher. Now days kids gotta have cell phones so their parents can check with them all day and make sure they're not watching R-rated movies, back then you just left them on a pig farm for weeks to fend for themselves while you went to kill a couple guys. "Kill a chicken if you get hungry" is the equivalent of "there are chicken nuggets shaped like dinosaurs in the freezer." And he didn't have to worry about them looking at porn on the Internet.

But as usual I digress. We know from what people say that Munny was this badass killer, but we see with our own eyes that now he's old and washed up. He can't shoot a pistol straight so he has to use a rifle. Whenever he tries to get on his horse it tries not to let him, making him look like a jackass. He tells his kids it's because he used to be cruel to animals before he met their mother and they're getting back at him. The first time he's confronted by Little Bill's deputies he's in a saloon, hunched over like the sick old man he is, staring at the drink he knows he can't have. You almost believe he's gonna lose.

But you also know there's this bad motherfucker in there somewhere. English Bob exaggerates his stories, so does the Schofield Kid, but Munny actually underplays his. His old friend Ned (Morgan Freeman) reminds him that in a story where he supposedly killed two people he actually killed three. This is one of the few movie badasses who's embarrassed by what a badass he is. He keeps saying "I'm not like that anymore," as if trying to convince himself, and Ned keeps agreeing with him, like a friend reassuring a friend that the new hair cut looks fine.

The ugliness of violence is always a theme. Munny is haunted by it to the point of breaking down and crying about it, *First Blood* style. The Schofield Kid idolizes killers and thinks it would be cool to be one, but quickly learns otherwise. I think the genius of the movie is the balance between being honest about the ugliness of violence and satisfying the audience's need for it. I mean, if he knew it was gonna be Best Picture maybe he would've known to get all high and mighty and not make it a satisfying western. But this is Clint we're talking about here. That's not in his nature. So even in a Best Picture he has one of the all time great OH SHIT IT'S ON moments.

For the whole movie Munny has been avoiding alcohol and associating it with his wicked past. When Schofield kills a guy for the first time and is obviously upset about it Munny tells him to take a drink, like that's the only way to numb the pain. Then, as the prostitute tells him the story of Little Bill beating Ned to death for what he did, Munny starts to swig off a bottle. It's so casual it took me a second to even realize it. And as you're seeing him switch back into cold-blooded killer mode, it just so happens that the story she tells is also the all important "just how badass is he?" monologue, because she's recounting what Little Bill said about Munny, that he's a killer of women and children and police and etc.

And he gets his revenge and has multiple classic lines ("Well he should arm himself if he's gonna decorate his saloon with my friend," "Deservin's got nothin to do with it," etc.) but when he storms out of there threatening to kill and burn the family of anyone who shoots at him or who doesn't properly bury his friend or who cuts up or otherwise harms a whore he's like a vengeful demon. This man who's been quiet and hunched over for the whole movie is now yelling like a madman as the rain pours down on him. And he's finally commanding the respect of his horse. He's a fuckin maniac. The evil twin of the old Clint Eastwood movie persona. He does not ride off into the sunset.

But, you know, if a guy goes on a rampage when he drinks, and you call your town "Big Whiskey," you gotta expect problems when he shows up. Put two and two together, people.

Man, what a great set of characters, and what a great story. I'm not sure why they never made the sequel about him prospering in dry goods in San Francisco. That sounds pretty exciting.

I'm sure most of you have seen *Unforgiven*, but I know I have a younger generation of readers that maybe was not of age when this came out, or were abandoned on a pig farm to fend for themselves and did not have access to it. If for some reason you haven't seen this one I say put it on the top of your list.

Believe me, I know what you're thinking. Just because it was Best Picture doesn't mean jack shit. So was *Crash*. *Dances With Wolves* won over *Goodfellas*. *Driving Miss Daisy* won and *Do the Right Thing* wasn't even nominated. I think one of the *Look Who's Talking* movies won one year, and it was the same year that *2001: A Space Odyssey* and *Taxi Driver* came out. I might be remembering that last one wrong but the point is these people are fucking lunatics.

Okay, well played, young readers. But how about I point you to an award with a little more meat behind it, one that I can personally vouch for the integrity of? Well my young friends, it just so happens that *Unforgiven* is #4 on the Badass 100. Number four, man! You can't beat that, other than to be numbers one, two or three. It's behind only Clint's own Man With No Name trilogy, the *Lone Wolf and Cub* series, and *Yojimbo*.

Forget about how "important" it is or any of that shit. Even if it wasn't saying anything it would still be some top shelf Hollywood movie making. *The Godfather* is important too but you don't give a shit about that while you're watching it because the thing is so fucking entertaining, that's all that matters. This movie is much smaller and more intimate but it's the same way.

I can practically guarantee you will love this movie. If not, kill a chicken. I'll be back in a couple weeks.

YOJIMBO
and
A FISTFUL OF DOLLARS
and — why the hell not —
LAST MAN STANDING

I've been doing a lot of themed movie-watching lately and I don't want that to grow stale, so I decided to mix things up a little. Three movies starring my favorite badasses, but from different years and different countries. Just a real variety of material here. *Yojimbo* is about this bad motherfucker who wanders into a small town torn apart by two warring gangs, and he goes back and forth working for them, plays them against each other, rescues a woman from them then gets beaten up real bad but escapes and hides out and then tricks them some more and also I forgot to mention there's a lot of good jokes about the town coffin maker getting business from his activities. A *Fistful of Dollars*, on the other hand, is about this bad motherfucker who wa— *hey, wait a minute!*

Nah, I'm just fucking with you. Actually I thought it would be a good experiment to watch *Yojimbo* and its two remakes all in the same day. See what happens. This is kind of a miracle of badass cinema we have right here. Three of the greatest badass icons — Toshiro Mifune, Clint Eastwood and Bruce Willis — all starring in the same story. Plus you got the directors: Akira Kurosawa, Sergio Leone, and Walter Hill, who ain't in their league but he's no slouch either.

You know, I've seen *Yojimbo* before and I liked it, but it wasn't until watching it this time that I really realized what was right in front of my nose: this is WITHOUT A DOUBT ONE OF THE MOST BADASS MOVIES OF ALL TIME (or WADOOTMBMOAT). And definitely one of the most badass characters. I mean I always think of Clint Eastwood as the very top of the badass totem pole, but you gotta take into account that the role that started that persona was based on Mifune in this movie. So he's the grandaddy of it all.

Toshiro plays a badass ronin motherfucker with no name (he introduces himself as Sanjuro something something which means "Thirty-year-old Mulberry Field") who wanders at random into this small town. And while he's drinking some water he bummed off an old man he eavesdrops on a conversation about the gang war that's ruining the town. The old man pointedly says "hungry dogs always come when they smell blood" and Sanjuro gives this look like "ouch!" But a little later he sees an actual dog with a severed human hand in his mouth and I wonder if it occurs to Sanjuro that that maybe the guy actually wasn't insulting him, his eyes just wandered while he was speaking literally about the local dog problem.

As soon as he walks into town a goofy dude sees he's a ronin, runs up and starts giving him advice about which side to choose in the gang war, tells him where to go to sign up and make lots of money. "I'd show you myself but I'm the law around here!"

How badass is Sanjuro? Well, we don't have all day so I'll just scratch the surface. He has pretty much every great badass quality: superb fighting skills (sword), dry sense of humor even when threatened with death, full of clever tricks to play on the enemy, casual in the face of danger to the point of ridiculousness, keeps on going even after being beaten so bad he can't walk. And this is all made even more badass by the fact that he's not really a hero, not even a reluctant one. There's no good reason why he has to fight these guys. He's cleaning the town of gangsters but not out of any sense of duty — he thinks he can get some money out of it and he seems to think it would be amusing to kill these guys. And he's not even in town for any particular reason — he threw a stick in the air to choose his path and it pointed down this road. So what the hell, when in Rome...

After demonstrating his skills by killing three men on one side Sanjuro joins up with the other side. They're worried he might take the money and leave at night so they schedule their big gang war for that afternoon. He even overhears them talking about their plans to kill him and keep the money, and he seems to think it's funny. As soon as both sides arrive at the appointed battleground he says he quits, climbs up the watchtower and sits with a big stupid grin as they all face off with their swords and giant hammers and shit, too embarrassed to back down.

As he plays more games with the gangs he doesn't really tell people what he's doing, he keeps most of it to himself and you just have to watch the plan unfold. After he saves some people and gets a thank you letter he almost seems embarrassed or disgusted by it — in fact he leaves it laying unread on the table and that's what gets him caught and beat up by a giant. He just doesn't give a fuck.

There are different translations so it's hard to know exactly what the original lines were, but in this Criterion version it's got some of the all time great badass lines. A lot of them to the coffin maker. One of my favorite parts is when he tells a dude to go get help because six men are dead. Then he busts into the place and kills six guys. That's how confident he is, he starts the rumor before he even does it. It gets even better though — he wrecks the place and when the backup gets there he says it "must've taken fifteen or sixteen men." So by his own estimation one Sanjuro is equal to roughly 15.5 regular men.

The end is another classic moment in Badass Cinema history. He's wiped out both gangs so he tells the old man he was staying with that the town will be a little quieter now. Then he tells the corrupt lawman to hang himself. Suddenly he lifts his sword and the old man thinks he's gonna kill him — but he swings the sword and merely cuts the ropes from the man's wrists. Then he struts away and says "See ya around." The end.

There are different translations of it but I think "See ya around" is the best. I mean it's so casual and at the same time kind of threatening — yes, this guy who killed everybody else in town, you may run into him again.

Even if Mifune didn't have these great lines and badass activities he might still have turned this into a badass icon because his performance is topnotch. He looks so physically imposing (except when standing next to the giant). Just the way he moves is interesting to watch. He has this weird way he moves his shoulders up and down sometimes — I took it to be a stretch because it reminded me of Ichiro Suzuki on the Mariners. But I learned from a documentary on the DVD that Sanjuro does that because he has fleas! You hear that Mickey Rourke? I know you pride yourself in being grimy but do you have fleas? Sanjuro does. How are you gonna top that?

The way he moves his shoulders, the way he scowls, the way his eyes look at everybody else like they're no concern to him. And the way he's often scratching his chin or the back of his neck makes him look relaxed, like Dirty Harry holding that hot dog while foiling a bank robbery. Even a corrupt town torn apart by greed, filled with young psychopaths and giants with hammers, where stray dogs walk through the streets snacking on human limbs — even there this guy is not intimidated. And the very fact that people think they pose a threat to him would make him smile... if he was the kind of guy who smiled.

A Fistful of Dollars is one of the all time greats too, and it's gotta be one of if not the most influential remake of all time. The only way you can ever make it look bad in any way is to do what I just did and watch it immediately after *Yojimbo*.

The basic story stays pretty close to *Yojimbo*, with guns instead of swords. (Note: the guy in *Yojimbo* who has a gun, that guy does not have a sword in *Fistful*, he still has a gun.) But even when the scenes are directly based on *Yojimbo* there are always little variations that make it interesting. If I had an Oprah's Book Club type deal for discussing the films of Badass Cinema I would ask the question "Which coffin joke is more badass?" In *Yojimbo* he tells the coffin maker to prepare two coffins, then changes his mind: "No, better make that three." This is because he killed two guys and cut another guy's arm off, and he thinks about it and I guess he decides the third guy is gonna bleed to death. But in *Fistful* he tells the guy to prepare three coffins before he kills anyone. After he ends up killing four guys he says, "My mistake. Four."

That's pretty fuckin badass in a different way, that he is trying to be polite about it, like it's a normal transaction. Like "How would you like your cash back? Is a twenty okay?" "Sure." And then, "You know what, actually I have to do laundry, could I get a roll of quarters in there?" It's as casual as that. Plus the fact that he ordered the coffins before killing the people to go in them. That kind of thinking ahead gets you badass points. So I can definitely see an argument for either version being more badass.

Another good twist is in the scene where he first picks a fight with a group of thugs in order to get involved in the clan war — he tries to make them apologize to his mule. Then when they laugh he says that his mule doesn't like to be laughed at. You could almost argue that this is my Theory of Badass Juxtaposition in action, that he is very sensitive about the feelings of animals. But I think he's just fucking with them. Otherwise there would be a scene later on where he fixes the wing of an injured hawk or nurses a sick baby goat back to health or something like that.

Another good addition is the graverobbing. The Man With No Name may not have fleas like Sanjuro, but since he plays with dead bodies and you don't see him wash his hands I think it's fair to say he has his own hygiene issues. He takes two dead soldiers out of their coffins, sets them up against a graveyard, tells one side that two soldiers are camping out there and gets the other side to watch when they come shoot them. *Weekend At Bernie's* would've been child's play for the Man With No Name. He's a master at this shit.

(By the way, how do we really know that that body in the opening of *Texas Chain Saw Massacre* wasn't part of a similar playing-one-gang-against-the-other scheme? Think about it.)

From what I understand, *Yojimbo* was revolutionary in Japanese cinema at the time, the music was really unusual, some of the camerawork was groundbreaking and the violence and the portrayal of a scruffy samurai were shocking. Supposedly it was the first movie to use the sound of a sword going through flesh, for example. A great cinema landmark. *Fistful* does the same thing to the style of westerns and the image of the western hero. But this one is more noticeably stylish and hip. It's got the animated opening credits like a James Bond movie, the catchy Ennio Morricone music, the shots of the bad guys' ugly mugs with one guy in closeup in the foreground so you can stare at all the interesting lines on his face. All this stuff got more extreme in Leone's later movies, as his movies also got longer, his settings got more epic and the stories got more operatic and emotional. But I could see how some people could like this one even better, to see all that in its earlier, tighter form.

p.s. Good poncho

Last Man Standing on paper sounds like some kind of badass supermovie. I mean you got the story of *Yojimbo*, the star of *Die Hard*, plus you got the *King of New York* in there, from the writer of *The Getaway*, the director of *The Warriors*, and with the bottomless gun clips of *Hard Boiled*. That oughta add up to a giant foot bigger than the ass it's gonna kick, but I don't know. It's a little hit and a lot of miss. It may be a giant foot but it has poor aim and only brushes the side of the ass rather than punting it.

It's not a total loss. Bruce, obviously, is cool. The cinematographicry is spectacular. There's a couple scenes where it's pouring down rain but most of it is in the dustiest small Texas town you ever saw, the whole thing tinted a pale orange like there's even a layer of dust over the screen. A lot of times the camera's pointing through a window covered in dirt or steam or bullet holes, and sometimes when it's not it still looks like it is.

But I think maybe where the movie goes wrong is in the very premise of turning the *Yojimbo* story into a hard boiled/film noir type of story, because it changes the tone too much. I mean he drives into town in a car, there's an Italian gang and an Irish gang in from Chicago, they got tommy guns and fedoras and they talk about Prohibition, that stuff is all fine. But the voiceover narration? That kind of blows it. Both Mifune and Clint's characters are great because they're stoic, they have this big plan but they keep most of it to themselves and you watch them play all their cards one at a time with confidence. When they get beat to a pulp halfway through you wonder if this is gonna foul things up, but you kind of get the sense that it's not gonna stop them. And it doesn't.

Bruce's "John Smith" plays it quiet a lot of the time too (although he does have more dialogue than the other two), but then he explains everything he's thinking and planning in this narration. It fits the genre they're going for but it undermines the story.

Worse, to fit the noir conventions he has to be pessimistic, always talking about how fucked he is, how he's doomed but he has to take his lumps, "you have to play the cards you have," etc. So you completely lose the attitude that made the original story so enjoyable. Sanjuro and Man With No Name come in and outsmart everybody and strut out suppressing a smile, Bruce goes in and gets his ass kicked and he's lucky to get out alive. And the whole tone is more gloomy. Ry Cooder's score has a good upbeat theme at the beginning and end, but it's mostly just low notes to make everything seem grim. And instead of being shocked and in disbelief about getting their asses kicked, the bad guys just get pissed off. It's not as fun.

Luckily, there are some pretty good scenes of badass ridiculousness. In one scene, Bruce is having sex with Judd Apatow's wife when some guys come in with guns. He hops out of bed holding two handguns, as if maybe he had them in his hands while screwin. And he blows the guys away while buck naked. Obviously this is an attempt to one up *Die Hard*, where he had no shoes on, now he has no nothin on. He even has less hair than in *Die Hard*. But he has the Chow Yun Fat Signature Series .45s so he sends these guys flying five to ten feet in the air when he shoots them. Later he gets attacked while naked again, when he's in the bathtub, but he can't quite reach his guns this time. That seemed like a pretty stupid mistake not to have his guns underwater in the tub with him. Fuckin amateur.

This one is specifically based on *Yojimbo*, and credited as a remake. But when he gets beat up it's his right eye that is swollen, which I'm pretty sure is the same eye as in *Fistful of Dollars*. In *Yojimbo* it's his left eye though. Caught ya, Walter Hill. You and your damn westerns.

Anyway, I'm sorry to report that *Last Man Standing* is most important as proof that the films of Badass Cinema are more than just a list of ingredients. You can have Bruce, Walter Hill, Walken and *Yojimbo*, you can still fuck it up. Oh well, we still got those other two.

Results:
AUDIENCE AWARD: *Yojimbo*
SPECIAL JURY PRIZE FOR ACHIEVEMENT IN REMAKE: *A Fistful of Dollars*

INTERLUDE: OUTLAW MUSIC

Well sometimes there comes a time in a man's life or in a Writer's career when he really has no choice, he must move on to explore the other Arts besides the films of Cinema. The Universe is pointing him in that direction and he does what he has to do. That is why I have decided to begin my studies in the medium of Music.

It is a great challenge to put into words the feelings a good chunk of music puts into a man's (or woman's) heart and soul. However I am not about to pussy out on this one in my opinion and that is why I have decided to challenge myself with the task of studying and discussing one of the most legendary and influential bodies of music in the world, the catalog of Motown records out of Motor City, Detroit Michigan, home of the American automobile and the geographic heart of soul music.

Motown is the label that brought us the Jackson 5 and Stevie Wonder for one, and on my budget it would probably be impossible to review their entire output at this point. However this is an important mission, and I am willing to put it on the line and say that over the course of the next few years I will attempt do just that, right here in Outlaw Music. I hope that my growing success as a film Writer will help me to fund this project, until then I will use the generosity of friends and the public library who share their love of the music with each and every one of us motherfuckers.

Piece by piece I hope my Motown essays will begin to paint a picture of how this one company has changed the landscape of music forever. Our journey will encompass many artists, many lives, many stories. We will visit giants like Marvin Gaye, Diana Ross, The Temptations, Smokey

Robinson & the Miracles, The Four Tops as well as people like Rick James, The Dazz Band, Jr. Walker, Brenda Holloway, Teena Marie, Rare Earth, even The Jazz Crusaders. We will see how these two prodigies Stevie and Michael could begin as child star novelties and still grow into, respectively, our greatest songwriter and our greatest performer. This will be an epic journey through American music and culture and what not.

To start things off on an interesting note I have decided to begin with a less obvious choice, an important but fairly obscure record from an otherwise slow period in Motown's history, the year 1987. Although this album features backup vocals by The Temptations and Siedah Garrett, and an appearance by Booker T. Jones on the Hammond organ, it is primarily performed by lesser known Motown studio musicians who take the opportunity to shine, giving a contemporized spin to many soul standards as well as a few originals. The album is mostly forgotten outside the halls of academia and the homes of Motown historians, BUT it has proven to be a VERY fucking influential work which stretches its reach even outside of the soul and rhythm and blues camps and as far as the genre of contemporary country.

This album in my opinion laid the groundwork for Garth Brooks's top selling 1999 concept album *In the Life of Chris Gaines*, in which Garth presented the "greatest hits" of a fictional goofball rockstar Chris Gaines which apparently the dude plans to make into a movie for whatever reason. This Motown album we are dealing with here today introduced the same concept more than a decade earlier. The songs represent different musical eras from throughout a character's fictional career, a career chronicled in the liner notes and in a little seen film. The name of the album is of course *The Return of Bruno* by Bruce Willis (MOTC-6222).

Many would argue that Bruno was fighting to jump out of Bruce long before this album. On *Moonlighting* he charmed the hearts of women and children with his impromptu renditioning of the old songs such as 'Doo Wah Diddy,' etc. And also on the television he and his band did a famous advertisement singing the song 'Seagram's Golden Wine Cooler.' The inside of the cover explains that Bruno first performed in 1967 with a band called "The Bad Boys". Then blah blah blah it tells how he recorded these great albums but the masters were lost, he was ahead of his time, invented all different styles of music, and idolizes Steve McQueen and everybody wants to jam with him blah blah blah. At least he doesn't take it as seriously as Garth Brooks.

I believe the only song on the album that received any airplay was 'Under the Boardwalk,' however you will recognize some of the other songs anyway — 'Respect Yourself,' 'Secret Agent Man' etc. He sings about "it's fun time" and "down in Hollywood" and "I'm a youngblood", "I wanna lose myself in love tonight" and etc. His voice is kind of halfway between singing and the recognizable Bruce Willis voice. I mean you will not forget that this is Bruce.

I gotta be honest though bud this album is pretty much unlistenable garbage. BUT I feel it is historically important for many reasons. Bruce was doing embarrassing singing projects before all the other action stars — Steven Seagal, Jackie Chan, Michael Knight, Hulk Hogan all followed in his footsteps. As a known TV comedian Bruce also broke the barrier for comedians who can't stop themselves from doing karaoke such as Michael Meyers, Adam Sandler, Jamie Foxx and I believe Eddie Murphy. Okay yeah you could say that the Blue Brothers was white comedians doing Detroit rhythm and blues karaoke a decade earlier than Bruce and even somehow against all odds turned into a classic movie. But so the fuck what man, what, you're trying to say I don't have a legitimate point about Bruce being ahead of his time? Cool it bud, jesus.

More importantly this album cleansed Bruce of his "Bruno" rock star ambitions just in time for him to leave that garbage behind and star in 1988's little seen action piece *Die Hard* and change the action world of Cinema FOREVER. In fact it is even possible that Bruce was so embarrassed by this garbagey album that he made the leap into action films to keep him from looking like a pansy. Well we'll never know. Anyway the album did the trick, Bruce never brought "Bruno" back again until a cartoon in the mid '90s and by then he had changed the idea so much that Bruno was no longer even a singer, he was a little kid who is a spy and flies around in a rocket. Before then Bruce was able to leave the prancing around behind and focus on his true work in Cinema, although he had a few lapses into baby movies and then did *Armageddon*. Still in my opinion he is one of the more important comedian artists in Motown history.

CHAPTER THIRTEEN
BRUCE

In his long and varied career, Bruce Fucking Willis has crossed paths with many of the subjects discussed in this book so far. He mingled with cartoons in Sin City, Beavis and Butthead Do America *and* Bruno the Kid; *he explored a still relevant social issue in* The Siege; *his* Twelve Monkeys *and* The Fifth Element *were some of the more interesting sci-fi movies of their decade; he could've made it into the Filth and Sleaze chapter with* The Color of Night; *and he most definitely pissed me off with* Armageddon *because I was so distracted by the unbearable editing that I could never forgive the moronic horse shit going on in all those 1-second long shots. But of course most significantly to me he blew shit up real good in one of the all time great not-dumbed-down summer movies,* Die Hard.

When you watch Die Hard *you don't say, "it's dumb, but I like it!" It completely holds up as a masterfully directed action movie with unforgettable heroes and villains, tension that builds to thrilling bursts of violence and destruction, and gallows humor that gets big laughs without taking away any of the drama. There is nothing to forgive or apologize for in the movie, except arguably the dated character of Argyle the limo driver. But a little Run DMC never hurt a movie in my opinion.*

The Bruce persona is full of contradictions. John McClane was a revolutionary action hero because he seemed like a regular guy compared to Rambo or John Matrix. His muscles were smaller, his body and mind were more vulnerable. He got cut and beat to shit and couldn't stop swearing to himself about what deep shit he was in. We were used to seeing Stallone single-handedly murder entire armies and Schwarzenegger walk around carrying a log with one arm, so John McClane felt like one of us.

But he wasn't because, let's be honest, you or I would probably not jump off the building tied to a fire hose. Or maybe we would if we were painted into that corner, but then you get into Die Hard 2 and Die Hard With a Vengeance and he starts to seem more and more like a super hero. So McClane is a regular guy and also the greatest guy ever. Just a man, and also The Motherfucking Man.

And Bruce Willis seems to have that same John McClane duality. Down to earth guy from working class Jersey, a real smartass but in a charming way, gets a little tipsy at basketball games and says "motherfucker" on live TV just like you or I would do. He seems like a guy we could hang out with. But think about it, if that hanging out scenario actually came about, how do you think it would unfold? The hanging out would be in progress, you'd be watching the game or whatever, he offers you some of his garlic fries or something, suddenly it hits you that holy shit, this is Bruce Fucking Willis, this is John McClane, David Addison, Butch Coolidge, the ghost who talks to kids, the voice that babies hear in their heads. He's worked with Walter Hill, Brian De Palma, Quentin Tarantino, Terry Gilliam, Alan Rudolph, Luc Besson, Robert Rodriguez, Rob Reiner, Steven Soderbergh, Barry Levinson, Richard Donner, Richard Linklater, even McG. For a movie nerd he's a guy you want to be your buddy but you can't help but be in awe of him. He's a dude and a god under the same bald head.

So we see ourselves in Bruce and also our potential, what we think we are and what we want to be. We want to be the guy that overcomes incredible odds without wearing a cape or a mask. The guy who can't stand bullshit and knows how to destroy it with a simple smartass remark. The guy who makes a receding hairline and a dirty undershirt look good. We want to be John McClane in Die Hard With a Vengeance because not only does he save New York, he does it reluctantly. Like, "Ah, shit you guys, I'm really pretty busy to be saving New York but… ah, hell. I guess so." He's hungover and suspended and doesn't even want to be involved in this shit, but does it anyway. You could be Superman flying around saving people or you could be John McClane and say, "well, shit, I didn't want to do it, but it was obvious nobody else knew how to handle it. Now leave me alone." You know which one is cooler.

That persona — along with his great acting talent, charisma and many, many wise or lucky career choices — is why Bruce Willis is a screen legend and to many of us an ideal of manhood. Also that movie Hostage was okay. Not great.

NOTHING LASTS FOREVER: THE BIRTH OF DIE HARD

If you're like me, you've wondered for years how much Bruce Willis's *Die Hard* (1988) owes to the book it was based on, *Nothing Lasts Forever* by Roderick Thorp. And then you bought the book on eBay but didn't get around to reading it for a while because of an addiction to Richard Stark novels. But now you finally read the whole thing, rewatched *Die Hard* and are ready to share with the world a comparison of the movie to the novel. Me and you, we're in this together, like Bruce and Sam in part 3. We're gonna do this.

The "ultimate *Die Hard* DVD" has little mention of the original novel, other than director John McTiernan admitting he never read it. And a quick Internet search (a research technique I expect to see in *Die Hard 4.0* if they ever really make it) brings up no detailed comparisons between the movie and the book. But I'm sure there must be one out there somewhere. Fortunately, I am a fuckin pro at this shit. I done this for myself with *Million Dollar Baby*, *Point Blank/Payback*, *The Outfit*, two Seagal movies, and others. Also I have a commitment to excellence. So I guarantee this will be the #1 *Die Hard/Nothing Lasts Forever* comparison.

Enter Joe Leland

The book is about Joe Leland (not John McClane), a retired (not vacationing) cop going to visit his daughter (not wife) in L.A. at Christmas time. In the movie he's estranged from his wife, in the book he was divorced from his wife and she later died. His daughter used to be married to a chump he didn't like and has taken his name, Gennaro (in the movie that's his wife's maiden name that she uses at work).

Like in the movie, Leland is on the outskirts of an office party with his shoes off (washing his feet though, because he was told it keeps you from being tired at the end of a day) when he hears gunshots, because terrorists have taken the office hostage. He spends the rest of the book as a fly in the terrorists' ointment, picking them off one by one, blowing shit up, communicating with them and police on the outside using a CB. Like in the movie, the terrorists are German, and sometimes talk in German so he won't understand. One major difference is that the book always follows Leland, it doesn't cut away for scenes on other floors of the building. So unless he's spying on them, we don't know what the terrorists are up to.

And of course there are some different subplots (a budding relationship with a stewardess he met on the plane, a survivalist type named Taco Bill who talks to him over the CB) and many of the details are changed, but the basic structure is pretty much the same. What really surprised me is most of the memorable action scenes in the movie are taken from the book:

— hanging into the elevator shaft by his gun strap

— throwing a dead terrorist out the window to attract cops (doesn't hit the car, though)

— putting a dead terrorist in the elevator with "NOW WE HAVE A MACHINE GUN" written on his sweatshirt (the movie changed it to "I" and had the welcome addition of "HO HO HO")

— dropping a C4 bomb strapped to a chair down the shaft and blowing out all the windows

— rappelling down the side of the building strapped to a firehose and shooting out a window to get back inside

— taping a gun to his back for the final showdown.

The same, but different

Most of the characters in the movie are from the book, give or take: trusty Al Powell, bureaucratic Dwayne T. Robinson, blonde beast Karl and his dead brother. Even the treacherous yuppie cokehead Ellis comes from the book. In the movie there's a vague hint that Holly could be having an affair with this guy, or at least that McClane's jealous mind could be worried about that. But in the book it's his daughter's co-worker, so it's more of a fatherly "I can't believe my daughter is fucking this asshole" kind of pain.

In the book the heavy isn't called Hans Gruber, he's Anton "Red Tony" Grueber, a terrorist who enjoys sitting people down and shooting them in the lapel. Also, the ages of most of the characters have been switched around at random for the movie. In the book, Leland/McClane is much older and retired. And he's going to visit his daughter, not his wife, so she's younger. Al Powell is twenty-two. The limo driver, who isn't named Argyle and who is never seen again after he drops him off, is older.

In the movie, McClane gets dirty from climbing through vents and elevator shafts. In the book he becomes completely stained, covered in black filth, which helps him to hide in the shadows. He thinks it makes him look more fearsome, but then when he sees himself on TV he worries that it just makes him look pathetic.

And Frank Sinatra as John McClane

After enjoying seventeen years of *Die Hard*'s bastard sons and inbred cousins, I notice one cliché refreshingly missing from the original. There's a point in the movie where the media identifies the terrorist leader as "this man, Hans Gruber," and another point where Gruber learns that his foe is "Mr. officer John McClane of the New York City Police Department." In almost all *Die Hard* type movies, this is now used for the two *Just How Badass Is This Guy?* scenes, one for the hero and one for the villain.

What they would do is have a bunch of military or intelligence guys standing around in a room with a bunch of computers and a big screen, looking at security camera photos of Hans Gruber. And they list the different terrorist groups he's been connected with, the bombings and assassinations he was involved in, and that he's an expert in marskmanship, explosives, improvised weaponry, etc. And how he's unpredictable and all that crap. Then there would be a scene for John McClane where Gruber uses a computer to find McClane's secret files and it lists off what a badass he is, he has this medal and this medal, he is trained in this and this and this, he was in Bosnia and Mogadishu, he can tear a phone book in half, etc. Or they would say this guy's file is empty, he has no history. It's like he doesn't exist. This guy has black ops written all over him.

Well *Die Hard* doesn't have either one of those scenes, there is only a little bit of backstory. For McClane, the bit of backstory you get is not about his achievements as a cop, just that his wife moved away for a career opportunity. Same thing with Gruber — we just know that the terrorist group he used to be in doesn't want to be associated with him anymore. Creative differences or something.

But *Nothing Lasts Forever* is a book, so you end up having a lot more backstory. In fact, the book is a sequel to an earlier Roderick novel, *The Detective*, where Leland is a P.I. investigating a weird sex crime. In *Nothing Lasts Forever* we get a summary of that case, and how he got the wrong man executed, his marriage was ruined, his wife left him and eventually died, he was an alcoholic for a while, his daughter wouldn't speak to him, life is shit, etc. Also we learn a little bit about Leland being a pilot during the war, and a cop, and a world-renowned security expert, which helps him out with this whole terrorists-in-a-building scenario.

The Detective was even made into a movie starring Frank Sinatra. So in a way, you can consider that movie to be a prequel to *Die Hard*. But only if you can accept that Frank Sinatra as Joe Leland becomes Bruce Willis as John McClane. Which might be kind of hard. But you should try though.

(*Nothing Lasts Forever* was actually written after the *Detective* movie so they'd have a basis for a movie sequel, like *The Lost World: Jurassic Park* or *Be Cool*. But Sinatra turned down the movie. Fifteen years later, when Joel Silver decided to make it, he first offered the role to Sinatra and Robert Mitchum. Apparently it was only after they turned it down that it was decided to make it a younger character visiting his wife.)

The joy of Die Hard
On McTiernan's DVD commentary track he says that his main objective was to find a "joyful" way to do a movie about terrorists. It's kind of a weird thing to say on such a dry and humorless commentary track, but it's a fair point. He says that if the bad guy is a terrorist killing people for some political cause you just have to hate them. But if they're just trying to get money you can have more fun watching it and admire the cleverness of their scheme. Which may be true, I don't know.

At any rate, this decision is the one that makes the biggest change to the meaning of the book. In the movie Hans Gruber and his gang are pretending to be terrorists fighting for some vague political cause, but actually that's a cover to help them in a robbery. In the book though they really are fighting for a political cause, and it seems possible that if Leland hadn't become involved they could have done it without killing anyone. They say that Klaxon Oil was involved in a shady deal with the ruling junta in Chile, propping them up and taking money away from the impoverished citizens. Leland not only believes their claims, but believes his daughter was willingly involved in this corruption. But she's still his daughter, and they're still holding guns on her.

The terrorists plan to make public documents proving that the deal took place, then they plan to dump $600,000 in cash (part of the deal) out the windows.

(Klaxon Oil is changed to the Nakatomi Corporation in the movie, to reflect '80s concerns about Japanese companies buying out American ones. Ironically, if they'd left it how it was in the book it would be more up to date, less dated than it is in the movie.)

But remember, the movie added joy to the book. So the book ends up much darker. When Grueber falls out the window, he hooks a finger onto Leland's daughter's bracelet — in the movie it's a Rolex given as a reward for her work. But in the book, he pulls her down. Even though he's already dead, he kills Leland's daughter.

So Leland continues his rampage, seeks out the other terrorists in the building and kills them. And it's not pleasant. Some of the terrorists are women, and at first this bothers him, then he starts to get used to it. The last one is described as "a little girl, plump, with rosy cheeks and green eyes." When he pulls a gun on her, Thorp writes:

"She started to scream. Leland could see that she had never lived, that she knew she was dying without ever having experienced most of the natural course of life. Leland thought of his dead daughter Steffie and shot this bitch in the forehead above the bridge of her nose."

At the end of the movie, there are a couple shots where the bonds and documents from the company safe blow out the windows and fall to the ground like snow. Not important at all, just a little detail. In the book, part of the terrorist plan is to throw the company's money out the windows to the people below. Leland stops them, but since he blames the company for his daughter's death, he himself throws all the money out the window.

And remember that scene at the end, where it seems like it's all over, then Karl (last seen hanging from a chain like a slab of beef) stumbles out of the building like a crazed zombie and opens fire on McClane and everybody else, only to be gunned down by Al Powell? Same thing happens in the book, except Karl first hits Dwayne T. Robinson, killing him. And Powell jokes and/or hints that Leland ducked behind Robinson on purpose. As Leland is carried away, wounded, he drifts away and thinks about flying — an ambiguous ending that could mean he's relaxing and enjoying the fact that it's all over, or could mean that he's dead. (There is no *Nothing Lasts Forever 2: Nothing Lasts Foreverer*, after all.)

The joy of Bruce

Another part of making the movie "more joyful" was in the casting of Bruce Willis. Not that Joe Leland is humorless, but John McClane is a lot more of a wiseass. Most of the smartass remarks, discussion of cowboy movies, etc. was not from the book. Some of those lines are a little corny now, years later, but most of it works as the kind of black humor people really use in grim situations. And he doesn't follow the standard kill-a-guy/make-a-pun formula of other action movies. It's more spontaneous. I like that Bruce, while going through impossible physical punishments, is not a stone-faced super-killer. He's scared shitless. He's running around yelling "JESUS CHRIST!" and "FUCK ME!" every time things get bad (which is always). He may be a bad motherfucker but he doesn't hide the fact that he's jumping rope on thin ice.

In fact, Bruce has one line about Rambo and another one about Schwarzenegger, as if to say, "this guy is not Stallone or Schwarzenegger. He's more like us and also speaks clear English." They're purposely trying to position him as the alternative to the two top musclebound he-men of the era.

Another major theme they dumped from the book actually wasn't so dark. In the book, Leland is trying to prove that one man really can make a difference. If this old fuck can singlehandedly stop a terrorist attack, then you don't have an excuse anymore. You CAN make the world a better place! Do it for Joe Leland!

In the movie, *one man really can make a difference* sort of becomes *this one man sure is a bad motherfucker.* Which I can't really complain about. And I guess you could argue that Bruce Willis being a normal guy with a receding hairline, not some lantern jawed Adonis shipped in from Europe, sort of gets the message across anyway. One Bruce Willis really can make a difference.

Take out the grey areas, add more fun and a happy ending

McTiernan's joy-ification of the book is a little offensive from one point of view. I'm not one of those dudes that thinks anything dark is AUTOMATICALLY better than a happy ending. Like, if Pinocchio was used as a fire log or carved into a canoe at the end, I don't think that would improve the movie just because it's dark. I do think the end credits of *Seabiscuit* should be a classroom of kids pasting their art projects together, but that's an isolated case. Anyway, dark does not always mean better, but Roderick Thorp's book already exists as a grim story with purposely ambiguous morality. You definitely side with Leland, but there's a part of you that wonders about some of the things he does. And, like in some *Die Hard* rip-offs, but not *Die Hard* itself, the bad guys actually have a noble cause that even Leland agrees with. It's just their methods that are fucked. So there's more grey area there.

So it's kind of what you expect from those Hollywood fucks, to take out the grey area, add more "fun" and a happy ending. Turn it into something it's not. On the other hand, it's not like they turned it into a goofy comedy. McTiernan doesn't seem to know it, but it's still a pretty brutal movie. The guy is running around barefoot on broken glass, covered in blood. That scene where he swings shirtless and barefoot through a broken window, then gets dragged across the floor... and what about that fight with Karl, he's pounding on him and grunting like an animal, says "Motherfucker! I'm gonna kill you! Then I'm gonna fuck'n cook ya! Then I'm gonna fuck'n eat ya!" and then he wraps a chain around his neck and tosses him off the stairs... I mean, shit. This is not the watered down PG-13 action movie bullshit we got today.

Come to think of it, I'm not a big fan of the '80s at all. But that's one thing I will say for the '80s — the days when Verhoeven was a mainstream filmatist. The movies may have been corny, the music may have been horrendous, the President may have been Ronald Reagan. But at least they didn't water down the action movies. Good job with that one, '80s.

McTiernan also talks on the commentary track about how he used *A Midsummer Night's Dream* as a guide for the plot, and had them rewrite the script so it took place all in one day, because *A Midsummer Night's Dream* takes place in one day. But, you know. At least he made *Die Hard*.

The movie has a couple weird nods to important plot points that have been dropped from the book. In the book, Leland flirts with a flight attendant named Kathi, gets her phone number, later calls her and even gets to talk to her on the CB while he's in the building, thanks to the media. None of this happens in the movie, but there's a little part at the beginning where a flight attendant looks McClane up and down like *hubba hubba* as he's getting off the plane.

What doesn't Last Forever?

Another weird connection between the book and the movie — they both got titles that don't make a lot of sense. Since 1988 I've wondered why the fuck it's called *Die Hard*. I mean sure, he's a bad motherfucker, he's hard to kill, etc. But usually a movie title should have something to do with the content, right? Like in *Out For Justice*, Seagal is out for justice, right? 'Cause they killed his partner. In *Hard To Kill*, they really do have a hard time killing him, 'cause he wakes up from that coma and comes back for them. In *Unbreakable*, the plot is all about how Bruce is unbreakable. It's important.

So I always figured *Die Hard* had something to do with that old saying, "old habits die hard." But what is the old habit then? He's not a retired cop, he's just out of his jurisdiction, so being a cop isn't really an old habit. Getting back together with his wife maybe. He's been away from her and things aren't going too well with the relationship, but then he loves her and wants to save her life. But I don't know man, calling that an old habit kind of diminishes the love story too, like he's just saving her because he's used to it. So I don't know about that interpretation either.

All you can really figure, it's called *Die Hard* because it sounds cool.

Nothing Lasts Forever I don't get either. What is it referring to that doesn't last forever? The takeover of the building? Leland's life? His daughter's life? Peace on American soil? The Klaxon Oil Company being unaccountable for their criminal ways? I don't know man, it's kind of vague. None of those really fit very well. I don't get it. So like with *Die Hard*, that leaves you with one option: it sounds cool.

Only that can't be it, because *Nothing Lasts Forever* doesn't sound cool. So you got me on this one. I got no idea.

Conclusion

Everybody knows what an influence *Die Hard* has been on the action movies of the past two decades. But what's surprising is how much of that comes straight from my man Roderick's book. That's why Roderick Thorp is truly The Father of *Die Hard*. I recommend the book to all fans of *Die Hard* and *Die Hard* type movies. It's interesting to see where it all came from, and it's a good read anyway.

MCCLANE. JOHN MCCLANE.
THE WORKING MAN'S JAMES BOND
BRUCE WILLIS'S DIE HARD 2

December 21st, 1999

Well hell man I guess for those of you who read the title there's no point in explaining my premise here. You see I just watched *Die Hard part 2* for the first time since you know what[62] and I realized that John McClane is a James Bond for *our* people. The people who *aren't* rich and who don't always get the breaks this motherfucker James gets.

Bond is the ultimate secret agent, who the government agencies go to for help. McClane is just a badass that happens to be there when the shit goes down, and the government agencies try to *stop* him from helping but they can't do it cause like the title says this mother fucker is HARD.

Bond has connections everywhere and can go anywhere and do just about anything he wants, but McClane has to save the whole fucking airport just to get these motherfuckers to let him out of a parking ticket. Bond drives snowmobiles and sports cars provided by the government and jumps off of them and blows them up. McClane steals the snowmobiles he uses but also jumps off of them and blows them up. Even when he drives a car at the beginning, it's a piece of shit borrowed from his mother in law, and that one gets impounded.

Bond wears expensive suits and dapper uniforms. McClane wears a dirty maintenance man snow jacket he *borrows* from somebody else. If McClane was *ever* in a casino, he'd be wearing a sleeveless undershirt, it would be on the Indian reservation, and he'd be losing. My man John doesn't know the *meaning* of the word dapper.[63] He's a rough and tumble type dude, and if I didn't know he was a cop I'd swear he done time, cause this is the type of motherfucker that knows how to bite a guy's hand during a fight. Thumbs up for that one, McClane.

Bond has a team of experts at his disposal, but McClane just has the

---

62 At that time I talked about incarceration a lot.

63 If you're reading, John, Random House defines the word dapper as, "neat; trim; smart: *[The motherfucker] looked very dapper in his new suit."*

fax number for Reginald VelJohnson who can run fingerprints for him. Bond has this Q dude who lives in a secret lab, makes fancy gadgets for him and helps him out. McClane has a crazy janitor named Marvin who lives in a basement and finds the bad guy's gadgets laying around and tries to sell them to McClane. Bond has the greatest possible technology at his disposal, McClane has to make a torch or tie a fire hose around his waist if he wants to get fancy.

While Bond travels the world in search of intrigue, McClane just sticks to one limited location and the shit comes right to him. Bond is on a fancy ass mission trying to stop a bad guy but shit man McClane just wants his fucking wife off the plane so he can go home. Women fall for both Bond and McClane but McClane is just trying to save his wife so he shows them his wedding band. He doesn't have time for off screen sex with exotic named gals.

McClane also has the vernacular, the language of the people. Bond is all elegant with the British type shit but McClane swears like an American.[64] Bond performs these fantastic, death defying type stunts but keeps cool and says funny one-liners in that accent of his. McClane does basically the same thing but instead of keeping cool he yells "OH SHHIIIIIIIITTTTT" or "MOTHERFUCKER!!!" Bond says "Bond, James Bond" and "shaken, not stirred." McClane says, "Yippee ki-yay, motherfucker!"

In short, fuck James Bond.

John McClane is the type of hero we can admire. To be frankly honest James Bond is a fucking baby he needs all that shit to stop the bad guys. Give me a fucking break rich boy.

Now *Die Hard part 2* is a pretty good movie in my opinion. At first it seems to be coasting on Bruce Willis alone. The story begins with Bruce getting his mother in law's car impounded by the pigs. Even though he himself is a pig with the badge to prove it they won't give him a break. This shows right off the importance of bad luck. Bruce is having a bad day

---

64 Fortunately, movie stereotypes have advanced since the time of this review. The prevailing image of an Englishman back then was somebody like Brosnan looking all prim and proper. Now days that image has been replaced by Daniel Craig and actors who can not only swear but transport things and take part in bank jobs or death races.

already and just wait till the mercenaries take over the airport.

There is also a theme of coincidence. By coincidence, Bruce bumps into the man who will later be revealed the leader of the merc terrorists. This fits because it's also a fucking big coincidence that Bruce would just HAPPEN to be coming to see his wife ON CHRISTMAS during a terrorist attack, just like in part 1. And Bruce himself points this out, "How can the same shit happen to the same guy twice?"

In this part of the movie Bruce is at his best acting in my opinion. He acts without words, watching suspiciously in the crowded airport as some military bastards are passing around suspicious packages. You see the curiosity in his eyes as he struts around, sucking a cancer stick, using his badge to get into the luggage department to follow these guys and see what's what.

The high stress level of the airport is something you can really feel floating off the TV screen. When the mercs take over the tower and make it impossible for the planes to land, there is a scene where the board full of ON TIMEs switches to DELAYED, DELAYED, DELAYED all the way across and you hear panic and anger spread across the crowd.

In a way this movie also has a little more of the Christmas spirit than the first one. John and Holly are back together now living in the same city but they are visiting Holly's parents and came into town at different times. So now instead of marital type strife we just have these two wanting to celebrate the holidays together as soon as they get these merc motherfuckers out of the way.

Through the whole movie it is snowing and I think you will agree that special twinkle of the winter snow is pretty fuckin Christmassy if you think about it.

One problem, I think they tried to force Bruce's humor a little bit. There's a couple scenes where I think they just dubbed the joke on later. Like when the parachute falls over him and right away he goes, "where the fuck is the door?" It doesn't really work. Sorry Bruce, no offense. There's also this Tom and Jerry type shenanigans on the plane where Holly happens to be on the same plane as that prick reporter from part 1, and she makes fun of him and then shocks him with a stun gun while he's reporting live. Kinda stupid although I remember it was funny at the time.

Also, the South American drug lord character is pretty fucking fake. At one point I think he calls Bruce a bandejo. I'm surprised he didn't say *ay carumba this John McClane is loco*. This time the bad guys aren't krauts, they're American soldiers and I like that. The movie acts like the "drug war" of the time was totally on the level, but this fits the movie because what the fuck does a working class James Bond like John McClane know about what goes on in the governmental CIA type shit? He just wants his fucking wife back, man.

One other thing about this movie and how it further proves Bruce Willis is one of the top action stars out there. You want proof Bruce is tougher than that kraut Schwarzenegger? Well go no further than the scene early on where Bruce takes on Robert Terminator 1000 Patrick, playing a painter that goes crazy from the fumes or whatever and decides to kill Bruce. It took Arnold the whole two hours of *Terminator part 2* to wipe out this little prick. Bruce dusts him off in about twenty seconds and the dude doesn't even morph or anything. I believe these were filmed around the same time so I'm sure Robert Patrick was at a similar level of physical and mental training during both fights. The answer is clear, Bruce could bite Arnold's fucking throat out with his bare hands.

Die Hard part 2 is a good follow-up to *Die Hard part 1*. It takes basically the same type of shit but puts it on a "larger canvas" you might say, establishing Bruce as James Bond for men. Sure it is flawed but it is one of the better action sequels and in my opinion like part 1 it will some day be a large influence on the action movie genre.

THE LAST BOY SCOUT
starring Bruce Willis

So let's say instead of being John McClane or somebody, Bruce was Joe Hallenbeck, a washed up, slightly overweight, cigarette-loving, booze-sucking, wife-and-daughter-arguing, disgraced secret service agent turned low-life asshole private detective. Also, for the sake of argument, let's say that Damon Wayans is Hallenbeck's one-time favorite football player but his career was ruined in a gambling scandal and now he's a drug addict dating a stripper (Academy Award-winner Halle Berry, in a step up from her role as a crack ho in *Jungle Fever*) who Hallenbeck was hired to protect by his former friend who he just found out was screwing his wife then saw get blown up by a car bomb and now Halle Berry has been murdered because she knew too much about a football team owner trying to blackmail a senator that Hallenbeck used to protect but punched out because he was torturing women and now they're trying to legalize gambling. Also I forgot to mention that Hallenbeck once saved the President's life, and some dudes are gonna set off a bomb at the football game, and there was this fucked up part at the beginning where an NFL player pulled out a gun on the field and started shooting everybody then said "Ain't life a bitch?" (to be or not to be, that is the question) and blew his brains out.

Well shit, I really don't know WHAT the fuck is up with this movie, but let's just go with it. The director is Tony Scott, who you can always count on to make a movie that's either not that bad or, more often, actually that bad. But the real auteur in this case is Shane Black, the former hotshot screenwriter who was the first to make $4 million just for writing a Renny Harlin movie. I feel like an asshole even bringing this up, but it's probably relevant to mention that this guy was between twenty-six and twenty-nine when the movie came out (depending on which articles you trust) and he got paid $1.75 million for the screenplay. In other words, more money than you and I together earn in fifteen years. In his twenties. For this.

The movie goes on Tony Scott's not that bad shelf, mostly due to Mr. Black's attempts to push this kind of crap in weird new directions. In many ways it's just the same old crap but then he tries to make it darker and more fucked up and more smart assed. I'm pretty sure he was thinking '80s action buddy movie meets hardboiled detective noir. Bruce doesn't do any voiceovers, but he's got the down on his luck, alcohol swilling, desperate for a case, in over his head private eye shit down pat. And he's got the sometimes-witty dialogue going at 300mph from beginning to end. If anybody ever says anything, I guarantee you the other guy will have a smart ass answer to that, except in one case where Damon Wayans just says "fuck you," and then Bruce says, "Nice comeback." It feels pretty forced and self-conscious at times but you get used to it and every once in a while there's a pretty good one. Like when a bad guy uses the word "exuberance" and Wayans says, "Ah shit, we're gettin beat up by the inventor of Scrabble."

Black has the most fun when he's beaning action movie formula in the back of the head with a curveball. (That was a metaphor I believe.) For example, Hallenbeck doesn't have your usual romance here. In the first scene with his wife, he pulls out a gun and shoots their family portrait. His wife is a crazy bitch who cheats on him with his best friend and then blames him for it. But in the twisted world of the movie, he's still able to love her and reunite with her at the end, while saying, "Fuck you Sarah, you're a lying bitch and if there weren't cops around I'd spit in your face." And they put that in a context where it's genuinely supposed to be romantic.

Hallenbeck is ironically "the last boy scout" because deep down he actually has some small sense of honor, etc., but the guy really is an asshole. Insulting people, even his family and his heroes, is his number one skill and passion. He gets trapped by "bad guys" as he always calls them (this was the '90s, everybody was a postmodernist), he starts doing a whole routine of fat jokes and I fucked your wife jokes to both distract and entertain them. Shane Black must've kept a journal of one-liners and snaps and dumped them all into this screenplay.

I don't get some of em though. Like, "I'm trying to figure out which one of you looks like my dick." What's that mean? And there's a part where somebody asks Damon Wayans if he's alone and he says, "No, I got the Vienna Boys Choir with me." They always got jokes like that in movies, but why is that a joke? In my opinion that is some weak sarcasm. Totally random and meaningless. It would make the same amount of sense to say, "No, I got a class of ESL students with me," or "No, I got two meter maids and a dog catcher with me," or anybody. It might as well be The Harlem Globetrotters or the Missouri State Senate or Run DMC or the surviving cast members of The A-Team. I mean what the fuck does Vienna Boys Choir have to do with anything? I don't get it man. I wish there was some way I could return that line to Shane Black. It's defective.

Another reason Hallenbeck is an asshole, he hates funk, rap music, and specifically Prince. But to be fair the only Prince song you hear is 'Gett Off' which is not exactly his masterpiece. Still, this guy should be thanking the lord he found a strip club that plays Prince and not 2 Live

Crew or fuckin Warrant 'Cherry Pie' type garbage. Plus, I don't know if the characters in the movie are privy to the music played during the opening and closing credits, but JESUS FUCKING CHRIST. There is a song about football games on Fridays that makes the song on *Pumping Iron* sound like Beethoven's fifth in comparison. (Or whichever one was Beethoven's best. I'm not up on that information.) It kind of seems like a joke but I don't know for sure. Whatever it is I'd rather listen to 'Gett Off' for three weeks straight than hear that shit again.

Anyway like I says, despite being such a fuckin prick, Hallenbeck's got a code of honor. (That's how Americans know he's the good guy. Also, because he's played by Bruce Willis.) They have him risking his life to save the guy who ruined his career and avenge the death of the guy who fucked his wife and tried to have him killed. Because it's the right thing to do, like in that movie *Do the Right Thing*. Unfortunately, they have to have Damon Wayans explicitly point out that Hallenbeck is risking his life for the people who fucked him. Because we're retards. And later on there's a bit where the bad guy steals the wrong suitcase, which is fine, but does Damon Wayans have to fucking SAY OUT LOUD that he got the wrong suitcase, five to ten minutes after we already figured it out ourselves? I guess if you're payin a screenwriter millions of dollars, you're not gonna want subtlety. Somebody might miss something and you won't get your money's worth.

Hallenbeck is a pretty good character. You sort of gotta like a hero who's introduced passed out in his car, neighborhood kids putting a dead squirrel on his head. Damon Wayans doesn't get that type of topnotch entrance though, and it gets kind of iffy when he learns from Hallenbeck's tough guy ways and starts pulling phoney action hero maneuvers. When they're at gunpoint he stages an escape that's pretty hard to swallow. I'm not the king of action movie scripts like Shane Black was at the time, but if I was, I woulda made a declaration that no character is allowed to perform an escape that involves knowing for sure that throwing a bullet in a fireplace will cause two people to catch on fire. And if some Wayans brother or other DID pull that one off, they would at least be surprised and amazed that it actually worked.

Also the ending is kind of sad because Bruce and Damon walk off into the sunset talking about how they're gonna be partners now, and you get the strong, uncomfortable feeling that Shane Black and company assumed

America would fall in love with these characters and beg for more of their adventures for many years. I mean shit, I woulda taken a *Next to Last Boy Scout* before *Bad Boys 2* any day, but still. It didn't happen, and Shane Black disappeared after a couple years and only recently came back from the brink trying to face the demons and prove himself against great odds, just like one of his characters. But with less guns.

In a way I think Mr. Black's screenplays were one a them self-fulfilling prophecies the Lord sometimes tosses at a motherfucker. A Chinese finger trap. Shane Black was always writing about these middle age burnouts, alcoholics and suicidals, people who hate life and worry they will never recapture what they once had, before the movie started. IMDb says the guy wrote *Lethal Weapon* when he was twenty-two years old, but if I'm doing my math right he was more like twenty-five. Either way the bastard's just out of college, should be workin at a record shop or something, instead he's richer than shit, getting flown around to meetings, people with fancy offices telling him he's the future of Hollywood. Probably doesn't even know how to do his own laundry, let alone understand how a real police department operates. He doesn't know what the fuck he's doin, he just does it. And I think with this movie and *The Long Kiss Good Night* he was trying to sort of rebel against the MILLION DOLLAR ACTION MOVIE KID slot that the Joel Silvers and David Geffens were shoving him head first into, maybe trying to justify it all to himself. So he makes the main character all fucked up and throws in some weird business like the NFL shootout, the hateful romantic climax, a little girl telling a guy to "eat shit," etc.

Well none of Shane Black's movies are an ingrown hair on *Die Hard* 's shaved nutsack, but that don't mean they weren't influential. I think it's safe to say that most non-kung fu Hollywood action movies today are poured into the jello mold of *Die Hard* and *Lethal Weapon*. (At least, from what I remember. I haven't watched that movie in years. That's the one with the black dude and the white dude, right? The white dude's all crazy and the black dude's all uptight and you're like come on black dude, be more like white dude, he's crazy he's gonna shoot everybody, why can't you be more like him he plays by his own rules, don't get tied down by the red tape let's let the bullets fly and see where they stick, but seriously though you have a great family let's be friends though I got all kinds of black friends I'm totally down bud.)

Anyway, I'm glad I went back and filled in this hole in my Bruce-watching. Not a great one but an interesting one anyway.

THE FIFTH ELEMENT

The Fifth Element is your usual Bruce Willis movie that starts out in Egypt in 1934 and ends up in some fancy space hotel in 2334 with this blue-skinned space opera lady singing opera and then busting off dance moves. Bruce is introduced down on his luck, pretty much like in the *Die Hard*s — his wife left him, he's trying to quit smoking, his mom won't stop hassling him and he's "five points away" from losing his job as a flying cab driver in space age New York.

In fact this is a lot like a *Die Hard* movie except in a cartoony comic book space world instead of a building. Instead of talking to a cop on a walkie talkie, he just talks to his mom on the phone, and instead of terrorists there's this big ball of fire hurtling toward the Earth that turns light to dark, life to death, sometimes has a giant skull for a face, eats missiles and satellites, and calls himself Mr. Shadow during phone calls.

It's a pretty simple plot. There are these four stones that, combined with a perfect being called "the fifth element," can stop the ball of fire. These stones are in Egypt but then these fat robot guys come down from space and take them away for safekeeping. But then 300 years later they try to bring them back but their ship gets blown up by these muppet dog men. But the government finds a glove inside the ship and they use it to construct the perfect being, a hot orange-headed gal named Leeloo. So then she and a priest and Korben Dallas (Bruce) have to pretend they won this contest and go to the space hotel and the rocks are inside the belly of a singer so after she dies they take them out of the belly and there is a shoot out so they bring them to Egypt and do the whole ritual and whatnot.

The appeal of this picture is mainly visual. It's a real spectacle like some artsy fartsy comic book some frenchy would do. Bruce doesn't joke too much and he gets some corny lines like, "There are some very good words in V: valiant, vulnerable, very beautiful."

But let's face it the man looks cool even if a little gay. He's got blond hair and he wears arm warmers. Later in the movie after the space opera there is a big shootout, so he is right at home in space.

Now this Leeloo is a pretty young gal with freaky ass hair like Lola in *Run Lola Run*. She's played by 1999 Outlaw Award Honorable Mention for Best Badass female Milla Jovovich from *The Messenger* and she seems completely real, hopping around like some kind of animal blurting out crazy Japanese or some shit. See she's this "perfect being" reconstructed by scientists, so she has to use computers to learn about Earth culture, and she only speaks "the divine language."

Now I might be imagining this but I seem to remember hearing a story about how this movie was made, I believe this girl was a wild child that they found out in the jungles of South America or something, they dressed her up and let her loose on the set and just filmed whatever she did. Now some would say this is cheating as far as acting like an alien goes and that's probably why she wasn't eligible for an Oscar for this piece. However if you've seen *The Messenger* I think her English has improved quite a bit after being out in civilization for a while and she seems to be learning all the social rules, how to stand up straight and eat food properly and what not, although you can still see she's a little crazy, a little wild. But I hope she is happy living out in the concrete jungle. Kind of a shame really, I think like Tarzan or King Kong this will inevitably lead to tragedy but what the hell, the little jungle girl makes a damn good Leeloo in my opinion.

There's a lot of comedy type shenanigans in the movie that I don't think are very good. There are three different parts where people faint, if that gives you an idea. At the end the President tries to talk to Bruce's mom on the phone but she doesn't believe he's the President, and it's just awful as far as being funny. But Leeloo is funny. And there is this scene, Leeloo has just been created in the lab but the scientists and soldiers are just busting her balls so she decides to just haul ass out of there, and the cops chase after her. Funny thing is, they know she's this alien being just created in the lab two minutes ago, but they call her "lady" and get mad at her for not having an ID. Fuckin pigs man. Nothin changes in 300 years.

The casting in this movie is good. Not just Bruce and jungle girl, but they got this HUGE motherfucker Tommy "Tiny" Lister playing the President. This is a dude I would vote for in my opinion. There's also this goofball

(Chris Tucker) playing Rhuby Rod, a superstar DJ that dances around, sings, rhymes, and dresses like a lady. When he's reporting live from the scene of a terrorist attack all he says is "Omigod, omigod, omigod, omigod." Rest of the time he's spinning around, going "bzzzt," "super green super green." I don't know WHAT the fuck this freak is blathering about but I'm not surprised that shit is popular in the future. I mean look at Pokeyman.

There's also Jean-Baptiste Emanuel Zorg (Gary Oldman), right hand man to the evil ball of fire. This guy's such a prick that when his adviser tells him they're worried about the economy and want him to consider laying off 500,000 workers, he says, "Fire one million." He has a Hitler type haircut and wears a fancy plastic thing on his head, but he talks like Andy Griffith. This guy turns out to be a puss, though. His big scene where he almost dies — and I'm not joking about this — he's sitting at a table flapping his big yap and then he chokes on a cherry. Like a true super villain he just barely survives that one by the skin of his teeth. But then he gets blown up by muppets before he even meets Bruce. And I mean why should Bruce have to bother with this pansy anyway.

It's a goofy movie, but it's a beautiful movie. It's like if you take *Die Hard*, plug it into a wall, paint it blue and red and teach it how to fly, that's *The Fifth Element*. You know what I'm talkin about.

SUDDEN DEATH

There are about three kinds of Jean-Claude Van Damme pictures in my opinion. There are the real experimental, artsy type like *Double Team* and *Knock Off* (the best kind), the real cheap and crappy ones like *Cyborg* and *Double Impact* (the worst kind), and the more expensive ones where he's trying to become a more respectable mainstream action star (the kind that *Sudden Death* is).[65]

I have a hard time reviewing this picture since it is an unofficial sequel to *Die Hard*. For those of you who don't know I am a HUGE fan

---

65 In Seagalogical terms we would call that a Silver Era movie, like *Under Siege*.

of the *Die Hard* pictures (starring Bruce Willis, look it up if you haven't seen it) because, as a fan do I want to support this as part of the *Die Hard* mythos or should I not support it since it is unofficial, it is hard to say.

For legal reasons, McClane's name has been changed to McCord, and he is being played by Van Damme instead of Bruce. He is now a fire marshal and instead of saving Holly he has two kids going to the hockey game while he's on duty. Hans Gruber (now played by a different guy[66]) has planted bombs in the arena and has taken over the vice president's VIP box seats. He's gonna blow up the whole arena with everybody in it if the feds don't transfer a whole assload of money to his bank accounts and what not.

Van Damme does not do the smartass one-liners that Bruce does, but he does a pretty decent job and he wears an undershirt like Bruce does. One complaint, I think they should have shaved his hairline to make him look more like Bruce.

Now at the beginning I didn't think I was gonna like this picture because it was too cutesy to be believed. For cryin out loud the guy sign languages "I love you" to his kids before he goes on his shift. When he's gone the kids have an argument about whether or not their dad is brave. And before there's any sign of danger he tells his son to stay in his seat no matter what, "even if the building is falling down around you, stay in your seat." Well gee willikers I wonder where this one is going.

There are some good tricks though, like they introduce this chef character who impresses the kids with a meat cleaver trick, and you're thinking, "Gee, I wonder if that's gonna come up later." But about three minutes later the guy gets shot and you never see the cleaver again. Good stuff.

In the beginning of a *Die Hard* picture what you gotta do is establish how organized and how vicious these terrorist bastards are. So one technique they use on this one is where Hans shoots a secret service agent and the vice president says, "That agent was named so-and-so, he has a five year old son, a three year old daughter, and his wife is pregnant." So

---

66 Powers Boothe.

that way you know that it is so bad that they killed him.

Of course McCord quickly finds out about the terrorist plot going on and it turns out he knows a lot of karate for a fire marshal, and doesn't have a problem beating people to death. Right away there is a good scene where he savagely murders a gal in a penguin costume.[67] His daughter becomes one of the hostages and this time it's personal. He doesn't try to pick the terrorists off one by one like McClane usually does, but if they try to stop him from defusing the bombs, he kills them using kitchen supplies, hockey gear, fire, or what have you.

One of the best parts is when he's running from some dudes, and he has no choice but to steal a guy's hockey uniform and go out on the ice and be goalie in the big game. It is a great way to hide but also I'm thinking wow, this is a good twist, now the movie's gonna be about will they win the game or not.

But again, the movie is not going where you think it is, actually it goes back to the terrorist story when the dudes notice him out on the ice. So then I'm thinking maybe they'll have to disguise themselves as players from the other team so they can get out on the ice and shoot him. But no, the dumbass gets kicked out of the game for a flagrant foul and has to fight them in the locker room where it is more difficult to wear skates, because there is no ice.

There is a really cool and ridiculous stunt that I won't give away, where McCord gets his daughter back and saves all the hostages. Hans has his perfect chance to run off and go collect his money. But instead he puts on an elaborate disguise with fake mustache and blond hair and kidnaps McCord's daughter, forcing McCord to come after him. It's just one of those stupid mistakes you make, you get nervous and you slip up you know. There is always some little way to drop the ball... the closer you get, the farther you are in some ways. I mean if I had a nickel for every stupid motherfucker that made it to the home stretch and then crashed into a parked car or got his pants stuck on a fence or dropped the money down

---

67 I should clarify that it is Van Damme's opponent wearing the penguin suit, not Van Damme, and that she's wearing it because she's disguised as a mascot, not because she just dresses that way. If you want to see a hero going into action wearing a bear outfit I recommend the remake of *The Wicker Man*, in which Nic Cage punches women while wearing a bear costume.

a sewer or slipped on a pile of wet leaves and broke his tailbone or, as in this case, put on a fake mustache and kidnapped the daughter of an overzealous fire marshal, I would be able to drop these reel.com banners[68] that's for sure.

I think McCord is the real jackass in this situation, though. He also has the chance to get away, he has his kids with him, he saved all the hostages, and the building is evacuated. But I guess it just chaps his ass to think he's busting his balls every day as this hockey arena fire marshal, changing light bulbs and what not, trying to raise two kids on his own on this measly salary, I mean really WORKING for a good, honest living — and then here's this German fuckhead Hans Gruber[69] getting all these billions of dollars for one day of work. And I mean he wasn't even planting the bombs or anything, he was just sitting on his ass up there in the box seats. He killed a few people but big deal, it was a gun and they weren't armed, it wasn't like hand-to-hand or anything. I mean if anyone deserves this money it's the blue collar terrorists, the guys who put their blood, sweat and tears into chasing McCord around the arena, the guys who ended up set on fire or blown up or steam pressed because this fire marshal happens to be so god damned ingenuitive.

I think this must be what McCord was thinking when he chased after Gruber and climbed onto his helicopter and made sure to kill the bastard. (The big surprise here is that even though McCord refers to the situation as a "game" throughout the movie, he doesn't say "I win" or "game over" when he kills him. Good restraint there bud, seriously.)

But I don't think this is good judgment on McCord's part and I think he should be ashamed of himself and so should the whole fire department. I mean maybe if he was a security guard he should chase the guy down, it would be his job. But he's a fire marshal, his job is to prevent fires which means he should NOT be blowing up helicopters while he's on the clock. I hope if there is another sequel it will start out with him fired and

---

68 Reel.com was a DVD-selling website of the late '90s that supposedly paid residuals if you ran their banners. They never paid me a cent though. That's why I have always been so independent and full of integrity — whenever I try to go corporate there is some accounting error or something and they forget to pay me.

69 Code named "Joshua Foss" in this one.

disgraced or at least on suspension like McClane in the beginning of *Die Hard: With A Vengeance*. If he gets away with this then I can only say that this kind of lenience by employers is the reason why the American work ethic is often so shoddy, they can get away with this kinda crap.[70]

FOX – VERN HAS SOME WORDS FOR YOU ABOUT THE PANSY-ASSING OF THE 4TH DIE FLACCID MOVIE

A reader named Ed Wilson tipped me off to the following outrageous lunacy:

"In June's *Vanity Fair*, it states that Bruce Willis was initially disappointed that his fourth *Die Hard* film will likely be cut to get a PG-13 rating rather than an R. 'I really wanted this one to live up to the promise of the first one, which I always thought was the only really good one.' And he's not happy about it. 'That's a studio decision that is becoming more and more common, because they're trying to reach a broader audience. It seems almost a courageous move to give a picture an R rating these days. But we still made a pretty hardcore, smashmouth film.'"

Dearest 19th Century Fox:
Howdy. Name's Vern, nice to meet you. I am writing to ask you one question. WHAT IN GOD'S NAME ARE YOU JOKERS TRYING TO PULL?

Before you blow me off to go bathe in that champagne/money/panda blood mixture you have in your hot tub, please be aware that I am not speaking as a member of the internet community, or associate of the nerd community. I think ALL communities agree with me on this, except maybe the Amish, who don't watch movies and are therefore neutral. I am speaking as an American, and as a citizen of the world. You can't fucking do that to *Die Hard*.

Correct me if I'm wrong, but I thought the movie was called *Live Free Or Die Hard*. But from what *Vanity Fair* is saying here, it sounds more like *Live Free Or Die—Well, Let's Not Die Too Hard, There Are Children Present*.

---

70 I don't know why I was down on American workers when I wrote that. I apologize to the workers, but not to McCord.

Which, in my opinion, is not as good of a title.

Now, I know what you're thinking. If we make a horrible movie for babies and make it PG-13, it will make lots of money. The movies that make money these days are worthless garbage intentionally designed to be of a low quality, intelligence and entertainment value, in order to lower standards, make people stupider, destroy our culture and make short-term, tainted money for our evil corporation. Okay, fair enough. You know your business, I can't argue with your money piles.

But let me remind you of a couple movies you guys had something to do with.

Exhibit A: *DIE HARD WITH A VENGEANCE*, aka *DIE HARD 3*
Exhibit B: *DIE HARD 2*, aka *DIE HARDER*
Exhibit C: *DIE HARD*, aka *GREATEST AMERICAN ACTION MOVIE OF ALL TIME*

There are many things these three movies have in common. Two of them: they made you all kinds of money (untainted money that you could be proud of), and they were Rated-R.

Die Hard is a name you're gonna have a hard time living up to, even with an R-rating. The world is already skeptical. Does organic John McClane have to be updated to the CGI world to fight computer hackers? We don't know. We're not sure about this role-playing vampire sissy being the director, either. Some people have trouble with the title *Live Free Or Die Hard*, even though it's awesome. The trailer is pretty good, but you've got a bald, fearless John McClane we have to get used to, plus you teamed him with that smarmy prick from the Mac commercials.

My point is that you have a lot going against you. I, as a die hard *Die Hard* die hard, am willing to give you a chance. I am praying for a real *Die Hard*. The world of action cinema *needs* a real *Die Hard*. Let me tell you something. I am not like Harry, I don't get sent the scoops all the time. But a while back, as filming was starting up on this thing, somebody sent me the script. People were up in arms against this thing, the word that was leaking out was not inspiring confidence, and I think the idea was that I would read it, I would be outraged at how it was a bad *Die Hard* sequel, and I would start some kind of online crusade against it and try to get them to stop and rewrite or something.

What I did instead, I didn't read the script, not even the first page. I was suspecting that this probably would be an unworthy sequel. But on the off chance that it wasn't I didn't want to ruin it for myself. I wanted to go into that theater, sit down and see a brand new fuckin *Die Hard* movie. And if not be "blown through the back of the theater," at least there would be a cool breeze of awesomeness blowing me lightly against the back of my seat, and cooling me off on a hot June day. What could be better than that? I'm keeping my hopes up. I've been rationalizing away all the parts that look bad and keeping my fingers crossed.

But if you cut the movie for babies, you finally lost me. I don't know if I would even pay to see that shit. If I did I might not admit it to anybody.

You know what a PG-13 action movie is? It's *The Marine* starring John Cena. Not a good movie, not a profitable movie. It's *Half Past Dead*, Steven Seagal's only PG-13 movie, which also happens to be his last theatrical movie. Hmmm, that's odd, I wonder how that happened? When people name their favorite American studio action movies, they're gonna talk about *Die Hard*, *Lethal Weapon*, *Predator*, maybe *Under Siege*, maybe *Speed*. If you want to go even more sci-fi than *Predator* you could include *Terminator 1&2*, *The Matrix*, *Aliens*, *Robocop*, *Total Recall*, etc. All rated-R movies, all good movies, all profitable movies. That's how you die hard. PG-13 is not dying hard.

As a measure of caution, I am asking all movie writers to pull a nerd-Hans-Gruber and hold the title hostage. Do not use the word "*Hard*" on the title until we have been given proof of a hard rating. As long as there is a chance of a dishonorable PG-13, please only refer to this one as *Die Soft, Die Limp, Die Weak, Die Feeble, Die Fragile, Die Compromised, Die In a Puddle Of Your Own Urine Afraid of Facing the Consequences Of Being a Man*, etc. I personally will follow this rule and I hope my colleagues will as well.[71]

If you make this PG-13, you might get your opening weekend, it might be as big as if it was R. On the other hand, people might say "What? A new *Die Hard*? Where he's bald? And the title is funny? And the Macintosh guy is in it? And it's PG-13? I don't want to see that shit!" Or,

---

71 Yeah, remember that epic name-calling campaign that forced Fox to change the rating on *Die Hard*? Me neither. Not one of my more successful ideas in my opinion.

"Bruce Willis said it was supposed to be R-rated, and he was really disappointed, I'll just wait until the real, actual adult version of the movie is available for free, illegal, non-Fox-money-giving download after some pissed off studio employee leaks it."

And the thirteen to sixteen year olds you're banking the legacy of *Die Hard* on will say "that old guy from *16 Blocks* is supposed to be tough? Ha ha" and then they will pout sullenly as they text each other and listen to crappy music on iPods. And this might make the Macintosh wacky sidekick guy happy, but it will not get you any money. Which, in this ugly scenario, will be the fate you deserve.

Keep in mind, a sixteen year old today was four years old when the last (and not even best) *Die Hard* came out. Do you think he or she gives a fuck about *Die Hard*? And if so, isn't that odd, that somehow he or she has seen an R-rated movie? It's almost as if it can be profitable to release R-rated movies. Weird.

And before you pull some kind of cheap "yeah, but *Grindhouse* was Rated-R and it lost money" bullshit, remember this: BRUCE WILLIS WAS IN GRINDHOUSE. What are you gonna do, cut him out of *Live Free Or Die Frail* just to be safe? Come on, people.

Best case scenario, moneywise: you make a ton of money on it. But everybody feels ripped off. Your precious franchise is dead forever. The shine on an American classic gets a little less bright. Everybody starts associating the real *Die Hard* with this horse shit and thinking it's not as good as they remembered it. You sell less copies when the old, actual genuine made-for-adults good *Die Hard* movies come out on HD-DVD, BLU-RAY and whatever other futuristic formats come into existence. Nobody will even consider making a new sequel or video game or downloadable ringtone or Happy Meal toy. When you die, you will realize that in the long run you could've made more money on this *Die Hard* thing, and without having to shame an entire country to do it. You could've held your head proud instead of saying, "yeah, but this is a business, we are not here to do good things for the world and humanity, we are here to steal their money and then rationalize it by saying that ultimately it is a business."

And the real kicker will be when you realize that the stress caused by knowing the damage you had done to cinema and culture had made you ill, causing your last years to be miserable. If only you had known now what you will know then. That you could've had it both ways. You could've lived free *and* died hard.

Yippee ki-yay, etc.

I'm not gonna call out any studio head names, I don't know who's responsible. But for God's sake — listen to Bruce. *Die Hard* is for grown ups. And for kids who are allowed to go to R-rated movies with grownups. It is part of a long tradition of dads taking their kids to see R-rated movies, and making them think their dad is cool. If you pull this punk PG-13 move their dads will no longer be cool. The American family could fall apart.

Do the right thing, pal. There is a clear path to follow here. What do you think John McClane would do? Would he sissy out? Fuck no. You know who you are in *Die Hard* — you're Ellis. Go back and watch it. I think you'll be interested to find out what happens to Ellis.

Don't blow it, buddy. Don't be Ellis. Be a man. Don't die soft. You know how you want to die.

thanks bud,

Vern

Obviously I was pretty worked up when I wrote that one. I had been really excited for the revival of the Die Hard *series, and it never occurred to me that it would fall victim to the modern trend of aiming all movies at children under seventeen. When the guy e-mailed me about it, it was an instant fight-or-flight reaction, like some junkie had snatched a purse down the block and I just started running after him. I closed the email, hit 'compose,' rattled off the rant you see above and sent it to Harry.*

To be honest it's not hard to rile up my fellow talkbackers there. They are quick to get angry and criticize any movie sight unseen, like I was doing there. If you need some new compound words with the prefix "fuck" or some filthy animal-orifice metaphors, they are some good guys to go to, they can take care of that no problem. So it's not a big deal to get them worked up, but it was nice to see how many people shared my passion for the Die Hard *pictures and felt sick about the new one potentially being watered down. The best emails I got were from the people whose dads had taken them to see* Die Hard *and* other R-rated '80s action classics when they were too young to go by themselves. It really was a common bonding experience in that era and it's too bad the studios are so happy to throw that tradition away. Of the many over-the-top accusations I've made over the years maybe the best was accusing Fox of destroying the American family by releasing this PG-13.

So we all complained and cursed and then went on to other things, except for one really persistent talkbacker called "9banned0.5furious" who even three days later kept posting over and over again to keep the discussion (and therefore the PG-13 Die Hard issue) on the front page of Ain't It Cool. He was even more militant than I was. I was kind of in a movie-nerd dilemma here now, because I was obviously dying to see the movie, but if it was gonna piss me off I didn't want to support that kind of shit by giving it my money. And now that I had incited a mob I was really gonna look like a sucker if I paid to see it. My fellow "die hard Die Hard die hards" would be disappointed in me. Shit, maybe I shouldn't have said anything. Paying money for a kiddified Die Hard could've been my private shame, for me alone to know about and deal with.

Then all the sudden there appeared a post from a guy called "Walter B" claiming to have worked on the movie and defending its honor:

"I am pleased to see Vern, and everyone who responded to Vern's rant exhibit such emotion over DH4. But as someone who worked on the picture, and has seen a cut of it, I would suggest that all the yakkin' over the PG-13 issue hang onto their weapons for now. This episode if *Die Hard* is as good, if not better than the first Movie. And I was there for that one too. In a Summer filled with CG/fantasy driven films, *Live Free or Die Hard* is an in-your-face, hard-ass Action movie that will satisfy Vern, and anyone else who is a fan of the *Die Hard* series. All PG-13 means is that you cannot say f*ck more than twice. Other than that, the Mythology of *Die Hard* lives.... I could not have been more pleased with how DH4 turned out. It'll be out soon enough, and I wanna hear what Vern has to say after he sees *LForDie Hard*.... Set your pre-judgement aside for another 7 weeks and then decide."

On the Internet, obviously, people are not always who they claim to be. Just ask those perverts they catch on Dateline NBC. Usually when some anonymous poster on a message board claims they worked on a movie it's safe to assume they're full of shit. But for some reason I immediately believed Walter B. I thought "am I imagining this? Could this be true? Is this really who I think it is?"

A little lower down I came to another post from Walter B, one that directly implied what I already suspected:

"Since they have existed, I always said the first *Die Hard* was the only good one. I will go on record here as saying that *Live Free or Die Hard* is better than the first one. Take it from a guy who was there for all of them. John MaFuckin'Clane"

So there were basically two choices of what was going on here. Either

a) I wrote a nerdy, pissed off essay on Ain't It Cool News, and then Bruce Fucking Willis signed up for a talkback account so he could assure me I was gonna like his new movie.

b) Some dude on the Internet thinks I'm stupid enough to believe that Bruce Fucking Willis would sign up for a talkback account so he could assure me I was gonna like his new movie.

Call me naive, call me optimistic, but for some reason I was convinced it was 'a'. I responded:

"I was honestly thinking I couldn't ethically pay to see this movie if it's PG-13, but if I just read what I think I read that seems like a pretty fuckin solid recommendation. I better not be hearing no Mr. Falcon in this one, though.

By the way, I've gotten a whole lot of emails in response to this piece, and almost every one related strongly to the part about bonding with their dads when they got to go see a *Die Hard* movie even though it's rated R. These were stories that would make you tear up, Walter. So if it's not too late you might at least throw one more 'fuck' in there just for the sake of our nation's young men so they can grow up strong of character, etc.

thanks a million"

There was absolutely no evidence to support that this was the real Bruce Willis, but I wasn't the only one who assumed it was. For four days, in between his reports supposedly from a looping session, we asked this "Walter B" about the new movie, about his old movies, about his favorite movies. He complimented Shane Black's writing and Mel Gibson's direction of Apocalypto. *He said he would never work with Michael Bay again. A couple people called him an imposter, called us morons for believing him, and attacked his spelling (he kept spelling "McClane" wrong). He told them to fuck off. We kept asking him whatever random shit you would ask Bruce Willis if you ran into him somewhere and he was really cool and stayed to talk — like that hypothetical hanging-out-with-Bruce-Willis scenario I mentioned earlier. In a quest to find common ground between my two all time favorite action movies I got him to praise* Hard Boiled *and call Chow Yun Fat "the boss of ass whoopin'."*

But there was that nagging feeling that maybe we were suckers and that the random dude on the Internet who implied but did not say in so many words that he was Bruce Willis was not, in fact, Bruce Willis. He didn't write much that seemed out of character for Willis, but I did notice that his answer as to why Len Wiseman was chosen to direct Live Free Or Die Hard *contradicted what he said in an interview I had read. People started to try to quiz him with questions that "only Bruce Willis would know the answer to," like which hotel he stayed at when he went to the Cannes Film Festival in such-and-such a year. I e-mailed Harry to see if he could verify Walter B's identity, but got no response until Moriarty, at that time the #2 guy at Ain't It Cool and my main contact, emailed to say that no, it wasn't him. I broke the news to the others:*

"I believe it was Darth Vader who said 'NOOOOOOOOOOOOOOO!!!!!!'
    (part 3, near the end.)
    I still haven't heard from Harry on a positive ID for Walter B, but Moriarty says it's not Bruce and that Harry would give him a black box if it was. He didn't give me any more explanation than that, but I guess 'Bruce Willis dissing Michael Bay in my talkback' would be near the top of my personal 'too good to be true' list, so he must be right.
    Which brings me to my next question for Walter B: what kind of a sick sonofabitch would put us through this? First 9-11, then PG-13 *Die Hard*, and now this. Why won't you let America heal?
    Also, what was it like working with Tarantino, and did you know *Pulp Fiction* was gonna be such a keeper. thanks Walter."

Moriarty came on and told us that we'd been duped. Walter B disagreed. Moriarty dared him to call Harry then. Walter first hedged, then claimed he had tried calling, but that Harry wasn't home. Moriarty wrote, "Guys... I

Repeat... this was not Bruce Willis. It really shouldn't even be a question, but in case you're still wondering... nope. Not him." I was feeling like a moron. Should've seen that coming. Oh well, it was a nice fantasy while it lasted. Now back to reality.

But some time early on May 9 when no one was looking, the posts by Walter B switched from black text on a white background to white text on dark grey. This is the "black box" Moriarty referred to, Ain't It Cool's way of marking talkbacks from their editors and contributors. Moriarty had a black box and I did too (a trophy earned from my Demon Dave wrestling challenge). Now so did this guy who we first thought was Bruce Willis and then thought was some asshole taking advantage of the world's love for Bruce Willis. I had told him that "Impersonating a police officer or a federal agent is a crime. Just ask DMX. But impersonating Bruce Willis is AN ABOMINATION AGAINST GOD."

What did the black box signify? Did this mean that God had nothing to be offended by? Did it mean what we thought it meant? No explanation from Harry. And then Walter B says he knows what to do, why doesn't someone with iChat talk to him on camera. For a few more hours, we stayed glued to the talkback waiting for someone with a Mac and iChat to step up, then to connect with Walter B. And sure enough, some guy named Jay made contact — a close encounter of the Bruce kind. The picture he posted online still makes me laugh — it's an unmistakable Bruce Willis pulling up a sleeve to reveal a shoulder tattoo (showing his identifying marks?). Inset in the corner is Jay, a young bearded guy in a baseball cap with an ear-to-ear grin that says "Holy shit, I'm iChatting with Bruce Willis!"

By this point the talkback had more than 1,000 posts. With word spreading that for some reason Bruce god damn Willis was answering random nerd questions, the server seemed to get crushed. Moriarty ate crow and then started a new "official" thread for Bruce Willis questions, which was an absolute avalanche of new names from all over the world telling Bruce how much they loved him and asking about their favorite movies. It was a lot to dig through and make sense out of.

But that was okay because for a dozen or two of us our faith had been rewarded. We had those four weird days where for some reason Bruce "John MafuckinClane" Willis stayed up late answering our stupid questions on the Internet, taking our shit and tossing some back.

It was a surreal experience, a weird drama played out in crude little text *boxes. What better example can there be of the connecting and equalizing powers of the Internet than a bunch of crass movie nerds stumbling across a bonafide cinema icon in their regular hangout? For me obviously it was a career highlight to know that somehow my essay had opened a window for John McClane to walk barefoot into the broken glass of the talkbacks.*

The cherry on top was an unlikely journalistic error where a quote from me was misattributed to Bruce. Early in the talkback someone had suggested Michael Bay would've been a better Die Hard *director than Len Wiseman, which inspired one of my usual ludicrous rants. Since we both had those black boxes somebody confused mine for something Bruce wrote, and that mistake spread from blog to blog. By the time I found out about it it had already spread to news sites in English, Spanish and French. Some even included an "oh yeah, then why did you ask me to direct* Die Hard 4?" *response from Michael Bay, hopefully just responding to Bruce's actual comments about* Armageddon *and not mine. Either way, there was a day or two when it was being reported around the world that Bruce Willis had said:*

"I would rather eat a live baby in front of my grandma than have Michael Bay direct a *Die Hard* movie. I would rather go hunting with Dick Cheney than let that car engine in a human skin leave his satanic fingerprints on John McClane. In fact, this new PG-13 thing is the only part of ruining modern action movies that Michael Bay is not personally responsible for. The rest of it is all him. Don't even fucking say those words in the same sentence, you're only gonna give them ideas for part 5. It's like saying Candyman in front of a mirror, that motherfucker will show up and snort John McClane's soul right in front of you and then piss it out on your shoes."

If at any point in your life you get a chance to have your words attributed to Bruce Willis, I recommend giving him some crazy shit to say like calling somebody a "car engine in a human skin." I mean, do it however you want, but I have found that's a good way to do it.

Anyway, my problem was solved. Earlier I said I didn't feel comfortable supporting a PG-13 Die Hard *with my money. But that was before I had a personal guarantee from Bruce Willis that I would like it. Personal guarantee from Bruce Willis takes precedence over any ethical qualms. That's one of the rules.*

LIVE FREE OR DIE HARD

"No one has that power. There is a much more powerful guy in Hollywood, and his name is Rupert Murdoch. It's his corporation. I only work there."
— *Bruce Willis to* Vanity Fair, *on not being able to do an R-rated* Die Hard.

"This city is like a big CHICKEN, waiting to get PLUCKED."
— Scarface, *edited for TV version*

Fellas—

Die Hard, the motion picture, characters and their likenesses, are the copyrighted intellectual property of the Twentieth Century Fox Corporation. To them *Die Hard* is a franchise, a license, a property, a brand, a tentpole, a consumer product, an opportunity for cross promotion with Arby's and whichever candy bar it was. To them *Die Hard* is a dollar amount for an opening weekend, a domestic gross balanced against a marketing budget. But to the rest of the world, to the people with beating hearts, *Die Hard* is something more.

There's a lot of ways you can interpret those two words. I used to think it had something to do with the saying "old habits die hard." But it sounds more like a command, like it's telling you to *Die Hard*. If you believe in something, die standing up, die with your boots on. Or in this case with your shoes *off*. Die hard.

I never really thought of it as a noun, like "John McClane is such a die hard," but that might make the most sense. If you look up "die hard" on dictionary.com (this new one's about computers so why not) it tells you it's "a person who vigorously maintains or defends a seemingly hopeless position, outdated attitude, lost cause, or the like." Obviously that describes McClane to a T. He's a die hard who dies hard.

Whatever the title was originally supposed to mean, over the past almost two decades it has taken on a new meaning. Of course you've got the "*Die Hard* on a blank" method of describing a movie where one man is forced to sneak around whatever the blank is to foil a terrorist attack. But to me anyway *Die Hard* is more than just a premise or a formula. *Die*

Hard describes the attitude and tone of the movie. Like John McClane, *Die Hard* has little patience for bullshit, a high tolerance for pain, and now it has a machine gun, ho ho ho. There is no such thing as *Die Hard* lite, or *Die Hard* medium, or a *Die Hard* that pulls a few punches. There is only *Die Hard*. You can't put *Die Hard* in a box or a cage, because we have known from the beginning that walls cannot contain *Die Hard*. To my dying day, whether that day is hard or regular, I will remember the newspaper ad that promised "It will blow you through the back of the theater!" and included a diagram of how exactly this would work. You hear that? *Die Hard* is not balls to the wall action — *Die Hard* is action that actually knocks your balls THROUGH the wall. That's just how it works. Be careful with the balls.

But now here we are in 2007 and even Walter B. Willis, John Ma(gunshot)Clane[72] himself, cannot sneak around and pick off Fox executives one by one to foil their plan to build walls around *Die Hard*, or to reinforce the back wall of the theater so nobody gets blown through it. As you can see in that quote above, Bruce felt an R-rating was a seemingly hopeless position, but he did not vigorously defend it like a die hard. In that article there's a funny story about a Fox executive giving Bruce notes about the Kevin Smith scene and Bruce listens and then says, "Let me ask you a question: Who's your second choice to play John McClane?" Unfortunately it was a bad play, he should've saved that card for the rating.

Because I believe they really did make a *Die Hard* movie here. Obviously, it's not as good as *Die Hard*. Nothing is. But if you like the sequels, this is in the same tradition, and it earns the description *Die Hard*. Almost. I think. In my PG-13 *Die Hard* rant I asked Fox, and by extension all mankind, not to be Ellis, the smarmy yuppie sellout bastard who tries to betray McClane to Gruber to save his own ass. But clearly those mister falcons are Ellis. Every last one of them is Ellis, holding the can of Coke and giving the thumbs up and everything. But they don't want to be Ellis, they want to be Gruber, so they are holding the real *Live Free Or Die Hard*

---

72 The PG-13 cut of Live Free Or Die Hard used the sound of a gunshot to muffle McClane's signature phrase "yippee ki-yay, motherfucker." So in those circles at that time it was common to replace any curse words with "(gunshot)".

hostage, saving the real movie that has blood and falcon-bombs for DVD so at that time you can be blown through the back of your apartment and lose your security deposit.

So, my friends, I dearly wish we were not in this ridiculous situation. I wish they had just done the right thing and released the movie as it was obviously meant to be, so I could recommend this movie without reservations or caveats or what have yous. I mean how ludicrous is it that we are actually put into the position of explaining how a flippin *Die Hard* movie is "really violent... for PG-13!" and "pushes the limits... of PG-13!"

It's preposterous and it's sad and it's a bad omen that we have found ourselves here, but it could've been worse. The movie could've sucked. But I am relieved to be able to tell you that, despite everything going against it, *Live Free Or Die Hard* is a pretty damn entertaining movie. It could and should be harder. But it's fun, it has a good villainous plot, it has many intense and well constructed action sequences, and other than the rating[73] it manages to overcome most of the worries I had about the movie.

Hey, you skipped over all that preamble stuff to find out if I liked it or not. That's cheating. Show me some respect man I'm a god damn artist. I was trying to create suspense and what not.

Anyway I guess I might as well go through piece by piece.

JOHN McCLANE.
I think they could've done more visually to show us this is our man John McClane. I understand the baldness, but he's wearing sort of a hip leather jacket that does not remind me of that working joe we love. So he looks different, and we must assume that he has become a Jehovah's Witness since there is no mention of his alcoholism, he never smokes and somebody cleaned his mouth out with soap. It's sad, like how Prince stopped swearing so he doesn't perform 'Sexy MF' anymore. Good for you, John, getting off the booze, but we want to hear that song. Are you worried your grandma is watching this or something? You're not as fun that way.

---

73 See footnote 75.

So that makes it hard to recognize McClane at first, but this is definitely McClane, with the same sense of humor, cynicism and with the *With a Vengeance* powers to manipulate vehicles and withstand vicious falls and hits. The super hero business comes in mostly at the end when they get to that jet fighter you probably saw on the commercials — that was a pretty big leap into ridiculousness. The rest of the movie is a little more grounded, in my opinion. And I'm happy to report that unlike *With a Vengeance* there is not a moment when you think he should just go home and let the professionals take over. This time around the philosophy is that if somebody else could do it he would be happy to go home, but he knows nobody else can do it. The fact that he is the one chasing these "cyberterrorists" and doing a better job than all the other government agencies seems absurd, but they use the almost-convincing trick of mentioning Hurricane Katrina. When you think of it that way you realize hey, it's true, maybe McClane really *is* the only one who's gonna have his crud together.

MAC KID.

I was as worried as anybody. I don't think McClane needs a wacky sidekick. I like McClane isolated, using a radio to talk to his allies on the outside or to taunt his adversaries. The guy doesn't need company. And if he must have a sidekick, how are you gonna top Samuel L. Jackson? You're not. This comic relief sidekick crap is more like the *Under Siege* movies, where Casey Ryback has to protect Erika Eleniak and Morris Chestnutt and teach them how to shoot a gun. Luckily, Justin Long (who plays a hacker McClane is protecting from people trying to kill him) is much less annoying than either one of those characters. In fact, I thought he was pretty funny, and he was only saddled with a couple chunks of computery exposition crap.

DAUGHTER.

This is another one straight out of *Under Siege. Part 2: Dark Territory*, that is. In that one Katherine Heigl played Seagal's estranged niece, who knows a few moves courtesy of her uncle, tells the bad guys they've messed with the wrong guy and mends her relationship with him as he saves her life. Lucy Gennaro/McClane does the same exact thing here, but

I didn't mind. It's kind of cute to see her take after her old man, her not speaking to him in the beginning is the last remnant of McClane's screwed up life, and if these bad guys didn't kidnap somebody in McClane's family they would be poor bad guys.

THE VILLAINOUS PLOT.

"Cyberterrorism" sounds really stupid on paper and on web, but in the movie I like the idea. Remember, Hans Gruber also had a corny movie-fied computer hacker on his team. These guys have a similar scheme but on a much larger scale. Instead of *Die Hard* in a building it's *Die Hard* in a country. Early on they manipulate the traffic lights to cause massive pileups all around Washington DC. McClane gets out, stands on top of his car and looks at the chaos as far as he can see in every direction, and it is a genuine "oh shit" moment. Later these jerkwads use the magic of the digital age to trap our guy in a tunnel between four lanes of traffic going both ways. The cybervillainy even creates some atmosphere in the scenes where they drive or fly through cities with all the lights turned off. Kind of eerie, kind of pretty.

And by the way, these aren't just computer guys, they also have a team of badass mercenaries. Which brings me to...

THE HENCHMEN.

I read Quint's review and I totally disagree with the guy, and especially on this front. I think the henchmen in this movie are topnotch. Maggie Q plays a sexy cold-blooded badass like she did in *M:I:3* and *Dragon Squad* (executive producer: Steven Seagal), and she has a great fight with McClane that is sort of a symbolic fight between modern action movies and the old style. (Don't worry, no wires as far as I noticed.) But my favorite henchman and one of the big surprises of the movie was the one apparently called Rand.

When the mayhem first starts, the movie is *Die Hard*-in-a-dude's-apartment, but when it moves outside is when you notice Rand. There is a really gimmicky but excellent shot of this guy jumping around, swinging across fire escapes and what not, and the camera follows his every move. It's very modern in that it's such a precise camera move that was either done digitally or with a very fancy computerized camera rig. But it's old school in the sense that you can tell exactly what's going on, it's not disorienting. Then you get a clear look at Rand's face and I realized holy bananas, that's that dude from *District B13*! Cyril Raffaelli is his name. He's the guy that played the cop, not the founder of free running guy, but he does those kind of moves, and he is the stunt co-ordinator for many Luc Besson movies. When I realized it was him I had to think *wait a minute, did he do that fire escape stunt FOR REAL?* Because I bet he could.[74]

Rand has a couple close calls with McClane but he keeps surviving. One of my buddies said he was "lucky," and Quint said he was "ridiculous." Both wrong. What he is is a die hard. A guy who vigorously maintains such hopeless positions as "if I get thrown from a car I think I can roll with the punches" and "if my helicopter blows up it would be a good idea to jump out." But he says those things in French because he is from France, where people run up walls and jump off buildings and know how to fall safely.

With these two characters you get a little martial arts, a little parkour, but neither enough to seem like they're showing off or trying to make it too modern. And McClane's tackle em, choke em, toss em down stairs, hit em with cars style of fighting wins every time.

TIMOTHY OLYPHANT.
Okay, I can't deny it, he is not an iconic villain like Hans Gruber, or even a fun over-the-top one like Eric Bogosian's Travis Dane in *Under Siege 2*. He has some good moments, especially when he gets the upper hand enough to dare McClane to "go ahead, say something funny." He's pretty good with the "I'm smarter than you" vibe, but it's hard to compete without a British accent. People are saying he is underwhelming, that's fair enough. I don't agree that he's bad, though.[75]

Director LEN WISEMAN.
I gotta give credit where credit is due. Wiseman gets the award for

---

74 Sure enough, he did.

75 At this point in my original review I had some criticisms of the character 'Warlock', played by Kevin Smith. Kevin Smith's books *My Boring Ass Life: The Uncomfortably Candid Diary of Kevin Smith* and *Shootin' the Sh*t with Kevin Smith: The Best of SModcast* are available from Titan Books. Ask your bookseller to order your copies today.

performing beyond expectations. I am not a fan of the *Underworld* movies and could not figure out why they would hire some dungeons and dragons nerd to do a *Die Hard*. And I'm not saying the guy is John McTiernan quality, and I'm sure I'm gonna get plenty of guff for saying this, but I honestly think he did a good job. Walter B told us that Wiseman brought John McClane into the 21st century, and thankfully that didn't mean any of the following things it could've meant: shaky cameras, quick cuts, Avid farts, whooshy camera sounds, wire-fu, matrixy outfits, electronical music, rockin guitar soundtrack, bullet time, gratuitous CGI. Yeah, there's a "modern" feel to some of the color tinting and there are some fancy camera moves here and there, but — praise be Jesus — the Lord heard my call and made an action movie where for once I CAN TELL WHAT THE HELL IS GOING ON! You guys can have your Michael Bay. Please, for God's sake, take him. I don't want him near my movies. Wiseman, at least in this movie, is Vern-approved. He designs his sequences in such a way that you can follow the geography of where the people are, where the vehicles are, what is headed in what direction, etc. These are images that involve you in the action instead of make you dizzy or explode in your face. And Wiseman uses these images to create tension and excitement in the audience. You know, like they used to do in action movies.

And that brings us to the main reason why this movie is worth watching: there really are some kickass action sequences. I am not saying this in a "there is a big explosion and it is AWESOME!" kind of way, I am saying that I love this character of John McClane and when he headbutts a guy or skids across pavement or falls down an elevator shaft it makes me grit my teeth. I usually hate it when people compare a movie to a "ride" or a "rollercoaster," but that's really how I felt watching this, there are many thrilling action sequences that if they don't send your balls through the back wall at least bounce them off the wall a couple times. It kind of feels like when you're on a rollercoaster hanging over a ledge staring straight down, and your heart beats fast and you can't help but smile. This movie gave me that feeling many times and, despite all my misgivings, I gotta be thankful for that. *Casino Royale* is probably a better movie overall, but to me this was more thrilling. Not that there's a lot to compare it to, but it's the best action movie of this type in quite a while.

Watching this movie you almost forget that they don't make movies like this anymore.

misc. notes

- The bad guys don't seem to bleed. There is one guy that gets shredded almost *Fargo* style, he bleeds a little, but you'd think there'd be a geyser. I almost wish they would've done green blood, that would've been funny. For the most part I was not bothered by the lack of blood though, because the number one rule is MCCLANE GOTTA BLEED, and he does indeed do all the bleeding in this one. There is one climactic moment though, and you will know it when you see it, where something pretty damn badass occurs, but the biologically impossible lack of blood actually made me think wait a minute, did I misinterpret that, is that not really what happened? So that wasn't good.

- Also I coulda done without the helicopter scene. McClane flies a helicopter which they use for quick transportation and to set up a joke that he took lessons to overcome his fear of flying. But there's no urgency to it, he doesn't really need to fly it, and it doesn't even lead to an action scene. So that was kind of dumb.

- The jet sequence has some phony looking digital effects, but most of the movie feels pretty organic. If you think this one is too digital you are pickier than I am. (And they don't look any more phony than Bruce propelling away from the explosion in part 2.)

- love the title *Live Free Or Die Hard* but it doesn't have much to do with the movie. It does take place on Independence Day, though. But it's not at all like the movie *Independence Day*.

Before seeing the movie I figured this had to be the last *Die Hard*. I'm not sure how many people are still interested in *Die Hard*, and of those that are, I know a lot of them that lost interest once they heard it was PG-13. And then next week you got that exploding robot movie coming out, it's the same rating so that's gonna suck away a lot of the audience. (And I do mean suck.)

But now that I've seen it I don't know. My experience was the opposite of Quint's — the audience was clearly into it, with lots of clapping and laughing and cheering. And maybe normal people don't care or notice about the PG-13 like we do. Maybe the world needs a shot of McClane in whatever strength they can get it. I'm sure some of my talkback pals will be disappointed in me for writing a mostly positive review and think I sold out or that I'm trying to be nice to Walter B so he'll send me the uncut version and autograph my cassette tape of *The Return of Bruno*. But I'm just being honest. I hate what they did with this movie. But I liked this movie.[76]

Okay, Bruce said this is maybe better than the first one, that's not even close to true. But it's an enjoyable action movie in the midst of a long enjoyable action movie drought. It could catch on. So I ask you, Walter B, if you're out there, and if you ever choose to *Die Hard* again. Think of us die hards. I won't even say you owe us one — you owe YOU one, because I know you want it too. You can do it. We believe in you. If you can jump off the side of a building tied to a firehose I think you can get those Dwayne T. Robinsons over there to understand that *Die Hard* must go out with a children under seventeen not admitted without a parent or guardian style bang. The backs of the theaters won't know what hit em. You'll make a movie like this times ten, and across the planet we'll all be yellin MOTHERFUCKER so loud it'll drown out all the gun shots in the world.

thanks Bruce,

Vern

---

76 In the Walter B talkback I vowed, "…if the movie comes out and knocks us on our asses and/or through the back of the theater, we're gonna say 'phew' and laugh at how wrong we were and all give each other high fives and set off some fireworks and erect a statue of Len Wiseman in the town square and watch *Underworld Evolution* again and try to figure out how exactly this happened." And I'm sure some of those things happened but I wasn't there to witness them so I can't say for sure.

AFTERWORD

OUT OF THE SHADOWS: CLINT EASTWOOD –

An American Masters Special

and

HOLLYWOOD SALUTES BRUCE WILLIS:

An American Cinematheque Tribute

from VERN TELL'S IT LIKE IT IS #49 — Man Stuff

I remember there used to be women who read my column. I won't say their names but there was a nice gal from the newsgroups who was an early supporter of my works.

'Nother one from the website for the director of *Running Time*, that Bruce Campbell movie all done up in one shot like *Rope*. She used to write me all the time, very encouraging, very supportive.

I haven't heard from any women in a while, and I wonder if I'm scaring them away with all this man talk. All this Badass Cinema, all this Bruce and Clint and breaking people's legs and bending punks over and smoking motherfuckers. Balls and dicks. Man stuff.

Well I hope some day my sensitive side will return, I'll lay off of the macho for a little while and I'll get a little more genderifical diversity in my readership. I mean who the fuck knows, even Clint Eastwood directed *The Bridges of Madison County* one time.

Sorry though ladies, this is not that column. Because today I've been pondering a question that only a fucking man would ever wonder about.

The question is:

What does it mean to be a man?

Seriously people, don't laugh. There are a lot of reasons I ask this question. One reason is the pair of TV specials that were on last week, that honored two icons of Badass Cinema from two different generations, Bruce Willis and Clint Eastwood. I look at a guy like Bruce, and especially a guy like Clint, and I have to wonder — what is it that I see in this guy that I want to see in myself? Why are these two actors such models of manhood to me? That's one of the reasons why I ask this question, *what does it mean to be a man?* The main reason I ask is because of how, earlier today, I got double penetrated.

So uh, this column isn't gonna be pretty folks. I hope you're sitting down. I hope you're not eating. You're really gonna wish you didn't read this one.

I guess I really started thinking it around 10:30 this morning. Sitting in a waiting room at the urology clinic, watching the sick people stumble up and down the hallway with breathing masks or wheelchairs they didn't know how to use. Everyone else is as nervous as me. Who knows what they're waiting for.

Over the intercom they say "MRS. CORA BELL PLEASE RETURN TO BLOOD DROP! CORA BELL, RETURN TO BLOOD DROP!" Sounding a little panicked.

I look around. Nobody else looks freaked out. Maybe they know what it means. I'm thinking, what the fuck is a blood drop? And where the hell did Cora wander off to? What kind of crazy shit is going on in this building?

I'm thinking any second now, Cora's gonna come running down the hall with no blood in her. "Come back Mrs. Bell! We didn't put the blood in yet!"

And I'm thinking about the paper they gave me when they signed me up for this caper.

1. Try to report for your evaluation with a comfortably full bladder. If you empty your bladder just prior to your appointment it may delay your test.

Okay, so it WAS comfortably full... when I came in for my 10:00 appointment. Now it's 10:30. It's uncomfortable. I'm staring at the restroom signs. Don't think of pissing. Don't think of pissing.

A guy goes into the bathroom holding a folded up shirt. He's got jeans and cowboy boots on but he's wearing a polka dotted nightgown on top.

They gonna make me wear a fucking nightgown?

Don't think of pissing.

Goes into the bathroom, comes out wearing the shirt and dangling the gown from two fingers like it's a dead rat he has to get out of the attic. What kind of psychological shit is this, putting polka dots on a man's hospital gown? Like boot camp or something. You have to break him down mentally, destroy his self-image, humiliate him. Then you can operate. Whatever they did to him in that nightgown, he probably didn't enjoy it. He's disgusted at even being associated with this gown.

I don't know what they did to him. But I know what they're planning to do to me.

You remember how a month ago I said it was good news, it wasn't chlamydia? Well, turns out it wasn't good news. If it was chlamydia, they woulda given me medicine. It would be over by now. I wouldn't have had to come in this morning for the urodynamic evaluation. *This exam can cost up to $1500.00.* Thank christ I have insurance. *The CPT codes for this procedure are as follows:*

51726—Cystometrogram-complex
51741—Complex uroflowmetry
51795—Voiding pressure studies
51797—Intra-Abdominal Voiding pressure
51785—EMG Urethral Spincter

It's gonna be okay Vern. Think about something else. Think about something tough.

Lee Marvin.

Clint Eastwood.

Outlaw Josey Wales.

Josey and the Pussycats.

Anything.

DESCRIPTION OF URODYNAMIC EVALUATION

Urodynamics is an in depth evaluation of the lower urinary tract (bladder and bladder outlet or urethra). These studies are important in diagnosing problems of loss of urinary control or urinary retention (inability to pass urine) or frequency of urination. This evaluation involves placing small tubes through the urethra into the bladder to measure the pressure inside the bladder.

Oh yeah, and a small tube inside the rectum to measure the pressure in the abdomen. Occasionally x-rays may be taken during the study. A complete evaluation may take up to 1 1/2 hours. You know, the length of a movie, with a tube up your ass, and one in your dick. No big deal. Ask if you have questions.

When I first read that, I was like, *holy fucking jesus*. Now it's a month later, and I was starting to get used to the idea. Well, it's gonna happen. Might as well get it over with. Might as well go in and get DP'd. Not sure how it works exactly, sticking a tube in my dick. Not sure I want to know how it works. Holy fucking jesus.

Steve McQueen. Sam Peckinpah. *The Getaway.*

Remember when he gets up and starts cooking a big pan of eggs for breakfast? Ever since I saw that I've always thought cooking eggs was manly.

Thunderbolt and Lightfoot. Rabbits jumping out of the trunk.

Fistful of Dollars. The Good the Bad and the Ugly. Once Upon a Time in the West.

I told the doctor wait a minute, you don't understand. That's a dick. You can't stick a tube up a dick, can you?

Okay, you can think about pissing.

So I keep looking at those restroom signs. The international sign of the man. A little man with a circle for a head, and rounded off nubs for hands and feet. His ladyfriend is identical, except her arms are splayed out to accommodate her triangle shaped dress.

Think about pissing.

Rounded off nubs.

Think about pissing.

What does it mean to be a man?

The nurse, or medical assistant or whatever comes out. Tough lady, like a gym teacher. "Vern?"

I look over my shoulder. It's not too late. I could make a run for it.

"Here," I say, getting up, my voice cracking.

No, I'm not making this one up, boys. They really did a number on ol' Vern. First they had me piss in this thing with a big whirring motor inside. Took care of the uncomfortably full bladder right away.

"Go back in there and wait for Dr. Mayo."

Dr. Mayo comes in and asks me a few questions about pissing. "Did they have you urinate already?"

"Yeah."

He peeks in the door, checks out the whirring thing.

"Oh yes, they did," he says, with a very elegant English accent. "It looks very nice, very nice."

They didn't let me keep my pants on, like the bathroom guy. But I had the polka dotted nightgowns on. Two of them. And little paper booties on my feet. In the examination room there was a big machine to sit in, with stirrups. And you sit your bare ass on cold metal, with a gap in the middle.

I walked in, my little paper booties pitter-pattering on the floor. I'm not sure why, but there's a big yellow piss stain in one spot on the floor. Like piss has dripped there so many times there's no way to scrub it off anymore. Fucking urology, man.

There's a lot of psychological shit they do to help you get through this, and they're good at that. They make conversation, and little jokes.

"Did you get my message?" the gym teacher asks.

Message? No. What did it say?

"That we had an intimate date today."

She delivers the jokes good, like they're spontaneous. I wonder if she always uses the same ones. Like a wedding DJ who every day plays the *Rocky* theme when the best man comes up for a toast, and every day people laugh.

She dims the lights. "Mood lighting," she jokes. I give a little fake laugh, trying to play along, because I want it to work.

I didn't even see anyone turn it on, but suddenly I notice this portable stereo on a table on the other side of a room, and it starts playing gentle music to calm me down. And I realize after a little bit that it's Elton John.

'Can You Feel the Love Tonight.'

Swear to fucking Christ.

First they stick a tube in your dick, then they pull it out. Then a different one. The lady says, "Yep, we have all sorts of catheters." Gallows humor. Next is the one in your ass.

And let me say this. No offense. But I don't know WHAT you gay guys are thinking! Same goes for the girls that let their boyfriends assfuck them. Or the straight guys who like a dildo up their ass. Yeah, I saw you on *Real Couples*. I know what you're into.

I'll never think of *The Lion King* the same way again.

Oh lord, please forgive me for all that business in prison. I was young and reckless then. It was a mistake. I know about karma and all that but fer chrissakes, I'm a changed man. Please consider my case. No more of these catheters, ever again. Fer cryin out loud I'll give up Cinema if I have to. I'll burn my DVDs and drown my computer. I'll travel to Hollywood to piss on Clint and Bruce's stars. I'll curse Steve McQueen and call Bruce Lee a shrimp and give Michael Bay a blowjob. Just never ever let them stick a tube in my ass again.

"It's a leaded room. It's okay to scream."

SHIT!!!

"You're doing good. You can wipe the tears from your eyes if you want."

I cried? Ha ha, I didn't notice.

"We make men cry. That's our job."

You don't know what to think about yourself after something like that. I'm a pathetic old man who's dripping piss. So pathetic they had to do THAT to me.

No, I'm a tough motherfucker, so tough I let them do THAT to me.

Maybe that's how I'll feel tomorrow. But today I still feel fragile. Have you ever farted from your dick? I guess there was some air trapped in there. And it burns a little when I piss. It's hard to forget a feeling like that, a tube up your dick. And then they make you piss through it. I still don't know how it works, exactly. I probably shouldn't have mentioned this in the column. Well, I'm too old to be dating anyway.

What does it mean to be a man? In *Hollywood Salutes Bruce Willis*, it means LOOKING tough, but being a nice guy at heart. The American Cinematheque was giving an award to Bruce Willis, so it was kind of like

The Bruce Willis Awards. Typical corny awards show, lots of celebrity presenters, but only Bruce Willis wins.

And Bruce sat there, his head shaved bald, not knowing how to react. What expression should you have on your face when you're the guest of honor for something like this? Sometimes he smiled, laughed at the jokes made at his expense. Then they'd start talking about how he bought ice cream for an entire neighborhood while shooting *The Sixth Sense*, or how he bought Michael Clarke Duncan the book *The Green Mile* and told him to read it over and over and start studying and I'm gonna make a few phone calls and this is gonna change your life.

Bruce is looking tougher at this age. More damaged. And when they said all this nice stuff about him, he didn't smile. He looked real serious. Maybe he's gonna cry though. Like I did when they stuck a tube up my dick.

Sorry about that.

Some of it was kind of embarrassing. Ol' Bruce has done a lot of shitty movies. And when you line them all up next to each other it starts to get embarrassing. *North. Armageddon. Blind Date.* etc.

But then you look at the good stuff. *Die Hard. Die Hard 2. Die Hard With a Vengeance. Pulp Fiction. The Sixth Sense.*

I liked *Fifth Element*, and so did a lot of folks on the Badass ballot. He was pretty cool in *Last Man Standing*, even if it's no *Yojimbo* or *Fistful of Dollars*. He was always funny on *Moonlighting* and you fucking know it. And he does those dramatic roles that are supposed to be good, but I've never seen them. *In Country. Nobody's Fool.*

He's not just doing the same shit all the time. Even in the bad movies, he gives it his all. He looks tough in *Armageddon*, it's just the movie surrounding him that sucks. And he's got longevity. He doesn't have to keep trying for comebacks. He's not making an ass of himself like "Fats" Stallone doing that *Get Carter* remake. Look at that fucking jackass in that bad suit.[79]

But then, he IS a man. In the bad sense of the word. In the sense that he does make his *Armageddon*s, and he wants to be the movie star, he wants to own the Planet Hollywoods. And he wants to be a rock star.

---

79 Man, I was mean back then. Well, I was still in pain. I was trying to reclaim my masculinity by bullying Stallone. Never saw that movie but that was unnecessary. I apologize.

There was a whole section on *Return of Bruno*. Ouch.

And that's why Clint Eastwood is so great. He doesn't want to be a rock star. He just plays jazz piano, on occasion. Real good, but only on occasion. It's my Theory of the Badass Juxtaposition. It's gotta be something sensitive, something emotional, or something cute if it's gonna amplify the Badass quality.

Jumping around doing 'Under the Boardwalk' karaoke doesn't work. Sitting quietly playing jazz does.

Clint is jazz. Everybody else is karaoke.

Out of the Shadows — Clint Eastwood: An American Masters Special is a ninety-minute overview of Clint's career, skipping through time for interviews with Janet Maslin, Walter Mosley, Sergio Leone, Don Siegel, even Clint's mom Ruth Wood. It shows how Clint went from a little boy who loved jazz to a bit player in b-movies; from the star of *Rawhide* to the Man With No Name, to an American icon, to a director.

More than anything it shows how Clint is a shy man, a quiet man, and the more he doesn't say, the more he tells about himself. It's how he tells you how he's gonna kick your ass. It's also how he tells you he has a soul.

My favorite parts in the special are when they show him actually directing. He doesn't say "Cut" or "Action!" He just says hey man, let's try this. Okay, that's good.

And then there's the part where he is honored. Not by Amanda Peet and the cast of *Friends* introducing clips of his recent movies. By a jazz concert.

Can you imagine that? A jazz concert, honoring you. And then he comes up on stage at the end. "My name is Clint Eastwood, and I love jazz." And he sits down and briefly grabs the spotlight, playing the piano. Out of the shadows. And then quietly he goes back in, and we don't hear much from him, except occasionally he releases a movie.

Maybe that's what it means to be a man. To let your manhood speak for itself. You don't have to prove yourself. Yourself proves itself. They talk about how Clint has the physical strength to stand still and be menacing. To not say anything with his mouth, but say volumes with his eyes. To lay it all out by holding it all back.

People will know you're a tough motherfucker. You don't have to explain the whole tube in the dick deal, why it makes you tough and not old. In my opinion.

By the way, maybe you guys shouldn't mention this to anybody else, you know.

Paying for the parking garage took a long fucking time. Two long lines, they started out about the same length, but I chose the wrong one. The cashier must've been new, typing all kinds of weird shit into the computer, taking five minutes for each transaction. Coming up with weird prices like $4, when it's supposed to be $3 a day. Everybody in line, straight from hearing bad news or getting shots or getting tubes stuck up their dick (me), is starting to get pissed. Swearing under their breath or making those loud sighs of annoyance.

Then this young couple comes up, gets in the other line, gets through it long before I get through mine. They looked like they were in their mid-twenties. Fashionably dressed. Lacking in sleep. Holding hands. The woman was whiter than I must've been earlier, when they thought I was gonna faint. She was skinny and her hair was mostly shaved off, growing back haphazardly in little blond patches.

What the fuck am I complaining about, getting sodomized in novel new ways. I bet this gal WISHES she had a dick to stick a tube up, rather than this. That dude would LOVE to get the urodynamic evaluation, rather than have to deal with this. It would be a fucking birthday party to him.

Part of his mind, the devious man part, I bet it's looking for a way out. Get her to do something wrong, find some reason to break up, to save himself the emotional damage of loving a girl that's probably gonna die.

But he stands there and holds her hand, and goes on with life.

Maybe THAT'S what it means to be a man. Even if he doesn't play piano. You just have to find your own definition.

—Vern

APPENDIX 1
THE THEORY OF BADASS JUXTAPOSITION

Early in my career of writing about the films of badass cinema I came up with "the theory of badass juxtaposition." Many people simplistically assume that a badass is an alpha male consumed with only stereotypically manly traits and with an aversion to anything feminine. But my theory states that the strength of a badass is in fact magnified by the presence of a sensitive hobby or a sentimental soft spot of some kind. The juxtaposition could be an image — like Chow Yun Fat holding a gun in one hand and a baby in the other in *Hard Boiled*, or Jean-Claude Van Damme carrying his late daughter's pet rabbit everywhere he goes in *The Shepherd: Border Patrol* — or an activity, like Clint Eastwood playing jazz piano in real life and in *In the Line of Fire*. A well-rounded badass is a stronger badass, he is clearly secure in his badassness if he's not ashamed of his artistry or his emotions.

APPENDIX 2
THE BADASS 100

In 1999 I read about the American Film Institute's list of the 100 greatest American movies of all time (*Citizen Kane* was #1 — that must've raised a few eyebrows. Way to go out on a limb, AFI). Nothing against their list but since it didn't have much overlap with the type of movies I'm most interested in I decided to put together the World Badass Committee, my own "blue ribbon panel of experts," to vote on the BADASS 100. In 2006 the list was revised and improved by a new WBC made up of 43 volunteer Badass Cinema scholars from 11 countries.

It's hard to keep a list like this entirely timeless (I don't think *Sin City* would make the list if we voted today) but overall this is a great checklist for people interested in seeing the most badass movies and performances of all time. And you get more than 100 because there are some ties and also I allowed people to vote for an entire series where applicable. For your convenience the name of the lead badass is included in parentheses.

1. The MAN WITH NO NAME trilogy (Clint)
(A Fistful of Dollars, For a Few Dollars More, The Good, the Bad and the
    Ugly)
2. The LONE WOLF AND CUB series (Tomisaburo Wakayama)
(Sword of Vengeance, Baby Cart at the River Styx, Baby Cart to Hades,
    Baby Cart in Peril, Baby Cart in the Land of Demons, White Heaven in
    Hell)

3. YOJIMBO (Toshiro Mifune)

4. UNFORGIVEN (Clint)

5. DIE HARD (Bruce)

6. 36th CHAMBER OF SHAOLIN aka SHAOLIN MASTER KILLER (Gordon Liu)

7. SEVEN SAMURAI (ensemble)

8. SANJURO (Toshiro Mifune)

9. RED RIVER (John Wayne)

10. HARD BOILED (Chow Yun Fat)

11. THE WILD BUNCH (ensemble)

12. THE OUTLAW JOSEY WALES (Clint)

13. MAD MAX 2 aka THE ROAD WARRIOR (Mel Gibson)

14. ENTER THE DRAGON (Bruce)

15. POINT BLANK (Lee Marvin)

16. BRANDED TO KILL (Jo Shishido)

17. THE LIMEY (Terence Stamp)

18. DIRTY HARRY (Clint)

19. CHOPPER (Eric Bana)

20. OUT OF THE PAST (Robert Mitchum)

21. THE KILLER (Chow Yun Fat)

22. LE SAMOURAI (Alain Delon)

23. THE STREET FIGHTER (Sonny Chiba)

24. RIO BRAVO (John Wayne)

25. ONCE UPON A TIME IN THE WEST (ensemble)

26. HIGH PLAINS DRIFTER (Clint Eastwood)

27. WHERE EAGLES DARE (Clint motherfucking Eastwood)

28. HANA-BI aka FIREWORKS (Takeshi Kitano)

29. THE DIRTY DOZEN (ensemble)

30. WHITE HEAT (James Cagney)

31. KILL BILL VOLUMES 1-2 (ensemble)

32. GET CARTER (Michael Caine)

33. FIVE DEADLY VENOMS (ensemble of five)

34. ALIENS (ensemble)

35. ZATOICHI series (Shintaro Katsu)

36. MASTER OF THE FLYING GUILLOTINE (ensemble)

37. PULP FICTION (ensemble)

38. THE BIG SLEEP (Humphrey Bogart)

39. SONATINE (Beat Takeshi)

40. FIST OF LEGEND (Jet Li)

41. ROLLING THUNDER (William Devane, Tommy Lee Jones)

42. RESERVOIR DOGS (ensemble)

43. TIE: THE KILLERS ('64) (Lee Marvin) & BAD DAY AT BLACK ROCK (Spencer Tracy)

44. KISS ME DEADLY (Ralph Meeker)

45. WHEN WE WERE KINGS (Ali)

46. OLDBOY (Choi Min-sik)

47. SWEET SWEETBACK'S BADAASSSS SONG (Melvin Van Peebles)

48. THE GODFATHER (ensemble)

49. THE DRIVER (Ryan O'Neal)

50. TIE: KNIGHTRIDERS (Ed Harris) & WALKING TALL (Joe Don Baker)

51. GHOST DOG — THE WAY OF THE SAMURAI (Forrest Whitaker)

52. PREDATOR (ensemble)

53. SCARFACE (Al Pacino)

54. BROTHER (Takeshi Kitano)

55. BULLET IN THE HEAD (Simon Yam, Toney Leung Chiu-wai)

56. ZATOICHI (Takeshi Kitano)

57. PICKUP ON SOUTH STREET (Richard Widmark)

58. DOLEMITE (R.R. Moore)

59. THE GETAWAY (Steve McQueen)

60. SUPERFLY (Ron O'Neal)

61. THE WAGES OF FEAR (Yves Montand)

62. NIGHT OF THE HUNTER (Robert Mitchum)

63. THE WARRIORS (ensemble)

64. MAGNUM FORCE (Clint)

65. PAT GARRETT & BILLY THE KID (James Coburn & Kris Kristofferson)

66. ESCAPE FROM NEW YORK (Kurt Russell)

67. A BETTER TOMORROW 2 (Chow Yun Fat)

68. THE SEARCHERS (John Wayne)

69. TAXI DRIVER (Robert Deniro)

70. GOODFELLAS (ensemble)

71. SHAFT (Richard Roundtree)

72. LADY SNOWBLOOD (Meiko Kaji)

73. THE THING (ensemble)

74. STANDER (Tom Jane)

75. FIRST BLOOD (Sylvester Stallone)

76. THE TERMINATOR (Arnold Schwarzenegger)

77. FIST OF FURY (Bruce)

78. THE LONG GOOD FRIDAY (Bob Hoskins)

79. ASSAULT PRECINCT 13 (Darwin Joston)

80. FIGHT CLUB (ensemble)

81. SEXY BEAST (Gandhi)

82. TIE: BRING ME THE HEAD OF ALFREDO GARCIA (Warren Oates)
& KING OF NEW YORK (Christopher Walken)

83. FRENCH CONNECTION II (Gene Hackman)

84. RAGING BULL (Robert Deniro)

85. SPARTAN (Val Kilmer)

86. SCARFACE aka SCARFACE, THE SHAME OF A NATION, 1932
(Paul Muni)

87. A HISTORY OF VIOLENCE (Viggo Mortensen)

88. LEON aka THE PROFESSIONAL (Jean Reno)

89. THEY LIVE (Roddy Piper)

90. TO LIVE AND DIE IN L.A. (William Petersen, Willem Dafoe)

91. LE CERCLE ROUGE (Alain Delon)

92. THE GODFATHER PART 2 (ensemble)

93. PATTON (George C. Scott)

94. SIN CITY (Mickey Rourke OR ensemble)

95. IRON MONKEY (Donnie Yen)

96. MAD MAX (Mel Gibson)

97. GUN CRAZY (Peggy Cummins)

98. PATHS OF GLORY (Kirk Douglas)

99. THE MALTESE FALCON (Humphrey Bogart)

100. THE GREAT ESCAPE (ensemble)